American Film Distribution
The Changing Marketplace

Studies in Cinema, No. 40

Diane M. Kirkpatrick, Series Editor

Professor, History of Art
The University of Michigan

Other Titles in This Series

American Film Distribution
The Changing Marketplace

by
Suzanne Mary Donahue

U·M·I Research Press

Ann Arbor, Michigan

Produced and distributed by
UMI Research Press
an imprint of
University Microfilms, Inc.
Ann Arbor, Michigan 48106

Library of Congress Cataloging in Publication Data

Donahue, Suzanne Mary, 1956-
American film distribution.

    (Studies in cinema ; no. 40)
    Rev. ed. of author's thesis (Ph.D.—University of
Southern California, 1984)
    Bibliography: p.
    Includes index.
    1. Moving-pictures—United States—Distribution.
I. Title. II. Series.
PN1993.5.U6D55   1987   384.8'3   86-24900
ISBN 0-8357-1776-3 (alk. paper)

Contents

Acknowledgment

Professor Melvin Sloan of the University of Southern California School of Cinema-Television has generously provided me with dedicated and insightful direction throughout this study. I profoundly appreciate his inspirational passion for filmic expression and his respect for the highest ethical standards in the business of the collaborative art of filmmaking.

Introduction

A feature film must be viewed by as many people as possible for its potential power of communication to be fully realized. Whether the motivation for production is communication, financial reward, or aesthetic, the more people who see a picture, the greater is the film's opportunity to be successful in achieving its aim. Distribution is the means by which a film becomes available to the public, and is, therefore, a crucial factor in the ultimate success or failure of a film.

Motion pictures today are too expensive to produce without consideration of how they will reach and be received by the public. Because of high costs of distribution, the studios find it unprofitable to distribute a film with a gross rental potential of less than $10 million. "Film rentals" is defined as the portion of box office receipts returned to the distributor after the theater overhead and profit have been deducted and is generally 40 percent of the box office gross.

Because of production and distribution expenses, fewer films are being made by the studios. Although an audience may exist for various types of films, the studios cannot afford to risk money on producing and distributing films aimed at an esoteric audience. They therefore try to appeal to the mass market. Independent producers, however, are able to make films at reduced costs, either by sacrificing quality or through the dedication of people who will work for less money to get the film made. They may attempt to secure studio distribution, but more often, find themselves with an independent distributor.

A major advantage of independent distributors is that their lower overhead and less conservative standards permit experimentation with new ideas and concepts that may serve as a proving ground for new talent and subject matter. If the independent distributor has not invested his own money to produce the film, he has much less at risk than a studio. Even though the majority of independently produced and distributed films are aimed at a smaller and more predictable audience, the potential for a huge success always exists.

Whether a film is distributed by a studio or by an independent, the company needs to make money to survive. If a filmmaker wants to continue to make films, a financial success will more likely secure one that opportunity. It is, therefore, imperative that a film be distributed to realize its maximum financial potential.

An increasing potential source for the recoupment of production and distribution costs exists in the ancillary markets (e.g., network and syndicated television, pay television, video cassette rental and sales, video discs, hotels, airlines, the military, colleges, cruise ships, sale of 8mm and 16mm prints, music, merchandising). However, the maximum exploitation of these markets is still contingent upon the initial success of the film in theatrical distribution. Once a film has proven itself a money-maker at the box office, its value in other markets is greatly increased.

Every film is different and should be individually and creatively distributed to guarantee it the opportunity to be seen by the greatest number of people. Only then does the film have a chance to communicate to an audience and be judged on its own merits.

1

The Evolution of the Theatrical Distribution of Motion Pictures

Communication by visual images has fascinated man throughout the ages. After creating rudimentary depictions of motion, man sought a means of making the replication more realistic. Many artists and scientists imagined the value of a new dimension of moving pictures and worked to realize the vision, while others viewed the stages as nothing more than mere novelty. The eventual reproduction and distribution of motion pictures evolved along with the technological changes in society into the newest of the mass media. Though motion pictures require the physical accoutrements such as a projector and electricity, they are now capable of reaching and influencing more people than ever before. Throughout history, motion pictures have evolved from affecting an individual to being able to reach millions.

The first movements on a screen were those of the silhouette puppets of China, Java, and Turkey that were imported to Europe to entertain audiences. Man was now capable of controlling motion while an audience watched.[1] By the seventeenth century a crude projector called a "Magic Lantern," which utilized a mirror with lens and candles or reflected sunlight serving as a light source, was being used. It projected a series of slide pictures onto the wall of a darkened room and soon became an entertainment device. Itinerant showmen began to carry them throughout Europe and entertained audiences with slides portraying contemporary plays.[2]

Illusion of motion experiments and Niepce's development of the first crude photograph in 1822 stimulated experimentation that would ultimately culminate in motion pictures. People in many countries were borrowing information from each other and discovering new techniques simultaneously. Many new devices were developed during the nineteenth century that used a disc or wheel and showed the same action repeatedly. By 1898, 109 "scopes" and "graphs" were for sale. Small theaters were set up to demonstrate these devices for people who could not afford to own one.[3]

A very popular device was the Zoetrope, or "wheel of life." This cylindrical synthesizing apparatus was sold as a toy for years and evolved into the Praxinoscope developed by M. Reynaud of France. His use of angled mirrors increased illumination and created a smoother flow of images.[4] He adapted its principles to create other forms of rotating mechanisms harmonizing progressive drawings to show movement.[5] Reynaud was constantly improving upon his invention. After he added a frame and tiny settings, he converted the device into a parlor theater. By combining it with the Magic Lantern he created a form of projection. By 1889 he had enlarged his pictures and synchronized them with music, which enabled him to present them to a paying audience.[6] Variations on similar inventions were being created in different countries.

In 1882 Marey introduced the "fusil photographique," or the photographic gun, that took twelve photographs per second, enabling him to analyze the movements of a bird in flight.[7] His aim was not to create entertainment but to create a tool to aid scientific investigation.

By the twentieth century, the development of motion picture techniques had diverged into two paths. One, using photographs, was to become live-action and the other, using hand-drawn pictures, would become animation.[8] Many people in various countries were in pursuit of creating a projector to throw these moving images onto a screen. Between 1885 and 1887, Louis Aime' Augustin Le Prince projected moving pictures in a New York workshop with a single-lens camera and projector.[9] W. Friese-Greene in 1888 developed the machine to take and project film, which is essentially the prototype of all the varied patterns since brought out.[10] But there is no proof that it was ever used for successful projection.

The date of the first live picture show before an audience is usually taken as December 1895, when the Lumière brothers opened their cinema in the Boulevard des Capucines in Paris. They had developed a singular instrument that served as a motion picture camera and projector they called the Cinématographe and screened "La Sortie des Ouvriers de l'Usine Lumière," or "Workers Leaving the Lumière Factory." They soon began showing their popular invention in the salons of Paris. However, in 1897, when a fire caused by their projector killed several prominent people at a Paris charity bazaar, severe regulations were enacted and audiences afterword avoided cinemas for awhile.[11]

Many showmen realized the commercial possibilities of their creation and wanted the rights to their process. Not interested, the Lumières continued making filmstrips they viewed as scientific experiments. They did, however, open cinemas themselves and gave licenses to friends and associates. The scientific community appreciated the new process. In 1899 Dr. Doyen in France used film to record his surgical techniques.[12]

It was Thomas Edison, however, who further perfected the motion picture and brought about the most successful means to commercially exploit it. Edison's initial aim in working with film was to improve his phonograph by supplementing it with pictures.[13] The first motion picture item in his laboratory is dated 8 October 1888, which is also when he declared, "I am experimenting upon an instrument which does for the Eye what the phonograph does for the Ear."[14] Edison's assistant, Dickson, linked up the pictures with the phonograph and showed what he called the "Kinetoscope" to Edison on 6 October 1889.[15] It consisted of a brief film in which Dickson appeared and even spoke. Dickson envisioned this new device not as a form of mere entertainment or personal expression, but as the "foremost" instrument of reason, for now people would actually see empirical truth.[16] Shortly afterward, the Edison laboratory began turning out short story filmstrips. In April 1891 Edison applied for patents on the Kineograph as a photographing camera and the Kinetoscope as the viewing apparatus.[17] He did not, however, want to project motion pictures to groups of people, as he believed the effect would be lost. He did not even market his invention but licensed Raff and Gammon to distribute it.[18]

Many entrepreneurs quickly perceived this machine as a way to make money. In 1894 Edward Holland opened the first Kinetoscope parlor in what had been a shoe store at 1115 Broadway in New York City.[19] Approximately 480 people paid twenty-five cents each for admission to the Kinetoscope debut.[20] Suddenly, new films were now in great demand. Having invented the machine, Dickson was put in charge of making new films to show. He photographed bits of vaudeville and even recreated historical incidents.[21]

In an attempt to retain control over the production and sale of the movies, Edison's company refused to sell or rent cameras, while renting and later selling the projectors. Since Edison had neglected to obtain foreign patents, France and England soon put out similar peep-show cabinets and cameras that ultimately came to the United States to meet the demand for equipment. Holding the patents controlling the equipment and film, Edison's company claimed all other versions were patent violations. Their lawsuits, however, were of no consequence. Because of the voracious appetite for films, the opportunity for quick profits was too alluring. Mae D. Huettig wrote, "Without an understanding of the intensity and suddenness of the demand for movies, much of the history of the industry is incomprehensible."[22]

The Kinetoscope was so successful that it soon appeared in department stores, hotels, and salons in all major cities and was soon marketed abroad. The Kinetoscope's limitation was that only one person could use it at a time. An American, Jean Aimé Le Roy, borrowed ideas from Edison and various French inventors and on 25 February 1894 projected an image to a paying group of people.[23] Thomas Armat and C. Francis Jenkins created the

Phantoscope, which projected images onto a screen in a room so that they could be viewed by many people simultaneously. Edison acquired the rights to it, renamed it the "Vitascope," and presented it in vaudeville theaters in 1895.[24]

Before 1896, businessmen who wanted to book a projector were protected by exclusive exhibition rights to carefully defined geographical areas. In 1896, however, Edison sold his Edison Projecting Kinetoscope without any geographical restrictions. Theater operators were initially uncomfortable with his policy, but its success soon forced other companies to adopt similar practices. Dramatic sales of the projectors gave a significant stimulus to the entire motion picture industry in the United States. At last, films were being distributed all over and seen by entire audiences.[25]

As the technique of the mechanical projection of motion pictures continued to be improved, theaters sprung up around the country. There were not only store theaters but movie houses built especially for motion pictures.[26] By 1900, motion pictures, called "chasers," became so repetitious that they were often used merely to bridge live performances or were moved to the end of the bill as a signal that the show was over.[27]

When the nation's vaudeville actors formed a union and went on strike for higher wages, theater managers refused to recognize the union and either had to close their theaters or keep their houses open by presenting programs consisting solely of motion pictures. Projection equipment was in great demand. At the end of the strike, manufacturers were overstocked and the theater owners wanted to sell the equipment they had bought. At bargain prices, the equipment was picked up by smaller entrepreneurs who had longed to compete but had been unable to do so due to the high costs and scarcity of product.[28]

Audiences were quickly losing interest in motion pictures which were usually just short bits of filmed action. What finally saved the movies from the increasing apathy was the introduction of the narrative. Duped by American manufacturers and sold outright, Georges Méliès' *A Trip to the Moon* in 1902 was the greatest box office hit to that time.[29] His artificially arranged scenes combined with imagination were far above the standard. Edwin S. Porter introduced drama in 1902 in *The Life of an American Fireman*. He perfected his techniques in the first American dramatic film, *The Great Train Robbery*, which became a huge success at the theater. Finally, the audiences were given drama in which they could become involved.

Experiments with the content of films and filmic techniques became numerous as scientists and entrepreneurs sought more effective means of psychologically involving the viewer in motion pictures. George C. Hale, realizing the importance of involving the viewer, sought to do it through sensation. At the St. Louis World's Fair of 1903 he showed his *Hale's Tours,* which made the audience feel as if it were in a swaying railroad car.[30]

Experimentation continued within the limitations of the short film. By 1905 the standard length of movies was one reel of eight hundred to one thousand feet of film, lasting approximately fourteen minutes. Short subjects of three hundred to five hundred feet in length were being made by small and less established companies.[31]

Nearly all of the early films were made by companies that produced films essentially to maintain and increase demand for their equipment. Films were then sold outright at about ten to twelve cents a foot, regardless of the quality or subject matter.[32]

With a steady supply of films available for rental, establishment of theaters solely for showing motion pictures became a sound business venture. In 1905 Harry Davis and John P. Harris of Pittsburgh turned a storeroom into a theater by adding decorations and installing a projector, piano, and approximately one hundred seats. They charged five cents for admission to their theater, named "Nickelodeon."[33]

Films were sold outright to any buyer. As the number of exhibitors grew, films quickly saturated the market. Because audiences now had easy access to motion pictures, exhibitors had to change the films more frequently. Smaller exhibitors could barely afford to continue buying films that became worthless after a few days of showings. In order to operate theaters successfully, owners had to have three to five one-reel pictures on the program and had to change this schedule several times a week. Finding it cheaper to relocate and set up "black tent" shows around the country, others bought several films and traveled from city to city with them.[34]

To keep up with the great demand for films, exhibitors began trading films among themselves. It became apparent that some type of organization was necessary. In 1902 in San Francisco, Harry and Herbert Miles organized the first "exchange," which functioned to supply exhibitors with a constant supply of new pictures. They purchased films from producers and rented them to exhibitors on a weekly basis for one-fourth the purchase price and provided them with a new picture when one was returned. In 1904–5, distribution systems were created which allowed exhibitors to rent films individually or in groups or blocks. Exchanges ensured that competing exhibitors did not have the same films. The majority of early exchanges were independent and became known as "state's rights" exchanges of "state's rights" distributors. These exchanges had exclusive rights to sell pictures in a certain territory, usually corresponding with the boundary of a state. Contracts with exhibitors were made for all or a portion of the product of a producer for the year, with prices agreed upon at the time the contract was written.[35] Exchanges needed volume, regardless of quality, and accepted product from many producers. Because of this, some producers felt slighted in favor of other producers, which led to a desire for a definite link to particular distributors and exhibitors.

By 1907 there were 125 to 150 exchanges serving the entire country. Producers even favored this method because they no longer had to deal with thousands of small exhibitors. Exchanges bought films at a good price, which also pleased producers. Exhibitors benefited by their cut in costs and the more frequent program changes that they could now afford. Exchange operators also profited greatly, as they could continue renting a film long after the purchase cost had been recouped.[36]

Nickelodeons were initially cheap entertainment enjoyed by the lower and immigrant classes. Immigrants without knowledge of English could not understand theatrical plays and thus sought entertainment from motion pictures. There were about fifty theaters in New York in 1900 and more than four hundred by 1908, showing movies to approximately 200,000 people daily.[37] In 1909 approximately six thousand nickelodeons were showing a thirty-minute program of three one-reel films that changed daily.[38]

When the middle class began to frequent nickelodeons, the market greatly expanded. *Scientific American* claimed that there were "fully 20,000 nickelodeons in the northern cities by 1910, and they seemed to be expanding daily."[39] By 1910–11, attendance was estimated at ten million people. However, no records of attendance were compiled until the Federal Government collected a war tax on tickets in 1918.[40] Exchanges, however, did not provide satisfactory service. Films were commonly scratched or worn, deliveries were often late or missed, or neighboring theaters were given the same program. The distribution service was in grave need of reform.[41]

The mass production of motion pictures allowed this form of entertainment to grow rapidly. Costs of producing and distributing films could be spread over the entire country while charging a small admission fee to the patron. Broadway theaters were charging more than a dollar, but for a mere nickel or dime one could see a film. Exhibitors only paid twenty-five dollars for a license, while theatrical competitors paid five hundred. "While it cost $2,500 a week to run a theater in New York in 1910, it only cost $500 for a nickelodeon. Moreover, a theater-owner was not limited to only one or two performances a day. Rather, he could run the story ten to fifteen times in a row."[42]

Going to the movies became a weekly habit for many families. Serials were created to involve audiences with a particular story to ensure their patronage. *The Ladies' World* magazine simultaneously released its short stories in conjunction with a series of films. It proved profitable to synchronize weekly publications with a screen version at the nickelodeon.[43]

As the number of exhibitors grew, added competition led to the creation of more lavish theaters to attract customers. The exteriors of nickelodeons were often Moorish, Gothic, or Oriental in style. New theaters were built to seat thousands of people, with entire symphonies replacing the solitary piano in the nickelodeon. Live shows were now staged between the movies instead of the other way around. Interiors of the theaters contained ornate marble columns, oil paintings, Wurlitzer organs, and other accoutrements that could only otherwise make up the environment of the most wealthy members of society. Some theaters even had soundproof "crying rooms" where mothers could leave their children with a supervisor.[44] The "Roxy's" owner, Samuel Rothafel, was a master in creating spectacular environments in his theaters. He did not believe, however, that movies had much of a future. Predicting that vaudeville acts would eventually take over, he staged extensive shows along with the motion pictures. Sid Grauman decided to build a theater on the West Coast since Hollywood had become the capitol of the movies. Unlike Rothafel's stage shows that were unrelated to the movie, Grauman put on shows that tied in directly with the theme of the film.[45] These movie palaces thrived as a novelty. Even though people continued to go to movies during the Depression, they could no longer afford the extra prices these luxurious houses charged. Instead, they attended the cheaper theaters.[46]

Before 1910, several open-air theaters called "airdromes," existed. Before World War I, Marcus Loew attracted 21,000 people to Ebbets Field in New York to see Thomas Ince's *Wrath of the Gods* along with vaudeville acts.[47] However, weather conditions kept open air seating an unprofitable enterprise until the automobile could house the patrons.

Theaters came to be classified by their size and quality. A double standard was created whereby films permitted in one kind of theater were not allowed in another. For example, cheaper nickelodeons were prohibited from showing sex education shorts while first-class theaters had such permission.[48]

Producers discovered audiences were often attracted to lurid films. This incited protesters to intervene before the films were distributed. The nine principal producing companies that would organize the Motion Picture Patents Company with the intention of creating a monopoly over all phases of motion picture production, distribution and exhibition, decided to try to prevent outside interference by forming a regulatory body of their own choice. The People's Institute, a New York reform organization which recognized the value of movies as a popular form of entertainment, organized ten other New York civic groups to sponsor a motion picture censorship board. In 1909 the producers agreed to submit all films to them prior to making release prints and to cut out any footage the board deemed offensive. This New York Board of Motion Picture Censorship changed its name to the National Board of Review of Motion Pictures to stress the point that it did not approve of censorship.[49]

Motion pictures proved to be a new influence in society, of which many people disapproved. These were only the first attempts at controlling this powerful channel of communication. People were fearful of the environment that was being created around the nickelodeons. Worried about acquiring reputations as ethnic theaters, nickelodeon operators in large cities were advised to avoid booking programs slanted toward any one nationality, to avoid ethnic vaudeville acts, and to eliminate songs sung in foreign languages. The operators preferred to attract the larger, middle-class family trade that had been the domain of vaudeville and the legitimate stage.[50]

In 1912 the Motion Picture Ordinance created stricter licensing requirements and gave police additional manpower to perform periodic inspections. The licensing fee was increased from twenty-five to five hundred dollars in an effort to lure more respectable businessmen into the movies. The law also set up safety standards for theaters, such as requiring fire exits. It also dictated that children under sixteen had to be chaperoned by an adult.[51]

As the motion picture business grew and people became more secure that movies were not merely a novelty that would soon wane, competition in all areas of motion picture production and distribution grew. By 1897 Edison had instigated several lawsuits against those he believed had violated his patents, and he was innundated with just as many countersuits. These suits were temporarily resolved in January 1909 with the foundation of the Motion Picture Patents Company, which was composed of the nine major producers, Edison, Biograph, Vitagraph, Essanay, Selig, Lubin, Kalem, Méliès, Pathé, and George Kleine, and became known as the Trust. All of their individual patents were pooled. Edison received royalties on all of the films produced and George Eastman agreed to sell his filmstock only to members. If a distributor handled films of other companies, he would not be granted any of the Trust's films. For the privilege of renting licensed films, an exhibitor had to pay two dollars a week. Edison was the prime recipient of the royalties and his net profits soared to more than $1 million a year.[52] In an attempt to enforce its regulations, the Trust filed hundreds of lawsuits and even hired private detectives to search for patent violators. Regardless of their efforts, other producers continued to make movies and found exhibitors who were eager for new product.

The Trust's failure to control the business spurred them into national distribution themselves. In 1910 they created the General Film Company and bought out fifty-seven of the fifty-eight exchanges across the country. Exchanges that were granted licenses had to agree to buy films only from the Trust. The Trust aimed to drive other exchanges out of business by eliminating their supply of films, price-cutting, and other forms of intimidation.[53] Because of a seemingly unlimited demand for motion pictures, independent producers and exchanges managed to survive and even the licensed exchanges of the Trust did not always remain loyal.[54]

William Fox operated theaters and was the owner of an exchange called the Greater New York Film Rental Company that refused to be intimidated by the General Film Company. Since he was denied films, he opened his own studio and began to distribute his own pictures nationally. He was successful and bought more theaters in the New York area. Carl Laemmle, also an independent producer and head of Independent Motion Picture Company (IMP), chose to fight the Trust in the market and in court.[55]

The Trust was unable to control the independents who kept getting stronger. In 1910 Laemmle, Kessel, and Baumann organized the Motion Picture Distributing and Sales Company, designed to consolidate the movement of films from producers to exchanges. After initial resistance by some small companies to join, the Sales Company became the sole outlet for independent films, except those of William Fox. The Sales Company continued to grow in power and within five years they were able to offer exhibitors a choice of twenty-seven films a week. They had strong relationships with owners of small nickelodeons and soon began to lure licensed exhibitors away from the Trust.[56] Robert C. Cochrane, an associate of Laemmle, waged a campaign against the Trust in the trade papers, attacking their two-dollar-a-week royalty and strong-arm tactics.[57]

After the novelty of motion pictures wore off, exhibitors and the audience wanted quality pictures. Marcus Loew, an operator of a string of nickelodeons, was one of the first to realize that production needed to be improved. He demanded films that told stories and appealed to a more intelligent audience. The Trust, however, argued that better films would increase production costs, necessitating higher film rental from the theaters and creating higher admission prices. The Trust believed that the five- to ten-cent admission was the maximum that audiences would pay.[58]

The Trust also resisted films longer than one reel, believing that audiences did not have the mental capacity to appreciate them.[59] Before 1911, a few longer films that had been imported from Europe were successful. The Trust, however, did not allow any longer productions to be made in the United States.[60] The Trust considered motion pictures to be merchandise and chose to mass-produce films at the lowest cost in standard lengths of one-thousand-foot reels. Their stubbornness in maintaining uniform regulations did not allow films to grow in quality or length to meet audience need. Independents were the ones who took risks and experimented in the hopes of pleasing the public. Independent companies produced features and sold exhibition rights to state's rights distributors.[61]

By 1912 the independents nearly equalled the Trust in their film production output. The independents, however, split into two factions. Harry E. Aitken, a Wisconsin distributor, organized the Mutual Film Corporation with a goal of buying exchanges and becoming the sole distributor for several production companies. Ten independent producers went with Aitken and seven others formed their own corporation, the Universal Film Manufacturing Company, to continue supplying films to independent exchanges.[62] Adolph Zukor decided to experiment with an imported French film, *Queen Elizabeth,* starring Sarah Bernhardt. Americans saw their first feature-length film and paid the unprecedented price of one dollar per ticket. The film proved to be a major success, which Zukor attributed to the star featured in the movie.[63]

In 1912 the refusal by General Film to distribute *Quo Vadis,* a nine-reel Italian picture, led to the distribution technique of "roadshowing" or "four-walling" of a film. George Kleine, one of the Trust's founders, bypassed the distributors and dealt directly with the exhibitors. He opened the film himself in a theater in New York and received 10 percent of the gross receipts.[64] Like Zukor, he charged a one-dollar admission, ten times the previous rate charged. This first roadshow was a success and in several months was playing in nearly two dozen cities in the United States on the same terms.[65]

In roadshowing or four-walling a film, the producer would either rent his film on a percentage basis or he would take over the operation of the theater for a limited time period. This was often used to place a movie in a large legitimate theater instead of the nickelodeon. D.W. Griffith perfected the roadshowing method in 1915 with his distribution of *The Birth of a Nation.* This picture had exceeded all production costs, making the Trust fearful. When heads of the industry seriously considered dividing the twelve-reel film and issuing it serially, one reel a week, Griffith adamantly refused. He opened it at a theater in New York City, accompanied by a symphony orchestra, and ran it twice daily with an intermission.[66] He sold tickets in advance on a reserved-seat basis for the highest admission fee yet, two dollars. After roadshowing the film in the big cities, he then sold the exhibition rights to distributors in different areas.[67] Nearly ten years later, *The Birth of a Nation* was still breaking attendance records in large movie houses. Though the Patents Company had realized the success of the film too late, independent producers were influenced by it.[68] The financial success of *The Birth of a Nation* set the pattern for the "blockbuster," where a huge investment is made with the hopes of even greater returns. *The Birth of a Nation* cost $110,000 and eventually returned $20 million or more. Since the film was distributed on a state's rights basis, the actual cash generated by the film might have been as much as $50 million to $100 million.[69]

William Fox instituted a lawsuit against the Trust under the provisions of the Sherman Antitrust Act, charging unlawful conspiracy in restraint of trade aimed at monopolizing the industry. The suit went to trial in January 1913 and took five years for the final dissolution of the Trust. In 1915 General Film Company contracts were declared void by Federal Courts. In 1917 the United States Supreme Court held that the Motion Picture Patents Company could not enforce exclusive use of licensed film on patented projectors in theaters. The Trust was finally legally dead. But by then, they had already lost their power.[70]

After solving the problems of procuring equipment to make and project films, concentration was then upon distribution and marketing. Although the motion picture industry could not be controlled by patents, the legal battles demonstrated that control of the industry rested with distribution and that a national network of distribution was necessary to maximize profits. Exhibitors were dependent upon distributors for films, and producers were dependent upon distributors for outlets.[71]

When certain actors became well-liked by the public the Trust, fearing that they would gain power and demand salary increases, attempted to thwart their fame by refusing to give out the names of their actors. Carl Laemmle, the head of IMP, capitalized on this practice. By offering Florence Lawrence more money and fame, he lured this popular actor, known by her admirers as "The Biograph Girl," from Biograph and succeeded in creating the first movie star.[72]

The motion picture industry was becoming increasingly more lucrative. Film costs had advanced from $500 to $1,000 for a two-reel subject in 1912 to between $12,000 and $20,000 for a five-reel feature in 1915. The longer specials or films with popular stars cost even more.[73] It became apparent to most companies that the old practice of renting a picture simultaneously to as many theaters as wanted it would lead to briefer runs at lower prices in half-filled theaters. With the increasing number of lavish theaters, it no longer seemed feasible to treat all theaters on the same terms. The state's rights distributors had already been classifying theaters by quality and profitability. Between 1914 and 1916, an elaborate class system for theaters was created. It was believed that the run of the picture could be extended and its rentals increased if the film were first released for exclusive showing at the most prestigious theater charging the highest price. Only later would the smaller theaters get to play the picture. Zones were established around theaters that would compete with each other. Schedules for staggering the release dates were also created. A "run" indicated the priority rights in the exhibition of a film in a particular class of theater in a designated area. The time between a first-run and second-run opening date was called "clearance."[74]

As films became longer, they were in release longer and not as many screenings a day were possible. This allowed unscrupulous exhibitors to bicycle prints from one theater to another while paying rental on only one print. It became evident that a national distribution network was needed to protect the producers.

Exhibitors rarely used cuts in admission prices to compete with other exhibitors, because the reduction in rates would lower the standard of their theaters. If third-run theater operators lowered admission prices to increase attendance, their theaters might then become fifth- or sixth-run theaters in the eyes of the distributors. Competition between theaters, therefore, usually involved double, triple and even quadruple features, prizes, and games.[75]

Few exhibitors could afford to pay rentals on two quality films and usually resorted to showing one quality film and one cheaper "B" picture. To make up for this extra expense, rentals for both kinds of films tended on the average to decrease. Production budgets were concomitantly lowered as the studios moved to quantity over quality.[76] Larger theaters paid higher rentals and created a demand for the films. Owners of smaller theaters would then pay more to secure the subsequent run, since they knew people were pre-sold by the film's advertising. They would also agree to play the film longer and at the most favorable time of the week. Producers who could not book their films into a large theater found it difficult to earn back their investment since no demand existed for the films.[77]

William Wadsworth Hodkinson of the Trust's San Francisco exchange believed that above-average films could run longer than a single day. His idea was rebuked by the Trust.[78] In reaction to this resistance against longer films and to the state's rights method of distributing films, Hodkinson in 1914 consolidated five regional distributors into the first successful distributing organization covering the entire country. This company, which he named Paramount Pictures, only financed and distributed features produced by affiliated independent studios.[79] In 1912 Zukor and Daniel Frohman, one of the biggest theatrical producers, formed Famous Players and subsequently distributed their films through Paramount.[80] Zukor was the principal manufacturer of feature films and organized his Famous Players Company around the slogan "famous players in famous plays."[81]

Paramount entered into a contract with his Famous Players under terms stipulating that for a period of twenty-five years, the distributor agreed to advance to the producer $20,000 to $25,000 for each five-reel negative, and the producer agreed to distribute exclusively through them. Paramount also agreed to advance the cost of advertising. Gross rentals were to be divided with 65 percent going to the producer and 35 percent to the distributor. Paramount eventually wanted one picture a week from Zukor.[82]

Because of the success of the films, Paramount was able to charge higher rental fees than ever thought possible. General Film charged $100 to $150 a week to the best theaters for a total of seven programs of four to eight reels and $10 to $15 to theaters with less audience drawing power for each program of four to eight reels, changed daily. Paramount rented five-reel features for $500 to $700 a week to the largest theaters, $100 to $300 to secondary theaters, and as low as $5 to old theaters. Rentals quickly escalated to a total of $125,000 a picture.[83]

People became curious about the earnings of Paramount and realized that producing features was the richest field in the industry. Paramount charged a 35 percent distribution fee on rentals averaging $100,000 per picture. Out of the producer's $65,000, production costs averaged $35,000.

The producer's net profits per picture averaged $30,000. Foreign sales also earned rentals of $10,000 to $20,000 a picture.[84]

Hodkinson realized actress Mary Pickford was entitled to more money. He increased the advances to Famous Players on the Pickford films, charging exhibitors higher prices for her pictures. When Pickford's mother heard a Paramount salesman say "as long as we have Mary on the program we can wrap everything around her neck," she realized that Mary was entitled to greater compensation.[85] On 15 January 1915 Pickford received a new contract from Famous Players, under which she was to make ten pictures a year for $2,000 a week and half the profits of her productions. This led to increasingly higher salaries for other performers and increased admission prices at theaters, which the public was willing to pay. The theater admission price had risen to twenty-five cents. Many exhibitors doubted that further increases would be tolerated.[86]

Films were being distributed on a program system. Exhibitors were given complete programs for a week based on the population, without distinction between small and large theaters or cities. Limitations of the program system would not allow Pickford higher compensation without modification of the entire system. Hodkinson suggested to Pickford that one day her demands could be met by introducing a percentage system of paying film rentals for important films. In 1916 it would have been possible in only a few theaters and would have been impossible to induce five to ten thousand exhibitors to install the necessary accounting methods. Since Hodkinson could not appease Pickford, she threatened to go to another studio that would meet her demands.[87]

Not all distributors rigidly adhered to the program system as did Hodkinson. Lewis J. Selznick was selling his product in units made up of one star and occasionally rented an important picture separately.[88] Zukor, too, began an open booking policy, with rental based on individual films desired by the exhibitor. In 1916 Pickford formed her own producing company and planned to distribute her films through "Artcraft," which was affiliated with Zukor. Each of her films was to be sold separately. Her films, which earned United States rentals of $100,000 under Paramount, increased to $300,000 or more. Exhibitors loudly condemned Zukor, alleging his intent to monopolize stars and destroy competition. The exhibitors, however, remained unable to get together and effect any change. Pickford's salary rose to $10,000 a week and half the profits of her pictures, adding up to $1 million a year.[89]

A national distribution network that could handle feature films still did not exist. Zukor's pictures were distributed on the state's rights basis, in which exhibition rights were sold to distributors operating within a particular geographical area. Mutual, Universal, and Fox still sold shorts that changed daily or every other day. A producer would sell his movie to a state's rights buyer for a flat fee in exchange for the exclusive right to market the film in a specified territory. The buyer then would lease the picture to individual theaters on a flat rental or percentage-of-the-gross basis. By this method, if a film were extremely successful and earned a great amount of revenue, the distributor would profit but not the producer. This disadvantage was later overcome by selling the distribution rights for a limited time or on a percentage basis instead of outright.[90]

Zukor was the first to capitalize on this idea. His pictures featuring the most popular stars were in great demand, but since they were distributed by Paramount Pictures he did not reap the benefits. Half of the films Paramount distributed were supplied by Zukor, while Jesse L. Lasky and others contributed the balance. Although Famous Players earned more than a million dollars in its third year of existence, Zukor was unhappy with Paramount retaining 35 percent of the gross.

The success of the General Film Company with national distribution demonstrated that the production of films could be more profitable if the producers controlled the conditions of sale. Because Zukor disliked Hodkinson's power to replace his product whenever he chose, Zukor suggested to Hodkinson a merger of Paramount, Famous Players, and Lasky. Hodkinson did not believe in the integration of distribution and production and argued that better films would be made if competition for markets existed. Within a year, by the end of 1916, Zukor had bought control of Paramount and deposed Hodkinson. Zukor announced the formation of the "25 million dollar" Famous Players-Lasky Corporation, with himself as president, Lasky as head of production, and Paramount as the distributing subsidiary. Zukor's aggressive policies foreshadowed the pattern of what would come.[91]

Within a year, several new combinations of exhibitors, state's rights exchanges, and producers were following the Hodkinson-Zukor-Lasky plan. Most lacked strong management and went out of business or merged with larger companies.[92] With costs increasing greatly, Zukor needed to be assured of markets for the films. Direct control of theaters seemed remote then, so he controlled talent for leverage.[93] Zukor instituted distribution practices that still exist. In order to secure the Pickford films, which many exhibitors wanted, he made them take all of his films by "block-booking." A few powerful theater owners only took a portion of his pictures, but they still had to comply with Zukor's demands for preferential dates and higher rentals. Zukor had too many popular stars for the exhibitors to be able to ignore his demands.[94]

Up until this time films were sold for a flat price with higher prices for better grade movies. Those exhibitors who had better theaters and paid more were given priority known as "first run." These first-run exhibitors were protected for a week or more against exhibition of the picture in other neighboring theaters, and were nearly always located downtown in the center of the amusement district.[95]

By 1912–13, nearly all producers ceased trying to sell films that did not feature a star. Competitive bidding for stars increased, with the inadequate supply of experienced actors only making them more valuable. News of how much one star was making traveled quickly, making others demand even more. Better stories and directors were also now in demand. During the war years, financiers became cautious, allowing risk-takers to steal away stars. A few performers deserved the salaries since costs were passed on to the willing audience. However, severe losses were sustained by producers who bid for players whom they subsequently discovered were not in great demand by the audience.[96]

Extravagance and waste in the business was omnipresent. Each producer or each group of small producers operated a distribution system of thirty to thirty-five branch offices, costing $500,000 to $600,000 a year. Each producing group had its own studio, involving unnecessary costs of $250,000 to $500,000 annually. Two hundred or more producing and distributing companies were actively engaged in business in 1915.[97] Zukor was distributing about 220 features a year and kept increasing rentals.[98] In reaction to Zukor, twenty-six of the largest first-run exhibitors who owned several hundred theaters in the country organized in 1917 the First National Exhibitors Circuit to act as the purchasing agent for them and to finance and distribute their own features.[99] Unlike Zukor, who began in production and expanded into distribution and finally exhibition, First National united to form their own distribution channel and would ultimately move into production. They desired to combat high prices of star pictures by providing their own constant supply of pictures to members.[100]

The First National circuit operated by buying exclusive national rights to a film and apportioning the cost among the twenty-six members. Since market conditions were known, a percentage of the total income of a film was estimated from a given territory and each member paid a percentage of the film's cost calculated on the revenue in the territory of the member. Since the members also owned the first-run theaters, they had choice of product and play dates. Independent theaters in the area, partially dependent upon them for films, were often forced to sell out or face a dearth of films to exhibit.[101]

First National threatened Zukor's power by luring Charlie Chaplin and Pickford away. Chaplin was given a contract making him his own producer of eight two-reel comedies a year. He would be given a salary-inclusive $125,000 advance to make each negative. The cost of distribution was set at 30 percent of the total rentals. After all costs, profits were divided equally between First National and Chaplin. This served as the standard contractual agreement for years. [102]

First National realized that they needed a studio to ensure a constant flow of films to fill the chain of theaters and subsequently merged with Warner Brothers Vitaphone. [103] By January 1920, 639 theaters were controlled by First National. Of these, 224 were first-run houses, 49 were subsequent run houses, and 366 were operated by subfranchise holders. [104]

Fearing his market would be gone if First National became independent of his product, Zukor was motivated to enter the theater business. [105] After two years of analysis and study, Zukor in 1919–20 decided to set about acquiring theaters. He quietly bought into the Stanley Company, the Saenger Amusement Company, and the Black-Gray-Gordon Corporations in New England. He acquired not only the theaters and booking offices and interests in corporations owning three memberships in First National, but was also in the position of receiving information to study the operations of his main competitor from the inside of its organization. [106] Zukor fought to maintain control of stars and other talent for his productions while creating a national booking organization based on the Stanley Company of Philadelphia. This company selected pictures for dozens of independently owned theaters. It also set rental prices and charged the exhibitors 5 to 10 percent above rentals for the service. This company was the most powerful single element then in existence in the theater branch of the movie industry. Some exhibitors claimed they were forced into the company which threatened otherwise to build opposition theaters. Zukor's men, whose job was to acquire theaters, became known as the "wrecking crew" and the "dynamite gang." They either gave exhibitors the opportunity to remain in business if they agreed to show only Paramount pictures or they bought or built theaters nearby, making it impossible for the exhibitors to compete. Producers alleged that the Stanley Company was an oppressive monopoly that decided which pictures could be shown in its territory and that insisted on prices so low manufacturers could not make profits. [107]

In 1918 the Federal Trade Commission had issued an order against the Stanley Booking Corporation of Philadelphia, one of the largest combinations, declaring it guilty of unfair competition. The corporation was ordered to cease and desist from screening films which competitors had advertised to be played at a later date, making contracts conditional upon the exhibitor agreeing not to rent films from any competitors, employing threats and intimidation to induce exhibitors to play the film, or forcing producers to agree not to supply product to competitors. [108]

Like the Stanley Company of Philadelphia, the Saenger Amusement Company of New Orleans had succeeded in employing the "booking-office system," under which theater owners paid them for selecting the films for their screens. Stanley and Saenger, collecting 5 or 10 percent from the exhibitor and from the distributor, became the most powerful exhibiting organizations. Their consolidation of the purchasing power of many theaters enabled them to obtain better prices for the best films. Smaller, powerless exhibitors welcomed an alliance with this power. While the Stanley Company owned or controlled most of the important theaters in Philadelphia and eastern Pennsylvania, the Saenger Company commanded a similar position in Louisiana and portions of other states served from New Orleans. Each also owned the First National franchise for its territory.[109] The power of these two companies demonstrated the value of theater control. Although there was an abundance of films, by 1919-20 the producers who had not been aligned with these two companies had very few theaters in these areas in which to play their films. Litigation was too slow to be effective.[110]

The Stanley and Saenger system was followed by that of Alfred S. Black, who operated Black's New England Theaters, Inc. and Exhibitors Film Booking Office. After calculating in 1919 that there were 6,500 theaters in towns of less than 5,000 people, he decided to bring 4,000 of them under his control. He told possible financiers:

> Control of this great industry is coincident with the control of its source of revenue, namely, the theater. . . . It is only fair to assume that, at the present time, the destinies of the United States—social, commercial and political—lie largely within the power of the motion picture theater.[111]

Although Black was not able to induce Wall Street capitalists to invest in his idea, he proceeded with a small amount of money and soon persuaded or frightened thirty or forty theaters in New England into his control. He then formed alliances with others who controlled groups of theaters. Throughout the country, people were similarly aligning theaters for greater control and security.[112]

Zukor's initial idea was to extend this booking system of the Stanley Company to the entire United States. If he had been able to implement it, he could have remained in power without ownership of theaters. When he presented this plan to First National, however, many of the exhibitors objected on the grounds that it would eliminate their power to select pictures for their own houses. Even though it may have protected their theaters by a connection with Zukor's product, it had been rejected.[113]

In only a few years, five thousand to six thousand theaters were showing Paramount films. Other companies envied their profits. When a representative feature film was opened on a first-run basis, it would generally gross from $60,000 to $100,000, whereas it would only gross $30,000 to $40,000 without an adequate first-run exhibition, thus failing to even cover costs.[114] Other production companies were anxious to compete with Paramount. To ensure first-run theaters for their pictures, they began to buy theaters in strategic locations. Like Paramount, Fox began to build its own theaters. The independent theater owners, who were being charged ever increasing rental fees, were frightened for their existence.[115]

To be assured an outlet for their films, Goldwyn Picture Corporation in 1921 bought a half-interest in thirty theaters. Conversely, Loew's Inc., a theater chain, bought Metro Picture Corporation to be assured of first-run films for its screens. Since the majors became dominant in the 1920s, the independents and smaller studios, such as United Artists, had to do business with one or more of them in order to book their movies into first-run theaters via distribution organizations the majors also owned.[116]

Most theaters were independent but had the least power, as they were generally unorganized and in smaller cities. Large theater chains developed great buying power as producers aligned with them for security. As production companies grew financially, the independent distributor became less significant. Producers now either integrated with the existing distributors or more often established their own district and branch exchanges. By 1929, there were 444 producers' exchanges that accounted for more than $200 million worth of business. Approximately 95 percent of the total volume of business reported by all exchanges was accomplished through these exchanges. Also, four of the fourteen exchanges that exported films were owned by producers and worth more than an additional $5 million.[117] In the early twenties, as the studios integrated producing and distributing, first-run theaters took on a new power, away from the distributors.[118]

The last phase in integrating production, distribution, and exhibition was described as the "battle for theatres."[119] The advantages of national distribution over the state's rights system were so great that the integration of production with distribution was inevitable. Theater operators quickly realized the merits of the system and formed alliances with producer-distributors. Mae D. Huettig wrote, "The logic of the entire situation pointed in the direction of vertical consolidation." She believed that the motion picture industry is unique because of the interdependence of the majors which results from each being simultaneously buyer and seller of films. "Reciprocity of dealings between the majors is the key to understanding the motion picture business."[120]

The studios began buying as many theaters as they could because, as well as being profitable operations, they also afforded the studios a link with the audience, functioning as a barometer of the public's tastes in films. Owners of lucrative theaters were given the choice of selling according to terms offered by the majors or of having to compete against a new theater that would be built in the vicinity and that would secure the best films. Most theater owners sold under this pressure. If a theater was not too profitable, the majors would not necessarily purchase it but would persuade the theater owner to give preference to the films of the particular major.[121]

This indiscriminate, zealous drive to acquire or control as many theaters as possible often proved excessive and unprofitable. Initially, Paramount and Universal bought as many theaters as they could without regard to quality, size, or location. However, managing these numerous theaters proved unprofitable and even burdensome. As soon as it was realized that the audience would pay more to see new films, they began to institutionalize this demand for novelty through first-run theaters.[122]

Since the studios had acquired so many theaters, they needed outside films to keep the theaters supplied. To remain profitable, Paramount showed its own films and Metro pictures released by Loew's. Loew's reciprocally had to show Paramount films; however, Loew's stars were in greater demand, enabling Loew's to have a stronger bargaining position than Paramount. Therefore, when Paramount sold films to Loew's, the terms were conditioned by their need for Loew's films.[123] This "seller's market" situation did not exist in towns where a theater or chain of theaters had no competition. In these situations, the distributors competed while the theater owner could select the best films and the best terms. These situations, however, were quite uncommon.[124]

Even though most independent distributors disappeared from the industry, independent theaters did survive. Since lawsuits against the majors by the Federal Trade Commission were commonplace, the majors were not about to absorb all the theaters. More importantly, the majors realized they could still control the theater market and collect revenue from the most lucrative theaters by absorbing only the first-run theaters.[125]

The initial struggle in the industry involved patent control and monopoly over the market, but it was replaced by a fierce battle for theaters. Many theaters strengthened their bargaining power. Since real estate on which to develop theaters required a large financial backing, the three branches of the industry integrated for power. By the early twenties, most individual and independent corporations had been eliminated and had been replaced by a few powerful organizations.[126] In 1926 there were an estimated twenty thousand theaters with a total seating capacity of eighteen million and annual box office revenue calculated at $750 million.[127]

The majors had great strength in the exhibition field, even though they did not directly own a majority of the theaters. Of the twenty-three thousand theaters operating in 1930 in the United States, the majors owned or controlled only three thousand of them. They were, however, the best first-run theaters in the large cities and they accounted for almost 70 percent of the nation's box office receipts.[128]

Public relations concerns and restrictive legislation posed severe problems which led in 1922 to the formation of the Motion Picture Producers and Distributors of America (MPPDA).[129] Much confusion had arisen over the multitude of contracts between distributors and exhibitors. Attempts to enforce any contract by litigation were too time consuming and costly, and rarely were they effective. Some exchanges organized film clubs which collected information on the business practices of their customers and established credit ratings. If an exhibitor employed questionable business practices, the clubs refused to do business with him. It is believed "that the initial impetus toward a standard form of contract came from exhibitors."[130]

In 1923 a contract was agreed upon by distributors and exhibitors which was supposed to be applied uniformly. Individual distributors continued adding clauses which modified or amplified the contract. In 1925 the exhibitors called for a contract that would be uniform in practice, and one was adopted in 1926. A year later the Federal Trade Commission adopted fifteen rules governing trade practices. Arbitration was adopted along with provisions for negotiation of a new contract which would provide for periodic reconsideration and revision of the contract. In 1928 the new contract was adopted. An exhibitor now had to sign an application for a license to exhibit films in accordance with the distributor's copyrights. The sale was not consummated if the exhibitor did not receive notice of the acceptance of this application from the distributor's offices within a certain number of days. This allowed centralized control of sales.[131]

The license allowed an exhibitor to run a film at a particular theater for a number of successive days. In return, the exhibitor agreed not to allow the film to leave his possession during the specified period nor to exhibit it in any other theater. The distributor granted "protection," or agreed not to play the picture in any competing zone for a designated time afterward. The distributor did reserve the right to roadshow not more than two of the films licensed to the exhibitor. An exhibitor was not required to play a film he had leased when the distributor presented a film based on a different book, or which featured a different star or different director from the time the agreement was made. The exhibitor agreed not to alter a film. If an exhibitor found a film racially or religiously objectionable, he could submit it to the board of arbitration. If the board ruled in his favor, the picture was excepted from the agreement and the distributor had the right to license the film elsewhere, free of the exhibitor's claims. The contract also defined play dates, payment of fees, return of films, advertising, and minimum admission prices.[132]

A statistical analysis by the Hays organization regarding the work of the arbitration board from 1924 to 1929 revealed that the greatest source of complaint on the part of the distributors was the exhibitors' failure to show films for which they had contracted, by refusing to accept delivery and make payment. This complaint accounted for 81.7 percent of the claims filed. The principal complaint of exhibition was the failure of distributors to deliver pictures. This amounted to 38.5 percent of the cases. Violation of protection and clauses regarding runs accounted for 18.2 percent of the cases. Failure of a distributor to designate play dates amounted to 7.5 percent of the cases.[133]

The Allied States Association of Motion Picture Exhibitors was made up of approximately 6,000 independent exhibitor associations. More than 1,375 independents belonged to local associations which in turn belonged to the Motion Picture Theatre Owners of America. The Allied States Association was the spokesman of unaffiliated or independent theater owners in negotiations regarding contract standards.[134]

Exhibitors claimed that the contracts served to grant distributors control in the industry. On 25 September 1929 the government in *United States v. First National Pictures Inc. et al.,* began proceedings against producers and distributors who were members of the Hays organization for maintaining a conspiracy in restraint of trade. On 15 October 1929 in *United States v. Paramount Famous-Lasky Corporation et al.,* the government attacked the arbitration system as a conspiracy in restraint of trade on the grounds that the standard contract compelled exhibitors to submit to arbitration by waiving the right to settle disputes in courts. The government also claimed that the contract compelled exhibitors to put up cash or suffer the loss of their supply of films when they refused to submit to arbitration. The rules governing arbitration were also attacked. In 1930 a new contract made arbitration voluntary.[135]

Competing studios discovered that price competition was not beneficial to the industry as a whole. Since price cuts were rapidly met by competitors, no permanent advantage was maintained by anyone and the profits for all were merely reduced. Cooperation was seen as a means to prevent additional competitors from joining in and disturbing their interests.[136] Block-booking and related practices became common means of maintaining control of the industry and limiting any independent power. Block-booking was the practice used by producer/distributors of selling groups of films to an exhibitor before they were completed and only as a package deal. This began as a mutual need for producers to be sure of a market for their films and the exhibitors' need to have a constant supply of motion pictures.

The studios claimed block-booking reduced overhead costs, saving money for all. An argument by analogy was offered equating block-booking of motion pictures to subscriptions of magazines.[137] They claimed this service provided advantages not possible on an individual film booking basis.

Theaters owned by the studios received the best pictures and chose not to play the weak films. This was acceptable since the studio's profit was directly linked to that of its own theaters. Large chains were powerful enough to refuse to buy in blocks. They used the threat of not showing any product of a particular studio in any of their theaters. It was, therefore, the small exhibitor who had to acquiesce to any studio terms to secure films to play. Warner Brothers generally was denied access to first-run theaters. However, when Warner Bros. became exclusive agents for sound, they easily negotiated deals for those theaters in exchange for the right to use Vitaphone and Western Electric equipment.[138]

Exhibitors disliked buying blocks because it left them powerless in making decisions about which films would be played. Blocks of films often included unnamed pictures and pictures without a story line or stars. This also served to increase the value of the stars and creative talent, as this was often all the information they were given on a particular film. If a star in an already contracted for film became more famous before the movie was ready for exhibition, the exhibitors were powerless when the studio decided to remove the film from the block. The studios had no qualms about increasing the rental on these films or replacing them with inferior pictures.

Small exhibitors also claimed that the large chains and majors wanted to maximize their profits at their expense and the public's. In addition to block-booking, they complained about blind-selling, whereby they had to agree to play a film without having seen it. They had no recourse if the film was different from what they expected or even was not what they believed to be in good taste for the public interest. They also objected to being forced to take short subjects along with the feature film. They claimed they often did not want the particular short or did not want to play shorts at all. They believed they should have the right to schedule their own theaters.

Small exhibitors also complained over "designated play dates" or being told when they had to show the film. Studios, of course, wanted their films screened on holidays or weekends when attendance is greatest, while exhibitors wanted the option of showing a popular film midweek to bring in an audience that would not regularly attend. The small exhibitors also claimed the large exhibitors controlled the setting of admission prices, which they believed should be negotiated on an individual basis. Overbuying was a practice whereby large exhibitors licensed more films than they could play to prevent their competition from playing the films. The smaller exhibitors, therefore, were at the mercy of the larger chains. The distributors cooperated in exhibitors' overbuying for fear of a boycott by these large exhibitors.[139]

The small exhibitors believed they, particularly, were being adversely affected by zoning and clearance practices. If an exhibitor, usually a large chain, was playing a film, he could demand that the film not be played in the particular vicinity where it would draw customers away from his theater. He also could demand that a certain period of time elapse before any other exhibitor could play the film. Small exhibitors were thereby excluded from playing new motion pictures when they were most desired by the public.

In 1927, although a cease-and-desist order in regard to block-booking was issued, the practice continued. Studios argued that no exhibitor was ever forced to show a picture. They claimed that an exhibitor could cancel 10 percent of his commitments, could cancel any picture which might offend local tastes, and could afford not to play a film he did not want to run. They stressed that the pictures the exhibitors generally did not want to show were the pictures good for society, and only if these were included in blocks would they ever be shown. [140]

In 1932 the Federal Trade Commission decided it would not enforce the block-booking order. The matter, however, was not settled. Congress passed the National Recovery Act in July 1933 which suspended antitrust efforts by the government and returned power to the businessmen to regulate their own industries by codes of trade practices to be set up under the National Recovery Administration (NRA). Instead of the goal of allowing the majors to control the industry smoothly, the small independent theater-owners protested. They organized into the Allied States Association of Motion Picture Exhibitors. Initially, they were against the way the NRA created the division of interest between affiliated producers, distributors, exhibitors, and the nonaffiliated exhibitors. The independent exhibitors believed the division should be between sellers and buyers. [141]

The majors were interested in reinstituting block-booking and also wanted to stop the playing of double features. The independent exhibitors created an intense lobbying campaign against the proposals and won. The code ultimately made no reference to double features or block-booking. However, it adversely affected independent exhibitors by outlawing a practice they had implemented to entice customers to their theaters—it eliminated all rebate schemes such as lotteries, free gifts, drawings for cash prizes, "Bank Night," "Race Night," and "Screeno." Only severe protest from pottery manufacturers led to permission of premium gifts as prizes. In 1935, when the Supreme Court declared the NRA unconstitutional, the lotteries and drawings quickly reappeared. [142]

A common sentiment by those linked to the studios was that the motion picture industry was a "purely private enterprise engaged in furnishing the public a service of amusement and entertainment and is not affected with such a public interest as to justify federal regulation and control." [143] Charles C. Pettijohn, Counsel for Motion Picture Producers and Distributors Association, stated in a hearing in the House of Representatives in 1936:

> They say, "Show samples in advance." We are not in the business of mass production. We cannot make pictures in mass like soap or shoes. We do not know when a picture is made; not until after shown can we tell whether or not it is going to be a successful picture. That can only be determined after the picture has gone out and is before the public. Pictures are not alike; no two are alike; we cannot make them alike. [144]

Many national organizations, however, opposed compulsory block-booking and blind-selling. They included the American Association of University Women, Associated Church Press, Association for Childhood Education, Film Audiences for Democracy, Motion Picture Research Council, National Congress of Parents and Teachers, National Education Association, and the National Motion Picture League.[145]

The government strongly believed each picture should be able to seek a place in the open market and that theaters should be able to bid competitively for pictures. They found collusion existing between the five companies, which created a closed market for independent producers, distributors, and theaters.[146] After years of charges and countercharges of unfair trade practices, the Department of Justice on 20 July 1938 filed a petition against the five major producer-distributor-exhibitor companies—Paramount, Loew's Inc., Radio-Keith-Orpheum, Warner Bros., and Twentieth Century-Fox—and against the three large producer-distributors—United Artists, Columbia, and Universal. They were charged with combining and conspiring to restrain trade and commerce in the production, distribution, and exhibition of motion pictures in the United States and with monopolizing such trade and commerce in violation of the Sherman Antitrust Act.

In an amended petition on 14 November 1940, the Department of Justice listed the offenses charged against the companies. They included the mutual loaning of personnel and equipment while excluding these privileges to independent producers, fixing license term contracts before licensees can judge the film's value, fixing of minimum admission prices, fixing of runs and clearance, licensing one group of films on that of another, licensing of films to a certain theater based upon licensing it to other theaters under common control or ownership, making exclusive contracts with circuit theaters in some localities, withholding prints to give circuit theaters clearance not agreed to in contracts, setting of minimum admission prices so independent theaters could not compete with circuits, forcing independent theaters to take shorts and newsreels, charging independents higher film rentals than circuits in equivalent situations, and partially defraying the costs of circuit theaters and not of the independents. Additional charges made against the five producer-distributor-exhibitor companies included excluding independent productions from their affiliated theaters, excluding independent exhibitors from operating first-run theaters where affiliated theaters were located, using affiliated theaters to control film supply and admission prices, coercing and intimidating independent exhibitors into licensing films on arbitrary terms by threatening to build or acquire a competing theater, coercing and intimidating independent exhibitors into giving up their part or whole interest in a theater to one of the affiliated companies by threatening to build or acquire competing theaters, eliminating competition by jointly operating theaters, and dividing available films between two or more affiliated theaters in the same competitive area to eliminate competition.[147]

The Department of Justice found that for the years 1934 to 1937, more than 95 percent of all pictures shown in the first-run metropolitan houses of each of the majors consisted of the releases of the eight companies. And over 99 percent of the films exhibited in Loew's first-run theaters were released by the majors.

> As a result...the independent producer does not have access to a free, open, and untrammelled first-run market in metropolitan cities in which to dispose of his pictures. Entrance to this market by an independent producer is only at the sufferance of (the defendants herein) who control it.

These sobering conclusions did not even address the issue that if this market were closed to the independent, the remainder of the market in subsequent runs would also be closed.[148]

In 1940 Paramount, Loew's, RKO, Warner Bros., and Twentieth Century-Fox, without admitting guilt, consented to change their practices so that the Justice Department would drop its suit. The Paramount defendants were enjoined from (1) granting a license with minimum fixed admission prices by any means, (2) agreeing with exhibitors or distributors to maintain clearances, (3) granting clearance between theaters not in substantial competition, (4) making a formula deal, an agreement in which the license fee for the theaters covered by the agreement is measured by a specific percentage of a picture's gross, or a master agreement, which covers the exhibition of features in a circuit, (5) entering into block-booking and, (6) licensing other than theater by theater.[149] They also agreed not to offer more than five films in a block to exhibitors, not to rent a film without a trade screening, not to require theaters to rent shorts as a condition of renting features, and not to acquire any theaters for a period of time. The government retained the right to reinstitute the suit if the companies did not live up to this Consent Decree. In 1944 the government stepped in again.

The government wanted Paramount, Twentieth Century-Fox, and Warner Bros. to sever their theater interests and wanted Loew's and RKO to stop producing films. Columbia, Universal and United Artists refused to sign the Consent Decree since they owned no theaters. The government then gave the five that did sign until 1 June 1942 to persuade the other three to sign or the Decree would be void.

By 1945, 3,137 of 18,076 motion picture theaters in the United States were either solely or jointly owned by the majors. They, however, comprised 70 percent of the first-run theaters in the ninety-two largest cities and 60 percent of the first-run theaters in smaller cities.[150] In 1947, 107 distribution companies were in business in the United States.[151] However, the eight majors dominated eleven of these companies, which were the only ones to distribute nationally.[152]

The majors clearly had control over the production, distribution, and exhibition of motion pictures, and the independents continued to protest. In 1949 the Department of Justice finally achieved what it intended in 1938. The majors were forced to choose between either retaining their production and distribution channels or their exhibition channel. The Supreme Court ordered RKO and Paramount Pictures to split their production and distribution operations from their theater chains and to sell enough of their theaters to allow for competition. In June 1950 the same decision was applied to Loew's Inc., Twentieth Century-Fox, and Warner Bros. It also established voting trusts to prevent shareholders in the former integrated companies from exercising common control over both successor companies.[153]

The majors chose to retain production and distribution. Columbia, Universal-International, and Republic Pictures had been successfully making money for years without owning a single theater. This observation, along with the fact that theater revenues had been dropping sharply in the preceding years, greatly influenced their decision.[154] The studios now had to market each film individually without regard to any other films or theaters. This was a practice in which they had little experience. Without the security of a guaranteed income, each film had to be financed individually. Stars and script changes now carried more weight in getting a film made, and greater emphasis was placed on the marketing of the film. Since an assured market no longer existed, the studios began to reduce production.

The governmental decision, therefore, aided independent production since a possible outlet for films now existed. Studios also began renting space to independents in addition to financing independent production. The studios were able to save interest on independently financed pictures while still distributing a film or even purchasing it outright after it was completed. The independent exhibitor gained more freedom, yet was confronted with the reality of product shortages and resultant higher rentals.[155]

United Artists had historically functioned as a distributor for independent producers. Between 1953 and 1957, they released approximately fifty pictures per year. The majors began following United Artists' pattern. By 1958, 65 percent of Hollywood's features were made by independent producers.[156]

In addition to the changes created by the Consent Decree, the industry was faced with the growing impact of television. During the late thirties and early forties, television broadcasting was in the experimental stage. A wartime ban on the manufacture of receivers interrupted progress. However, once the restrictions ended more than forty-thousand television sets were being produced each month.[157] The studios did not want to accept the fact that television would increasingly replace the moviegoing habit. They viewed television as a threat to their means of distributing pictures and sought to fight it by resurrecting the wide screens, the three-dimensional format, and other gimmicks that had been used in the past in an attempt to maintain dwindling audiences.

The television networks, CBS and NBC, were primarily in business to manufacture television sets.[158] When the studios would not supply motion pictures, the networks were forced to produce product for their television receivers. Columbia Pictures, owning no theaters, was the only company to begin television production immediately and set up Screen Gems TV production in 1950.[159]

Between 1941 and 1946, the last years before the impact of television was felt, the studios' income had doubled from $809 million to $1.692 billion, as approximately 95 million Americans attended the movies each week.[160] By 1953, only 32.4 percent of all theaters were making a profit on admission income. Another 38.4 percent were losing money at the box office but making a profit through concession sales. The remaining 29.2 percent were losing money.[161] Small independent theaters had to compete for first-run films by raising their prices. Concomitantly, as the prices went up, the lower economic groups of people who were considered to be the most faithful moviegoers could no longer afford to go to the movies. In the decade from 1946 to 1956, more than four thousand theaters closed. Their loss was, however, balanced by the construction of new drive-ins.[162]

By the late fifties, the studios began to sell their pre-1948 libraries to television and even began to produce for television. The studios now were mere suppliers of product to television and television series became their main source of revenue.[163]

Power in the industry shifted in favor of the talent. When the studios cut back on their production, they also terminated long-term contracts that appeared too costly for the fewer films being made. In an attempt to save money they lost control of the talent. When laws made it more profitable to operate as a corporation than an individual, stars became involved in negotiations and increased demands to include participation in a picture's profits.[164]

Frank E. Rosenfelt, past chairman of Metro-Goldwyn-Mayer, believes the income tax rate, in addition to television, helped to destroy the studio system. During the war years, taxes greatly increased for stars, directors, and other highly paid people. The studio, with talent under contract, would open independent production companies for them to avoid the payment of these taxes. A few years later, those independent companies were supplying the studios with most of their films.[165]

United Artists was created to offer to talent creative control and a share in the profits, but it lacked sufficient product to sustain the cost of a distribution arm. In 1951 United Artists was reorganized by Arthur Krim and Robert Benjamin who began a new policy of being involved in as many films as possible, regardless of whether it was a low or high budget picture, to build up business. Realizing that talent was no longer tied to studios but instead had their own producing companies, United Artists could offer what they lacked—financing and distribution, in addition to autonomy if the film would be made within budget. Leading producers were attracted to United Artists. Although United Artists had been in the red in 1948, by the end of the fifties it was among the leading money-makers in the entire industry. By 1955, other studios began welcoming independents to their lots.[166] United Artists had given independent producers and filmmakers creative control and participation in net profits. By 1960, sharing revenue with filmmakers became standard.[167]

In the fifties, television firmly became the mass entertainment despite the motion picture industry's attempts to defeat it or compete with it. Finally, in the sixties, the studios had to adjust by trying to provide audiences with what they could not find on television. The majors offered the big musical and costume epics for the mass audience, while the independents offered the low-budget "B" picture geared toward a select audience. Foreign films gained wide acceptance on college campuses. Many small film societies were created in addition to New York's Cinema 16, which had thousands of members. By the late sixties, many small theaters that were started to accommodate this new audience had to resort to screening pornography to survive. The novelty of foreign films waned as new themes were being explored in television.

As fewer pictures were being distributed by the majors, the independents were able to secure a larger share of the domestic box office, rising from 5 percent to 15 percent. When the majors began to dominate certain periods of the year, the independents were left with the rest of the playing time.[168] Though independents had been thriving at this time with their "B" pictures, the films generally were limited in audience appeal. *Easy Rider,* produced for a little more than $500,000, was a success at the 1969 Cannes Film Festival. Since it grossed $60 million worldwide, it became clear that an enormous profit could be made with obviously little risk.[169] Consequently, many low-budget youth movies were produced; however, the financial success could not be replicated. By the next year, the high-budget *Airport,* with big-name stars, broke box office records.[170]

Because of erratic earnings, stocks in the film companies were undervalued during the 1960s. Conglomerates were, therefore, attracted to the studios and realized that procuring them would prove to be a wise investment. The studios owned valuable real estate, music publishing houses, and theaters in foreign countries. Their film libraries were also highly attractive with the coming of cable and pay television. Taking over the studios, therefore, involved more than just the desire for a motion picture production-distribution company. The conglomerates succeeded in buying up the major studios, making films a minor part of their disparate industries.[171]

In 1962, Music Corporation of America (MCA) acquired Universal Pictures from Decca Records who had controlled it since 1952. In 1966, Gulf and Western bought Paramount and TransAmerica acquired United Artists. In 1968, Warner Bros. went to Seven Arts and then in 1969 to Kinney National Services which changed the parent company's name to Warner Communications Inc. Avco bought Embassy and Coca-Cola bought Columbia Pictures Industries. Avco ultimately sold Embassy and TransAmerica released United Artists to Metro-Goldwyn-Mayer. Twentieth Century-Fox, acquired by Marvin Davis and Marc Rich, was converted from a publicly held corporation to private ownership in 1981.[172]

At the end of the 1960s, excessive amounts of money were spent in an attempt to make successful musicals such as *The Sound of Music*. This was a factor in the industry depression from 1969 to 1971. From 1969 to 1972, the seven majors lost a total of $500 million. During that period, the studios did not recognize that television movies were satisfying the public and that they, therefore, had to make what could not be seen on television.[173] Hence, the studios increasingly began to produce for television. In January 1972, Universal reported a ten-year production peak, with five thousand employees working, yet no features were being made. All were involved in television production. Independent producers of theatrical films were able to thrive. In 1970, 42 percent of the films started were by independents. By the end of 1970, independent filming was up 225 percent from 1969 levels. By 1975, independents accounted for nearly $100 million worth of production and approximately three hundred features.[174]

In the seventies, the "blockbuster," the large-scale picture aimed at a huge audience, took on great significance. Film production and distribution became increasingly too costly for the majors to justify making films aimed at a limited audience. Instead, they chose to gamble on blockbusters, which demanded that a film appeal to the broadest mass audience. These costly productions, when unsuccessful or even marginally successful, were financially devastating for the exhibitor in particular. Studios frequently demanded 90 percent of the box office net while requiring a blind bid on the film, in addition to a hefty guarantee. *The Economist's* David Gordon said:

> When a picture is a success, that reward is too high; and when it is a disaster it is too low.... The only way distributors can survive is by setting the super-profits of one production against the super-losses of another and the nothing profits of the average picture.[175]

In June 1975 *Jaws* opened in five hundred theaters. For a twelve-week run to reduce competition against it, Universal did not release any films.[176] It was the first film to amass more than $100 million in domestic film rentals. Though the industry was amazed that one picture could generate such large revenue, it was still to be surpassed in the eighties. Now, because of increasing fixed costs, pictures need to reach a wider audience to break even. Films, therefore, are produced with the belief that they will be appreciated by more than a small audience. Less effort needs to be exerted with the hope of generating great profit on a few blockbusters than by aiming to make small profits on more pictures.

In the 1970s the distributors grew in power as the number of theaters increased and the high cost of film production reduced the number of films made. It became a "seller's market." During the mid-1970s, distributors received an average of 34 to 36 percent of box office receipts. By 1979, they were commanding 39 to 40 percent.[177] Alan B. Snyder, an entertainment analyst in the investment banking firm of Cantor, Fitzgerald and Co. Inc. stated, "That swing in power . . . is over. You've gone as far as you can go and keep some theaters in existence. . . ."[178] A product shortage was the result of making fewer films at greater and greater costs. This encouraged chains of theaters to grow in strength as independents found it difficult to secure any films to exhibit and nearly impossible to get the few blockbusters.

It is generally believed that seven out of ten pictures lose money, two out of ten break even, and one is a huge success, or that two out of three pictures do not generate enough revenue to pay for the prints and ads, with less than one out of three pictures making more than $10 million in film rentals. It is generally stated that for every dollar spent on production, the film must recoup three times that cost before there is any profit. This rule, however, does not apply similarly to a $10 million and a $30 million film. The expenses for marketing and distribution, employees, prints, and advertising are generally not that much greater for the higher budgeted film. It does not follow that a $10 million picture needs to recoup $30 million and a $30 million film needs to generate $90 million to break even.

In the past, below-the-line costs exceeded above-the-line expenses. Today, major stars, directors, and scripts can command fees in the millions. In 1972 the average negative cost was $1.9 million.[179] In 1983 the average production cost for a feature produced by a major was $11.5 million, with a range from $5 million to $40 million. The average cost for an independent that was picked up by a major was $5.8 million, ranging from $2 million to $10 million. Pay-cable budgets averaged $3.5 million and network TV budgets averaged $2.1 million.[180] Moderately budgeted pictures kept the average relatively low. Pre-opening and opening advertising costs, however, added an additional average of $5 million to $8 million to a picture. This cost varied greatly from marginal to wide releases.

In 1974 the average feature cost $2.5 million to produce and $1 million to market. The break-even point was $7 million box office gross from 3.5 million admissions. By 1984, the average picture cost $12 million to produce and $7 million to market. The break-even point was reached with $38 million box office gross from 12 million admissions. The ticket prices increased only 65 percent while production costs rose approximately 500 percent.[181] The nation's average ticket price in 1983 was $3.15.[182] Average weekly attendance was greatest in 1945 to 1948 with 90 million admissions weekly. Weekly admissions in the eighties are around 20 million. Historically, more than 70 percent of the theater public has been under thirty years of age. However, because of changing demographic characteristics of the country, the size of this group has been decreasing.[183] Box office gross receipts in the 1970s grew by 7.7 percent annually to $3.5 billion in 1982, while the number of admissions only grew by approximately 2.1 percent to 1.18 billion. Film rentals stayed constant until 1982 when they jumped 20.5 percent to $2.4 billion. Theatrical showings accounted for 65 percent of the $3.6 billion grossed. By 1987, according to Merril Lynch's Harold Vogel, rentals will only bring in 44.5 percent of overall revenues.[184] In 1983, theaters sold $3.7 billion worth of tickets in the United States and Canada, setting a record for the third year in a row.[185] While each studio used to produce fifty pictures a year, the majors are now producing approximately half of their release schedules or a combined total of sixty in-house pictures a year. In 1972, 70 percent of the majors' product, 150 films, were produced in-house. In 1982 the number was only 54 percent and appeared to be decreasing.[186] By 1983, only 44 percent were produced in-house.[187]

Over the past decade, the majors and independents have released a combined average of 450 pictures annually. To handle the product domestically, approximately 180 major and independent distributors with an aggregate of 492 film exchanges listed in forty-seven cities exist. This averages less than three films per distributor. There are also seventy-four exchanges in seven Canadian cities and 380 non-theatrical film distributors in the United States.[188]

Regardless of the number of independent distributors that exist, from 1972 to 1982 independent distributors accounted for 11.7 percent of the market, while the seven majors (Universal, Warner Bros., Paramount, Twentieth Century-Fox, Columbia, MGM/UA, and Buena Vista) accounted for 88.3 percent.[189]

Since, generally, ten or fewer films are generating 60 to 70 percent of the business at all theaters at any particular time, the competition for these films is highly intense. With this exhibitor demand has come the increase in film rental terms.[190] Because of the product shortage in the seventies, distributors were able to demand greater advances and guarantees, longer runs, and higher percentages of the box office revenue. Alan Hirschfield, however, claims the studios' share of the box office revenue has declined 10 percent during the last ten years from approximately 50 percent in 1974 to approximately 40 percent in 1984.[191]

Lacking accurate means of predicting the success of a motion picture, the studios sought means of minimizing their risk up front. They sought to employ proven box office stars, directors, and formulas. The increasing importance placed on actors gave more power to their agents. Eventually, larger agencies began packaging films among their own clients. Andrew Sarris wrote in 1978:

> Nowadays, producers, agents, and moneymen meet indiscriminately with bankable stars, bankable directors, and bankable writers to discuss bankable projects. The "Deal" becomes the instant "Studio" and as soon as the Deal is either fulfilled or broken off, the Studio vanishes in the mists like Brigadoon.[192]

In "The Me Decade and the Third Great Awakening," Tom Wolfe felt that only one line of credit was necessary for any movie: "Deal By."[193]

The studios have lost control over the financing of pictures. Innumerable means of financing exist and the studios have chosen to protect their downside. They even are involved in coproduction deals with other countries and other studios. New suppliers are entering the marketplace, creating additional competition for creative talent. By overpaying talent, others demanded more and more, escalating costs for all. The studios needed to cover all costs by relying on ancillary markets. David Londoner stated:

> Theatrical distribution used to be seventy-five percent of total Hollywood revenues in 1978, and will be about fifty-seven percent for 1983. The relative importance of worldwide theatrical distribution is diminishing. The power of the majors is also decreasing, as an independent has access to the other forty-three percent of the non-theatrical market.[194]

Though the theatrical audience is not growing, the studios are releasing more films each year. In 1977 MPAA members released 112 first-run features. In 1982 150 were released in addition to 25 MGM and UA classics. Londoner stated, "It's not only that there will be more films in the theatrical market splitting what is roughly the same pie, adjusted for inflation. There will also be a change in terms that come [sic] about between the exhibitor and the distributor." The box office revenue increased yet the distributors' share decreased.[195]

Foreign rentals have been reduced 12 to 14 percent because of foreign exchange rates. Londoner also expects advertising costs to increase because the more films in the market the greater the competition for the audience.[196]

William Bernstein, executive vice president of Orion Pictures Corp., finds that the industry has always been plagued with problems. He believes the majors must be ready to quickly capitalize on new opportunities instead of accepting the new after it is already firmly established by others.[197]

The history of the motion picture industry demonstrates that distribution practices have been influenced by the paramount goal of extracting the greatest revenue from a picture. When the studios were forced to divest themselves of their exhibition arm and reform common distribution tactics, government dictates only served to suppress specific practices. The powerful producer/distributors merely created new means of retaining control they had ostensibly relinquished. Studios, divested of their theaters along with the concomitant demand for product, were no longer obligated to provide any new films to keep the machine working. Exhibitors who had brought the monopoly suit against the studios had wanted better prices. However, after they became independent, exhibitors found that the dearth of product created bidding which only increased prices. The majors discovered they could make greater profits with fewer pictures. The decreasing need of studios to produce a greater output and the resultant shortage of product have inspired many independent productions. These films, of varying quality and often of limited audience appeal, have allowed for the growth of independent producers and distributors to supply exhibitors' needs. Exhibitors find that they often can make more money with a less crafted film made for a certain audience who will respond immediately to directed advertising. Such films also provide opportunities for new filmmakers to gain experience.

When independents have proven successful in a particular genre, their areas of domain are invaded by the majors. When independents proved highly successful with youth comedies, the majors quickly began producing them. When the majors realized that profit was being made from art and foreign films, they began their classics divisions and rapidly succeeded in dominating the market. Producers of low-budget pictures in these genres often feel it is difficult to compete with the majors and either raise their budgets or discover new genres to exploit. Yet there is always a market in any genre for independent films, regardless of how low the budget, which has a unique intangible ingredient that cannot be predicted. It is often independents, needing to keep ahead of the trends, that produce and distribute the watershed film that the majors begin to copy once it is proven safe. With the majors' concentration on mass audience films, independents may ultimately be the ones to fulfill adult audience needs. Independent producers and distributors have always been flexible enough to fulfill the needs of disparate audiences neglected by the majors. Though costs must escalate to meet increasingly sophisticated tastes, independent films are able to be created and distributed with minimal interference. Independent distributors can be truly independent—of content restrictions, quality restrictions, and restrictions of the spirit.

2

Censorship

Movies from their inception have been looked upon by the upper classes as a form of cheap entertainment for the lower classes. Although groups of people were wary of the influence of motion pictures from the start, when films reached the middle classes protests began to be heard. *Dolorita in the Passion Dance* in 1894 aroused a protest in Atlantic City.[1] In the Kinetoscope days *The Kiss* shocked audiences. In 1908 certain times during the day were devoted to exhibiting pictures for men only.[2] Intrigued, women dressed up like men to attend. This further inflamed those lobbying against the evils of the motion picture.

Censorship in the cinema became organized in the nickelodeon days. The mayor of New York City was pressured by Protestant denominations to use his licensing power to shut down theaters that violated Sunday closing laws. The denominations were convinced that the cinema would "corrupt the minds of children." On Christmas Day 1908, police moved to close the 550 movie houses and nickelodeons in the city. When the mayor noticed that many theaters exited into salons, he demanded that all cinemas close and reapply for licenses "in order to avert a public calamity."[3]

The People's Institute, a New York reform organization, nevertheless was aware of the value of movies. It brought ten New York civic organizations together to sponsor a motion picture censorship board. In 1909 producers agreed to submit all films to the board prior to making release prints so that any offensive footage could be extracted.[4] Within a few years, several states passed laws creating review boards to establish films' suitability for exhibition. In 1915 the name of the National Board of Censorship was changed to the National Board of Review of Motion Pictures and the slogan "selection, not censorship" was adopted. Their objective was to oppose legal censorship while encouraging support for worthwhile films.[5]

In a positive manner, community groups fought for one or two nights a week of family entertainment programming. Since sound had substituted talk for action, the children were often bored by the new style of filmmaking. Exhibitors wisely cooperated by providing special matinees and by organizing family night programs. [6]

Gradually, the upper classes accepted the existence of motion pictures. In 1920 publication of *Cine Club* magazine was begun and Ricotto Canudo instituted the first film club showing all pictures that were considered "good." England's "Film Society" showed movies and presented lectures on films from other countries. Not only were motion pictures being accepted, but people were even interested in studying them. In 1927 the University of Southern California Cinema Department was created to satisfy this need. In 1929 European avant-garde filmmakers from thirteen countries met in Switzerland to form an international league of cine clubs to advance film appreciation. [7]

Terry Ramsaye claimed that the legitimate theater was mainly for upper classes in sophisticated metropolitan areas who were not shocked by but instead loved candor on the stage. When sound became part of the movies, material from these plays was used. However, the other classes, unaccustomed to hearing such discussion, took offense. [8]

Some groups were worried about the image of America portrayed in films which were seen in other countries. They believed the films would be taken as an exact representation of life in the United States, and they did not like the image they saw being projected. [9] Religious, social, professional, and racial groups were crying for censorship. Public officials, therefore, had to respond to the complaints.

In the early 1920s public disapproval in conjunction with a series of scandals involving motion picture personalities led to the fear in the industry that, even though several states had censorship laws, the Federal Government would institute censorship. Therefore, the industry in 1922 instituted the Motion Picture Producers and Distributors of America, Inc. (MPPDA) with Will H. Hays, then Postmaster General and Chairman of the Republican National Committee, heading the organization. The MPPDA ostensibly quelled the censorship drive by inducing voluntary restraint. [10] However, by 1927, forty-five censorship bills had been introduced into state legislatures though none passed. [11]

The MPPDA, known as the Hays Organization, exemplified the cooperation of large business units for self-protection by delaying regulation of the industry and being dedicated to keeping outsiders from dictating policies affecting the industry. [12] The Hays Organization passed a self-regulatory policy in 1924 known as the "Formula." Members were asked to submit a summary of a proposed film adapted from a novel or play to receive advice about possible objections. This, however, applied only to original screenplays. [13]

To appease the public, Hays arranged a conference with outside organizations and groups interested in motion picture problems. These groups developed into the Committee on Public Relations, composed of more than seventy organizations. On 30 March 1925, the Hays Organization adopted a resolution establishing the department's "open door" policy, inviting every organization to send a representative to make suggestions for improvements in the motion picture industry.[14] The Hays Organization adopted a second code in 1927. These "Don'ts and Be Carefuls" listed subjects and themes that should be handled with discretion. It, too, could not be legally enforced.

In 1930 the Production Code was formulated by Martin Quigley, publisher of the *Motion Picture Herald* and Reverend Daniel A. Lord, a clergyman who acted as advisor on many films.[15] Nevertheless, groups were becoming increasingly angry over what they saw in the neighborhood and in the theater. Edwin Schallert stated:

> Miss West was nominated the queen of 1933, and right after that came the deluge as typified by the Legion of Decency. She was no more than the last straw, if she was that; the camel's back had already been bent to the point of breaking.[16]

Pressure groups were becoming increasingly agitated by the unsatisfactory results. Parents even focused anger at the drive-in theater for the immoral conduct brought about by the new privacy afforded by the automobile. In 1934 the Legion of Decency announced its plans for a crusade against the immoral and irresponsible motion pictures. Priests were instructed to preach on the evils of film and to put pressure on local exhibitors. The Legion gained attention when Catholics in Philadelphia boycotted all theaters. Non-Catholic groups, both religious and social, joined in. The Legion's efforts were so successful that in 1934 the Hays Organization organized the Production Code Administration Office, with Joseph Breen as its head. This was the first time the Hays Organization had the power to enforce its regulations. If any studio member released a film without their certificate of approval, the studio was fined $25,000.[17]

The Production Code Administration was formed to review all scripts and advertising, with fines being the mode of discipline when a picture created sympathy for evil or ridiculed "correct standards of life."[18] Martin Quigley wrote:

> The code is based on the objective principles of morality in their relation to public entertainment. It involves no doctrinal distinctions. Its address is simply and solely to the fundamental criteria of human obligation and responsibility as set forth in the Ten Commandments.[19]

Not only were motion pictures themselves attacked, but advertising as well. A report by the Federal Council of the Churches of Christ in America stressed that much confusion existed because the advertising of motion pictures induced the public to see a film, even though the picture might have been in poor taste. The report claimed that responsibility in the motion picture industry was greatly needed.[20]

After the divestiture of theaters from the majors, the theaters did not have the freedom to play films of their choice. In 1943, when Howard Hughes exhibited *The Outlaw* without the code, the film was soon withdrawn from distribution.

In 1945 Will Hays retired and Eric Johnston took over. The Hays Organization (MPPDA) then changed its name to the Motion Picture Association of America (MPAA).[21] Its predecessor's Production Code remained effective and was adhered to until Otto Preminger refused to remove certain words from *The Moon Is Blue,* a 1953 comedy. Although he released the film without the seal, the film nevertheless attracted huge crowds and made money.[22] In some small towns, however, police recorded the names of those who viewed the picture. In 1955 United Artists pulled out of the MPAA when the Code refused a seal to Preminger's *The Man with the Golden Arm.*[23]

Foreign films capitalized on sexual content and further led to acceptance of new subject matter on the screen. As television was becoming widely viewed, movie producers needed a new dimension to attract audiences, which they found in more risqué situations. The Code became increasingly antiquated and was therefore amended and reinterpreted.

Jack Valenti succeeded Eric Johnston as president of the MPAA in 1966. On 22 April 1966, in *Ginsberg v. New York,* the Supreme Court ruled that material which was not obscene for adults might be obscene for children. That day, *Interstate Circuit v. Dallas* declared that a classification system for films could be constitutional if guidelines were clearly defined. Together these two decisions would grant every city or state the right to devise its own classification code.

To replace the old Production Code, the MPAA created a voluntary film rating system, the Code and Rating Administration, with the National Association of Theatre Owners (NATO) and the International Film Importers and Distributors of America (IFIDA). According to the new system, any film could be made; however, it would be subjected to a rating. The ratings were to serve parents in making informed decisions on whether their children should attend a particular film.[24]

Their initial plan remains relatively the same today. They created four categories, "G" for general audiences—all ages admitted; "M" for mature audiences—parental guidance suggested; "R" for restricted—those under 16 must be accompanied by parent or guardian; and "X"—no one under 16 admitted. The "M" rating was later changed to "PG"—parental guidance suggested—and the age limit for "R" and "X" was raised to 17 years of age. The name was also changed to Classification and Rating Administration. Though no one must submit a film for rating, Valenti judges that 99 percent of producers of non-pornographic films do submit their films for ratings. Most pornographic film producers self-apply an "X" rating, which is allowed. The "G," "PG," and "R," however, are registered with the U.S. Patent and Trademark office as certification marks of the MPAA and cannot appear in advertising for a film that was not submitted officially for a rating. NATO states that approximately 95 percent of the exhibitors in the United States participate in the rating program and do enforce the admission restrictions.[25]

The board rates approximately four hundred films a year. For this service, the filmmaker pays a fee based upon the cost of the film and the size of his company. The fee, ranging from $800 to $8,000, is occasionally waived if the filmmaker has depleted his funds.[26] The seven-member board reviews each film and grants it a rating by majority vote. The producer may inquire as to the reasons for the decision and may also re-edit the film and try for another rating. A producer may appeal a rating at the Appeals Board, which consists of twenty-two members from MPAA, NATO, and IFIDA. After a screening of the film and a discussion, a secret ballot is taken. A two-thirds vote is needed to overturn a rating board decision.[27] Richard Heffner, administrator of the ratings board, stated that they have rated approximately 3,500 films in less than ten years and in that time only fifty-five films have gone to the Appeals Board. Out of that fifty-five, only on twelve occasions has the vote been overturned.[28]

Also subject to the self-regulatory system is film advertising. All advertising material, including trailers, radio spots, pressbooks, and the title for rated films, must be submitted to the Advertising Code Administration for approval prior to release. Such items must individually conform to the ratings and must not misrepresent the film. Trailers are either rated "G," allowing them to be shown with all feature films, or "R," limiting their use to films rated "R" or "X." At the head of each trailer, a tag designates for which audience the trailer has been approved, and the rating of the picture being advertised. The tag for a G-rated trailer has a green background. A red background is used for R-rated trailers. The color serves to alert the projectionist of the rating of the trailer.[29]

In 1983 an Opinion Research Corporation poll indicated that 66 percent of parents with children under age 12 found the ratings system useful.[30] Jack Valenti on 26 January 1984 endorsed the plan by the National Association of Theatre Owners to provide more information to the public about the degree of sex, violence, and/ or profanity in PG- and R-rated features.[31] The outcry over excessive violence in *Indiana Jones and the Temple of Doom* hastened the inauguration of a new rating, PG-13, which became effective 1 July 1984. This non-restrictive designation reads, "Parents are strongly cautioned to give special guidance for attendance of children under 13. Some material may be inappropriate for young children."[32]

NATO is seeking to reduce the age of those admitted to R-rated movies from 17 to 16 years of age, the usual age required to obtain a driver's license. While many exhibitors complain about the difficulty in checking ages for R- and X-rated films, theaters exhibiting unrated adult pictures are required by law to refuse admission to anyone under age 18. However, there is no legal requirement to enforce the age limit for an R-rated picture. Budco Inc. and Budco-Goldman were sued by the father of two daughters who were admitted to see *Private Lessons* without a parent or adult guardian. However, previously, in November 1983, the Philadelphia Court of Common Pleas ruled that exhibitors are not subject to civil penalties for failing to stop juveniles from viewing R-rated pictures, and "just by advertising an arbitrary rating selected by the Motion Picture Association of America, the defendants have not assumed a duty to enforce the suggested guidelines."[33]

Since ratings serve to warn people about the contents of a film, those very elements that people are being warned of may serve as the main attraction. The fact that children under 17 years of age are barred from certain films may increase their desire to attend. In 1947 a study found that among moviegoers who felt censorship in general was "too strict," 58 percent of them said they were more inclined to see movies that had "trouble with the censors." Only 15 percent stated they were less than inclined to view such films.[34]

Dr. Bruce A. Austin in 1980 found that more than half of the high school students he surveyed indicated that a film's rating was either "very important" or "important" in making their decision about whether to attend a particular movie. Austin performed a study on college students asking them to indicate their likelihood of attending four films with the same plot, same actors and same filmmakers, but only with different ratings. He found that the likelihood of attendance at both PG- and R-rated movies was significantly greater than for both G- and X-rated. However, he did not find any statistically significant difference in likelihood of attendance between "PG" and "R" or between "G" and "X." From a take-home questionnaire, he found that 97 percent of respondents reported to have attended an R-rated movie and 58 percent claimed to have attended an X-rated film. When asked to report the movie they had most recently seen, respondents claimed 13 percent were G-rated, 39 percent were PG-rated, 48 percent were R-rated, and none was X-rated.[35]

Since research has proven that people prefer to attend motion pictures rated either "PG" or "R," the rating is very critical to a film's ultimate success. During the system's fifteen-year history, the "X" and "G" ratings have almost disappeared. The "G," which comprised 32 percent of 1968 releases and only 3 percent of 1983's releases, has come to be associated with children's movies. In the last ten years, the board rated more than 3,500 movies, about 80 percent of them being in the "PG" and "R" categories.[36] A shift to R-rated films is evident. In 1968 they accounted for 23 percent of the films rated, in 1983, 59 percent.

The ratings system was attacked in 1978 for granting the majors more "PG" ratings and more frequently giving independents an "R." The House Subcommittee on Special Small Business Problems deemed the claim groundless.[37]

The ratings board is a tacit form of censorship. Since a "PG" or "R" rating is so intrinsically linked to box office revenue, producers are apt to self-censor their scripts with this in mind. Even though a person is free to make any film, the aim of the filmmaker is generally to have the film viewed by a wide audience. If most distributors refuse X-rated films, the motion picture will not have the opportunity to reach the audience for which it was made.

Occasionally films are released in two versions. For example, *Saturday Night Fever* (1977) was originally rated "R" but was later released in a "PG" version to reach an even greater audience.[38] Since it is accepted that a rating can have an influence on the film's revenue, attempts have been made to circumvent the ratings board. New World in 1983 was accused of submitting one version of *Escape 2000* for rating and subsequently slipping a more graphically violent rendition into theaters, quite different from the version rated "R."[39]

The MPAA filed a federal trademark infringement suit against the theatrical and home video distributors of *I Spit on Your Grave*. The suit alleges that the seventeen minutes of violent footage excised in 1978 to secure an R-rating was restored in the video cassettes.[40] To counteract such practices India's policy requires film producers to submit a print of the film when it is presented for censoring. The print is kept for comparison with the release print as a means of ensuring that no additions are made.[41]

Low-budget independent films frequently depend upon the graphic depiction of sex and violence to entice audiences to the theater. Since an audience exists for material that cannot be viewed on television, that material itself often becomes the focus of the film. Producers frequently test the limits of ratings in their zeal to depict more and more of what they perceive the audience desires. The filmmaker must be concerned with the reality of ratings and censorship, as they limit the potential audience. Since X-rated films are barred from being advertised on television, in certain publications, and from being exhibited in certain theaters, the audience is severely limited. A filmmaker must realize the repercussions of the material he chooses to include in the motion picture.

The *New York Times* announced in June 1977 that it would restrict movie ads deemed unfit to print to one inch, unillustrated notices of time and place.[42] The idea has spread and grown. On 23 August 1977 the *Los Angeles*

Times announced its decision to refuse advertising for hardcore pornographic movies. Any X-rated film is generally considered as obscene as the rest, particularly where ads for X-rated films are segregated, and theater chains generally refuse to play them.

Low-budget, sexually oriented motion pictures playing to a limited audience have existed for nearly fifty years. In the early days of the industry, large studios and fly-by-night operators produced these films. The eventual public outcry over "sex in the movies" led to various self-regulatory procedures. Early exploitation movies were usually short one-reel films showing nude women, yet were made in 35mm. Small independent producers who called themselves the "forty thieves" catered to the exploitation market during the 1930s. They often sold the exhibition rights to established theaters and independent distributors. Traveling showmen rented theaters to show the films and moved on before being apprehended.[43]

The producers of exploitation films were not bound by the industry's self-imposed Production Code of 1934, yet exploitation films were relatively circumspect throughout the thirties and forties. Total nudity was seldom shown, in contrast to the practice of the 1920s, and erotic activity was avoided. Common themes included a grieving young girl out of place in the "wicked city." Nudist camps were also frequent settings for these types of films. Among these pictures were pseudodocumentaries of non-white cultures that were imported with nude scenes inserted. Nudity was the focus of the film yet was concealed by the story or locale. During the middle and late 1930s, exploitation movies played in at least two thousand theaters.

Roberto Rossellini's *The Miracle,* first shown at the Venice Film Festival in 1948, caused great controversy because it was considered "sacrilegious." The Supreme Court ruled that motion pictures are within the constitutional protection of free speech and press. The court, however, recognized that motion pictures are not necessarily subject to the precise rules governing any other particular method of expression. The Supreme Court did decide that a state violates the constitutional guarantee of free speech and press if it bans a motion picture on the basis of a censor's conclusion that it is "sacrilegious"[44] or that it is "of such character as to be prejudicial to the best interests of the people."[45]

The first exploitation film of lasting influence was *Garden of Eden,* professionally made in a Florida nudist colony in 1954. After a long court battle in 1957, the New York Court of Appeals ruled that "nudity in itself and without lewdness or dirtiness, is not obscenity in law or in common sense." This film and others opened the way for a breakthrough in the exploitation film market. In 1959, Russ Meyer spent $24,000 in four days to produce *The Immoral Mr. Teas* which grossed more than $1 million. It concerned a man unable to see clothing, and was followed by a rash of copies. Between 1964 and

1968, exploitation films went in several directions. Strip films without plots emerged. Others began to mix sex and violence in the "roughies." The transitional film was *Lorna,* by Russ Meyer. This changed the role of the passive female in a pleasant setting to one of a victim of violent, "unrestrained lust." A series of pseudoscientific movies in the mid-1960s exploited sexual deviations. Sex in films became increasingly more explicit and bizarre.[46]

A whole new industry of films went further than before. Self-proclaimed "triple X" ratings were created with various kinds of sexual behavior documented explicitly on the screen. Even though most films rated "X" limit the box office, some independent exhibitors have chosen to exhibit pornographic films to survive economically. A first-run film would cost them $10,000 a week in guarantees, and the exhibitor might be lucky to gross $40,000 a month. Instead, one could acquire a pornographic film for $350 a week, all of which could be recouped in one night.

In June 1973, the United States Supreme Court handed down a landmark obscenity decision.

> Three guidelines were provided by the Court for the preparation of anti-obscenity legislation: (1) the average person, applying contemporary community standards, must find that the challenged work appeals to prurient interest, (2) the work must depict or describe in a patently offensive way sexual conduct explicitly defined by the law, and (3) taken as a whole, the work must lack serious literary, artistic, political, or scientific value. (Previously, the court had held that a work must be proven *utterly* without redeeming social value in order to be judged obscene.)[47]

Justifications offered for terming certain expressions "unprotected" are the protection of individuals from an immediate threat of harm or shock to their sensibilities, and the protection of societal order. If expression falls into the unprotected area, it may be completely regulated and even prohibited by the government. If the expression is protected, it may only be limited by reasonable regulations of time, place, and manner. Problems arise as to how much regulation is permissible where there is a mixture of protected expression regulated by the government. *Erzoznik v. City of Jacksonville* struck down an ordinance banning all nudity on drive-in movie screens. The court dismissed the privacy rights of those viewers on the street because the offended viewer could avert his eyes. It was held that clear reasons for discrimination on the basis of content must be shown.[48]

Surveys of community views can be taken to show the preferences, but it is ultimately the decision of the court. Municipal laws can define the things they do not want to be shown but it has to be done within very narrow constitutional limits. "In the *Jenkens v. Georgia* case in 1974, the U.S. Supreme Court reversed a local decision declaring the movie *Carnal Knowledge* obscene. Localities, therefore, don't always have the final word."[49] The Michigan State Supreme Court decision in *Detroit v. James Llewellyn* makes the state's obscenity statute binding over local ordinances. As of 1 May 1978, statewide obscenity laws may preempt passage of local pornography laws within a state.[50]

Studies have shown that people of lower socioeconomic status rated nudity as obscene, even if no genitalia were shown. They were more likely than subjects of higher socioeconomic and educational strata to regard any nude photo as being sexually exciting. Black and white photos were judged as being more obscene than color photos; pictures of poor photographic quality as more obscene than those of higher quality; unattractive models as more obscene than pretty ones, regardless of the pose; and, erotic scenes in an indoor setting as more obscene than those in an outdoor setting.[51] These psychological factors may also affect the perception of films that are of poor technical quality because of the low budget.

The major motion picture studios are also aware of the grosses that explicit sex films have generated. One cannot deny the fascination that is evident, as *Deep Throat,* shot in 1971, continues to make money. Sex in the cinema is becoming increasingly more common in all productions.

Throughout history, many books have been censored according to the morals of the population at the given time. Books have been seen as "evil" and a "danger" to society. Such conceptions were based on the belief that suggestion will lead to action. It was believed that the reader could easily be tempted to change his life-style or become like a character in a novel. To impede this occurrence censorship was believed to be imperative. Such objections to literature are now targeted at films.

With the diversity of beliefs, it is difficult to create laws that appease everyone. Vast and rapid changes in acceptable behavior have occurred. For example, *Last Tango in Paris,* an X-rated film, has made several attempts to acquire an "R" rating. It has not yet been successful in this endeavor; however, the fact that it now considers its material not as explicit as to warrant the "X" rating is significant. Standards of morality have always been in constant flux and have become less stringent as sex is more explicitly portrayed in films and television. With depictions of sex being a greater topic of controversy due to its prevalence, people are being forced to take a stand on this issue. People and institutions with power may believe that it is good for public relations to oppose pornography. However, with the stable demand for freedom the controversy will remain.

Continued attempts at censorship are being made. In Wheeler, Texas, an exhibitor has been showing R-rated movies to stay in business. He has met with protest and harrassment from a pastor who finds such movies immoral and intends to close him down. The theater owner, Ed Nall, has received $2,500 from NATO's Texas branch and $1,500 from the Adult Film

Association and Pussycat Theaters to help his battle.[52] There have been attempts to harrass movie patrons, and groups of people have organized to protest films by sending messages to the producers. It is a risk to make films that have the potential of attracting controversy. This fear, in itself, is a form of censorship.

The most overt censorship restrictions are in foreign countries, where more severe penalties may exist for violence or political content than for sex. The filmmaker must be aware of the censorship laws of the countries in which the film will be exhibited. If the picture will not meet the standards and editing out the offensive elements will not be possible, one must not include the territory as a potential source of revenue. In the United States, films are affected by the influences of the MPAA rating, by governmental laws, and by public opinion. There is constant pressure, though varying in intensity and organization, from religious, political, and social groups who take offense at some aspects of movies. Cable television, too, is not free to air just anything, as censorship is ruled by community standards. To circumvent protests that children will watch adult programming on cable television, the "lock box" has been devised as a security system to limit who watches the television. This has come under scrutiny by those who claim children can circumvent this device.

Censorship has always existed, with new and varying targets. It is dependent upon a person's or group's convictions that deem the dissemination of a work to be morally wrong and detrimental to society. William Lock's Manchester (N.H.) *Union Leader* has for years banned ads for X-rated films and in 1977 extended the prohibition to R-rated films such as *The Exorcist* and *A Star Is Born*.[53] This only further demonstrates the myriad opinions and resources for action concerning films. Yet courageous books and art have been produced in spite of any pressure. If motion picture producers and filmmakers believe in the value of their work and produce a film with integrity, without letting the box office censor the vision, they will have to accept the fact that the audience may be limited.

Jonas Mekas stated in regard to his arrest with the film *Un Chant d' Amour:*

> Like *Flaming Creatures,* the Genet film, *Un Chant d'Amour* is a work of art and like any work of art it is above obscenity and pornography, or, more correctly, above what the police understand as obscenity and pornography. Art exists on a higher spiritual, aesthetic and moral plane.[54]

3

Methods of Securing Financing and Distribution

The very means of financing a picture may increase or decrease the possibility of securing distribution. A filmmaker needs to focus on the goal of distribution to ensure the picture properly reaches the public. A filmmaker can produce a picture by using his own money, winning grant funds, or by making deferred deals with cast, crew, laboratories, and equipment houses. He can then distribute the film himself; however, much time, money, and expertise are needed to succeed. If a filmmaker needs to raise money to finance a picture, distribution will often have to be secured prior to production. If he has the revenue to finance the picture, distribution may be secured before, during, or after the picture is completed. The possibility always exists, however, that no distributor will want the picture at any stage.

Myriad methods of securing motion picture financing exist. Studios are mainly distributors and then financiers. However, they will not readily finance a risky feature, particularly one to be made by an inexperienced filmmaker. If they will not finance the picture outright they may offer a negative pickup deal. A producer can secure a negative pickup deal from a major or an independent distributor. The distributor agrees to pay the producer an advance against the distribution proceeds when he is given the completed picture, the "negative." These contracts can be taken to a bank to secure financing. It is in essence a pre-sale of the picture. Or, the distributor may advance the proceeds to produce the picture. When a distributor provides an advance, he will likely acquire all rights in addition to more stringent financial terms than if no advance were given.

In negative pickup deals, studios or banks will require a completion guarantee. Completion guarantors generally charge 6 percent of the budget for their service of overseeing the finances and cosigning all checks. If the film is going over budget or over schedule, completion guarantors have the power to take over and complete the picture themselves.

Since union signators cannot fund or control the destiny of a non-union film, studios use negative pickups to secure low-budget films. Though unions are skeptical about the funding of guarantees for such pictures later distributed by the majors, negative pickups are common.[1]

Lewis Horwitz, lender, warns that in a deferred negative pickup, half is paid when it is delivered and the other half a year later. Yet a clause that states the film must be "in exact accordance with the script" gives buyers an escape clause. In foreign pre-sales, usually 10 percent is paid up front. Even when the print is delivered, if it is no longer desired by the buyer, there is little chance of collecting the remainder.[2]

Pre-sales to various ancillary markets can also be used to finance a picture. Any element, such as the script, director, producer, or actors, may be sufficient to sell a script or even an idea to various markets. Competition for product also might lure buyers to make a pre-sale. Pre-sale contracts serve as collateral and can then be taken to a bank to secure loans. Sales representatives charge a 15 to 20 percent commission to attain pre-sales in film markets. They can, however, acquire the total cost of production.

Continental Pictures is a production company that utilizes film markets to secure pre-sales. Often offering only a title, the head of American marketing, Helen Sarlui, stated, "It's the artwork that attracts buyers. We have the one-sheets and a one-page synopsis ready, and in some cases the scripts are available. The directors and stars are less important." They specialize in action films geared for the foreign market, budgeted in the $1 million to $3 million range and shoot their pictures in English with Americans in major crew positions.[3]

During the 1980s, pre-sales of a script or package became available. Often revenue generated from pre-sales would determine whether a film would be produced. As the ancillary markets grew in diversity, the money collected added to and sometimes exceeded the box office gross. The foreign market, often responsible for more than one-half of a film's rental, became another factor to consider in the production of a film. Many distributors who paid large amounts in pre-sales to acquire pictures that turned out to be financially unsuccessful soon became wary. Pre-sales are becoming less common. This shift greatly affects independents who rely on the contracts to secure bank financing to produce a picture.

A filmmaker must be aware that if any rights are sold to ancillary markets in order to secure financing, it may be harder or even impossible to secure distribution after the picture is made. Even if a distributor wants the picture, the producer will have minimal power in negotiating favorable terms. A distributor would most probably want to recoup all expenses before any revenue would be returned to the producer.

Securing a loan to finance a picture instead of selling percentages of the profits to investors can prove most profitable. The Lewis Horwitz

Organization is a company that specializes in lending and packaging loans for the entertainment industry. Horwitz stresses that if one borrows money to produce a picture, once the interest is paid, the producer owns the films. If investors finance the picture, the producer must split the revenue with them for perpetuity. Non-bank lenders charge more interest than banks, but will consider less structured projects using various forms of collateral. A bank generally charges 1 to 2.5 percent over the prime rate, whereas a non-bank lender charges 4 to 5.5 percent.[4]

Bankers are not investors but are lenders who make loans on proven assets. William Thompson, executive vice president of the First National Bank of Boston, stated:

> As a banker, I'm more interested in the quality and experience of the people involved, than I am in the movies they want to finance or the financing structures they want to use. In twenty-nine years of lending in this business, I've never once read a script, nor do I intend to start now. More specifically, I'm interested in who is going to pick the pictures and who is going to distribute them.[5]

Banks prefer that the borrower has funding to produce and distribute ten or twelve films a year, ensuring that a few successful films will balance the inevitable losses. Some banks do finance single films by discounting receivables and contracts due a producer upon delivery of the film. However, the First National Bank of Boston focuses almost exclusively on "large volume, long-term, corporate-type financing." They insist that borrowers have secured distribution plans; they demand sufficient financial resources, $100 million to $120 million, to produce and distribute a lineup of product; and they frequently restrict the size of the production budget per film while requiring that all the financing be lined up before production.[6]

Terry Semel, president and chief operating officer of Warner Bros., stated:

> In this business, you have to play upsides and cover downsides, and your downside coverage shouldn't take away your upside capability. If you lose your upside capability, it becomes difficult to survive in this business.... Yet, because of greater costs, there are greater risks. And the balance between the two is crucial, not only to survival, but to profitability. If you overcover the downside, you can give away the upside. And if you do that, there's not much point in being in this business. To me, that would be the worst position of all.[7]

If sufficient funding is secured to begin production, the filmmaker still has the option of trying to sell the picture at any time. A few completed scenes may be enough to entice a distributor to either purchase the film outright or finance the remaining costs. The independent must decide when the specific project should be shown to distributors and whether the film should be for sale during pre-production or at a film market. He must decide whether to sell to the highest bidder, to the best distributor for that particular picture, or to a major for one or more territories.[8] Because news travels within the industry, he should also consider the order in which he approaches distributors. For example, it may be dangerous to show his film to all the majors first and then to the independent distributors. By this method, independents might realize the desperation of the producer to make a deal.

Financing and distributing a picture are often closely associated. Securing financing can be contingent upon a distribution deal, and a distribution deal may depend upon the amount of money acquired to produce the picture. Innumerable variables must be considered when deciding when to seek a distribution deal. If a filmmaker has the means to finance a picture and believes that once it is produced many distributors will be bidding for it, the most advantageous deal will then be made. However, he must be realistic and acknowledge that what he believes will be a great film may not materialize and that tastes differ. If his main priority is to make a profit while covering the risk, he should attempt to secure distribution prior to production. Yet the independent filmmaker whose goal is often to merely get the film made, generally does not want to be concerned with such matters until later, when it is often too late. Though a picture may not be distributed, it will have been made without outside influences. A question to consider is whether it is preferable to keep a film intact exactly as the filmmaker meant it to be, containing elements such as excessive length that will considerably reduce the size of the audience, or whether it is preferable to compromise and maximize the number of people who will view the picture by making the film more accessible. A filmmaker must decide whether the benefits, such as more money to make a film that a distributor can contribute, merit relinquishing creative freedom.

In 1909 Sol Lessor, a partner in a San Francisco nickelodeon, wanted a $500 bank loan to install more seats. The Bank of Italy (now The Bank of America), operated by its founder's younger brother Dr. A. H. "Doc" Giannini, made this loan. New York was the center of the film business, yet banks were reluctant to lend money to help this new industry. The first actual movie loan was a $50,000 unsecured credit by Giannini to the Famous Players-Lasky Company of New York in 1918. Giannini instituted the practice of using the negative of one film as security on the loan of another. He advanced $250,000 to a New York movie company, while retaining the negative of the Charlie Chaplin film *The Kid* in his bank vault. Six weeks later, the loan was repaid when *The Kid* opened to instant success.[9]

Between 1919 and 1927, very few producers went to the stock market for funds. Independents often paid 40 percent interest on short-term loans to get films produced. They were usually financed by distributor and exhibitor combines at great cost. Around 1926, when the acquisition of theaters by the majors was in progress, the banks and investment houses finally regarded motion pictures as a legitimate field of activity. Unlike films, theater property was real estate and a more secure investment.[10] By 1927, reckless spending and extravagance were commonplace. Financial dependence on Wall Street increased enormously.[11] In 1929 the United States Commerce Department reported that high retail sales were correlated with greater film distribution. It suggested that theater attendance was a luxury indulged in with increasing frequency as one's income increased, measured by increased expenditures in retail stores.[12]

During the 1930s and 1940s, up to 70 percent of a film's budget could be borrowed from a bank on a picture-by-picture basis. Since the producer/distributors controlled the theaters, they could more accurately determine how much money the film would earn. Yet after the studios divested themselves of their theaters, they were no longer assured of a certain revenue. This, compounded with the encroaching television boom, made bankers more cautious. The 1950s once again brought on the need for collateral to acquire a loan.[13]

With the arrival of television, double features and "B" movies were no longer in demand. Because of the drop in box office receipts, Warner Bros., Paramount, and RKO sold or licensed their film libraries to other film companies or television syndicators. By 1960, the studios conceded the permanence of television and began viewing it as another market for their product. In 1967 United Artists licensed approximately seventy films to National Broadcasting Company for a total license fee of $125 million, including four films at $5 million each. A television sale was perceived as a guard against theatrical losses. Studios then accelerated production.[14]

From 1962 to 1970, the average cost of an American film doubled from $1.7 million to $3.4 million. Credit lines were increased to accommodate the escalated costs. Interest rates also reached a high of 8 percent. In 1970, the production boom was confronted with recession and inflation. Huge film inventories were faced with fewer people spending money on movies. Since domestic and foreign theatrical rentals remained relatively constant from 1966 to 1971, even a network sale could not alleviate the financial pressures. Studios reduced their spending, lowering the average cost per film to $2 million. Film companies also reduced spending in foreign distribution. In 1969, 1971, and 1973, the total foreign gross revenue exceeded domestic theatrical rentals.[15]

The United States government does not offer assistance to producers while the governments of other countries offer direct subsidies and indirect subsidies through significant tax incentives to aid the investor. In the United States, however, the film industry has created and perpetuates the image of extreme affluence. Because of enormous production and distribution costs, outside investors are often sought. Non-recourse financing evolved out of a Supreme Court decision in the late 1960s, "It involves the use of an instrument on which the buyer is not obligated to make payments to the seller in case of a default." The seller can only look to the property he has sold for security for repayment, but the buyer gets tax credit for the full amount paid.[16]

Tax shelters became popular when a 1973 decision in a Walt Disney case rendered motion pictures to be tangible personal property eligible for the investment tax credit. These deals became prevalent, generally involving a cash contribution of 25 to 35 percent of the negative cost of a film, with the balance of the cost of production or acquisition covered by non-recourse notes issued by the tax shelter partnership.[17] One could take tax deductions for up to five times the initial cash investment by depreciating all of the film's production, distribution, and advertising costs. Deductions were being taken on a business that was not entered into for economic profit.[18] Investment attorney Tom Pollock believes tax shelters added $150 million in production capital between 1971 and 1976.[19]

The Tax Reform Act of 1976 eliminated those benefits by limiting the deductible losses to the amount the investor actually had at risk. Film investment, therefore, became much less attractive. Congress succeeded in ending non-recourse leverage financing and required that the investment tax credit follow true risk of loss rather than the sole ownership of the copyright and negative of the film. In reaction, sophisticated new formulas were devised to meet these new restrictions while still offering an advantage to the investor. Foreign tax shelter money from Australia, England, and Germany began to replace domestic sources that had disappeared after 1976.[20] In 1981 the Economic Recovery Tax Act eliminated the large front-end depreciation of films by tax shelter groups. It required a straight-line method of amortization. Since their leverage was reduced by almost half, such investments were no longer appealing.[21]

In the late 1970s through 1980, many people from other businesses entered the industry and began financing films. After several successes, they continued spending money on film production. In an attempt to attract big names, they paid substantially higher prices for all talent. As Mae D. Huettig wrote, "They wound up displacing the cost structure of the industry upward by a fairly substantial magnitude."[22]

A drastic increase in marketing costs led to a national advertising campaign for some films, costing as much as the production of the film itself. Print and advertising costs of more than $5 million were common. Therefore, production, interest, and marketing costs combined, were in the $16 million to $18 million range. Since theater attendance domestically and overseas remained relatively constant, film companies once again had to reassess spending. Once again, film libraries recouped revenue from domestic and foreign syndication, with pay-cable providing needed cash.[23]

A new means of luring investors to the motion picture industry was needed. A method was devised that allowed investors to participate in a partnership that instead of financing a single film included ten or more films. This was intended to decrease the risk and increase the chance of one film becoming a huge success. These partnerships also were formed not only to produce but to distribute and own the rights to the pictures that would be released over a five to seven year period. Minimum investment was approximately $3,000 to $10,000 dollars. Revenue was expected after the first film would be released, generally in eighteen months. During that time, the investor could take a loss on the investment, writing off a portion of the initial cash outlay for tax purposes. The tax advantages were not as enticing as before, however, the potential existed for huge profits if any film became a blockbuster.

Many new partnerships were formed, with many investors losing all their money. John Kao, a Harvard Business School professor who specializes in the entertainment field, stated, "Until recently, the public deals that have come through the pipeline have been advantageous for the promoters and the distributors at the expense of the investor."[24] In 1981, Irving Levin and Sam Schulman of SLM Entertainment Ltd., organized the first public film financing offering. They raised $40 million for production and distribution of a dozen MGM/UA films through Merrill Lynch and Dean Witter's sale of limited partnerships to three thousand investors.[25] Many more of these public offerings have appeared.

Silver Screen was developed by Time Inc.'s Home Box Office (HBO), the nation's largest pay-TV system, for the purpose of spurring production of movies that will play in theaters and then be shown exclusively on HBO or its companion service, Cinemax. Though HBO has guaranteed to pay back at least the initial capital invested, they will receive an 8.5 percent commission off the top. Silver Screen Partners was formed to raise $75 million and to finance only English language theatrical motion pictures, with the average budget being approximately $10 million. The investors are always clearly warned of the risks of investment in motion pictures in the prospectus.

> The success of a film in theatrical distribution, network television and other ancillary markets, is dependent upon distribution arrangements and public taste which is unpredictable and susceptible to change. The theatrical success of a film may also be significantly affected by the popularity of other films then being distributed.[26]

Investors will have to wait at least three years and possibly ten years to find out if they have made a wise investment.[27] Even though they are guaranteed a 100 percent return by the fifth anniversary of the first film's release, it is based on present dollar value.

Motion picture partnerships have taken advantage of investors in the past, making them skeptical of any further involvement. It became imperative to make partnerships more attractive to investors by devising such creative arrangements. Yet Robert Stanger, a tax shelter specialist who evaluates limited partnerships in his monthly newsletter *The Stanger Report* claimed, "There is simply no way you can rationally judge the economic merits of the limited partnerships in the movies. . . . It's all a question of the vagaries of the box office. And if you want to take that kind of gamble, you might as well go to Las Vegas."[28]

Even in the deals where partners are assured their money back, it is generally after five or seven years have passed with the concomitant loss of interest. Tony Hoffman, head of the corporate finance department at Kralin and Co., a venture capitalist firm that raises money to set up companies, stated, "We're just now coming out of a period in which exceptionally large amounts of monies were raised for films on the basis of limited partnerships." He stresed that the majority concentrated on the "write-off aspects" of the tax advantages. The upside, even on a successful film, was quite limited. Many people invested in these partnerships in 1979, 1980, 1981, and to a lesser extent in 1982. However, recently, film financing on a limited partnership basis is not so appealing. People discovered that even if a film in the package they financed was a blockbuster they were not the ones to reap the profits. Any money they would receive would be withheld for years, reducing the value of that money. Since so few films become profitable, the upside potential on the few films is rarely great enough to cover the losses on the others. Hoffman believes limited partnerships structured as they have been will fade. He believes that an equal sharing arrangement on the upside and downside between the limited partners and the film company is necesary.[29]

Outside investors have been attracted by their desire to be connected to what they imagine to be a glamorous business. A possible investor can be swayed to invest by being introduced to a star, attending Hollywood parties, or by being in the film, even though his part may be only that of an extra. These possibilities may be promised to give the investor a fantasy of hope. All too often these expectations are not fulfilled and the investor is even more surprised when the film does not become a blockbuster but, instead, is a financial failure. The motion picture industry holds a lure for people who continue to want to be part of it, even if it means putting aside their rational business sense for a gamble on a dream.

4

Critical Acclaim, Film Festivals, and Film Markets

Critical Acclaim

Public interest in motion pictures has existed since their inception and over the years information about films and the filmmakers has been voraciously consumed. The prediction of the ultimate financial success of a film has been and remains inaccurate, based upon the written word of reviewers, critics, and gossipers. And yet filmmakers, distributors, and the general public act as if reviews are important and thereby are affected by them in subtle to drastic ways. Unlike the legitimate theater whose audience tends to be heavily influenced by reviews, the cinema cannot rely solely upon the judgment of critics to influence its audience. Numerous films with high critical acclaim have often produced poor audience response, while pictures disregarded in critical circles have earned the greatest commercial success. In addition to the print medium, critics are now able to reach a wider audience by presenting their reviews on radio and televison.

In the thirties, forties, and fifties, gossip columnists Hedda Hopper and Louella Parsons in Hollywood and Walter Winchell in New York wielded great power. The columnists, who were celebrities themselves, could generate great interest in a film.[1] Gossip is still demanded by the public. Columnists, however, do not have the clout they once possessed. Columns devoted to information about the motion picture industry survive and thrive, but the emphasis has shifted from the persona of the columnist to the factual basis of the information presented. The wide circulation of tabloids such as the *National Enquirer,* the success of the novel *Indecent Exposure,* and the publication of novels about film and news people demonstrate the expansion of interest in the entertainment industry.

Since moviegoing is no longer a habit for the majority of people, the blockbuster that draws enormous attention is of special interest today. While word of mouth is the cheapest and most persuasive form of advertisement, published box office grosses have become an effective means of drawing further attention to a particular film. If someone believes that everyone else has seen a specific movie, he may feel a need to see it to belong to the group. Advertisements will continue to exploit the snowballing box office grosses as evidence of a film's worth, leading even more people to believe they must see it.

While the financial success of a film is a recent catalyst in arousing the audience to go to the movies, the Academy Award, or Oscar, remains a prime motivating factor. The Academy Award can add millions to a film's gross revenue. Great sums of money are spent in advertising the film in trade papers in an attempt to secure the award. In addition to the financial incentive, the prestige of winning the award is sought. Ads placed in the trade papers also serve to appease contenders for the Oscar. If the talent feels the studio is supporting them, they may develop a loyalty to the studio or its executives and make additional pictures with them. The films competing for the Oscar are even shown on pay television in the Los Angeles area to provide the voting members of the Academy access to the films. The amount of potential revenue lost at the box office by this airing is minimal compared to what can be gained by winning an Oscar. The televised Academy Awards ceremony itself provides valuable publicity. Winning the award ensures higher salaries for the individual winners and the film may be given an extended run or may even be resurrected from dormancy. The nomination and/or winning of an Oscar is then incorporated into the advertising campaign of the film, serving as a validation of the quality of the motion picture.

While criticism ranges from simple reviews that synopsize the plot to profound analyses aimed at the film scholar, the critic performs an invaluable function and has an impact on his readers and the industry as a whole. Many readers familiarize themselves with a particular critic's perspectives and rely on the critic's reviews to aid them in their selection of a film.

While a reviewer's goal may be merely to summarize the plot of a film, the very elements he chooses to stress in his description may influence the reader, listener, or viewer. Even if a reviewer negatively mentions elements such as sex and violence, the audience that exists for such material may be moved to see the film. A reviewer must also be aware that certain foreign, political, or experimental films require specialized knowledge for complete under-standing. If a critic does not take this into consideration, a film may be given an undeserved negative review. Reviews of independent or foreign films can have great impact, as the people who frequent these types of films generally pay closer attention to reviews.

Film reviews can play an important role in the securing of distribution. For example, filmmakers of *Endless Summer* opened the picture without a distributor in New York. After the film had been playing for four weeks, favorable reviews in *Time* and the *New Yorker* inspired Don Rugoff of Cinema 5 Distribution Company to see it. Cinema 5 then agreed to distribute the picture.[2]

Wayne Wang made *Chan Is Missing* for just over $22,000. Though New Yorker Films liked it, they waited to hear favorable critical reviews before making a decision to distribute it. The film ultimately played in art houses in forty-five cities and grossed nearly $1.1 million.[3] Critical acclaim was also responsible for the wide showing of the independently produced *Northern Lights*. Though *Northern Lights* was initially successful in the region it was produced, lack of well-known actors, black and white photography, lack of sex or violence, use of foreign languages with subtitles, and a political theme were not attractive to distributors. An article published by *Mother Jones* in February 1979 on the film proved a catalyst for an invitation to the Belgrade Film Festival in Yugoslavia and new interest by exhibitors. Randy Finley, a Seattle theater owner, agreed to play the picture on an open-ended run if it brought in $5,000 a week or more. After six weeks of promoting the picture, it ran in Seattle for seven weeks and grossed $35,000 in an art theater of 220 seats. *Northern Lights* won the prize for the Camera d'Or Best First Feature Film at 1980 Cannes, which brought invitations to other international film festivals. The filmmakers were then able to secure bookings at the best art houses in the major American cities. Though a year and a half had been spent to distribute *Northern Lights,* the picture had still not played in New York. The ultimate acclaim and favorable reviews finally made it feasible.[4]

Film journals chronicle the making of a film and provide interviews with those involved. This information entices the selective reader to see a particular film. An article in *Film Comment, American Film,* or *Cahiers du Cinéma* implies that a picture is important.

Critics, realizing their potential power over the fate of a film, may strive to review a film objectively. However, subtle factors such as respect for a filmmaker's past work, friendships with those involved with the film, and personal concern for the subject matter of the film may all subjectively color and influence a critic's perceptions. Blatant attempts at influencing critics may be manifested by a company providing trips to locations, arranging for special screenings, and creating a feeling of privileged concern for the critic. Vincent Canby stated that Andrew Sarris once said, "The worst blackmail is not money offered under the table, but seeing the director and his wife and two small children walking down the street and looking rather poorly."[5]

From the point of view of the distributor, it is wise to create as many positive impressions about a film as possible in an attempt to move the public to see it. Excerpts from reviews are often used in advertisements for the motion picture. Even if the critique was negative, an experienced distributor can creatively use any review to exploit the film. Phrases or individual words may be extracted and manipulated to create an unintended connotation. In a desire for their name to be publicized, a few reviewers may make comments for the sole purpose of being quoted. This system may be detrimental to the industry as a whole, as real critical acclaim may be diffused by such hyperbole.

The distributor needs to use reviews and word of mouth to his best advantage. If a distributor is sure that a film will be critically acclaimed, he may hold selective press screenings even earlier than the usual several weeks prior to the release date. However, if he believes that the word of mouth will be more favorable, large audience screenings will be held to generate public interest. Bad reviews seldom hurt a film with favorable word of mouth, although they may tend to slow down the initial momentum. A film with bad reviews and poor word of mouth will not last long in theaters, often no more than one week, inspiring the distributor to recoup as much money as possible before the word spreads.

Some of the most significant reviews written on film are those the public seldom reads. These critiques often influence the types of motion pictures available to the general public. Many small independent and foreign films that open in single theaters in New York or Los Angeles are reviewed and critiqued in trade papers. While the reviews in these publications have little impact upon major films that have already secured distribution, they can have a great effect upon the life of the independent film. These reviews are read by distributors who may be looking to pick up such a film. If a review is extremely negative, the distributor or exhibitor may pass on the film without bothering to see it. A favorable review, however, may catch the interest of a distributor or exhibitor and ultimately play a role in the opportunity for the film to find its audience.

Film Festivals and Film Markets

If a filmmaker has independently produced a film, he needs to find a distributor or independent exhibitor who will play the picture. One means of having his film viewed by many people is to submit it to a film festival. Hundreds of film festivals exist and can provide an opportunity for an unknown filmmaker to have his work viewed. The festival can aid the filmmaker by providing feedback in the form of audience response and can also be a means of acquiring critical analyses of the film.

Film festivals originated out of a desire of filmmakers to meet to discuss their art. These types of festivals still exist; however, if a filmmaker's goal is to find a distributor or exhibitors, the value of a festival is measured by its prestige. It is imperative that a filmmaker investigate the festival before incurring the expense of submitting a film when there may be little to be gained. Since film festivals form and dissolve rapidly, it is prudent to know how long a particular festival has existed, the types of films preferred, the amount of exposure it provides, and the value of its awards. Certain film festivals attract important critics who may be able to create a positive interest in a film. An award from a prestigious festival will, at least, attract attention from distributors. Even if distribution is not secured, the film at least had the opportunity to be viewed.

Filmmakers must also be aware that some festivals require that films have not been exhibited in any other event. The filmmaker must therefore set up a priority of festivals and read the rules for entry before indiscriminately submitting the film to just any festival.

Distributors who acquire films after private screenings may be influenced by the producer, the cast, the reputation of the film, advertising material, or statistics that claim the subject matter is popular. However, unfavorable festival reviews and/or an audience's negative reaction to a film at a festival may deter a distributor from picking up the film.

Except for the few festivals with highly prized awards, studios generally do not enter their films in such competition, as they have nothing to gain. Their films are already set for distribution. If they are certain a particular film will be a commercial success, they more likely would preview it at a local theater than gamble on acquiring any negative reviews a critic might bestow upon it. If they are unsure how audiences will react to a film, exhibition at a festival would be too large a risk since negative reviews and poor word of mouth could reduce the picture's revenue potential before its release.

Filmmakers generally believe in their creation and want an audience to experience it. It is the independent filmmaker who can enter festivals and judiciously use them to study the audience reaction his film creates, meet people in his field, develop a reputation, and possibly acquire a distributor. Since hundreds of festivals exist, most are of very little positive or negative value and influence. However, the possibility always exists that an influential person will see the film and spread positive word of mouth. Roman Polanski attributes Charles Champlin's seeing *Tess* at the Cannes Film Festival as being instrumental in the picture securing distribution. Francis Coppola had offered a $1 million advance for his Zoetrope distribution company to handle the picture; however, Coppola wanted to refocus the film by reshooting, re-editing, and even eliminating entire scenes. More than a year after the successful release of *Tess* in Europe, Columbia Pictures began to show some interest. Polanski wrote:

> Their change may have been triggered by Charles Champlin, the *Los Angeles Times* film critic, for whom I'd screened *Tess* while he was serving on the jury of the 1979 Cannes Festival. "The best film of the year," he wrote afterward, "hasn't found a distributor in the United States."

Columbia acquired the film, hoping it might win awards even if it would not make any money. *Tess* received eleven Academy Award nominations and Polanski received his best U.S. reviews.[6]

Whereas a film festival serves to celebrate film and often grants awards, the film market serves as a meeting ground where films are exhibited for the sole purpose of being licensed or sold. Film festivals and film markets are often combined, with both activities occurring concurrently. Film markets are similar to trade shows and conventions in other businesses. Filmmakers, producers, talent, distributors, exhibitors, and buyers from around the world meet at one location for one to two weeks. Individuals or companies set up offices, often in their hotel rooms, to conduct business while films are screened in theaters easily accessible to the central meeting place.

Film markets attract people with a diversity of concerns, from those with merely an idea for a movie to those with pictures in varying stages of completion. Producers bring stories they want to test on various distributors from around the world. A writer's treatment or script may be passed around with the hope of generating enough cash from pre-sales to produce the movie. Some producers shoot one scene from a script or use a trailer of a proposed motion picture to attract production capital. Filmmakers and producers with unfinished pictures attend markets in search of completion funds.

A much sought-after commodity at a market is a completed film that has not been exhibited at any other festival or market. From reading a script, no one can envision exactly what a completed picture will look like. In acquiring a finished motion picture, the buyer's risk is reduced and he can rely on his judgment to reject the picture or to license it.

Though buyers are seemingly omnipresent and films are in limited supply it is not necessarily a seller's market. Hundreds of thousands of dollars are spent by both producers and distributors in publicizing and advertising their products and services. However, only a limited number of sought-after films exist. Distribution companies battle among themselves for the few prized films, while producers fight to attract the more valuable distributors. It is therefore wise for an unknown filmmaker to form an alliance with an established or reputable person who knows who the real buyers are and realizes the chances of selling a particular film to a specific organization.

The majors have their own foreign distribution networks but increasingly attend film festivals to acquire independent films for their inventory and to sell to other media around the world. Markets, like festivals, also serve the social function of providing an occasion where people in the same business from locations throughout the world can meet and exchange ideas and information on the attitudes, trends, and conditions of their art and business.

The oldest of all international cinema festivals is the Venice Film Festival established by Mussolini in 1932. This annual event sought "to raise the new art of the film to the same level of the other arts." In the late thirties many critics claimed the festival was run by Mussolini and his German allies. To counter this notion, the festival stressed its artistic aims. Yet, when Leni Riefenstahl's *Olympia* won the best film award, the British and the Americans argued that it was Nazi propaganda. Finally, in 1943, the war stopped the festival. In 1946 the festival resumed under new regulations. Shorts, documentaries, and retrospectives were added, and artistic merits were emphasized over commercial standards.[7] Maoists claimed giving prizes was bourgeois elitism, and Venice became less competitive in 1970.[8] The Venice Film Festival consists of the competition and retrospective and thematic information conferences. There is no market, yet a high volume of business is generated by the festival's ability to attract new films. Its awards are few and prestigious. Other important festivals in Italy include the Taormina Festival where first and second films of new directors are sought and exhibited.[9] The Florence Film Festival, begun in 1979, usually has small Italian distributors present to look for product.[10] Though both festivals welcome independent films from the United States, they are relatively small and not heavily attended.

Since the Berlin Film Festival was disrupted in 1970 by left-wing agitators, it has survived as a second-rate festival.[11] Yet it offers special events for young filmmakers and filmmakers from the Third World, in addition to other "alternative events." It is still one of the best in recognizing the crucial role of independent films. In 1983, ninety independent films from around the world were premiered, the largest single component of the festival.[12] Ken Wlaschin, artistic director of the Los Angeles International Film Exposition, believes the Berlin Film Festival is the best for the American independent cinema. The festival pays all the costs, including subtitling, and also provides the pictures with a non-theatrical release in Germany.[13]

The European festivals are generally funded by the city or state governmental organizations that believe the arts need to be subsidized because the product may not be profitable.[14] Since the government does not fund these in the United States, festivals are usually in need of money. Established in 1963, the New York Film Festival is considered to be the most important festival in America. It is presented by the Film Society of Lincoln Center in cooperation with the International Film Importers and Distributors of America, Inc. and the Motion Picture Association of America. *New York Times* reviews of the films shown are perused by distributors looking for films to acquire. A negative review, therefore, could eliminate a film's chances of securing distribution. Bernardo Bertolucci claimed that the New York Film Festival was a "slaughterhouse" for unusual foreign films.[15] In 1983, the first time in the festival's twenty-one year history, domestic rather than foreign films held the spotlight. There had been a resistance on the part of the major studios to premiere films at the festival, because it would interfere with release schedules and for fear that the festival's art-house image could taint a film.[16] Since the majors now have classics divisions, they attend the festival to compete for awards and to secure the most popular films.

Gary Essert, the founder in 1971 and former director of the Los Angeles International Film Exposition, or Filmex, as it is referred to, believes it is vital for Americans to see foreign films as they are "the most insulated people on earth."[17] Ken Wlaschin, the director of Filmex, stated, "It was no little achievement to start a festival in a town where film was not considered culture."[18] Filmex aims to reflect as much of world cinema as possible, by showing all genres of films from all over the world. In 1983, a total of 404 films were exhibited. Fifty-four nations sent films, 140 new films were screened, 219 features were presented, and 74 American films were premiered.[19]

In 1983 the nineteenth Chicago International Film Festival took place with every type of production represented, including features, shorts, student films, posters, animated films, television commercials, television productions, and documentaries. The founder and director, Michael J. Kutza, Jr., wrote, "The Chicago International Film Festival leads the search for the latest trends in cinema." They show films that do not receive U.S. distribution.[20] It is also highly respected by Europeans, as films are judged strictly on artistic merit.[21]

Other film festivals include the United States Film and Video Festival founded in 1979 and devoted solely to the works of the independent American film and video makers. As films become more commercial, there is greater interest from distributors. The Utah Film Development, the Utah Media Center, and Robert Redford's Sundance Institute are responsible for the festival's existence. Many supporters of the festival include established Hollywood people, the same people whom these filmmakers try to avoid emulating.[22] The New York Filmmakers Exposition provides filmmakers with written critiques. Nick Manning, the founder, stated that the festival's aim is "to provide recognition, unbiased critical feedback, and as much money as possible to innovative independent filmmakers."[23] The U.S.A. Film Festival established in 1971 and held in Dallas is a critic's film festival. Its objective is to show the work of some of the promising new American filmmakers and to recognize quality films. The Teluride Film Festival in Colorado, established in 1974, provides a captive audience, as it coincides with the meeting of the Association of Specialized Film Exhibitors, representing owners of art houses and independent theaters.[24] The Museum of Modern Art in conjunction with the Film Society of the Lincoln Center presents an annual series of new films by new directors around the world.

Small festivals overseas are also numerous. The Festival of American Cinema held in Deauville, France, is nine years old. It is gaining in importance as a provider of contacts and for the promotion of films soon to be released in the foreign market. Andre Halimi, co-founder of the festival, stated, "Unlike

Cannes, which is becoming more of a film market, Deauville is more a real celebration of the cinema."[25] Many film festivals, such as Cracow, Delhi, Dutch Film Days, and Göteborg, exhibit films from their own country, while attempting to lure buyers from around the world.[26] The Montreal Film Festival "seeks to discover and promote films of outstanding quality produced as an alternative to the conventions and commercialism of the established film industries."[27]

A great variety of other festivals exist in the United States where a filmmaker can easily submit a film without incurring the cost of subtitling and shipping overseas. The larger festivals are devoted to feature films, generally American and foreign. Others, however, are more esoteric, exhibiting films strictly of one region or emphasis, such as animated, children's, science, educational, dance, psychiatric, safety, industrial, sports, experimental, religious, fantasy, or horror.

Film festivals have been increasing in number since 1946. The fascination with watching films, learning about films, and making films is growing. Film festivals provide an atmosphere for people who love film to meet with one another, educate each other, and share their films. Films are shown that may never be released commercially, but may have as much or greater meaning to the specific audience. Film festivals attract people who appreciate these works of love and provide the positive reinforcement for filmmakers to pursue their art. In contrast to film festivals where the art of cinema is celebrated, the film market is a marketplace. Here, the film is merely a product to be bought and sold. Film markets or film festivals with a strong market are not as numerous as pure festivals, as their success depends upon buyers from around the world congregating at one time and at one location. Since such people are limited in number and cannot afford the time and expense of attending innumerable film markets, only a few markets have taken on any major significance.

Cannes Film Festival

The French government scheduled the first film festival at the beach resort of Cannes for September 1939. Because of the invasion of Poland by the Germans, it was cancelled and the Cannes Film Festival opened in September 1946. Approximately four thousand professionals and four hundred representatives of the press attended. The festival was cancelled in 1948 and 1950 because of financial problems, but resumed in 1951.[28] In 1968 filmmakers, critics and students, led by Jean-Luc Godard, Louis Malle, François Truffaut, and Claude Lelouch, forcibly closed down the international film festival. With the slogan, "Cinema of Freedom," the New French Cinema sought to make Cannes a non-competitive People's Film Festival, free of commercialism. Their goals, however, did not become realized.[29]

The goal of the festival is to contribute to the progress of motion picture arts and to encourage development of the film industry throughout the world. For a film to be accepted in the competition without a special waiver, it must have been produced during the twelve months preceding the festival, its exhibition must have been limited only to the country of origin, it must not have been presented in any other competition or exhibited in any motion picture event, and it must respect the aims of the festival. All of the films must be presented in the original language version with French subtitles. The awards given in the main competition for features are The Gold Palm of the International Film Festival for the best film; the Grand Special Jury Award for the film that shows the most originality and spirit of research; an award for Best Performance by an Actress; an award for the Best Performance by an Actor; and an award for Best Director. In addition, the jury may attribute an award for Best Artistic Contribution to a technician, and one other award the nature of which is determined yearly.[30]

Three non-competitive screenings are also held. For La Semaine Internationale de la Critique (International Critics' Week), members of the Cinema Critics Association choose seven films from first and second features of international directors to present during one week at the festival. La Quinzaine des Réalisateurs (Directors' Fortnight) presents twenty-five independent features from all over the world. Films showing innovation in format and ideas are preferred. The Perspectives du Cinéma Français (French Cinema Perspectives) aims to reveal new talents and new directions in French film.[31] At the Cannes Film Festival the Marché du Film, or the market, offers several hundred additional films for sale to international buyers. Any film is accepted for exhibition if a fee is paid. The former director of the Edinburgh Film Festival warned, "The Cannes Festival is a jungle. . . . Unless your film is officially in the festival, it's hard to get attention."[32] The Marché films are shown in the less exotic commercial cinemas along the town's main shopping street. Some of these theaters have their own specialties, playing films from one country or of one genre exclusively.[33]

The awards granted at the festival are the most prestigious, and second only in increasing the box office revenue to the Academy Awards. A win at Cannes of the best film, the Palme d'Or, can increase the picture's chance of success in exhibition. *Narayama Bushi-Ko* won the Cannes Golden Palm in 1983. The producing Toei company admitted, "Our asking price went up at least tenfold after the film won the prize."[34]

In the last decade, Cannes was transformed from a cultural festival with some peripheral buying and selling into a frenzied marketplace. The recent development of independent producers raising money to finance their films is believed to have generated this direction.[35]

Menahem Golan stated, "Cannes is our Christmas. . . . We count our year by Cannes. We start projects immediately at the end of Cannes and have them ready by the next Cannes. It's our day of judgment."[36] At the 1984 festival, Golan claims to have signed more than 255 contracts with a combined value of $20 million.[37] However, one AFMA official said, "If the members were told that they would have to pay 1 percent of their sales to the AFMA, you'd be surprised how drastically the figures they submit would change. . . ."[38] Since people from all over the world attend Cannes, very small business, often as little as $5,000 for the rights to a picture and not worth visiting the country for, can be conducted.[39]

The festivities at Cannes epitomize the Hollywood image. Competition to impress people and to make deals is keen. Companies claim they may spend close to half-a-million dollars to present a property properly at Cannes. Since press from around the world cover the event, competiton also exists for the publicity they can generate. Art Jacobs, vice president of JAD Films International, which specializes in foreign sales, had such a good year at the American Film Market that he would not have had to attend Cannes. However, pressure from producers who wanted to be represented at Cannes necessitated his attendance. Jacobs commented about the expense of parties at Cannes, saying:

> We had 200 people and paid about $200 a head, and at dinner we did a deal right there and then on the English rights to the picture. Encouraging. On the other hand, the French buyers who saw the film at the AFM (American Film Market) came by my office the next day and made the deal on the spot and I didn't even have to buy them a Coke.[40]

Irving Shapiro, president of Films Around the World, believes that people begin deals at the American Film Market and finish them in Cannes. He said, "It's a kind of continuous movable feast, and this is the main course." Eddie Kalish of Producers Sales Organization commented, "Of course you can make a deal in Cannes . . . whether it holds up four months later in Los Angeles after the lawyers and the accountants come in is another question."[41]

It appears that Cannes will revert to its more traditional role as a festival, with the market taking a secondary position to the American Film Market in Los Angeles and MIFED in Milan. American sellers now view Cannes as a soft market, with less emphasis on sales and more emphasis on making personal contacts with people and launching films for foreign release.[42] Cannes has maintained its prominence by metamorphosing and adapting to changes in the film community and motion picture business. It remains the most prestigious festival for exhibiting a feature film in addition to being a vital film market.

American Film Market

Frustrated by the hectic atmosphere of Cannes, the enormous costs, and the arduous tasks of getting films to France and shown there, a decision was made to have a market in Los Angeles. The American Film Marketing Association (AFMA) was formed in 1981.[43]

According to estimates by Robert Meyers, first president of the AFMA, U.S. films account for 80 to 85 percent of films in worldwide distribution, and a large percentage of those are produced independently. Meyers believes this statistic makes a film market in Los Angeles a necessity because the product and creative people are in Los Angeles.[44] Since member companies were spending $8 million to $9 million each year at Cannes, with some individual firms expending $600,000 to $700,000, they believed the risk of starting a market would be justified.[45]

The American Film Market (AFM), supported by the participating companies without any government or commercial sponsors, is for the sale of English-language films exclusively and is not a festival. The goal of the market is to become the most comprehensive and efficient film marketplace in the world, while striving for harmony among independent companies in the world.[46]

More than 150 films were up for sale to one thousand potential buyers at the first American Film Market in March 1981. Sellers must belong to the AFMA and buyers must be accredited by the AFMA committee.[47] The first ten-day market cost almost $1 million to put on. Thirty-eight companies paid $2,500 to join the association and thirty-four of them paid an additional $12,500 to $22,500, depending on the size of their company, to exhibit films at the market.[48] Buyers paid $250 if pre-registered, and $300 at the market. Between $50 million and $60 million in film sales were written at 1981's AFM.[49]

The AFMA and AFM members are composed either of large independent distributors who produce their own films and control their own foreign sales, foreign sales agents or licensing firms, or "peddlers" who sell one or a few exploitation films that are occasionally successful.[50] Filmmakers and producers even attend disguised as buyers to meet with distributors. Filmmakers with motion pictures made inexpensively and in need of foreign sales, but unable to afford the joining fee and cost of office space, sent their films to members of the association for possible representation, and several were successful.[51] Irwin Yablans, whose Compass International was regularly represented at the Cannes and Milan film festivals, elected not to join the AFMA. He, however, was screening *Hell Night* for foreign buyers at facilities not connected with AFM. Yablans believed market entry fees were too heavy and was confident that buyers would seek him.[52]

The majors decided against participating in the first market. Yet Meyers expected it to be an industry event. Since approximately half of what the majors distribute domestically comes from pickup deals with independents, and since many of the buyers of independent pictures around the world are the same people the majors deal with when they rent their films abroad, he had expected them to be interested.[53] In 1982 Universal Pictures International Sales, the foreign sales division of Universal Pictures, was the first studio to have an affiliation with the market by becoming a sponsoring member.[54]

The market was scheduled for the spring, since many independently produced American films are then completed for a domestic summer release. The markets are in hotels, with suites turned into showrooms. Posters, merchandise items, and other advertisements of completed or proposed films are omnipresent. The scheduled screenings of the films are the main event. Increasingly, video cassette samples are substituting for film. Manson International Films reportedly collected more than $3 million in guarantees for Charlton Heston's film *Mother Lode,* based on a short trailer of the unproduced film. Heston even invited distributors to his home to aid in securing guarantees.[55] To avoid the lavish competitiveness of Cannes, all suites at the hotel holding the festival are assigned by a draw. No company is allowed to invite more than twenty-five people to an event unless they invite the entire market. Though they claim they are not trying to compete with Cannes, a reported "gentleman's agreement" has been created by the sponsors of the AFM, requiring participant sellers not to screen, advertise, or hold parties at Cannes.[56] AFM director, Tim K. Kittleson, stated:

> In 1980, it cost one independent film distributor I know $500,000 to fly to Cannes and make sure his films were visible. Now he does 80 percent of his business here for only $55,000 and then goes to Cannes to play tennis.[57]

Meyers commented on the American Film Market's effect on Cannes. "There was very little business done at Cannes last year, and I think there will be very little done this year." He stressed his love of Cannes for the publicity and that they did not attempt to create a parallel, "Cannes just isn't the best place for a market." Harumasa Shirasu, a Japanese distributor, believes Cannes is best for artistic films. He usually goes to markets to gather information but bought at the American Film Market.[58]

An International Arbitration Tribunal of the AFMA was presented at the third market to arbitrate financial disputes among member companies. The arbitration system includes standard contract provisions, an Arbitration Advisory Committee to administer the program, and approximately seventy-two entertainment lawyers from more than a dozen countries to be the actual arbitrators in disputes arising from the international buying and selling of films. Continuing problems in international distribution include buying a clear title to a film, expansion of business in territories, and the growth of new media.[59]

Regardless of precautions, certain members still employ unscrupulous practices. Wolf Schmidt, former vice president of the AFMA, believes too many "one-man foreign sales companies" have been granted membership.[60] Distributors have experienced paying deposits for films that were never delivered. Alex Massis, president of Isram Film Corp., even prepared a warning list of foreign distributors for his fellow AFMA members.[61]

At the third market, sixty members of the AFMA exhibited 277 films to almost 1,100 buyers from 646 companies and 63 countries.[62] More than half of the films screened had never been screened at any other film market.[63] More than 15 percent of the features screened were films from other countries.[64] AFMA members were allowed to screen foreign films that they represented, while foreign sellers of competing product were barred. The AFMA board has since decided to permit foreign sellers to participate in the Los Angeles market. The official estimate arrived at by an anonymous poll of members of the "gross volume" of business generated by the market was $130 million.[65]

In the third year, the majors realized the value of the market. It is convenient for them to acquire pickups which make up a greater number of their releases. They can also make contacts for the future with producers and creative people. It also serves as a place for them to read additional treatments and scripts. Majors also search for films to fill a specific slot on their release schedules in foreign territories.[66] Orion Pictures put up a "sold out" sign after having made arrangements for its ten films.[67] Equally successful, Cannon said their company did $22 million worth of business on ten pictures.[68] One producer was even accepting American Express credit cards as a form of payment.[69]

AFM is valuable for acquiring rights to foreign home video, whereas, domestic video rights are often tied up with theatrical rights. Since the foreign home video is a newer market than the U.S. home video market, in 1982 there was a scramble to acquire product to build up a catalogue. High prices could then be secured for these precious items. But by 1983 things had quieted down.[70] At MIFED and Cannes, video was hailed as important in rescuing companies from financial disaster, with half the buyers from video.[71]

In countries with government-controlled television programming, average or below-average American films are sought on video cassette. Video sales accounted for nearly 50 percent of total business at the 1984 American Film Market. Just two years ago, the video sales were less than 25 percent. In countries with the most rapidly expanding video markets, such as Australia, Japan, and Germany, the buyers will purchase the theatrical rights to a film to secure the video rights. Theatrical release performs the function of an advertisement for video release.[72]

Of the approximately 125 new films that were to be screened at the 1984 American Film Market, nearly half the films announced for screening had a U.S. distributor and many had already played domestically. As the focus of the market, foreign and ancillary rights were the main order of business. Jonas Rosenfield, executive director of the AFMA, stated that with approximately $800 million of the estimated $1.7 billion the majors were to spend on production in 1984 coming from independent or outside investors, more big pictures would go to the AFM for assistance. By licensing a film territory-by-territory without cross-collateralization, the major producers learned they could realize a greater profit.[73]

The 1984 AFMA membership had seventy-four constituents, an increase from the first 1981 American Film Market with thirty-two members. The 1984 AFMA's increased membership caused some dissension, principally among the smaller firms. They opposed the acceptance of fledgling foreign sales firms and producers who had decided to sell on their own instead of signing up with a foreign sales agent who charged a commission of 10 to 20 percent.[74]

Independent distributors in New York believe the AFM neglects their interests. They find that the organization has expanded into a representative organization that desires to act as a bargaining agent by establishing standard contracts and displaying a unified front. They believe that admitting representatives of the majors who have divergent interests from the independents and admitting representatives from foreign countries who may gain bargaining power is detrimental to the interests of the independent. Stanley Dudelson, president of New Line Cinema, stated, "The West Coast guys do what they want and then inform us about it—we have nothing to say."[75]

Though the smaller, less powerful companies complain that their needs are of low priority to the AFMA, membership has almost doubled since the market's inception in 1981. In only a few years, the American Film Market has become a world event, organized and efficiently operated for serious business.

MIFED

In addition to Cannes and the AFM, MIFED is considered one of the world's major film markets. Since its inception in 1980, MIFED's object was to provide filmmakers with an efficient event at which to sell their films. It is divided into three sections. MIFED Traditional is for all media, including old and new features, home video, documentaries, animated films, and miniseries. MIFED East-West encompasses trade between Eastern and Western countries. MIFED Indian Summer is the market for features released within the past year.

MIFED is strictly a market. Director of the market, Dr. Michele Guido Franci said, "People do not come here to have a good time but to make money."[76] In 1983, 1,207 companies registered, 1,830 participants attended from seventy-seven countries, and 344 films from thirty countries were screened.[77] This market is believed to have fewer social diversions, making business more serious. Films may be offered for less money than at the first- and second-bid markets of Los Angeles and Cannes. Even if deals are not concluded, many transactions are begun or options are taken.[78] Since festivals draw people together from around the world, it is a convenient place to hold seminars to disseminate information.

Cannes, AFM, and MIFED are the major markets in the world. Michael Goldman, president of the AFMA and Manson International, claims his company does approximately 50 percent of its business at the AFM, 30 to 35 percent at MIFED, and only 15 to 20 percent at Cannes.[79] According to another member of the AFMA, Cannes constitutes 20 percent of all market business, while the AFM and MIFED constitute approximately 40 percent each.[80] Regardless of which market is most productive for a particular company, Cannes, AFM, and MIFED are important industry events.

Film markets whose main emphasis is not the commercial Hollywood feature also exist. For example, the Manila Film Festival "aims to be the Cannes of the East," placing a large emphasis on Asian talent.[81]

Started in 1979, The American Independent Feature Film Market in New York takes place at the same time as the New York Film Festival. Some of the films were presented at other festivals, yet still lacked a distributor.[82] From the 1983 market, participating films such as *El Norte* and *Android* were domestically released.[83] Representatives from the classics division of the majors along with other independent distributors attended.

Across the street from the third AFM was the first Extra Film Market. Since the AFM will not allow adult films to be sold under their auspices, the Extra Film Market was created. Fifteen sellers offered 150 films to approximately 300 buyers.[84] Chuck Vincent, coordinator of the event and president of Platinum Pictures, estimated that more than $3 million worth of business was transacted at the market.[85] One-third of the business accomplished by the fifteen participating companies selling X-rated films was for the video cassette market to overseas buyers.[86] Vincent was urging his industry to produce more "hard 'R'" acceptable on cable, instead of the X-rated fare. He also stressed the need of a story and predicted, "I think pretty soon we'll converge with the pictures from the major studios."[87]

Though many film festivals and markets were created to generate money for the local economy by attracting participants and visitors, they still serve as a celebration of film for a specialized audience. This common denominator is the basis for social and business contacts at these centralized locales.

Festivals and markets need new product, whether it is art or entertainment. A distributor is provided the opportunity to pick up a film at minimal cost from a desperate seller. A company may even purchase a completed film outright, add exploitative elements to the film, and make substantial profit at the box office. Festivals and markets also provide a distributor with the opportunity to acquire a film that may become a blockbuster, as in Corolco's acquisition of *First Blood* which generated a worldwide box office gross of more than $100 million. Since one cannot be sure from where a commercial film may come, wisdom dictates that distributors look at all films presented to them.

The distribution pattern of *Hester Street,* made for $365,000 in 1973 by Joan Micklin Silver, demonstrates the power of film festivals and critical acclaim.[88] Because of an enthusiastic response at Cannes the film was sold to several foreign countries. In the United States, however, the picture made the rounds of the majors three times and was rejected. The majors felt the black and white photography, low budget, and ethnic orientation were detrimental to box office success. Silver and her husband decided to distribute it themselves.[89] Because of the film's success at festivals, some exhibitors were willing to book the picture in a few theaters. When the actress Carol Kane received an Academy Award nomination as best actress, hundreds of smaller communities that would not have shown the picture opened up to it.[90] The picture ultimately grossed more than $4 million.

Critical acclaim, festivals, and markets can be used as tools in the financing, distribution, and release of a motion picture. A film festival itself can be viewed as a celebration of the business conducted at a film market. For if deals were not put together allowing films to be produced and distributed, festivals would have nothing to exhibit.

5

Publicity, Advertising, Promotion, and Research

Research, publicity, advertising, and promotion are tools that can be used prior to production to better predict the odds of a film acquiring distribution and ultimately becoming successful. Publicity directs attention to a product in the media using time and space that has not been purchased, either directly or indirectly. Because the competition is so keen, it takes money to create and place publicity. Advertising is an announcement brought to the public by a paid appearance in a communications medium. The studios used to have "exploitation" departments. When "exploitation" came to be associated with unfair use, the term became referred to as "promotion." Any means created to call attention to a film is promotion, such as film festivals, parades, books placed in supermarkets, albums, and merchandising. Promotional gimmicks provide motivation to prospective buyers. "Motivation . . . aims for the heart while advertising aims for the head."[1]

At the beginning of the motion picture industry, films were novelty items aggressively sought by the public. This intense demand for pictures was far greater than the supply. Since audiences were anxiously awaiting new product, little promotion was needed. With increased competition and more stability in business, advertisements were created to inform people of a new film and where it was playing.

The first movie ads were an outgrowth of carnival announcements. The advance man would precede the show to a town, giving away free tickets for the privilege of nailing up posters. It became obvious that he could achieve greater "reach" with the advertising if ads were placed in a newspaper. These were the first entertainment ads.

In 1910 Carl Laemmle promised Florence Lawrence screen credit to make her leave Biograph to work for him. After acquiring her services, he performed what is considered the first publicity stunt. He circulated rumors that she had died in a streetcar accident, and subsequently published large ads in newspapers announcing that she was in fact alive and was working for him on the best movies of her career.[2]

Harry Reichenbach was one of the more famous publicity men. During a lull in Rudolph Valentino's career, Reichenbach convinced Valentino to grow a beard. He kept him on the front page of newspapers to create protests that culminated in his shaving.[3]

Motion Picture Story Magazine, the first fan magazine, was published in 1911. It was originally intended only for exhibitors, but became so popular that it was sold on newsstands. *Photoplay* appeared in 1912 and *Motion Picture Stories* in 1913. These magazines summarized movie plots and soon expanded into behind-the-scenes glimpses of filmmaking. By 1914 *Motion Picture Story Magazine* had a circulation of 270,000.[4]

Fan magazines were important places in which to advertise. Audiences eagerly read them to find out about their favorite stars and to scrutinize the lives of people in the "evil" town of Hollywood. The lives of the wealthy had been of interest to the public for generations before movie stars were popular.[5] Around 1913 the movie premiere was created to contribute to the illusion of status. Wealthy and influential people came out for these events.[6]

As competition among exhibitors increased, novel means of attracting the customer to a specific theater were employed. Theaters began placing women, horses, and costumed people outside to attract audiences. Theater fronts were adorned with lights, and lobbies were transformed into environments corresponding to the film's theme. Handbills given out at the door were kept by patrons, prolonging the advertising impact. Free passes, poster contests, treasure hunts, drawing contests, and scrambled movie star contests were all used to entice people to a theater.[7]

When motion pictures began, producers provided exhibitors with promotional material. In the 1920s, when the flat rental method of distribution was common, the film exchanges bought films a year in advance and had their own staffs make trailers out of excess footage. The Famous Players-Lasky Corporation had an advertising department in 1918 as large as its production and distribution departments. They wrote ads and instructed exchanges on their proper use. The Pathé Exchange used an advertising agency to place local and national newspaper advertising and sold advertising accessories to exhibitors. United Artists created a yearly advertising budget prorated equally to all pictures. If a producer exceeded his allotted amount, he did so at his own expense.[8]

The studios regulated the press' access to stars and created images for them. Very little appeared in print by chance. Louella Parsons dominated Hollywood gossip through most of the 1930s. Though Parsons was extremely inaccurate and often fabricated information, she still wielded power and influence by forming images of stars in the public's mind. In the late 1930s, Hedda Hopper wrote a column in the *Los Angeles Times.* The struggle between studios aided the gossip columnists. Parsons and Hopper were able to manipulate personalities by speaking for the morality of the American small-town resident. Knowing how to make behavior appear moral or immoral, they became powerful forces when ostensibly working merely for publicity and promotion.[9]

Growing concern over the honesty and effect of advertising led to cries for censorship. The director of advertising for Paramount Famous Players-Lasky in 1930, Russel Holman said:

> Barnum is supposed to be the father of show advertising. He favored a flamboyant type of advertising, most of which was bunk. He had to deal with the circus which comes and goes in 24 hours. There is a difference in advertising a circus and a motion picture, for the motion picture is there day after day. We cannot afford to fool the public and we are gradually getting away from the Barnum type of advertising.[10]

In 1930, to ensure that motion picture advertising would reflect the same high ideals and aims inspired by the Production Code, an Advertising Code was created by advertising and publicity directors in the industry and was adopted by advertising directors.[11]

During the 1930s, conflict over the control of advertising took place between distributors and exchanges. Distributors inserted ad control into contracts, claiming they knew the picture better and could do a less expensive job. The distributors sold the material to the exchanges for a profit. On the other side, the exchanges believed they could do a better job with their own local audience. They also disliked the fact that distributors gave more advertising emphasis to poorer pictures. In the 1930s, RKO Productions was representative of the major studios. All ad material was prepared by an agency. The cost was shared on a cooperative basis with exhibitors. Generally, three different newspaper advertisements were created from which the exchanges could select. Approximately 3 to 5 percent of local grosses was designated for local advertising.[12] Fictionalizations of screenplays written in serial form of six installments were also provided to exhibitors to give to local newspapers. A week prior to a film's release the paper would run them, giving the picture a week of free publicity and the opportunity to claim, "You've read the story—now see the film."[13]

Motion picture advertising was being studied increasingly for its effect on the success of a film. Unlike other products, motion pictures could not be judged by their production companies but had to be sold on an individual basis. No picture had a guaranteed success for all exhibitors and very few films were made that some exhibitor by ingenious showmanship could not turn into one of his more profitable engagements.[14]

John Waters, the director of *Pink Flamingos* and *Polyester,* for which he provided the audience with a card to scratch off scents at particular points in the film, wrote of the gimmicks that used to be created to attract audiences to theaters. For example, Joe Solomon used four-walling to exploit *Mom and Dad,* a pseudosex documentary from the forties. He employed a phony nurse handing out sex education pamphlets to the sexually segregated audience. He also released a noxious gas through the air vents until a person passed out. He would then call an ambulance and the local media. William Castle took out a policy with Lloyds of London insuring every ticket buyer to his *Macabre* (1958) for $1,000 in case they died from fright in the theater. Hearses parked outside with phony nurses provided additional publicity. Castle then came up with "Percepto" for *The Tingler* (1959). Small motors were installed under the theater seats which were activated by the projectionist at appropriate times. For *Homicidal* he utilized the "Fright Break." Several minutes before the film ended, the screen would go black and would allow the too frightened to leave with a refund. Castle created "Coward's Corner" to humiliate the 1 percent who asked for a refund. For *Mr. Sardonicus* (1961), Castle created the "Punishment Poll" which allowed the audience to hold up cards of "Mercy" or "No Mercy" as the verdict for the villain. Castle had supplied two endings; however, the audience always voted "No Mercy." To promote *Straight-Jacket* (1964), Joan Crawford was sent to theaters and bloody cardboard axes were given away to fans. Believing the industry still has room for showmanship, Waters wrote, "Every time an expensive Hollywood bomb opens, theaters could profit by letting the audience in for free and making them pay to get out." He added, "People are getting bored with the theatergoing experience!"[15]

Regardless of the publicity, advertising, and promotion used to attract audiences to the movies, box office revenue kept dwindling during the late forties and fifties. Television was viewed as the enemy and not as an advertising medium. Exhibitor boycotts were threatened if films would be sold or licensed by distributors to television.[16]

In the sixties a study prepared by Daniel Yankelovich for the Motion Picture Association of America revealed that publicity contributed little to the success of a motion picture. Pre-release publicity, unless the film had a tie-in with a familiar book, play, or musical score, did not create extensive public awareness. It was advertising three days prior to the opening that was effective. Since this study came out when studios were struggling to cut overheads, they eagerly reacted by dismantling their large publicity departments.[17]

In the late 1960s, if initial box office response was small, advertising was cut back and sometimes eliminated. Not much study was done prior to or after release. It was not unusual for films in 1970 to go into production without publicists or still photographers.[18]

After the motion picture industry realized that television was not merely a novelty, but instead had a secure future, and when studios were suffering great financial losses, they had to start selling films to television. This novel idea was met with resistance. In 1966, Otto Preminger sued Screen Gems and ABC over the insertion of commercials in *Anatomy of a Murder*. He believed the commercials degraded the film and damaged his reputation as a filmmaker. The court refused to restrain NBC from showing *A Place in the Sun* with commercials but warned that commercials should be inserted with care not to adversely affect the artistic quality of the film.[19]

Finally, the motion picture industry not only sold their product to television, but began using it to advertise their films. Marketing executive Richard Lederer recalled the first national television buy for a Clint Eastwood movie, *Dirty Harry*. At that time, in the early seventies, it cost $250,000. For the same rating points ten years later, it would cost around $800,000 without a great increase in the size of the audience.[20]

As release patterns changed, so did the advertising. Because of the great demand to see *The Godfather,* Paramount broke the exclusive release pattern and opened the film in hundreds of theaters.[21] Since few theaters could afford television advertising, exhibitors gave up their exclusive territorial rights in exchange for a pooled-funds television campaign.[22] To be under the television umbrella provided greater hope for increasing the audience.

Four-wallers, those who rented out theaters, became experts of advertising campaign experimentation. By spending more money on advertising than production, they achieved great results. In the late seventies this practice became common.[23] New companies came to rely on media campaigns and distribution skills to extract profits from marginal pictures. Avco Embassy purposely produced films that were easy to market in terms of advertising. Instead of competing with the majors, they hired better sales representatives and young filmmakers. They proportionately spent more money than the majors on advertising. For example, $3 million might be spent to launch a $500,000 film.

Shopping malls became prominent places for publicizing movies. For example, characters from *Return of the Jedi* visited more than 150 large shopping malls across the country.[24] Since shopping malls were increasingly becoming centers of activity, and were often owned by conglomerates that also produced motion pictures, theaters were built in the malls. Promotional tie-ins became an added attraction. At the same time and in one place, a person could see the movie and buy records, books, toys, and other merchandise relating to the film.

In the 1970s the length of the line at the box office became a barometer of success. The first people interviewed in lines for the sake of publicity were waiting to see *The Exorcist* (1973).[25] People camped out days ahead of time on Hollywood Boulevard for the opening of *Return of the Jedi*. Pictures of these lines were novel means to publicize the film. When looking at low-per-theater averages, Frank Yablans, chief operating officer at MGM/UA, told one vice president, "Cut the number of theaters down. I want pressure. I want lines around the block. A customer comes into a half-empty theater and feels like a jerk."[26]

With general growing interest in all aspects of the motion picture industry, critics have increased in power and visibility. Critics' opinions have become increasingly common in advertising copy. With the growth of entertainment news on television, electronic press kits provide well-crafted material technically far superior to what a local station could produce on a daily basis. Though it costs more than $100,000 to produce and distribute the kits to about two hundred television stations, hundreds of thousands of dollars of free air time is commanded. It is now possible for any television reporter to insert himself into the interviews prepared by the film company. Such new techniques question journalistic integrity, as a reporter gives the impression that he performed the interview. The large number of bad pictures that are publicized as good films can lead to audience disappointment, greater suspicion of film criticism and future films, and less actual attendance.

Though varying degrees of importance have been given to research, publicity, advertising, and promotion, their techniques and importance have remained relatively constant throughout the history of the motion picture industry. What has changed has been the gradual relinquishing by the studios of their domination in the creation of advertising, publicity, and promotion. Henry Rogers of Rogers and Cowan stated that years ago studios had their own publicity departments. Now, companies like Rogers and Cowan work for all of the studios on long- and short-range campaigns. They become involved in long-range campaigns if the studio feels a particular picture is very important. In such cases they become involved before principal photography begins. In a short-range situation, they are brought in after the rough cut is completed, or three to five months prior to release of the picture.[27] Most stars are handled by independent publicity agencies. Fees can range from $1,500 a month at boutiques to the average $3,000 per month at Rogers and Cowan. An important star or producer can demand an outside agency supplement the studio publicity staff at fees from $40,000 to $200,000 a picture.[28]

Public relations firms are growing to meet changing needs in the industry. Since many films are produced independently, these companies have the expertise to completely market a picture. These firms also create campaigns that can make a picture appear more attractive in finding a distributor and can also arrange product tie-ins and broad promotions. Because they are hired on individual films, they are motivated to do a good job to ensure being able to work on the producer's next film.

Independent marketing consultants perform market research, develop the advertising campaign, and even advise on the release pattern for the picture. They are also involved with funding, finding distributors, lining up pay-TV sales, and even acquiring properties. Charles Powell and Buddy Young began their own business of selling their professional marketing expertise on the open market. Powell, former marketing vice-president at Universal, does not want to reveal the campaigns he has worked on. "The name of the game is to let the studio think they did the campaign themselves." Consultants are paid in various ways. A flat fee can range from $12,500 to $100,000 depending upon the amount of work involved. Some will accept a part ownership in the film, with 3 percent of the producer's net profits being common. Receiving a film one month before release could cost more "just for having to second-guess the distributor." It is easier and less costly to begin work early in the film's production. They are then able to advise on setting up special ad shots. Powell said, "We cannot make a picture successful; we can only maximize its potential." They can also provide a projection on how the film is expected to perform.[29]

Publicity tries to create the illusion that the public discovered the film on its own. A unit publicist is generally hired for a specific film before production begins and stays with the picture until its release. A publicist must focus completely on getting a picture into the minds of the people and generating a desire to see it. The publicist serves as a liaison between the production company and the world and thus needs to be diplomatic in dealing with the stars, the press, and the public.

The goal of a publicist is a national magazine cover, a news item on network television, or a photo or news story in *Time* or *Newsweek*. Though *Last Tango in Paris* was an X-rated film, it generated enormous publicity. The film was extensively reviewed around the world. It is wise to get the film into sections of the newspaper other than the entertainment page by staging events or benefits for publicity value.

Awards can generate publicity around the world. Three hundred reporters were present at the fifty-sixth annual Academy Awards in 1983. They each represented publications with a circulation of at least 150,000 unless they were trade-oriented or school publications. Attracting attention at this event alerts the world to the existence of the film.[30] If a film is nominated for an Academy Award, theatrical revenue may increase 5 to 10 percent. In the case of a small or lesser-known film, the incremental increase is generally 10 percent but could reach 25 to 30 percent. An Oscar could add 50 to 100 percent to a film's value in cable and network markets.[31]

Producer Sam Spiegel acquired *Betrayal* and spent more than $2 million distributing and advertising the independent production. After grossing $4 million, it was no longer in major release. He believed it worthy of an Oscar but was angry to find the distributor would not spend the money to advertise it to the industry. He commented:

> Films are honored for their quality and for the prestige they bestow on the motion picture art. We've spent years converting that art into an industry. And now comes a new generation of businessman who decides whether a picture deserves an award or not on the basis of its income.[32]

Exhibitors complain about publicity that emphasizes the high cost of a picture. They fear that average or low-budget pictures will be equated with inferior films.

The typical means of publicizing a picture includes press books or kits created and distributed to the exhibitors who will play the film. They include all of the necessary information to exploit the film, including stories and stills to be planted in newspapers along with advertisements for the film. Independents making films without adequate funding generally put all of their money into the actual production of the film. Frequently, they neglect publicity which may be crucial to their film acquiring distribution. If they do not have adequate publicity material, such as stories, stills, and articles, much time and money has to be expended to create these necessary items after production.

Samuel Z. Arkoff prefers to distribute films that come with publicity having been created during production. Arkoff stated, "No picture has ever been made that it is good enough to sell itself." Arkoff believes publicists should supervise the film from the beginning, by tailoring and restructuring the script's content and selecting stars for the tastes of the audience. Arkoff concluded his speech to the publicists:

> There are too many people in Hollywood that believe that movies are now *film* and must therefore be sold as culture with the soft sell.
> We used to be a business of Barnums. Unfortunately, today there is more razzle dazzle at the corner supermarket and MacDonalds [sic] Drive Ins than at our movie palaces.
> I can remember campaigns that were so exciting that the comment was "put the sprocket holes in the campaign and shelve the picture."
> American International Pictures couldn't live without you. The very soul of our existence from the beginning has been emphasis on publicity, promotion and advertising. And in my opinion our industry can't live without you either.[33]

Publicity departments have diminished in prominence at the studios. Publicists have been greatly replaced by public relations people.[34] Robert Evans is skeptical about the effect of production publicity. He wrote, "I don't believe in production publicity at all; it's forgotten by the time the picture comes out and distracts the actors from making the film. Publicity counts most in the month before the picture opens." Yet he believes a ninety-second teaser trailer should play in theaters six months before a film's release to plant an image in the audience's memory.[35]

Publicity can make people feel that it is a social necessity to see a film. Only then can they participate in discussions with friends. This feeling also makes people see a movie again, often taking a friend to join the experience.

Publicity strives to create positive word of mouth. Other people's opinions have always had a great influence on motivating others to the theaters. Pathé, the distributor of Robert Flaherty's *Nanook,* had difficulty in getting big theaters to show the film. They suspected that showing the film cold to Roxy, the exhibitor who ran the largest theater in New York, would be disastrous. Instead, they arranged for friends to applaud through the screening and discuss the merits of the film. After it was over, Roxy eagerly booked it.[36]

Publicity can be created to influence exhibitors to book a film. For example, *Snuff* was the Argentine film that supposedly showed a woman being dismembered on camera. Monarch Releasing Corporation itself invented protests by decency groups. The movie was booked and became a success in New York, Los Angeles, Philadelphia, and other cities. However, in Boston, organizations and press were suspicious over the exhibitors' desire to incite fury and decided to ignore the film, which quickly closed.[37]

Publicist Mac St. Johns claims that $1 million of free publicity can be created by paying a publicist $100,000 for one year of work. Audience studies can be used to pinpoint ages and types of audiences that like the film. Julian F. Myers blames the waste of advertising dollars on the practice whereby distributors, to outbid other distributors for the picture, promise producers that they will spend a certain amount on advertising to open the film. The amount they contract to spend on advertising usually reduces the publicity funds. The result is an enormous amount of money being spent on a film that no one has previously heard about. Myers wrote, "No 'want to see' has been engendered until an ad suddenly says 'Buy it now. We say you want to see it.'"[38]

Advertising can cost more than the production of the film and be responsible for getting the picture seen. If an ad campaign reflects the true nature of the film, audiences who go to the movie will not be disappointed, but will get what they expected and wanted. However, ad campaigns often reflect one element in a film that is believed to be most exploitable with a certain audience. This is often successful for one or two weeks and can help a producer recoup money from a low-quality movie. Generally 50 to 60 percent of the negative cost of a picture is expended for advertising. Though advertising costs vary with different pictures, an average of 6 percent of the box office gross is expended in advertising dollars.[39] Since the majors take their distribution fee off the first dollar, it may be advantageous for them to spend $12 million to recoup $14 million in rentals. Such expenditures, however, may not be the most profitable strategy for the producer.

Charles Powell said that 80 percent of all advertising money is spent in two weeks, the week before and the week of the picture's opening. A film generally has ten days in which to make money.[40] Richard Lederer, head of advertising and publicity for Orion Pictures, claims the advertising costs for the pre-opening and the first week average $4.5 million. If the film shows any success and is situated in 800 to 1,200 theaters, $1.2 to $1.3 million is spent the second week. In the third week only $700,000 to $800,000 is spent. The advertising expenditures continue to decrease in the following weeks. However, in the seventh or eighth week, $1 million may be spent in the effort to renew interest in the picture.[41] A blockbuster, however, may expend $20 million in marketing costs to sustain a long run.

Films can generate 90 percent of their revenue from 50 percent of the country. Since the majors often use nationwide advertising and releases, 30 to 40 percent of the advertising budget may be wasted. Independent distributors can focus the advertising dollars on specific areas that will be most responsive to maximize income for pictures with less than national appeal.[42] To determine the amount of the advertising budget that should be spent in a local area, the domestic film rental must be projected. No more should be spent on advertising than a proportional amount of what the local area generally earns of the national rental. For example, if the average Washington, D.C. exchange generally provides 3.6 percent of domestic film rentals, and the picture is expected to earn $2 million in rentals, then 3.6 percent of $2 million should be the maximum expended for the entire exchange area. However, one can "buy a gross," or spend excessively to generate huge grosses as a form of advertisement in itself.[43]

The release pattern of the picture is a prime influence in the advertising campaign. If the film is an exclusive run, it must be advertised as having enough merit to warrant people traveling long distances to see it and pay higher admission prices. Since it costs as much to advertise one theater as many, the exclusive run is becoming less common. In a saturation-booking release, an enormous amount of money is spent and demands that the film perform immediately. Since a film is a perishable product, the campaign is aimed directly before the film opens and advertises when the picture will open and where it will be shown.[44] The bulk of advertising cost is spent the opening week. In the second week the size of the ads is reduced and television spots are reduced or eliminated.[45]

Release schedules are flexible. First runs may open over a two- or three-month period around the country, depending upon the availability of the right theaters and right deals. Films are only locked to dates for prime times of the year, such as Christmas/New Year's and the opening of summer vacation. Otherwise, pictures are opened in sequence. A picture generating the minimum box office holdover figure can have an indefinite first run thereby holding up the next picture. For example, which films will open in Los Angeles and in which order they will play may be known but not the specific opening and closing dates. The cost of advertising at the prime season is virtually the same as at other times of the year. Although the summer is an optimum time for a wide release because of large audience attendance at theaters, the competition is great. Before United Artists experimented with *Lenny,* no one opened a major film in October or November. Suddenly, a void in the marketplace was realized. People now also open films in October or November for Academy Award consideration.[46]

New York represents a potential of 10 percent of a film's domestic gross. New York, the traditional launching city for films, is increasingly being bypassed because of the high cost of advertising and the fear of a negative review. Foreign and art film distributors, however, realize that New York reviews are essential to generating national publicity for their films, which encourages bookings elsewhere. A saturation release in New York of a seventy to one hundred theater booking generally requires $250,000 in advertising. Horror or youth pictures aimed at a specific age group may not have to spend that much. These costs are twice that of a launch in Los Angeles and considerably higher than in the rest of the country.[47]

Generally, a theater has a fixed amount they will spend for advertising, with the distributor paying the difference. Cooperative advertising, common elsewhere, is not used in New York. Since an opening in New York theoretically opens the film for the entire country, exhibitors do not believe they should pay for this national advertising. Because of costs, unless a film is widely released nationally in a thousand prints, release in New York is questionable. Exploitation films can gross $1 million in a saturation booking in New York for two to three weeks. However, harder to sell films have trouble earning back the marketing costs. A small launch of twenty to twenty-five theaters is only sensible if the film is pre-sold as a reissue of a successful film, or is an exploitation picture. Since a new film needs to compete with other releases, it may cost the same amount of money to open a film in twenty theaters as in one hundred.[48]

Alan Hirschfield was determined to introduce modern marketing techniques into the motion picture industry. Regional analyses were performed to determine the parts of the country that might be most receptive to a particular film. With a belief that millions of dollars in potential revenue had been slighted, he wanted to focus more attention on the rest of the country.[49] For example, Chicago's costs for advertising are less than one-third those of New York's. A film that has been played in the rest of the country is sometimes given exclusive New York runs to give the film a potential second life and to establish, by national reviews, its fully released status that is important for ancillary markets. In the seventies, weak films were played off in New York on first-run double bills. This has been replaced by reissues of successful recent films that offer the exhibitor more security.[50]

Gordon Armstrong, marketing vice president at Universal, said that all marketing executives agree there is little chance of making a profit in New York with a selectively booked film. One does not play there for large film rentals. He recalled that if a film played Radio City Music Hall successfully, one would get thousands of other theaters to book the movie. Now, when a picture opens in one theater, the effect of lines around the block creates similar exhibitor interest.[51]

Producers used to open a picture in Loew's Tower East on the East Side of Manhattan, Loew's Astor Plaza in Times Square, the Bruin in Los Angeles, and the Chinese on Hollywood Boulevard. Full-page ads were taken out in the *New York Times* and the *Los Angeles Times* beginning a few days before the picture opened and extending a week into its run. If the film was performing poorly, the ad budget was doubled. They believed no motion picture was so bad that it could not be sold by aggressive studio advertising. Since the money was the studio's, the producer did not complain.[52]

Since more films are independently produced with creative talent often having a percentage of the profits, this attitude of spending as much money as possible on advertising is no longer attractive. It is often wiser to spend advertising dollars more prudently to maximize the profits for all.

Motion picture "trailers," known as coming attractions, are the most effective and cost-efficient form of advertising. A captive audience proven to attend that specific theater is directly hit. Before 1920, exhibitors showed their coming attractions on slides or "stills." Trailers made from discarded footage came to be used and were given to exhibitors without charge. Eventually companies were formed specifically to produce and distribute trailers.[53] With cost reductions in the 1960s, studio in-house trailer departments were eliminated.[54] Independent trailer producers offered lower overhead. Intense competition exists for these contracts, now awarded on an individual basis.

Though a successful film may play ten thousand engagements in the United States, only first-run and first multiples are supported by distributor advertising. The majority of theaters do their own advertising with their own money, and use material provided by National Screen Service, the national distributor of trailers and accessories such as posters, still photographs, and mats used for newspaper advertisement.[55]

Since a trailer is a prime method of advertising, it is prudent for the producer or filmmaker to increase the odds of it being shown, particularly throughout the run of the preceding film. However, some theaters do not know what the next film will be and are understandably reluctant to advertise a film that may end up in a competing theater. A producer or studio can splice a trailer for their next film onto the current release. However, exhibitors can easily cut it out if they are not sure they will be exhibiting it. Prestigious films such as *Apocalypse Now* did not appear with trailers. Much valuable audience exposure to a future film that a trailer can provide is also lost because a projectionist may be too lazy to show it.

The new and growing practice of exhibitors playing commercial advertisements in their theaters may reduce the screen time previously allotted for trailers. Approximately four thousand of the nation's more than eighteen thousand movie screens carry national advertising. As the numbers of advertisements increase, controversy over their appropriateness and the rights to advertising revenues will grow.[56] The screening of commercials before movies, accepted in European and Latin American theaters, is increasing in the United States. Tests have shown that theater audiences remember products and brand names three to four times more frequently than from television commercials.

Screenvision, the largest distributor of advertising trailers in the United States, gives theater owners one-third of their gross profits in exchange for running thirty-second to two-minute ads. None of the revenue earned will be passed on to distributors. Screenvision maintains that the ads for their clients have entertainment value.[57] However, in the exhibitor's desire to make extra money, if the time allotted for the playing of trailers is reduced, more money might be lost in the long run.

The advertising campaign and the advertising budget are crucial factors in the selection of a distributor. If a filmmaker's priority is earning a profit, a company that will spend the average amount of $6 million to $8 million on advertising may not return a profit. Yet if too little is spent in total or at inappropriate times, a large segment of the audience may not be reached. An infinite number of variables exist in the planning, creating, and execution of a successful advertising campaign. A filmmaker needs to have a vision of what the advertising campaign should accomplish and then investigate the optimum method of achieving this goal. When the majors owned the theaters, it was paramount to keep people habitually attending theaters to see their favorite actors. The picture was secondary. Since films are now licensed to exhibitors on an individual basis, advertising must sell the motion picture.[58] An executive said, "The role of advertising today is very limited in comparison with previous years. More and more dollars do not result in more and more business. We can't even buy an audience the way we used to."[59] One or several advertising campaigns must be uniquely created for each picture. A decision must be made on the "handle," or emphasis to exploit, and how to "position" or place the film most advantageously in the marketplace.

Advertising campaigns have to be created specifically for other countries, emphasizing the particular elements most popular in a region. Foreign marketing campaigns should be considered at the beginning of production. They generally rely heavily on input from local distributors who know their audience.

Celebrity tours are much more effective abroad than in the United States. For example, Kirk Douglas did one television show in Germany to promote United Artists' *The Final Countdown* (1980) and an unexpected $3 million was attributed to his one personal appearance.[60]

Foreign sales agents are often an integral part of the marketing of a film. Sales agents advise on all aspects of distribution, from marketing strategies to censorship laws on a territory-by-territory basis. In some foreign countries, film advertising is not allowed on television. The audience must therefore be reached by other means. In some cases covering a city with posters is effective.

Each country's ad campaign is separate and can cost from a few thousand dollars to $100,000. Manson International President Michael Goldman stresses the importance of customizing advertising campaigns for foreign territories and of choosing the right distributor. He finds that different distributors are preferable for different types of films. A large company may be better able to give a picture a lavish release, whereas a small company may specialize in exploitation films. Manson creates original campaigns for approximately 50 percent of the films it handles, some of which have no domestic deal and no ad campaign of any kind.[61]

Ad campaigns and theater bookings are more beneficial to a picture if arranged in sufficient time prior to release of the film. Film buying for the majority of theaters is performed by circuits and cooperatives. A common complaint by exhibitors is that they do not receive immediate notice of bookings and receive publicity materials too late. Therefore, much revenue is lost because potential customers never learn about upcoming pictures.[62]

The day it is decided that a film is going to be produced, the advertising can begin. Ads are placed in the trade papers and talent searches are often publicized. During production, one overall strategy should be determined when the primary audience is defined. During post-production, sneak previews can be used to confirm the target audience. Trailers and ads are then created and tailored for this audience.

If one ad campaign is obviously failing, other campaigns are tried. Producers may have a third advertising campaign option. The first two are generally paid by the distributor and the producer is given the opportunity to pay for a third. The filmmaker often believes he knows the film best and therefore should have a voice in the advertising. Only rarely, when the person commands great power, is this the case.

Universal, following the practices of other distributors, has established a relationship with twenty-six advertising agencies across the United States to report to three regional field managers. Previously, six regional representatives covered huge geographical areas. Their new setup gives Universal greater representation on the local level. These agencies are responsible for advertising, publicity, and promotion. Paramount has used fifty-five similar regional agencies nationally which report to management in New York. Warner Bros. and Orion have comparable systems.[63]

Many independent distributors are experts in making money from a film solely based on the advertising. Many films produced by New World were excuses for an ad campaign. A New World employee claimed, "The bottom line was sixty seconds of good action for the trailer and a hot concept. That was enough to sell the picture and everything else was suspect." And when this was not enough, deceptive measures were employed. Trailers were artfully edited to suggest a different plot. Footage was shot exclusively for a trailer or a trailer was created from footage from another movie.[64]

Distributors feel a campaign is successful when no more than 15 percent of the box office receipts has been spent on advertising.[65] In 1980, $750 million was spent by motion picture companies to advertise and promote films, an increase of $100 million from 1979.[66] With advertising costs so high, it is very risky to attempt several campaigns. David A. Lipton, vice president of Universal Pictures, said:

> The difficulties arise from the fact that one is dealing with something very intangible: the public interest at a given moment. We have found through many years of effort that the public cannot tell you in advance what their tastes will be.[67]

Since advertising is so costly, security of investment is sought in market research or by producing sequels, remakes, or films similar to popular films. Yet a film always comes along that is a success, defying research. Gabe Sumner claims that whenever one spots a trend, it has probably already passed.[68]

Pre-testing is still not as common as surveying after a film is finished, even though the survey may reveal disappointing facts that can no longer be changed. In 1979 Associated Film Distribution (AFD) encountered a problem with *Saturn 3*. The producers believed stars drew audiences to theaters and thus hired Farrah Fawcett and Kirk Douglas. It was discovered after the production that Farrah Fawcett was not a star who would attract audiences but instead was a deterrent. They had already spent much money on a cast that a marketing survey told them not to advertise. They therefore concentrated on other elements in the film without mention of the actors.[69]

If preview cards show unanimous hatred for a film, it will probably be "shelved," not released, and sold to television and/or cable. If mixed response is found, re-editing or even reshooting may be necessary. Research can aid in title changes. Though this is resisted if a former title has been publicized, it can benefit the film in the long run.

A preview must be shown in a theater where a film of a similar genre is playing. The audience, already attracted to that type of picture, is a good sample. If one sneaks a musical in a theater playing a horror film, the audience reaction may not be representative of those who would be attracted to the film on its own.

Previews for saleswomen, hairdressers, cab drivers, and waitresses are arranged since they come into contact with many people. These are the desired people to spread word of mouth.[70] It is believed that for moviegoers under the age of twenty-four, men decide what movie a couple will see, and that for moviegoers over that age, it is the woman who selects the film.[71] Different ad campaigns are often slanted to sexes in addition to ages and genres.

Ronald S. Rugoff and his Cinema 5 distribution company resolved to effectively advertise Milos Forman's Czechoslovakian comedy, *The Firemen's Ball* (1968). They had purchased the United States distribution rights for $50,000 and decided to premiere the film at their own theater in New York. Regardless of excellent critical reviews, the film performed poorly for weeks. The distributor, however, believed the viewers enjoyed the film, and Cinema 5 decided to experiment by using an unprecedented ad campaign for a foreign language film released by an independent. They took out full-page advertisements in New York papers in addition to costly subway and bus ads. The experiment was successful. The film played for more than twenty weeks. Had he not owned the theater, Rugoff would probably have closed it after the initial weeks of failure.[72]

The most common places for advertising are newspapers, magazines, radio, and television. Sixty-five percent of an advertising budget is spent on broadcast media when a film opens. Print advertising accounts for nearly 100 percent at the end.[73] Advertisements for films appear in newspapers to alert people of the existence of the film and to reveal the location and time of exhibition. In the 1930s and 1940s graphics were cluttered in print ads. This has been replaced by a singular, more striking image. In the 1960s and 1970s, the graphic element as a symbol was introduced.[74] With identical print ads and posters people are then exposed to the same image in various forms, reinforcing it with the film.

Credits in advertising are valuable in attracting audiences if the name is well-known and the person is liked by the public. Generally, actors and top directors are the only recognizable names that can influence a person to see a particular movie. However, credits in advertising are given to innumerable other contributors to a film. Credits are personally important because a name is advertised to the industry itself. These credits that do not directly help to sell the film often cause clutter which leads to a less effective advertisement. During negotiations, credits are bargained for, compromised with, and given away. Credits and billing have become points of negotiation.

In the beginning, after actors' names became known to the public, above-the-title credit was reserved for stars and the producer, and in exceptional cases, the director. After World War II and the decreased power of studios, everything became negotiable. Stephen Poe, former lawyer for Twentieth Century-Fox said, "billing is generally the hardest part of a deal, because of all the egos involved." The order of names, location on the ad, and size in relation to the title or other names are all considered. It is difficult to create an ad that satisfies everyone, as it can never be equal. In *Boeing, Boeing,* neither Jerry Lewis' nor Tony Curtis' agents would accept second billing, so their names were printed diagonally, crossing to form an "X." Charles Powell recalled, "As a result . . . no one knew who was in the picture." When the agents of Val Bisoglio demanded special billing in *Saturday Night Fever,* the director wrote out the part, eliminating the actor's role and that of an actress.[75]

A most-favored-nation provision may guarantee an actor that no other actor will get better billing from the producer. The name originated from nineteenth-century China. A most-favored-nation treaty guaranteed a country that no other country could get a better deal from the Chinese. Because of most-favored-nation provisions in the motion picture industry, credits of many people are linked together. If one is printed, all must be printed. To avoid printing so many names that the size of the artwork would be reduced in the ad for *Raging Bull,* only the word *Raging* was used with a large photo of Robert De Niro. If the whole title had appeared, the director's name would have had to appear as dictated by the Directors Guild with all of the other credits that were contracted on that name. Possessory credit is also a point of conflict. Some people feel that designating the film to be that of one person is unfair. In 1963 the Writers Guild secured a deal with the producers to grant possessory credit only to writers. By 1970, however, the directors had become more powerful and turned it around. The writers were promised that these forms of credit would be restricted to greats of the industry. Yet it is now common to see "a John Doe film," "John Doe's . . . ," or "A Film by John Doe."[76] Studios also feel a need to spend sufficient advertising revenue to assure directors or stars that the studio is actively supporting the picture.

Newspapers are not believed to be too valuable in motivating people to attend a film though ads in them may appease creative talent. Julian F. Myers of Hansom and Schwann Public Relations claims that only 39 percent of those who read the *Los Angeles Times* are between the ages of 11 and 30.[77] People do, however, use newspapers to check the time and at which theater a film they have already selected is playing.

National Promotion and Advertising has practiced "wild posting," or the placing of posters all over cities, for sixteen years. They perform it in seventy cities nationwide while trying to maintain a low profile because it is not always appreciated. When a large film opens in Los Angeles, they put up five thousand posters to advertise it.[78] Posters serve to reinforce images from other advertisements.

Ads were widely placed in magazines until the demise of general-circulation publications such as *Life* and *Look* in the late 1960s and early 1970s.[79] Magazine advertising was most effective when films were released on the same date throughout the country. Since this is generally not the case, magazine advertising is too costly. Trade journals are read more closely than general magazines and newspapers; however, their circulation is quite limited. Art theaters needing to keep costs down cannot afford to run large ads in papers. They effectively distribute newsletters with monthly schedules of the films. Radio is experiencing a renaissance, while television is growing more expensive and delivering fewer viewers. Key demographics are more efficiently reached on the radio. Even within music categories, stations break down into specific age groups. For a primarily youth-oriented picture, television may not be the ideal choice. Some studies show that young people listen to more radio than they watch television.[80]

Television advertising, upon which the greatest expense and effort is spent, is accepted as the most effective means of getting people to want to see a particular film. Twentieth Century-Fox contracted for $10 million worth of television time during the 1984 Summer Olympic telecasts.[81] Network is a more efficient buy than local television because it reaches more people for less. In addition, commercials are shown during a program with a network purchase rather than between programs. In 1976 the majors paid $14.79 million on television network advertising; in 1979, $64.1 million; in 1980, $103.3 million. However, national advertising necessitates a wide release, which is not always possible or the best strategy.[82]

It is 30 percent cheaper to buy network ads than to buy regional ads if the picture is opening with a large number of prints.[83] Exhibitors, however, do not generally share in the cost of network commercials as they might in local spots. Since network commercial time must be secured in advance of the release date, up to one year, the scheduled time would dictate the release date, possibly forcing a distributor to book less desirable theaters.[84]

The advertising campaign of pictures that open on Friday begins the preceding Sunday. Network television advertising is used only if a picture is playing in more than 50 percent of the country. Radio accounts for less than

10 percent of the advertising budget. Four or five thirty-second commercials and a few sixty-second commercials comprise the $2 million to $3 million television expenditure.[85]

To advertise *Jaws,* Universal decided to create a massive television saturation three days before its opening by buying thirty-second spots on every prime time show on all three networks for three consecutive nights. The bid contract to exhibitors contained a rider that required each theater playing the film to contribute to the television ad campaign, in addition to any cooperative advertising on a local level at a later date. Universal would assess each theater's share of the national advertising campaign based on potential local earnings. The exhibitors were unhappy about the situation because they were being asked to share in costs over which they had no control. The exhibitors still had not seen the picture, though the book had been a best-seller. Universal was successful and obtained 85 percent of the time they sought.[86]

Bartering is the exchange of a trailer, documentary, or news item for commercial air time. For example, a featurette on the making of a picture can be aired on local stations for free. This television exposure is significantly cheaper than buying time for commercials.[87]

It is valuable to have stars appear on talk shows to publicize a picture. A mention of the film in a comedian's joke can also be powerful. A feature on the star of a picture on shows such as ABC's "20/20" is estimated to be worth around $20 million in advertising.[88]

Music Television, known as MTV, began in August 1981. Similar to a radio station in operation and in demographics, MTV is a market for advertisement aimed at a select young audience.

Several films masterfully used publicity and advertising to reach audiences. *Gandhi* incorporated myriad forms of research, advertising, publicity, and promotion for the three-hour movie to win eight Academy Awards. The film cost $22 million to produce and $18 million to market. One and one-half years before release, an educational campaign was launched in high schools and colleges. Three original books were published on Gandhi and two television documentaries were produced. Hundreds of advance screenings were held for newspapers and magazine editors. To generate awareness for the picture, Columbia rented a theater in every major city where the film would play and carefully selected an audience to watch the film with the theater owners.[89]

Close Encounters of the Third Kind attempted to avoid publicity, and wound up creating intense interest. Since little information was given out to the media, curiosity escalated.[90] To launch *The Deer Hunter,* initially no television commercials were used. Aided by positive reviews, the film was positioned as a high-class event. It opened in Westwood and in New York in closed theaters, ostensibly for Academy Award consideration. Yet the goal was to create a special quality about the picture.[91]

After Mark Buntzman made *The Astrologer* in 1976, he solicited outside reactions to the film at markets. He refined the picture after seeking advice from overseas buyers and theater owners he respected. He was eventually able to create "the type of product there was demand for."[92] The movie *Surf II* used "If you missed *Surf I*, you owe it to yourself to see *Surf II*" in the advertising when in fact no *Surf I* existed. They were capitalizing on the experience of audiences wanting to see hits and to be part of a group.

Promotion brings the film to the audience's awareness generally after the production is completed. Gifts of T-shirts, coasters, buttons, and posters serve to alert people to the film. Back-end promotion is common with merchandise tie-ins such as cereal boxes, games, fast-food restaurants, ice cream chains, college activities, and school newspapers.

Products are increasingly being placed in the motion picture itself. Twentieth Century-Fox was the first major studio to charge fees of $10,000 to $40,000 per movie for products to be placed in their films. In the past, products were generally given or loaned to motion picture companies. The production company saved money and the time of acquiring the items and the product manufacturer took the chance that the product would be seen in the film. Product agents now exist who receive fees from manufacturers to place the products in films.[93] Robert Kovoloff, owner of Associated Film Promotions, will guarantee a product five movies a year for $50,000. After Reese's Pieces candy was used in *E.T. The Extra-Terrestrial*, sales increased more than 65 percent. Irwin Yablans, producer of *Tank*, said Kovoloff saved him $1 million. When he needed three thousand extras a day for seven days, Kovoloff provided stereos, appliances, candy, cigarettes, motor oil, and even a car to be advertised on the radio as a giveaway to attract free extras.[94] Kovoloff, however, works for a yearly retainer and will not accept one-film deals. He has access to scripts in advance of production to identify scenes where products can be used. Kovoloff also manages to keep his clients' products out of undesirable movies. If a character in a film is negative, the character will not be seen with the product.[95] Yet not all manufacturers want to be involved. Kovoloff recalled, "Gillette said to me, 'We won't deal with you come hell or high water, because we can't control the message.'"[96]

The money and time to be saved by hiring a product agent is very enticing to a producer. Though seemingly beneficial to both parties, the motion picture content is influenced. If scenes are rewritten to include or exclude certain products, the film itself may be adversely affected.

Stanford Blum, a licensing agent, declares that "merchandising rights are potentially among the most valuable of the ancillary rights that flow from a motion picture, second only to book publishing rights in revenue potential."

Film merchandising had been largely ignored until *Star Wars,* licensed by Twentieth Century-Fox. Up to 1983, *Star Wars* products have grossed more than $1 billion retail from merchandising rights worldwide. Posters and T-shirts are the most lucrative items to merchandise, unless a character in the film can be made into a toy. For this, preplanning is necessary as toy manufacturers require at least a year to supply new toys to stores nationally.[97]

The rights to the title and artwork of the film are the essential merchandising elements. These must be licensed from the owner, usually the financier/distributor. For the rights to sell a product centered around a film, the manufacturer must pay the owner of the film a licensing fee and/or royalties, with usually a guaranteed minimum. The most paid up front for a license is around $100,000 and royalties are generally 10 percent of the retail price of the item manufactured. For security, some companies purchase the license and wait until a film proves itself in the box office before manufacturing anything. For the filmmaker, money from a merchandising deal is secondary to the promotional value. Disney, however, is one company that does make money on merchandising.[98]

Independent producers can make a deal with a licensing company to handle all the merchandising. This licensing agent usually charges 40 to 50 percent of all money due from the manufacturing company. Licensing agreements usually grant a 5 to 10 percent royalty to the producer. Licensing agents are concerned with the script, lead actors, and who will be advertising and distributing the film. If the picture is family-oriented, youth-oriented, or heroic, it is more desirable. They can even provide advice at the screenplay stage about elements that would enhance the merchandising potential of the picture. The country's main mass-merchandising stores with strength in their volume, such as J.C. Penney, K-Mart, Sears-Roebuck and Montgomery Ward, want to know when and where a picture is breaking so that their stores can be stocked at that crucial time. A producer must not assume that licensees will seek films out, but must actively pursue buyers or hire someone to do it.[99]

As the value of promotion is so important, manufacturers have asked studios to pay them to merchandise products.[100] The studios, however, feel their risk is already great enough. Since the merchandising industry is in its infancy, it is wise for a producer to consider the potential of this ancillary right.

Promotion can also be used to influence buyers in other areas. Exhibitors request that studios send top stars to their conventions. When the pictures of these actors are in their theaters, they might then do a much better job of generating interest and enthusiasm. The motion picture has to be sold on all levels before its inception, to those in the industry, and to the public.[101]

A filmmaker needs to investigate strengths of particular distributors in marketing a picture. Robert Laemmle, president of Laemmle Theatres, believes that the people who created ad campaigns for commercial films did not know how to market intimate pictures.[102] The wrong choice of distributor to handle the picture can severely limit the audience. And an ill-conceived ad campaign can actually keep audiences away. Before an acquisition, the sales department is asked if it would be profitable to handle the picture. Since they have experience, they can accurately describe how and why they would handle a picture in a particular way. The results, however, still cannot be predicted.

Motion Picture Research

Motion picture research is increasingly being implemented to aid in prediction of success before, during, and after production. It is often used as a tool to objectively justify an executive decision to produce a film or to use a certain ad campaign. If relied upon too heavily, research affords the possibility of stifling art and creativity.

Motion picture research was not actively employed in the early years of the business. The market was expanding so rapidly that the enormous volume of business did not warrant the need for analysis.[103] In England motion pictures were finally studied because of their suspected influence on trade. The upper classes in England and Europe had neglected the cinema. However, in 1912, English and German traders noted that American merchandise was beginning to supersede theirs in markets that they had controlled. After investigation, they concluded that American films showed goods that the audiences wanted and ultimately bought. Since more than 90 percent of pictures shown in foreign countries were American, they believed the films influenced trade in the territories where they were exhibited.[104]

In the United States, motion picture executives relied upon intuition and public demand to dictate their decisions. Research itself was viewed as a threat since it employed an independent, outside authority that could interfere with an executive's own power. "They saw in audience research not an instrument for their use, but a substitute for their executive acumen."[105]

Irving Thalberg, however, employed a form of audience testing of films prior to release. He screened the films for audiences, then re-edited and even reshot. The film was again previewed until audiences laughed or cried on cue. Thalberg himself used to sit in different seats in a theater to observe and hear reactions from varying age groups and types. He and others covertly watched for signs of restlessness or misplaced laughter. Additional clues about a film were obtained by standing in the lobby, visiting the rest rooms, and questioning attendants.[106]

Neither radio nor motion pictures needed to be concerned with the characteristics of the audience until broadcasters began delivering audiences to sponsors based on the number of people listening or watching. Experiments in audience measurement began in radio. The Nielsen system attached a tape to the radio receiver and recorded every use of the radio. It provided data on the flow of audiences from one program to another. The Radox method employed an electronic device to instantaneously report every turn of the radio dial.[107]

In 1940 the first significant step toward greater sophistication was the Lazarsfeld-Stanton program analyzer. Originally constructed to test radio programs, it enabled a subject to record his reaction to a film in terms of "like," "dislike," and "indifference."[108]

Albert E. Sindlinger created Teldox, a refinement of the program analyzer which permitted the respondent to draw a curve of likes and dislikes. This method was tested with plays and novels at various stages of writing by submitting them to selected groups. Out of eight plays voted likely to succeed, seven were actually successful on Broadway, and sixteen out of seventeen which were voted failures did fail when produced.[109]

Before World War II, film audience research was in its infancy. As intuition proved less and less dependable, research grew in importance. In 1946, the Audience Research Institute was set up as a Department of Research of the MPAA.[110] Its objective was to educate the public, eliminate the inaccurate industry statistics, employ research to formulate industry policy, and study the value of the motion picture as a cultural force.[111] It closed in the early fifties never having been approved by the MPAA member companies.[112] Sidney L. Bernstein, through the Granada Theatres, made the first contribution to film audience research by extensive studies of young moviegoers. The major difference between the British and American approaches was the British use of questionnaires, compared to the American use of personal interviews.[113]

Since films could no longer be block-booked and were instead being rented on an individual basis, the public became more important. Theaters could now refuse a film. The producers, therefore, wanted to be sure that they were making a film that was desired by the people.

World War II greatly contributed to the progress of research because many government agencies used new techniques.[114] The Research Bureau of the War Department, established to determine the effects of orientation films to be released to the Armed Forces, furthered film research.[115]

The motion picture industry had been criticized for failing to engage in any systematic compilation of factual knowledge. Much erroneous information was called "fact" when based on one person's opinion. The highly competitive nature of the business and accompanying reluctance to divulge operating data were factors.[116]

There were still certain people whose judgments of films were counted on for an accurate measure of the box office potential. Independent motion picture exhibitors relied on "Harrison's Reports" for advice as to what pictures to book and when to book them. When asked for the secret to the exhibitor's success, P.S. Harrison said, "It's no secret at all; if a picture makes me laugh and cry, it is a good picture, the public will like it and it will do well at the box office."[117]

Even though Dr. George Gallup's Audience Research Inc. conducted studies for several studios from 1935 to 1952, the reaction of a powerful executive often carried greater weight.[118] Gilbert Seldes wrote:

> In practice, the managers of the two most important media arrived at the same ends by different routes, the movies retreating from the consequences of their researchers and the broadcasters embracing them. Without the spur of competition for sponsors, the movies decided to let the audience vanish and to play for the adolescents they could hold rather than make any change in the quality of pictures or the system of distribution; radio went into a deeper analysis of the audience, determined to factor out all the complex equations of listening until it isolated the prime ingredients on which ever larger audiences could be built.[119]

Tests can signal a problem area that might negatively affect the box office potential. For example, if a film is tested to have a core audience under 17 years of age, and if the film is rated "R," it may be wise to pursue a "PG" rating. However, if the film is re-edited to meet the rating standards the film's content is altered.

Motion picture research attempts to predict what audiences want to see, when they want to see it, and the best means of motivating them to go to the film. Though the tests are heralded as being valid and reliable, the execution of a motion picture can create the most successful film when it would have tested as being very undesirable. For example, *Raiders of the Lost Ark* was turned down by all the studios except Paramount while Universal passed on *Star Wars*. Though Columbia had spent a million dollars developing *E.T. The Extra-Terrestrial*, when a survey told them the audience was too limited to make it profitable they passed on the picture and Universal picked it up.[120]

Research can be used as a barometer of the changing marketplace and can predict general responses. Other industries make use of as much information as possible in making decisions. Producer Keith Barish said, "As the larger and larger companies take over the studios, they start treating film as a product no different than soda pop or potato chips. Same cost controls, same reporting structure, same market testing."[121]

R. Ben Efraim's *Private Lessons* brought in nearly $45 million at the box office. Aimed at the 15- to 16-year-old weekly moviegoer, *Private Lessons* tested high on concept with a strong reaction from 15- to 25-five-year old people who wanted to see a young boy fulfill his sexual fantasies with an older woman. Because of its success, Efraim then decided to make *Private School* based entirely on market research. He hired Joe Farrell, head of National Research Group, former chairman of the Harris Poll, lawyer, Washington lobbyist, and marketing research expert who had assisted in the preparation and distribution of approximately 150 movies, to perform a phone survey in five cities of 510 moviegoers from ages 13 to 30. Tests were made on heavy sex versus a more romantic, innocent approach versus a comedic approach. Stars and plots were also tested. They found their audience, ages 12 to 16, and the most popular story to be two girls competing to seduce the male lead. Girls selected the actors up for the lead role while boys chose the actresses for the picture. Ads were tested with their target audience. During and after production, scenes were tested for their effect. Efraim stated, "Even if the movie doesn't deliver, you just open it everywhere and make your $8 million or $10 million until word of mouth catches up with it." Efraim was not pleased with Universal's advertising plan to buy network ads. Efraim, believing in exploitation, finds it is necessary to have full-page ads in the papers and national magazines. He also finds local television more cost effective than national television, believing the ad agencies do not want to buy locally because it means more work. [122] Regardless of the research in all areas, *Private School* was a disappointment at the box office, grossing only $14 million instead of the predicted $30 million. [123]

Research is often difficult to perform and is neglected because there may be very little time between the completion of the film and its release. A film's acceptance may also be a function of competition from other films. The emphasis of research is therefore generally confined to pre-testing concepts and postproduction advertising research. The execution of the film involves an infinite number of variables that are uncontrollable.

The easiest tests to perform are for a commercial title and actor likability. Titles are often changed for different parts of the country and when released abroad. A title may mean something completely different to the general audience than what was intended. Or the title may prove not to convey any information at all. Known stars are easy to test. However, it is possible for a dull subject and unknown stars to create a great film.

A concept study involves an interviewer talking to hundreds of people on the phone or in shopping malls. Infrequent moviegoers are eliminated. Lists of the stars and the plot of an upcoming movie are tested for degree of interest. Yet, from the time of the concept test until release, several years may have passed, along with a change in audience tastes and interests. Four-wallers usually rely heavily on concept testing. It is believed Sunn Classics did research leading them to put a bear as opposed to another animal in the film *The Life and Times of Grizzly Adams.* [124]

Harris Goldstein, vice president of market research at Columbia, claims that they begin "tracking a film," or making phone surveys, a month before release. "If awareness is building on a competitor's film but not on ours, perhaps the advertising campaign we've planned is wrong." [125]

People generally pay to see a film based on its advertising. If it is unrepresentative of the film, the viewer feels cheated. Unlike purchasing an item of merchandise, the viewer has to pay for an unseen item and is unable to secure a refund. It is therefore wise to ensure that the advertising is actually selling what will be delivered in the theater.

Sneak previews are used to test the rough cut of a film. Attention has to be paid to attracting a representative sample of the target film audience. It is also possible that the people in the audience (regardless of how representative it is) who fill out the questionnaires may be more skewed to either liking the film or disliking it. These tests can be crucial to an independent who is trying to find a distributor. Irv Ivers, president of worldwide marketing, motion picture division, at MGM/UA, claims that nearly every studio tests independently produced films before acquiring them for distribution.[126]

Tests have been made to study if ticket price influences theater-going behavior. Theaters have tried reducing ticket prices at slow times and on slow days and have attracted a different audience. Though it is possible that the gross box office receipts will go down by this practice; however, the concession sales would likely increase because of the greater attendance. This is of the greatest benefit to exhibitors.

Warner Bros. lost a lawsuit brought by an exhibitor for misrepresenting the potential success of *The Swarm*. During the trial, executives for Warner Bros. claimed that studies indicated viewers did not see bees as a real threat but as a Hollywood gimmick. They also testified that such studies are "unreliable and studio executives paid scant attention to their conclusions."[127]

Paul Lenburg of ASI Market Research claims research could help production respond to the aging population of moviegoers. He estimates that between 1980 and 1990 there would be eight to ten million fewer consumers in the prime film age group of 12 to 29. While ticket prices may go up, overall revenue will not necessarily. He stresses it is important for the industry, therefore, to monitor demographics and to find pictures with a broader base of appeal.[128]

Gilbert Seldes wrote about the public: "To talk of giving them what they want is nonsense unless we know the capacity of the giver to satisfy wants—the essential question—how people come to want what they want."[129]

Recent studies have concerned motivations for attending pictures. In the past, mere speculation attributed motives to people's behavior. Bruce A. Austin conducted a study to determine the motivations for movie attendance. The study revealed the main reason people attend movies is for an "enjoyable and pleasant activity." In descending order of importance were: to pass time, to socialize, to escape, to be aroused or excited, to learn and gain information, to enhance moods, to obtain communication ammunition, to learn about self, to relieve loneliness, to relax, and finally, to get behavioral ammunition.

Austin did not find any significant difference between the genders, but he did find that the movie motives had greater weight for those moviegoers who attended frequently, defined as "those respondents reporting attendance of three times a month or greater." As hypothesized, he found frequent moviegoers reported greater identification with the motives than the occasional, infrequent attender.[130]

Television Audience Assessment Inc. has found that not only is the greatest audience size valuable for advertisers, but that the quality of audience involvement is crucial. Therefore, a smaller but more involved audience may be preferable. Though motion pictures need to generate box office revenue, all films should not just be made with the sole goal of enticing the greatest audience.[131] John Harrington in *The Rhetoric of Film* wrote:

> Critics and spectators once thought that film viewing could be nothing but a passive experience and indeed at its worst it is. But a good film calls forth vigorous sensory and intellectual activity. The time of a film is a period of intensely concentrated experiences demanding the full attention and imagination of a viewer.[132]

It appears that research in its various forms is playing an increasingly greater role in motion pictures before production, in the execution of the film, and in the film's release. Because the studios feel a need to be secure before they make a commitment, sequels, remakes, and adaptations of films from successful books or plays are being pre-tested and approved by audiences.

Historical tracks are compared on the basis of other pictures that have played the same territories, the same time of the year, in the same theaters, and under the same terms. In domestic tracking, eight or nine local engagements can reveal a picture's potential success. For foreign projections, only three to five territories may have to be reported.[133] Researchers claim they can predict with a margin of error of 5 to 10 percent what the box office gross will be. Research however thorough cannot predict the coming together of elements that create a great film.

Publicists, advertisers, promoters, distributors, and exhibitors all attempt to influence a producer before the film is made. Each person has one's own interest and angle believed to be easiest to sell to the public. Films have been made solely on market research of actors and content; however, motion pictures are not replicable and are never perceived by everyone in precisely the same manner. Too many variables are involved for prediction to be reliable and valid. Producers who continue to rely upon their intellect and instincts to make motion pictures they believe are worthwhile, meaningful, and/or entertaining can then use these tools of research, publicity, advertising, and promotion as aids in presenting their films to the public.

6

The Distributor-Exhibitor Relationship

Although distributors and exhibitors cannot survive without each other, they are each suspicious of the control the other possesses. An exhibitor fears he will not be able to secure quality films for his theater while a distributor may fear he will not be able to book quality theaters for his pictures. In an attempt to protect their own interests, distributors and exhibitors have attempted to dominate one another. Distributors suspect the exhibitors of every form of cheating, from the underreporting of grosses to the withholding of rentals. Exhibitors believe that distributors control the industry and accuse distributors of unfairly increasing their profits with little regard for its effect on their existence. Since the exhibitors feel they are at greater risk, they often feel justified in employing any means to secure what they believe is their share of the box office revenue. In 1980, A. Alan Friedberg, president of the National Association of Theatre Owners (NATO), described the motion picture business:

> The relationship between the exhibitor and distributor is probably more adversarial and hostile than is true of the typical wholesaler/retailer situation in any other field of endeavor. I'm stating that as a fact! Why it is so, I would say pertains to the fact that the wholesaler, in this case the motion picture distributor—of which there are essentially six representing some 85 percent of total box-office revenues—in effect operates in a controlled environment... and that really is the crux of the whole matter. The fact is, if this was truly an openly competitive industry where the wholesaler, like other wholesalers, chases his customers and competes with other wholesalers... then you wouldn't have the situation where all the customers compete with one another for the favor of the very few wholesalers in the field... and that's why it's bitter, and that's why it's adversarial.[1]

The number of films produced is a factor in this power struggle. The majors have released fewer and fewer pictures. For a decade after 1959, the national distributors averaged only 250 films per year, down from more than 400. This low supply led to an accentuated demand from exhibitors between 1948 and 1967, resulting in a 10 percent share increase in the domestic split by the national distributors and a 30 percent rise in film rentals worldwide for these majors.[2]

Some exhibitors blamed the divorcement of theaters from the studios as the major factor responsible for the dearth of product and high film rentals. However, the Allied States Association of Motion Picture Exhibitors, which represented thousands of independent exhibitors, believed that the conditions had been intolerable for independents as they had been continually discriminated against in favor of the affiliated theaters. They also claimed that it was highly improbable that the film shortage was created by the theater divorcement.[3]

The Paramount decision required the majors to dispose of their theaters by filing consent decrees. Paramount was the first to apply on 3 March 1949 and Loew's was the last on 7 February 1952. Technically, final divorcement was not accomplished until March 1959. All five chains or circuits had been slow in completing divestiture because the market value of their theaters had plummeted throughout the fifties due to declining box office receipts. All five majors were granted extensions on their consent decrees, giving them more time to attract a fair price for their theaters. These extensions also gave United Paramount Theatres, National Theatres, the Stanley Warner Corporation, Loew's Theatres and RKO Theatres nearly an additional decade to dominate exhibition.[4]

From 1958 to 1963, exhibition suffered heavy losses, though the worst of the market turbulence was over by 1963. From 1964 until 1968, the industry progressed in a stable manner. Distributors were forced to decrease their share of the gross from approximately 35 percent to under 30 percent to ensure exhibitors', and ultimately their own, survival during this changing period.[5]

In the late 1960s, Cinerama, National General, Avco-Embassy and Commonwealth-United entered distribution and offered exhibitors lower than average splits in order to get established in business. These preferred terms that pulled down the competition's rates, in addition to the revenue losses in the industry between 1969 and 1972, aided in lowering the distributors' percentage of box office grosses to under 30 percent. By 1972 distributors were earning 31.6 percent of the box office. This continued to increase to 39 percent in 1977. Distribution's share of the domestic market increased from $500 million in 1972 to $1,215 million in 1978 or an increase of 143 percent, while gross domestic box office revenue grew only 67 percent.[6]

From 1975 to 1978, ten distributors collected more than nine out of every ten dollars flowing into distribution nationally, while their product output dropped 9 percent.[7] While the major distributors control the majority of rentals, a few exhibitors are beginning to command a greater share of exhibition's profits. Gary R. Edgerton wrote that the structure of the industry is reverting back to before the consent decrees. "The four major exhibition circuits are moving ever closer to the pre-Paramount days when the five major circuits then owned 17 percent of the screens and generated 40 percent of the revenues." By early 1980, the top four circuits, General Cinema, United

Artists Theatre Circuit, Plitt, and American Multi-Cinema had 2,719 screens or 16 percent of the domestic total.[8]

Since most of the box office revenue is generated by pictures from the major distributors, exhibitors compete for this product. Though the majors and exhibitors are not legally allowed to be connected, buyer and seller relationships have developed creating such links. For example, a particular theater chain generally plays films from certain distributors and rarely pictures from others.

Max Laemmle believes that since the divestiture it has been easier to release an independent film. He noted:

> Thus it is possible to see a fine quality picture one week at a particular theatre and the next week see the worst type of exploitational film imaginable. It is a "seller's market" as far as feature films are concerned.[9]

The mid-seventies' paucity of product caused exhibitors to panic. When from 1972 to 1975 the number of pictures released by studios dropped 36 percent, exhibitors began investing in films or producing their own. General Cinema Corporation supported several films, including *Capricorn One, Lost and Found,* and *Hanover Street.* United Artists Theatre Circuit produced *Sunburn, Kentucky Fried Movie,* and *Aloha, Bobby and Rose.* The Mann Theatre Chain produced *Lifeguard* and *Buster and Billie,* Henry Plitt was involved in the financing of *Bucktown* and *Seniors,* and Sherrill Corwin was involved with *Viva Knievel* and *The Poseidon Adventure.*[10]

EXPRODICO, the acronym for Exhibitors Production and Distribution Cooperative, was an attempt by exhibitors in 1975 to cease being at the mercy of producers and distributors and was one of NATO's greatest dreams. It was conceived of and founded by Tom Moyer, an Oregon circuit owner. Because of the dearth of films, exhibitors wanted to actively ensure product by pooling their money to produce films. Though the wealthy exhibitors backed this idea in theory, they chose to become filmmakers or investors in films on their own.[11]

In 1977, National Independent Theatre Exhibitors (NITE) devised a plan for generating capital. Cinemavision, a national network of advertising in theaters, was to be tested by exhibitors owning approximately one thousand screens in nine major markets. Proceeds from ads were to go to the Screen Advertising Film Fund Corporation (SAFFCO), an arm of NITE established to finance the purchasing and producing of features through their film cooperative. They claim the studios destroyed it by threatening to withhold their films from any theater screening advertisements, supposedly for fear the ads would alienate customers.[12]

Stanley H. Durwood, president of American Multi-Cinema and developer of the multiple theater concept, believes the exhibitor is "assigned the menial task of making the final sale, the collection of cash that is so necessary to fuel the tremendous creative pump." He claims the exhibitor performs these tasks and passes most of the cash on to distributors and is unable to accumulate enough capital to build attractive theaters or to make repairs. In discussing the factions of production, distribution, and exhibition, Sherrill C. Corwin, chairman of the Southern California circuit of Metropolitan Theatres, said, "We all remain inescapably interlocked, no matter how fervently each group protests this intimate relationship."[13]

After the divestiture of distribution from exhibition, entrepreneurs emerged from the ranks of the exhibitors who steadily aimed at rebuilding that structure. Since the early 1960s, fewer and fewer exhibition companies remain. Those that have survived have incorporated more and more theaters.[14]

The highly successful chains of the latter 1970s and early 1980s moved toward diversification to lend stability to the unpredictable rise and fall of market conditions. Loew's Theatres, founded in 1904 and the oldest chain in the U.S., is part of a conglomerate named Loew's, Inc. Though they have more than a hundred screens, theaters are a small part of the company which also has interests in insurance, real estate, hotels, and Lorillard Cigarettes.[15]

In 1960 General Cinema went public as General Drive-In Corp. with forty-nine theaters, twenty-six of which were drive-ins. Today, General Cinema is the nation's biggest theater operation with more than a thousand screens in thirty-nine states. The theater business accounts for 38 percent of their revenues and 33 percent of their profits.[16]

Though United Artists Communications, the second largest operator of theaters, is linked with drive-in restaurants, motor lodges, bowling alleys, and service stations, it collects 98 percent of its profits from its theater division.[17] Instead of diversification, it concentrated on theater acquisitions. All of the large chains, however, have multiplexed their theaters.

The Multiplex Theater

The high cost of operating single theaters, the greater cost of building new theaters, new rental terms, and the general change in the theater-going habits have led to the proliferation of dividing single theaters into several. This multiplexing has led to the virtual elimination of single-screen theater construction.

In 1963, Stanley Durwood of American Multi-Cinema (AMC) opened the first twin theaters in the world in a Kansas City shopping center. The theaters shared a common lobby, box office, projection booth, and concession stand. AMC opened the first four-theater complex in 1966 and the first six-theater complex in 1969. From 1969 to 1970, their circuit grew from twenty-five screens to more than 520 screens in twenty-five states. The initial aim was to construct four- or six-screen theater complexes, but as the success of the multiplexes grew, they expanded their policy to include up to twelve screens.[18]

An important factor in deciding to open larger complexes was the change in distribution pattern of wider openings. License terms demand longer periods for exhibition. This is ideally suited to the smaller multiscreen theaters, which because of their limited number of seats and shared cost of operation, have the potential to play a picture for a longer period of time. Because of this, suburban theaters have nearly been eliminated as they are no longer needed. A picture can open in the largest seating capacity theater in a multiplex and move to a smaller theater in the multiplex as it becomes less popular. The film, therefore, does not need to move to a suburban theater. Instead, after playing the multiplex, the picture can move to drive-ins and "dollar theaters" that admit all people at all times for one dollar.[19]

AMC established its own marketing department to analyze the market potential of all the cities in the United States. Cities with a population in excess of seventy-five thousand and having future growth potential are considered possible locations for multiplexes. Existing theaters are then analyzed to determine how many additional theaters can be economically supported in that particular city. All of their multiscreens are constructed in shopping centers, each have two hundred or four hundred seats per theater, and they preferably are located in middle-class areas inhabited by college-educated families and potential college-educated young people. AMC claims these people are the "backbone of the existing motion picture audience and of our future audience."[20]

Variety is the key to the multiplex concept. The policy was to change at least one or two of the pictures in a multiple-theater complex each week, but because of the heavy concentration of releases in six or seven periods each year, the same movies have played for six weeks or longer.

There is near unanimity among the leading chains in the United States that they have never had such prosperous times.[21] As of June 1983, the U.S. Department of Commerce and the Census Bureau found 18,772 screens in existence. Of this total, there are only 2,935 drive-ins as opposed to 15,837 walk-in theaters, also known as hardtops. California has the most screens, numbering 2,014. Texas is second with 1,339 and New York is third with 1,071.[22]

General Cinema Corporation is the country's largest exhibition chain, with 1,050 screens. United Artists Communications Inc. owns the second largest theater circuit, with 1,005 screens.[23] American Multi-Cinema, the third largest circuit, presently operates 734 screens.[24] The expansion pace of the nation's three largest circuits is an unprecedented boom in the exhibition industry.

Gary R. Edgerton found that the approximately twenty-three chains with more than one hundred screens each get the first-run films. The thirty to thirty-five circuits that have fifty to one hundred screens secure a share of the first runs and also participate in suburban runs with the one hundred to one hundred twenty-five circuits that have ten to fifty screens. The bottom tier of theaters consists of 95 percent of all exhibitors and 50 percent of all screens. There are more than five thousand independent theater owners with one to ten screens which exhibit the final showings of a film.[25]

The independent exhibitor generally cannot afford to make radical theater construction changes because of his inability to secure first-run films and subsequent lack of money. James Edwards of California, however, owns fifty-one screens at twenty-four locations and keeps ahead of others by winning contracts to build theaters in busy shopping centers. He now commands 60 percent of Orange County's box office trade while his dominance continues to grow.[26]

Multiplex theaters are also able to command more power in exhibition. Exhibitors have played several first-run pictures from different distributors on a staggered basis. For example, a multiplex with three screens can play four pictures with separate admissions for each. This existence of overbooking is not new. Theaters have even been known to play unauthorized mixed-distributor double bills without separate admissions. This practice is frowned upon but is tolerated by distributors, especially when dealing with powerful exhibition chains. Distributors attempt to check on "their" theaters and their competitors by comparing newspaper clippings with box office reports and watching the number of shows per day of each theater.[27]

Ira Deutchmans, executive vice president of distribution and marketing at Cinecom International, finds that his customers for independent U.S. and foreign films are increasingly major chains: Plitt, Loew's, General Cinema, and United Artists. He also finds that they will exhibit a picture for more than a week. Because of the increased number of screens, "filler" pictures are needed. Exhibitors also do not need to pay huge advances to secure these films. The multiplexes can afford the luxury of experimenting for a few weeks to see if a picture will attract an audience.[28]

Most plans now are for construction of multiple-screen theaters, and not too much more for multiplexing. A spokesman from United Artists Communications Inc. said, "I think we've multiplexed everything we possibly could." He also stated that they have retired virtually all of their single-screen theaters.[29] Whereas multiplexes have generally created small theaters, Henry Plitt is investing in the "blockbuster theater," believing "a theater has to be a theater, not a cracker box."[30]

The Drive-In Theater

In an attempt to create a new environment in which to watch motion pictures, on 6 June 1933 Richard Hollingshead, Jr., opened the world's first drive-in in Camden, New Jersey. On opening night, approximately six hundred people showed up and paid twenty-five cents per person or one dollar per carload to see a three-year-old movie, *Wife Beware*. Hollingshead had developed a system of ramps and grades to ensure an uninterrupted view of the screen despite the traffic of other cars. This first drive-in theater was built for sixty thousand dollars fifteen minutes from downtown Philadelphia, and accommodated four hundred cars. Two shows per night of shorts and "abridged features, with all dull or uninteresting parts removed" comprised the performances. After the initial week, Hollingshead opened a concession stand to sell hot dogs, ice cream, and beer. Hollingshead claimed the drive-in would benefit smokers, talkers, eaters, entire families, the aged, and the infirm. While some exhibitors viewed the drive-in as a fad, other distributors and hardtop exhibitors felt threatened. Distributors refused Hollingshead new films and charged huge rentals for old films. *Wife Beware* cost Hollingshead four hundred dollars for four days. The previous time the film had been run was in a small South Camden theater that had paid twenty dollars a week for it.[31]

Hollingshead also met with resistance from the public. He had to face irate parents, among others, who believed drive-ins contributed to immoral conduct.[32] Because of opposition to his novel experiment, Hollingshead sold his first drive-in in 1935. The man who bought it owned several indoor theaters and had easy access to films with lower rentals.[33] Since drive-ins were independently owned and outside the control of the studio-owned theater chains, the studios were reluctant to rent first-run films to them. They also were leery of the poor sound quality. Not until 1938 when the car speaker was developed did the majors begin renting films to drive-ins.[34]

Hollingshead's company, Park-In Theaters, had a patent on drive-ins. He licensed and attempted to collect royalties from all drive-ins built before 1950. In 1939 only ten drive-ins existed in the entire nation. Drive-ins, also knows as "ozoners," were popular after World War II when car registrations increased and suburbs sprang up.[35] The drive-in reached its peak in 1958. There were only 12,291 indoor theaters but 4,063 drive-ins.[36] The drive-ins offering playgrounds and diaper and laundry facilities were popular with veterans "who had new families and little money," said Melvin Wintman of General Cinema Corporation.[37] Since drive-ins were not able to secure first runs they turned to exploitation films, which became their staple in the 1960s.[38]

In 1982 indoor screens numbered 14,977 at 8,700 sites, while drive-ins dropped to 3,043 at 2,700 sites.[39] The MPAA, however, claimed that drive-ins accounted for 21 percent of the total U.S. movie business.[40]

Sumner Redstone, president of Northeast Theatre Corporation, which operates forty drive-ins in thirteen states, told *Newsweek* that "Drive-ins are rapidly becoming part of our nostalgic past—I foresee their extinction by the end of the decade."[41] "There is not a single drive-in we would like to preserve," he added.[42] Raymond J. McCafferty, executive vice president and general sales manager at Twentieth Century-Fox, claims drive-ins account for only 5 percent of their total billings.[43] Brandon Chase, a producer who made millions of dollars at the drive-in circuit with low-budget pictures such as *The Giant Spider Invasion,* said, "We haven't thought of the drive-in market for years."[44] Theaters in shopping centers have taken a portion of the audience away from drive-ins that previously had no competition. Teenagers now gather at shopping malls, video arcades, or fast-food establishments instead of drive-ins.[45]

Rising real estate values make land too expensive to be used only at night and not year around. Drive-ins are being rented as day-time parking lots and flea markets.[46] Cable TV is another factor in the decline of drive-in attendance. Families can now see a relatively new film in the comfort of their home. Regardless of the seemingly near consensus that the drive-in is heading for extinction, there are less vociferous people who believe the drive-in meets the unique needs of particular people.

Robert W. Selig, vice president of the three-hundred screen Pacific Theatres, including seventy-five drive-ins, most of which are in Southern California, claims drive-ins in non-sunbelt areas are going out of business because they cannot operate all year because of bad weather. He also said that those unsuccessful drive-ins do not play first-runs concurrently with walk-in theaters.[47] In the sunbelt areas particularly, drive-ins are still surviving and some are profiting.

In the past, drive-ins were popular for showing films that were too violent or sexual for television. However, these are now available on cable and video cassettes. This has eliminated part of the drive-in audience. There is still a large working-class audience remaining who cannot afford home entertainment. Also, a huge Spanish-speaking audience exists in Texas and other border states. In Fort Worth, for example, the drive-in with the greatest attendance plays mostly Spanish-language films. In California, the Spanish-speaking market is so great that the Pacific chain developed "bilingual sound." The car radio can be tuned into one of two frequencies and either English or Spanish can be heard.[48] Selig believes drive-ins will prosper in the Southwest because of the growing Latino population. The eight Pacific

Theatres showing Spanish-language films have the greatest per capita attendance record.[49] Texas is the drive-in capital of the world. There are 209 theaters in operation, many of which are multiscreened. Gordon McLendon, a Texas drive-in theater owner, built a six-screen theater in Houston that can accommodate three thousand automobiles. He claims that it is the largest drive-in in existence.[50]

Drive-ins no longer show only "B" pictures. The majors now release first runs to drive-ins, although the drive-ins still have to battle for quality films. Larger rentals and longer guaranteed runs are being demanded. Since revenues generally drop when "G" and "PG" films are screened, exhibitors turn to more R- and X-rated material.[51] Several chains are able to exist because of double features and concession stands. Selig reported that box office receipts in 1982 at Pacific's drive-ins in the Los Angeles area were up 22 percent. He finds attendance at drive-ins is directly tied to the success of films at indoor theaters.[52]

To combat the drop in attendance, multiplexing of drive-ins began. Twinning a drive-in usually increases revenue 30 to 50 percent. A third screen adds an additional 10 to 20 percent. More screens probably contribute another 5 to 10 percent of the box office and concession stand revenue.[53]

New innovations are being developed to help drive-ins keep their audience and attract more people. Modernized concession stands have been implemented. The new sound system, Cine-Fi, allows the movie sound track to be tuned in on the car radio. Population growth in areas near the once isolated drive-in has created light problems that diminish the picture quality. To remedy this, a new Protolite Screen was created to maximize the image by providing brightness three to four times that of present drive-in screens, allowing shows to start at any time of the day, not just after dark. This screen also appears blank to those outside the theater, which allows for screening of R- and X-rated films without regard for passersby.[54]

A study performed to determine the potential financial impact of the Protolite Screen divided the country into seasonal and sunbelt areas. The seasonal area had 2,170 theaters and the sunbelt had 1,100. The box office grosses in the seasonal area varied from $25,000 to $400,000 per year with $200,000 the average. Sunbelt theaters varied from $50,000 to $800,000, with $325,000 the average. They believe these gross figures could be significantly increased if the drive-in opened at 6:00 P.M. instead of 9:30 or 10:00 P.M. as is often the case. Additional revenue could also come from more people eating their dinner at the theater. Sixty-three percent of drive-in business is done on the weekends during the thirteen weeks of summer. Therefore, an additional show on Friday and Saturday nights could mean an increase of 25 to 60 percent of box office and concession revenues. However, they feel the greatest gains would be additional screenings during the week. People could go to the theater and be home earlier and it would allow drive-ins to offer a weekday early bird discount. Many hardtops that created these discounts found their weekday grosses increasing 25 to 60 percent.[55] Drive-in theaters still afford the patron a unique experience, different from that in the home or in a walk-in theater.

Selig found that 72 percent of those attending drive-ins were classified as young married couples with two or more children, who could not afford to go out and also pay for a babysitter. The average price of $3.25 for adults and children under age 12 free was economical for families. He found the remaining segments of the audience to be the handicapped, the elderly, and those who do not want to dress up for an indoor movie.[56] It is evident that a certain segment of the population enjoys the drive-in experience. The same argument of people wanting to go out of the house to indoor theaters for entertainment, even though it may be available to them in their home, applies to drive-in patrons as well. Drive-ins serve specific needs of its audience and allow them to leave their home for a unique evening of entertainment.

Drive-in theaters have traditionally been the market for independently produced and distributed features. In the early sixties and seventies the independents rented their pictures to drive-ins and downtown theaters which played mostly exploitation films. The independents also released on a regional basis, playing the picture only in the regions where it would be well-received. In the early to mid-seventies, changes in the marketplace altered these patterns. Drive-ins either began going out of business because the land was too valuable or were no longer playing independent product. As a consequence, old drive-in theaters were then torn down and converted to suburban shopping centers. Drive-ins of today are multiplexed, making the volume for any one screen reduced. In 1970 there were 3,770 drive-in theaters with single screens. In 1980 there were 3,454 drive-in screens, but only 1,000 to 1,500 drive-in theaters. The majors who had only released their product to drive-ins after the films were played out in walk-in theaters began releasing their first-run product to drive-ins, day-and-date, with hardtops. With the drive-in theater no longer available, the independent looked to the downtown theater for screen time. However, the number of these theaters began dwindling because of urban renewal and more advantageous land use. When downtown areas became associated with crime, audiences were deterred. When the makeup of downtown areas became dominated by ethnic groups, the remaining theaters began to cater to the local minority residents. The downtown theater thus ceased to be a profitable market for the independents.[57]

Independent Product

Independent exhibitors increasingly have to rely on the poorer films from independent distributors, since they cannot secure pictures from the majors or even from the larger independents.

The independent distributors try to compete with the worst pictures from studios for the best theaters. But since the studios provide exhibitors with more pictures per year, the independents have to convince exhibitors that their picture has great potential. In various areas, local exhibitors split the product of major and independent distributors. This results in fewer available theaters for the independents and reduces their ability to negotiate favorable rental terms.[58]

The major chains, however, have begun to play more independent product because their multiplexes require a variety of films. The majors have increased their number of pickups from independent producers. Instead of the majors making union pictures, they can buy non-union films made on small budgets. Chandler Wood, head buyer for Pacific Theatres, finds he is buying more and more drive-in pictures from the majors and is having to pay more. Robert Selig said:

> Distribution by independents is down about twenty-five percent, much to our sorrow. But independent distribution by way of majors (independently made features picked up by the majors) is up more than twenty-five percent—which means the majors are coming at us with independent product.

Selig prefers to deal with independent distributors, finding better promotional and advertising support from them. The majors charge greater overhead and have to be paid a substantial distribution fee which otherwise could be split between the distributor and exhibitor. When a producer deals directly with the theater, the income can be returned to the producer without the general 50 percent division of income to the distributor.[59]

Independent distributors used to complain that play dates were unavailable. Though play dates are available now, independent distributors do not have the pictures to release. The majors, relying increasingly on pickups, are not putting more features on the market. To meet the dearth of product, Pacific Theatres is pairing current releases with reruns, or with pictures it dropped quickly in first run. The independent distributors they used to rely on to supply them are no longer around. Chandler Wood believes that many independents went out of business not because of escalating costs of marketing but because of the increase in pickups by the majors. A. Alan Friedberg, chairman of NATO and president of Boston-based Sack Theatres, claims he does not play exploitation product even if it comes from the majors. He stated, "All our theatres are first runs, not drive-ins. It has been rare in the past ten years that I can recall playing a Crown International or New World film." Friedberg would rather handle a picture from a major because they are more likely to support it financially.[60]

The problems between distribution and exhibition are accentuated with respect to independents. Large theater chains traditionally pay independents less of the box office gross than they pay majors even when the pictures perform similarly. Circuits that are strong in one area can use their strength to secure product for their theaters in other areas that are inferior. Some circuits refuse to play independent films as a matter of policy. Though many circuits pay film rental over as long a period of time as possible, some take longer to pay independents. These pay delays can be for 120 to 150 days. This money that could be earning interest for the independent is used by the circuits to pay advances for product from the majors or for additional theater construction.[61]

Concession Revenue

Exhibitors often claim they are unable to make a profit on box office revenue alone and that concession profits are often their sole source of income. Distributors on the other hand claim that exhibitors earn a huge profit on their house nut, or what they claim is their weekly operating cost, and on the grosses, in addition to the profit at the snack bar. Some distributors feel they should be entitled to a percentage of this revenue since it is the film that attracts the patron. Concession revenue is important to the filmmaker because an exhibitor may choose to book a picture if it will be a big snack bar draw.

Operating costs of theater chains and individual theaters are the rental cost of the motion picture, the advertising costs for the picture, the direct cost of operating the theater itself, and if it is a chain, the overhead cost of the entire operation. Today, major chains are making money but increasingly have to rely on other means for profit. During the silent film days, first-class theaters refused to sell food. Gradually food came to be sold as a convenience for patrons. When in hard times it was discovered that candy and popcorn could return a 45 percent profit on gross sales, food became for many the means of staying in business.[62] Candy was sold, as it was easy to store and sell. In the mid-1940s, ice cream was sold in the aisles and became acceptable when it was found that it did not reduce candy sales. Popcorn and then cold drinks were added in the late forties. In the early 1950s, drive-in theaters began to sell full meals for take out.[63]

Approximately $750 million was spent at concession stands in 1983. National Association of Concessionaires (NAC) Executive Director Charles Winans acknowledges theater concessionaires charge higher prices than other

NAC outlets and is concerned that these escalating costs are reducing the number of patrons. Yet he attributes long lines as the main reason three out of four patrons pass up the refreshment stands.[64] New England-based Cinema Centers circuit has abandoned a two-year experiment in selling refreshments at half price. It did not produce an attendance increase to compensate for loss in concession revenue.[65]

As distribution commanded a greater share of box office revenue, exhibitors had to rely more on concession revenues. In 1972, 13.5 cents out of every dollar accrued by the exhibitor was generated at the snack bar. By 1980, the figure had risen to 20 cents out of every dollar that came into the theater.[66] Other sources say the average is 10 percent of the box office gross while others believe it is closer to 30 percent.[67]

Approximately 65 cents out of every dollar at the concession stand is profit. The cup, popcorn and oil that a customer pays $1.75 for costs the theater owner about 17 cents. A coke selling for one dollar costs the theater owner around 16 cents. A Hershey bar selling for 60 cents costs 20 cents. Popcorn accounts for slightly more than 40 percent of all concession sales and soft drinks for another 40 percent. Philip M. Lowe, former president of the NAC, claimed that popcorn sales gross as much as 800 percent above cost. This figure does not, however, take into consideration labor costs, equipment, rentals, and other expenses.[68] A National Association of Theatre Owners survey reported that theaters' pre-tax net income runs between 5 and 15 percent of admissions income, that refreshment sales range between 10 and 20 percent of box office income, and that an indoor theater's food cost varies from 20 to 30 percent of sales.[69]

A study compiled by the NAC in conjunction with Coca-Cola USA found that the average indoor theater generates 50 cents per person in concession sales and that only one out of six patrons purchases refreshments. The study found that G-rated pictures generate 27 percent more sales than PG- or R-rated films. Although 65 percent of total box office dollars are made on Friday, Saturday and Sunday, only 50 percent of weekly concession sales occur on those days. The study found concession sales to be 1,000 percent higher when an adult accompanied children than when children went alone. Even though pictures may generate the same box office gross, they do not necessarily generate the same refreshment sales. For example, though *Hot Stuff* and *Airport 79: The Concorde* earned the same box office gross, *Hot Stuff* produced double the concession volume of *Airport 79: The Concorde*. The top five refreshment-grossing films of 1979 on a per capita basis were *Hot Stuff, Sleeping Beauty, Sunburn, The Muppet Movie*, and *The Amityville Horror*.[70]

Concession sales are relevant to the filmmaker because an exhibitor would less likely book a picture that would not stimulate concession sales.

Young audiences are especially important for concession sales. For example, a Disney movie may account for concession sales of about 70 percent of the admission price. However, an art film would generally attract an older audience that might spend only 5 percent of the admission price per capita.[71]

Multiplexes serve to reduce operating costs while maximizing profits. The central concession stand can efficiently service multiple screens. When an extremely popular film is playing, the exhibitor must plan ahead and have ample supplies of candy and popcorn available. It may also be necessary to hire extra help to expedite the selling process. If these measures are not taken, huge profits could be lost.

As a means of reaching the people who pass up the snack bar, estimated to be six out of ten by concessionaries and five out of six by the president of the NAC, exhibitors have resorted to selling refreshments in the theater aisles. Some fear that this is in poor taste and that people do not want to be bothered once they get into the theater. They believe if the refreshment booths are properly staffed, there is no need for this. Others believe it would only work between double features or at long films where intermissions are provided.[72] Yet these "hawker trays" in the aisles generate 20 to 25 percent more sales in test marketing.[73] Exhibitors are also beginning to sell a greater variety of food and drink in addition to other items such as shirts and framed paintings.

Many people in the industry believe exhibitors underreport their lucrative concession earnings. Distributors thus do not sympathize with exhibitors' claims of losing money and barely being able to stay in business. Distributors have never been allowed to benefit from concession profits and feel justified in raising rentals to balance this injustice. Concession revenue is only one topic of disagreement between distributors and exhibitors.

Trade Associations

Exhibitors claim MPAA members use the MPAA as an information exchange and as a mechanism to fix prices, limit production, and impose uniform license terms on exhibition.[74] Exhibitors have formed their own trade associations to fight for their needs. There is, however, dissension within exhibition. The concerns of the large chains can be vastly different from the needs of the small independent exhibitor.

Exhibitors have always encountered problems with those outside of exhibition and those within. The National Association of Theatre Owners (NATO) was created on 1 January 1966 by a union of the Theatre Owners of America, the representative of the nation's larger and more prestigious circuits, and the Allied States Association, known as the trade association for the small, independent exhibitor. NATO represented an estimated fifteen thousand of the nation's eighteen thousand theaters.[75] NATO did not remain united, as in-house criticism arose in 1972 over the collection of dues. Conflict also arose because the independent exhibitors believed the interests of the large chains took priority over their concerns. NATO was also criticized for its uninvolvement in exhibitor problems. For example, a Georgia exhibitor, Billy Jenkins, had to fight an obscenity case over *Carnal Knowledge,* which he finally won in 1974. Jenkins, who received no help in his fight from NATO, called them "'gutless' for failing to back him 'until after the case was won.'" The National Independent Theatre Exhibitors Association (NITE) was born out of this lethargy and inaction. Exhibitors with nearly fifteen hundred screens met in September 1975 and drew up the charter of NITE. NITE began immediate social and political pressures to oppose the practice of blind-bidding, whereby exhibitors must bid for a picture without having viewed the film. In 1977, NATO began an anti-blind-bidding campaign out of what NITE started. NITE, however, was still concerned with the independent exhibitors' issues of paying more rental than the circuits, and with the independents' inability to acquire desirable films.[76]

Non-NITE independent exhibitors became increasingly dissatisfied with NATO. Many believed that eastern circuits and large chains controlled NATO. Robert W. Selig was one of the chief proponents of the California Plan, which called for NATO to hire a paid president, to transfer the national headquarters from New York to Washington, D.C., to create a federal lobbying presence, and to set up regional headquarters in the Midwest and California. When NATO claimed funds were not available for such reform, Pacific Theatres and other West Coast chains left NATO and formed Theatres West, with Selig as chairman. NATO of California, of which Selig was chairman, also resigned membership in NATO. In 1978 Selig moved from chairman of NATO of California to chairman of its independent statewide successor organization, Theatre Association of California (TAC). Selig claims they will all return to NATO when the organization adheres to the California Plan.[77]

In 1983 Selig was hired as the first paid president of the 1,900–member TAC. He is particularly concerned with impeding state and local efforts to institute admission taxes. He is also on guard against alterations in minimum wage laws. Selig still wants NATO to be unified but insists that the headquarters be moved from New York City to Los Angeles and that a full-time industry spokesman in Washington be hired to match the presence of Jack Valenti of the MPAA.[78]

ShoWest is an annual trade show and convention of Exhibitors West, the proprietors of houses in twelve western states. The representatives include the non-NATO members of the TAC and exhibitors from eleven other western states. The NAC and the Theater Equipment Association also attend.[79] The tenth annual convention in 1984 attracted more than 2,017 registrants and drew exhibitors from every state and from seventeen foreign countries.[80] NATO is becoming international, with the enrollment of five major circuits from four countries at the ShoWest 1984.[81] Show-A-Rama, emphasizing another exhibition interest, is a convention for people working in theater management. The showing of product reels from distributors is a principal ingredient of the convention. A prime emphasis at the convention is to encourage showmanship at individual theaters.[82] Although exhibitors believe they need to be unified against distribution, the exhibitors themselves are too disparate in their interests to form a cohesive association.

Distributor/Exhibitor Concerns

The exhibitor associations have encountered heavy opposition from the MPAA. On the most direct level, exhibitors and distributors accuse one another of blatant unscrupulousness. Illegal acts are committed that are rationalized with the belief that the other deserves what is being done to him. The withholding of film rentals from distributors by exhibitors is often suspected, as many means of hiding the revenue exist. Exhibitors are often accused of underreporting the box office grosses, thereby reducing the rental paid to distributors.

In October 1983, Twentieth Century-Fox, United Artists, Paramount, Columbia, Universal, and Warner Bros. were awarded $277,000 by a Federal court jury in Indianapolis for compensatory and punitive damages in an underreporting suit brought against a Bloomingdale, Indiana, theater operator. The verdict was the largest award ever won in legal damages for exhibitor underreporting of gross receipts. Distributors are hoping this will be a deterrent to other exhibitors. The bulk of evidence consisted of blind checks on attendance, ticket analysis, and estimates by theater employees of alleged underreporting. The underreporting amounted to 30 percent of receipts, which was roughly what the jury awarded.[83]

Exhibitors are notoriously late in paying rentals, enabling them to earn interest on the money. Some exhibitors do not pay rentals if the distributor does not provide a continuous line of product. An unscrupulous exhibitor may avoid paying rentals for a period of time and then sell the theater.[84]

Some exhibitors merely do not return films. In such cases, it is necessary to send prints to them COD. One exhibitor, believing he purchased the films for the rentals he had paid, was discovered with 150 prints. One cautious distributor sent a print $500 COD to an exhibitor, and it was returned weeks later to the distributor $1,000 COD.[85]

Columbia Pictures decided to require exhibitors to be personally responsible for their accounts even if their corporation went bankrupt. In lieu of a personal guarantee, Columbia accepted a detailed financial statement of the particular organization. A year after the policy was instituted, Columbia had significantly reduced the number of delinquent accounts it used to write off. Previously, Columbia received six or seven requests per week from branch managers to write off monies owed, while subsequent to the new policy, the number had been reduced to one.[86]

NATO is concerned about this unprecedented demand from distributors on small exhibitors who are randomly selected to personally guarantee film contracts and film rental due from their corporations. Many who have received the requests are not credit risks, while complying with the requests could involve great personal liability.[87] This new practice, however, demonstrates the concern over payment of rentals.

Theater employees can steal from theater owners by "palming" tickets, a procedure whereby a ticket can be taken from a customer and then resold. Customers generally do not care that they have not received a torn stub or do not notice if they are given the theater's half of someone else's ticket. A theater manager may sell seats from his own roll of tickets or from one not numbered sequentially with those previously sold. He can then remove the stubs from the ticket-taker's box, eliminating all evidence. "In many parts of the country, it's a tradition that the last showing on Saturday night belongs to the theatre manager."[88]

Theft is a major problem for exhibitors, who are losing between 10 and 20 percent of their gross revenue to employees. At ShoWest '84, exhibitors were warned to employ security systems and inventory control, and to control access to cash.[89] Distributors hire companies that specialize in the checking of theater attendance to make sure exhibitors are not underreporting attendance. Exhibitors themselves use these services for their own needs. For example, exhibitors claim that college campus showings of features are cutting into their commercial business. They state that little checking is done to ensure that only students are admitted. Exhibitor James Edwards employs checkers to sit in parked cars outside the theaters.[90] With binoculars they observe the cashiers and ticket-takers. Edwards wants to make sure his employees are not cheating him.

Exhibitors may also receive kickbacks from placing their advertising through an agency with which they have an "arrangement." The agency can command a substantial cost reduction from newspapers based on volume line buys. They charge the distributor the normal rate and the discount is divided between the agency and the exhibitor.[91] When cooperative advertising costs between the distributor and exhibitor are shared, the exhibitor can remit the standard charges and fail to report that he paid a reduced fee.

Exhibitors with several theaters may attempt to "bicycle" prints, using one print at several theaters. Not only can the exhibitor avoid paying additional rentals, he can also retain all the profits from the additional showings. When exhibitors are suspected of keeping a print extra days and blaming it on the courier, newspaper advertisements in the area can be checked. Unscheduled days when no film was contracted for can be detected. Yet many distributors do not have the inclination or the resources to make such checks. The new computerized box office makes it more difficult for employees to cheat the theater management and for individual exhibitors to cheat the distributors.

Exhibitors and distributors are concerned with these issues on the theater level. However, the practices that were supposedly outlawed by the Consent Decree still remain major points of conflict. Though price-fixing is illegal, it is possible for a distributor to set rentals in terms of a minimum per person charge. Typically, the film rental the exhibitor must pay to the distributor is a flat dollar figure per patron, regardless of the admission price charged by the exhibitor. Exhibitors claim this constitutes price-fixing. Distributors claim they are merely establishing a selling price and do not intend to influence admission price. Contracts cautiously state such terms are not to be construed as fixing or establishing admission prices.[92]

Block-booking is the practice of licensing one picture dependent upon that of another or only renting a film if the exhibitor agrees to rent others also. Block-booking is illegal because it extends the monopoly of the copyright owner by requiring his license to accept more films. A distributor may license many films at one time to the exhibitor, but he cannot license a group of films which the exhibitor refuses to license separately. Distributors employ master license agreements which cover several pictures and justify their use as a means of saving paperwork. It is argued that such contracts are in actuality tying arrangements.[93]

"Tracks" refer to certain theater groups that generally license the films from a particular distributor. The track system is evident in major cities where films from a certain studio play in particular theaters. Studios may even help pay for renovating a theater. Such upgrading, ostensibly done to enhance a picture that a distributor wants to be seen under optimum conditions, may be a tacit agreement making the exhibitor obligated to play the distributor's films in the future. For example, when Orion Pictures took over Filmways, Inc., thereby acquiring their own distribution network, they no longer needed to release their pictures through Warner Bros., which has a connection with Mann Theatres in Westwood. To secure a Westwood showcase for their pictures, Orion made an agreement with the theater chain owned by United Artists Communications, Inc., whereby Orion would pay for an $800,000 upgrading to state-of-the-art equipment at the four-screen UA Cinema Center.[94]

Baldwin Hills Theater in California was remodeled with the intention of creating a first-run house. After realizing the reality of the exhibition business, the owners finally charged in a lawsuit against Warner Bros. and Mann Theatres that an illegal set of relationships between studios and exhibitors prevented them from getting many first-run films. The owners of the Baldwin

Theater claimed that pressure from the Westwood chains nine miles away was behind their exclusion. Since Westwood is a showcase center, the theaters in Westwood do not have to bid for films but instead are pursued by the studios to play their pictures. Harry Swerdlow, attorney for Mann Theatres, said lawsuits have been attempted before and never won. He said:

> Upper East Side and Westwood are the two most important film exhibition areas in the United States. The grosses from films playing in those areas are reported weekly and are used by distribution companies to help sell their pictures all over the world. Film companies who cater to showcase houses don't wish to dilute their revenues with playing simultaneously with theaters which are relatively close.[95]

Other theaters, however, that are even closer than the Baldwin's nine-mile distance play day-and-date with Westwood. In similar cases, distributors have usually offered the exhibitor a picture as an out-of-court settlement.[96]

Motion pictures are licensed by a distributor to the exhibitor either directly or by the process of bidding. All theaters are supposedly granted the opportunity to secure a picture. In Los Angeles and New York, pictures are not bid for but are arranged between the exhibitors themselves and between the exhibitor and the distributor.[97] Exhibitors believe they are at the mercy of distributors, who release films in any manner they choose. Yet in a "closed situation," one area where all the theaters are controlled by a single chain, the exhibitors have the power. If a major wants to have its films shown in the closed situation, preferred treatment must be given to the entire chain. In areas of competition and where such arrangements are not made, bidding is used to select which exhibitor will be awarded a particular picture.

Blind-Bidding and Splitting

Blind-bidding is the practice whereby exhibitors bid against each other for the opportunity to play a motion picture without having viewed the film. Exhibitors guarantee to pay a certain amount of money to secure the film and state the rental terms and length of the play date. If a movie is not yet completed when bids come in, the guarantees may even be used as a source of financing. Theaters can suffer a huge loss if they misjudge how popular a film will be. This practice, however, ensures an immediate market for pictures. Blind-bidding began in the 1930s but was not the typical mode of negotiation. After the divestiture of theaters, studios negotiated directly with exhibitors instead of soliciting bids. They could thereby retain more control over the geographic area in which their film would be played. After block-booking was terminated, fewer "B" pictures were produced since there was no longer a guaranteed market and exhibitors had to compete more fiercely for pictures.

Before the actual trial of the Paramount case, blind-selling was temporarily ended by the original Consent Decree of 20 November 1940, a decree entered eight years before the first of what are now known as the Paramount Consent Decrees. It stated:

> No distributor or defendant shall license feature motion pictures for public exhibition within the United States at which an admission fee is to be charged until the feature has been trade-shown within the exchange district in which the exhibition is to be held.[98]

On 1 January 1969 a new stipulation of the Consent Decree became effective. The Justice Department restricted blind-bidding. The majors agreed not to blind-bid more than three films and roadshows a year and entitled exhibitors to terminate their blind-bid deals within forty-eight hours of viewing a film. Large chains were also required to bid for films on a theater-by-theater basis. Bidding became more vigorous because of the large number of competing theaters and because it was believed that the three blind-bid pictures would be the quality films. Independent exhibitors were aware that the exhibitors with closer relationships with the producers would have more information about the films. By 1975, the Justice Department allowed the agreement to expire, deciding it would not regulate in this area. Blind-bidding then increased greatly.[99]

In 1979, A. Alan Friedberg of NATO estimated that film companies were blind-bidding 90 to 100 percent of their films, while distribution estimates ranged from around 60 to 70 percent.[100] Exhibitors claim that blind-bidding makes unnecessary demands on them. They are asked to contract for a film that they have not seen. Distributors argue they are in an equally blind position when they produce or agree to distribute a film and are justified in making the exhibitor share in the risk.

Exhibitors claim they are denied the chance to select films for their particular audience if they must blind-bid. Yet screening the film to exhibitors only makes them predict the fate of a film. Even if they were accurate judges of public taste and could weed out mediocre or offensive films, exceptional films would then only command higher terms.

Exhibitors sometimes suspect that studios demand a large guarantee for a film they sense is poor, in order to get as much money as they possibly can before the film is released. Exhibitors believe films would have to be better if they were screened before they had a buyer. Producers believe the films are always made as best as possible, and such a practice would have no effect. Since production of a motion picture is so expensive, a producer generally cannot afford the interest accruing on the money if it is not released as soon as the film is finished. This economic situation necessitates that theaters be lined up ahead of time. Distributors claim if they had to show the film in advance to exhibitors, they would have to recoup these additional costs by charging more to the exhibitors, which would in turn make rentals and/or ticket prices higher. Some films that are best exploited during a particular time of year would be financially hurt by time delays which could necessitate waiting for the particular season to arrive again. If, instead, the picture were opened at the wrong time of the year, millions of potential dollars could be lost.

Since television advertising space must be contracted for months ahead of time, it is most practical for the producers to know where and when the film will play. States where blind-bidding is outlawed cause a problem for distributors planning national advertising campaigns that depend on a simultaneous nationwide release. A picture may not be ready to be trade-screened in time. This also poses a problem for the exhibitor. If a picture is available for viewing only a few weeks or days before the exhibition date, there may be nothing else available for the exhibitor to play in his theater if he does not want the picture.[101]

Blind-bidding adversely affects the independent distributors who do not have the power to demand bidding ahead of time. Their films do not generally have the desirable elements such as major stars to attract bids. They must therefore screen their films for theater owners before securing exhibition. Since many theaters are fully booked when independent films are ready for release, these pictures are often unable to secure the best theaters. This renders distribution less competitive and may deprive the audience of independently distributed films that would be more successful in first-run theaters.

Jack Valenti, president of the MPAA, stated in 1979, "As I predicted at last year's convention, the blind-bidding issue has turned into a war . . . causing more venom and more blood to be spilled than any other issue in the history of the industry."[102] Films are being bid earlier now to avoid any problems with states that may implement anti-blind-bidding laws. Studios have begun negotiating directly with the theaters in each state. NATO claims that this practice evades open bidding and ends competition. The studios claim the open-bid process takes weeks, whereas they are now able to negotiate over the phone. Since distributors do not have to bid competitively or negotiate when licensing their product, some exhibitors believe that the anti-blind-bidding laws eliminate any chance of their securing a film.[103] The distributors now merely contract with a particular theater without providing any opportunity for bidding.

In the spring of 1978 the MPAA was alarmed by the trend of states declaring blind-bidding illegal and began intense lobbying to fight back. The MPAA produced its own thirty-minute film to demonstrate its opinion to state governments. At the end of the film, the narrator, Charlton Heston, states:

> If blind-bidding is eliminated and the entire risk is put upon the studios without any investment to the exhibitors . . . the consequence to the viewing public would be severe. . . . Money available to finance new products may well dry up.[104]

Others believe that if blind-bidding is outlawed, more product will be available. Independent producers and distributors might have an equal chance of securing exhibition if the films are contracted for on the merits of the finished motion picture. The majors bid their product as much as a year in advance and secure large advances and guaranteed runs. With more anti-blind-bidding laws enacted, the independent is more likely to get playing time in these states.[105] To retaliate against states instituting anti-blind-bidding laws, studios have used boycotts as a threat.

The laws vary greatly from state to state. Twenty-four states have enacted various laws prohibiting blind-bidding. While guarantees and advances are prohibited in some states, criminal penalties exist in South Carolina.[106] Ohio law forbids distributors to require advances and guarantees as a condition of license.[107] Yearly attempts since 1979 to institute anti-blind-bidding legislation in Mississippi have been defeated. Its opposition is largely predicated on the contention by witnesses for the Film Commission and the MPAA that enactment would deter filming in their state.[108] Pennsylvania's anti-blind-bidding law, considered the toughest in the United States, was enacted in 1981. It forbids blind-bidding, prohibits advances and guarantees, establishes procedures for open bidding, and imposes a forty-two-day limit on exclusive first-run engagements to ensure rapid availability of a picture to other theaters. Distributors have attempted to instigate legislation to declare it unconstitutional. Enforcement was suspended in late 1981 but was reenacted in 1982.[109]

Exhibitors are also lobbying to outlaw blind-bidding to eliminate their having to lose money on films they contract for but do not meet their expectations. For example, when exhibitors saw *Cruising,* many who had already contracted to play the picture no longer wanted it. Some believed it deserved an "X" rating when they had bid for an "R" picture.[110]

In 1983 Warner Bros. lost one of the first lawsuits over blind-bidding brought by an exhibitor against a distributor. Warner Bros. was found to have misrepresented the potential success of *The Swarm.* It was ruled that the practice of blind-bidding on films violates the Texas Deceptive Trade Practices Act. Warner Bros. also had withheld information showing that they doubted the success of the film six months before the bidding began. Even though the state has no statute declaring blind-bidding illegal, a film that does not live up to a distributor's claim may violate the Deceptive Trade Practices Act. Distributors are warned that they blind-bid at the risk of a lawsuit.[111]

Even though blind-bidding is charged as unfair by exhibitors, it serves the majors by promoting efficiency. Requiring all films be trade screened for exhibitors might make licensing terms more competitive and increase the access of independently distributed films in theaters. Independent distributors, however, are not disadvantaged only by blind-bidding. The independent films would probably be disadvantaged under any system since they lack the attributes, such as top actors, writers, directors, and money, which created the power of the majors. One position is that the public interest may not be sufficient to warrant banning blind-bidding. Such state action might prevent national distributor concerns from being considered.[112]

Exhibitors are against blind-bidding, particularly where product splitting is banned. Product splitting is a practice used by exhibitors to reduce competitive bidding. Exhibitors in a given area clandestinely or openly divide up films among themselves and agree who will bid for a particular picture. Bids are submitted only after a picture has been allocated to a particular exhibitor and only by that exhibitor. Without product splitting, bidding is expected to generate increased guarantees. Plitt and Sack Theatres President A. Alan Friedberg stated, "There is no law and no decision in any splitting case requiring an exhibitor to bid.... sheer mathematics will match up product to theatres without bidding."[113]

Product splitting assures distributors of a certainty of play dates and market coverage, enables distributors to make adjustments when films do poorly, which is not allowed under competitive bidding, and enables a sharing of risk between exhibitors and distributors which competitive bidding would prevent. Some believe the small exhibitor, in particular, benefits from splitting because it keeps more theaters in business than if competitive bidding were the rule.[114] Sumner Redstone, president of Northeast Theatre Corporation, said that splitting is not only a function of exhibitors, but could not exist without the acquiescence of distribution. Distributors even split product among exhibitors and notify exhibitors which films they have been allocated.[115] The Department of Justice on 1 April 1977 said splits were "virtually indistinguishable from bid rigging practices, a traditional per se violation of Section 1 of the Sherman Act."[116]

Golden Theaters' Quad Cinema in New York filed an antitrust suit against distributors and exhibitors regarding an alleged Greenwich Village product split from 1972 to 1980. The Quad claimed the defendants conspired among themselves to undermine the fair bidding process, thereby excluding the Quad from obtaining first-run films. Quad Cinema, however, lost its suit on the basis of insufficient evidence.[117] Eighteen of the nineteen defendants had settled, leaving the Walter Reade Organization alone to fight. The Quad had received nearly $3 million in settlement, including approximately $375,000 each from Columbia, Universal, Paramount, Twentieth Century-Fox, Warner Bros., MGM/UA, Loew's Theatres, and Cinema 5.[118] Exhibitors criticized the film companies for settling. One of the exhibitors stated, "The distributors are out of their minds for what they did.... They're crazy. It opens the door for other nuisance suits."[119]

On 17 June 1983, the Milwaukee district court found that film product splitting by four exhibitors in that market was an obvious or "per se" form of illegal market allocation and price-fixing. Capitol Service Corp., Marcus

Theatres Service Corp., Marcus Theatres Corp., and United Artists Theatre Circuit were enjoined from participating in product splits anywhere in the country. NATO claims that the "issuance of a nationwide injunction against splits 'in any form' is too broad, and should be reversed."[120] To keep prices down, the four theaters had agreed not to bid for films, not to negotiate for a film with a distributor until it was split among the four, and not to negotiate for a film split to another exhibitor. By this agreement, one exhibitor would win the picture cheaply since no one was bidding against that exhibitor. In 1977, 317 competitive bids were made by exhibitors for seventy-four films. By 1981, the exhibitors had replaced competitive bidding with negotiated licensing deals, which are more advantageous to the exhibitor. In 1977 these four chains paid a total of $1,820,300 in guarantees. After their plan was implemented, they only paid $140,000 in guarantees in 1981.[121] The exhibitors' lawyers find product splitting to be efficient and "pro competitive." Believing there is no evidence that all splits in the country are of the same nature or entered into for the same purpose, they are seeking an appeal.[122] Encouraged by the Milwaukee product-split victory in the U.S. District Court in Wisconsin, the Department of Justice is now pursuing a national policy that such market allocation is illegal per se, notwithstanding any claims of local or special circumstances.[123]

Since the federal government ruled that United Artists Theatre Circuit, the second largest chain which operates more than a thousand screens, could no longer participate in splitting, exhibitors believe blind-bidding will resume. A. Alan Freidberg believes anti-blind-bidding legislation is even more imperative where splitting is outlawed. Some believe that splitting arrangements will only become more secretive. Friedberg stated, "If I couldn't split and if I couldn't see a film, then we're in some kind of 'Alice in Wonderland.'"[124] In 1975, General Cinema Corporation President Richard A. Smith privately circulated a letter to major distributors requesting a reduction in the distributor's share of film rentals and a curbing of blind-bidding because "some exhibitors feel justified misreporting grosses while others may consider litigation."[125]

Expected increase in bidding will probably increase guarantees. Therefore, exhibitors particularly want to see the film first. Jack Valenti stated:

> Maybe life will be a little more tedious for some theater owners. It's easy to sit back and split. Now they have to re-enter the marketplace. The business as a whole is not going to be affected one way or another. I can't think of a single exhibitor who hasn't done better last year than the previous two years.[126]

Richard Lederer wrote, "There are old-time exhibitors today who privately confess their wish that the legal action which forced the split of production companies and theatres should never have been taken." Without certainty of where their films would be shown, studios committed less money to production and the number of films diminished.[127]

Release Patterns

Exhibitors are greatly affected by the release pattern for a film that distributors choose. Regardless of the quality of a picture, once it is completed a plan is made as to how it shall be released in the marketplace. The strategy used can greatly increase a film's potential and in some cases completely destroy it. There are always innumerable excuses for a film's failure at the box office. The advertising campaign, holidays, weather, sporting events, world events, competition, and release patterns can be used to explain a film's success, but more likely, to rationalize its failure.

Sneak previews often play a part in how a film will be released. The most drastic effect would be the shelving of the film completely. If negative word spreads to exhibitors before bidding time, there may not be many desirable exhibitors who would want the picture. For example, because the film *Rolling Thunder* incited such anger in the preview audience, Twentieth Century-Fox sold the movie outright to American International Pictures. Barry Diller, chairman of Paramount Pictures, stated, "You can still have a sneak preview on an ordinary film, but you can't on any film to which attention will be paid. Today, movies being sneaked are no longer considered works in progress. Judgments are made and those judgments turn up in the press the next day." After Francis Coppola's *One from the Heart* was shown in San Francisco for bidding purposes to a group of exhibitors, their negative comments appeared in the *San Francisco Chronicle*. Diller said they did not take that risk with *Reds*. Instead, Paramount "hunted around for an obscure place in Canada where we could have a preview."[128] With the increase of blind-bidding, exhibitors often try to attend sneak previews. If what they see is bad, even if it is merely being tested for changes to be made, they spread the word.

If a film fails in a preview or at the box office of major cities, it does not mean that it cannot succeed elsewhere. A new or revised pattern of release could turn around negative beginnings. The time of the year that a picture is released is often crucial to the revenue generated by the film. A statistically significant greater number of people consistently attend movies at certain times of the year. It is wise to open a film at such times to have access to this larger audience. However, the competition from other films is keen, as everyone wants to attract a part of this audience. Exhibitors complain that the majority of commercial pictures are all opened at the same time, with little quality product left for the rest of the year.

Christmas, vacation from school, and the summer months are the times when the moviegoing audience is greatest. These times generally warrant huge national releases of the majors' best pictures. Approximately forty films were released in the summer of 1983 between Memorial Day and Labor Day. It was estimated that $200 million would be spent on television ads alone for these films.[129]

The summer season used to begin on July 4; however, summer films are now being released in May. By July 4, summer moviegoing reaches its zenith. Marketing consultant David Forbes said, "By July 15th, it's really clear who has made it and who hasn't. At that point, all the films that nobody is sure about will come in to fill in the gaps for the films that have failed."[130] Films released in mid-July or August have only a limited time to earn money. After Labor Day the accelerated moviegoing ends. In the summer, theater availability is a problem for smaller independent films. The majority of desirable theaters are taken up by the major films that have contracted up to a year in advance for that playing time. Blockbusters may have longer runs than anticipated, taking up theaters for an even greater amount of time. Only after the interest in these films has waned, or when a film that was expected to be a major hit proves to be a failure, can an independent think of getting into the theater. Many exhibitors, however, are fearful that an independent film will not draw a crowd and prefer to play old reruns of blockbusters.

During January, the Christmas releases of the majors are still in the marketplace. The only new movies likely to be released are foreign or independent films. Independents have the best chance of securing theaters in the times of the year that have the least audience attendance. April and May are generally considered the worst months to release a film. After Labor Day, total box office revenue is low, as school has resumed. The first two weeks in December are poor as many people are concerned with Christmas shopping.

Non-holiday weekends generate 75 to 80 percent of a week's business. Approximately 60 percent of weekly business is derived from weekend days during the summer and year-end holiday periods. During spring vacation 70 percent of a week's business is generated on weekends.[131] Exhibitors frequently offer bargain prices for the slowest days of the week and times of the day. The most profitable times of the year to release a film may be affected by the region. For example, in New York City the Labor Day weekend does not generate great box office business because residents typically leave the city. Tourists generally do not go to the movies.[132]

The topicality of a picture also affects the box office. If the content is new or popular it has a better chance of being well received than if it is released when interest in the subject matter is waning.

The social and political unrest in 1968 cost the film companies $100 million in lost box office receipts. People stayed home, afraid to go out. Theaters in larger cities, particularly those playing family films, lost the most, while roadshows and adult features suffered the least. In numerous low-priced neighborhood theaters, grosses were reportedly down 20 to 30 percent.[133]

The release pattern of a film must be decided upon prudently or millions could carelessly be spent and quickly wasted. Only two-thirds of all theaters are considered to be desirable and profitable.[134] Therefore, films have to be booked into theaters ahead of time while taking into consideration the time of year, the number of theaters to open them in, and the competition.

An "engagement" is a single-theater booking. One "play date" is one engagement. For example, a ten-week contract constitutes one engagement and one play date. Greenfield claims that the initial release of a major picture involves an average of 2,500 to 3,000 play dates. However, he finds it preferable to have 3,500 to 4,000 play dates.[135] After the percentage towns are sold (approximately 5,000 for a major picture), it does not pay to book the flat rental theaters. For these situations, mail-order bookings are used.[136]

Runs indicate a theater's playing position and define the succession of exhibitions of a picture. A first run is the first showing of the film in a theater or many theaters. First-run theaters are the most desirable because they draw the greatest audience and pay the highest rentals. A premiere, exclusive, or roadshow opening in one theater is followed by the general release, also known as the first run. A second run or intermediate break is the exhibition of the film for lower rental and often in independent theaters. In third, fourth, and successive runs, known as the underbelly break, the film generally plays in less desirable theaters or as part of a double bill. Films are played in first-run theaters in more than 50 percent of the country. Forty percent of total revenue of a film is recouped from first run and 50 percent recouped within the first ninety days of release.[137]

The first theater to play a film can recoup the highest revenue, and therefore has to pay a higher rental. For this privilege, a first-run exhibitor is granted protection over competing theaters. This consists of a stipulation that other competing theaters cannot show the same film for a specified amount of time. This period is called "clearance." However, if the clearance is too long, the effectiveness of the advertising may be diminished. "Zoning" is used to designate the area over which clearance is effective.

Distributors are increasingly less prone to give clearances. They now want to get the film in and out of a large number of theaters as quickly as possible. Films used to be licensed for first-run exhibition in a major city on an exclusive run, or at most, a simultaneous run at three or four theaters. After the initial run, it was then licensed on a sub-run basis to older suburban theaters or to multiplexes in shopping centers. Presently, films are licensed for first-run exhibition on a much broader basis because it is more lucrative. In a day-and-date first run, the film is opened in several theaters in a community on the same day, or is opened simultaneously in two or more markets. Multiple first runs play the film in exclusive and day-and-date theaters. A premiere showcase is a multiple run where the film has not yet been released. A second-run showcase is a multiple run where the film has already been shown on an extensive, exclusive, or general run. A double bill showcase multiple is a multiple run of two pictures. "Double bills," the playing of two films as one show, are generally not used in multiplexes. They are used for return engagements of two successful pictures as one show. Double bills are still expected at drive-ins. Shorts are used only if the film runs well under two hours.[138]

Patterns define the number of theaters or situations a film plays in within a given territory. In an exclusive pattern, a film plays in one theater in New York and Los Angeles with the goal of gaining positive critical reviews and generating favorable word of mouth. After the exclusive run is completed, a general run places the film in three or four theaters in a given territory. After the exclusive and general runs, the film goes into a multiple run of twenty to twenty-five theaters in neighborhood and drive-in theaters. In a platform opening, a film is opened in only a few major theaters in any given area. It aims for good reviews and word of mouth to grow. If the picture has "legs," or the ability to keep playing and draw a large audience, the film is opened in more theaters.

A saturation pattern opens the film in a thousand to fifteen hundred or more theaters simultaneously, with concomitant national television advertising. Independent distributors who cannot afford the nationwide expense employ the saturation method on a regional basis. A film can be released in one territory with great advertising expenditure in the area for a few weeks, and then be moved on to the next territory. This could be performed with fewer than one hundred prints.

Opening a film in a few theaters in a large city or in several cities can cost the same in advertising as if it were opened in hundreds of theaters. Therefore, it is often decided to release a picture wide to take advantage of the reach of the advertising. This does not necessarily ensure greater film rental. If box office grosses are low per theater, no profit is gained and the film may soon be played out. If it were carefully set in a few select theaters, the film might grow to greater success. Before 1972 when Paramount released *The Godfather* in six hundred theaters, it was common for "quality" pictures to play exclusively in one or two theaters in each city, whereas the saturation method was used for exploitation films.[139] In the summer of 1983, *Superman III* opened on 1,750 theater screens, *Porky's II* on 1,500, and *Octopussy* on 1,300. MGM/UA's Frank Yablans thinks there are too many prints in the marketplace. "There are too many marginal theaters being taken, and too many theaters in a given demographic area. No wonder some films can't compete."[140]

Release patterns have been altered because of high advertising costs and new strategies of saturation booking. If a film is of questionable quality, the area in which the picture is playing is saturated with heavy advertising to recoup as much money as possible before negative word of mouth spreads.

Though many high-grossing films dependent upon repeat business could play much longer in a theater and still earn a profit, they may be forced to leave if there is a locked booking of another film to open on a specific date. That successful picture then has to find another theater in which to be exhibited. Since the prime theater-going times of the year are of major importance, these periods are firmly booked by the majors in advance. During other times of the year, films that do not have locked bookings open in sequence, depending upon theater availability. If a film scheduled to play before another particular film is a failure, this next picture may be exhibited earlier than expected. If the previous picture is a huge success, the opening of the subsequent picture could be delayed for weeks or even months.

Once a film is opened, a quick decision has to be made in regard to keeping it in the theaters, pulling it out before more money is lost, or opening it wider and faster. National Gross Service can be an invaluable system to aid in such decisions. They are an independent supplier of computerized, overnight box office reports. For competition comparison, they provide statistics on all the theaters in one district and provide exhibitors with a week's bookings and grosses for each theater compared to the previous week. They also provide a record of daily reporting of individual bank deposits made by each of an exhibitor's theaters. For distributors, they provide a nationwide sampling of fifteen to twenty key situations per distribution branch to provide a full analysis of screen averages and trends in release patterns.[141]

The decision of how to open a picture is usually based on research of the audience reaction to a film. Tracking studies are performed on a weekly basis prior to a film's release. They measure how many people have heard of a film and their eagerness to see it. It can be predicted within a range of 5 to 10 percent how successful a film's opening will be. If a film receives a great response but the advertising is unable to create a desire to see it, an exclusive or platform situation is created so that critical reviews and word of mouth are allowed to grow and spread. If a film tests quite mediocre a wide release may be warranted to quickly gross as much as possible. And, even if the film has been released to poor results, it is still possible to reissue it and attain enormous profit.

Exhibitors are becoming more concerned with the rapid release of a picture to the ancillary markets. The first-run theaters are not affected; however, the subsequent run theaters are being eliminated from the pattern. Distributors increasingly find it more profitable to play the major markets and then capitalize on the success and advertising by a quick release to other markets. NITE President Robert Hutte advises small-town exhibitors who complain that they are squeezed out of first runs to wait and see how pictures perform before they book them into secondary release. A growing tendency of major studios is to sell to cable television while small theaters book the same pictures as second features. Hutte advises that instead of waiting for distribution to correct this practice, a theater play second features six months after they are on cable. If they are played while they are advertised as coming on cable, audiences do not go to the theaters. Hutte warned that early subsequent run bookings are usually "milked dry in their wide-breaking big-city openings." He also believes the four-week guarantees demanded by studios is of little value to small-town theaters because no film can play that long to a limited audience.[142]

Richard Childs of Embassy Home Entertainment described the sequential release pattern of a picture today, beginning generally with an opening in New York, Los Angeles, and Toronto. After two to four months of theatrical release, the picture is released to airlines; after six months, to home video; after eight to ten months, to the non-theatrical market; after twelve to fifteen months, to cable; after two years, for network play; and after four years, to syndication.[143] "Double window" situations are occurring, where a picture opens the same day in theaters and on pay-per-view cable.

Wide-breaking first runs have come to be known as showcasing, a method whose purpose is to prepare theatrical films for sales to pay-TV and/or home video. Jack Vogel, an independent exhibitor, contends NATO is run by and for big circuits who are willing instruments for distribution to use them as first-run or showcase vehicles for quick transition of product to ancillary markets. He views the rapid growth of multiplexes by the major chains as the acceleration of the showcasing of virtually all of theatrical exhibition. He therefore sees less possibility of survival for independent exhibitors.[144]

Branches/Exchanges

Major distributors and large independent distributors have branch offices in the various exchange areas throughout the country to handle the physical booking of films into theaters. Smaller independent distributors may employ independent subdistributors that function as branches. In the beginning of the motion picture business, the country was divided by railroad junctions to enable the delivery of prints. Because of modernization in all areas, the number of these exchange areas has been reduced. Howard Wilansky, director of branch operations for Warner Bros., said that the major studios each had approximately thirty-two branch offices in the United States and six in Canada in the early 1950s. These "exchanges" had a front room for the sales and bookings. In the back room, film prints were stored and inspected for shipment. In the late 1950s, when National Screen Service came to be used, the back rooms were consolidated. From 1969 to 1972, operations became computerized, reducing the number of branches to between twenty and twenty-six. In the last five years, further consolidation was implemented. The twenty to twenty-six were reduced to thirteen to twenty-six sales offices with 180 to 230 employees. As large exhibition chains grew, studios were able to cut costs. The independent exhibitors associate themselves in large buying combines and therefore can be handled as one entity.[145]

A distributor can make an agreement with a subdistributor that is similar to the distribution agreement between the distributor and producer. Yet the subdistributor can be cancelled at any time. The distributor's own branches serve the same function as independent subdistributors. Subdistributors generally receive a 25 percent commission for distributing a film. This fee is recouped after the advertising expenses from local newspapers are deducted and is based on the net cash received from the exhibitor.[146] Chains can demand that subdistributors pay advertising costs weeks ahead of play dates. Subdistributors sometimes use the money received from the exhibition of the previous pictures to secure another picture. Subdistributors can be slow to pay and if the subsequent picture is a failure, no money remains to pay the distributor the rental earned from the previous picture.[147]

The functions performed through the main office include control of prints, play dates, bids, settlement and contract review, branch operations, and non-theatrical distribution. The distribution sales manager's responsibilities include setting the time of year the film will play, setting the sales policy to ensure it plays in the theater with the best track records, and ensuring the public's positive perception of the film before it plays.

Branches are supervised by branch managers and are staffed with sales representatives, bookers, cashiers, and contract clerks. The general sales manager in a branch awards bids and is responsible for securing the maximum number of play dates for each picture and for extracting the greatest film rental for a minimum cost. The branch functions include booking, billing, collections, coordination of print shipments, confirmation of holdovers, daily gross and play date reporting, and "junking," or disposal of prints.

Before World War II, the Los Angeles exchange area generated less than 4 percent of rentals, while the New York City exchange area accounted for nearly 17 percent of the market share, now down to nearly 8 percent. The leading exchange area is now Los Angeles, contributing close to 13 percent of all U.S. film rentals. The Los Angeles exchange "runs from Santa Barbara east through Las Vegas to eastern Arizona, then west along the Mexican border and north through San Diego, Orange, San Bernardino, Riverside, Los Angeles, and Ventura counties." In the eighties, the top-ten exchange areas, out of thirty-one total, represent approximately 60 percent of all national rentals, and include Los Angeles, New York City, Dallas, San Francisco, Jacksonville, Washington, D.C., Boston, Chicago, Atlanta, and Seattle/Portland.[148]

The need for the number of branches decreased and continues to decrease as the many facets involved in distribution and exhibition become streamlined, computerized, and more organized. Distributors already make flat rental deals for pictures on the phone and ship the prints directly to these smaller theaters. Numerous branches were once necessary when travel and communication were slow. The need for these offices is being eliminated.

Exhibition Contract

Since distributors are no longer allowed to have exclusive contracts with certain theaters, films are supposed to be contracted for on a theater-by-theater basis. In areas of competition this is done through bidding. Since all theater owners by law have the opportunity to bid, each bid is supposed to be opened publicly. Exhibition contracts license a particular picture to a certain exhibitor on an individual basis. A number of films can be licensed on the same exhibition contract, provided their terms are not conditioned upon one another.[149]

A standard bid policy states "distribution reserves the right to reject any and all bids by exhibitors for any reason." For example, if all bids are unacceptable, the distributor will ask for new bids. If still unsatisfied, the distributor may negotiate with each exhibitor to try to secure the minimum terms.[150]

When a picture is to be blind-bid, bid letters can be sent out to exhibitors more than a year before the picture is scheduled for release. Bid letters inform exhibitors about the film's story line, the actors, director, and producers. It also tells them in what regions the picture will open and the available dates, and describes the advertising campaign.

The bidding process begins with the distributor sending exhibitors in the same competitive area a letter or form detailing that a specific film will be available in a given situation for a play date and requesting that each exhibitor make an offer. The bid requests the exhibitor meet or exceed certain minimum stipulations.

A bid letter may request a non-returnable guarantee or an advance as a condition for securing the picture. Distributors almost always request advances against the terms, known as "overages" in the business. As business declined in the late sixties and early seventies, exhibitors began remitting payments more slowly. The majors reacted by tightening their terms and blind-bidding more frequently. They also began requiring guarantees of up to $250,000 per screen in advance.[151] Guarantees are generally paid two weeks before a picture opens, while rental checks are paid sixty to ninety days after the film's opening.[152]

James Edwards put up a $150,000 cash guarantee on *The Blues Brothers* and lost nearly $100,000. Yet he paid a $110,000 guarantee for *Star Wars* which eventually generated $1.6 million during its 54–week screening at his Newport Cinema in California. Of the total, $1.1 million went to Fox and he kept $500,000 plus concession earnings. During the first week *The Empire Strikes Back* played at his theater it grossed $149,000, and the theater sold $28,000 worth of popcorn, candy, and soft drinks. Additionally, Edwards took in $7,000 on the sale of souvenir books.[153]

The minimum playing time for the picture is stated in the bid letter. A twelve-week minimum playing time may be demanded that will bind the exhibitor to play the film even if it fails. Twentieth Century-Fox reported that exhibitors were so eager to acquire *The Empire Strikes Back* that they were offering twenty-eight week minimum runs.[154]

In all bids, complete information about the allocation of grosses is requested. In weighing terms, distributors consider the exhibitor's "house nut," or the cost of running the theater for one week, which is recouped from the theatrical gross before the distributor receives any rental. The average weekly overhead of a theater is $1,200.[155] However, this average varies greatly, with house nuts of $20,000 in New York. Exhibitors may have two overhead expense figures, one for the majors and one for the independents. The independents will be charged more since they do not have the power to refuse terms. Distributors realize that the nut usually contains "air," or a certain amount of padding of the expenses to ensure the exhibitor that he will not lose money on the run.

The bid can also request clearance in days and specific theaters over which a priority run is sought. The number of daily exhibitions for each day of the week is also a factor. If a second feature is to be run in conjunction, the maximum deduction for the additional picture must be indicated.

Some distributors include in the bid letter a request to know how many minutes of advertising will be shown per performance (excluding the feature trailers) and stipulating that all income from the advertising is considered part of the gross receipts of the theater in computing rental terms.[156] In most small towns it is not profitable or efficient for distributors to pay for advertising. Theater chains and distributors can also contract to cross-collateralize box office receipts and advertising expenses for all of the play dates. The contract also states that the distributor has the right to determine at his sole discretion the nature, content and quantity of advertising, and to require that advertising expenses for each week shall be shared in the same respective percentages as are provided for the sharing of the gross receipts for that week.

Theaters may be awarded bids based on their seating capacity. The average seating capacity of theaters is five hundred seats.[157] A theater with more seats is not necessarily desired. Generally, the larger the theater the larger the house nut. If a picture is not going to draw a large enough audience, it is preferable to play it in a smaller house. However, if a theater has to turn people away, a portion of the audience is lost because of an unwise release strategy.

Licenses are supposed to be contracted for on a theater-by-theater basis to prohibit circuits from having an advantage over independent exhibitors. Widespread multiplexing, however, has generated a controversy over theater-by-theater licensing and "moveovers." A "moveover" involves a film's change in theater auditorium within or outside the same complex without any time elapsing between runs. Multiplex exhibitors can use their physical facilities as an advantage over single auditorium exhibitors to secure pictures in bidding. Competition is difficult when single-screen and multiple-screen exhibitors formulate bids without knowing how many screens the competition is putting up against them. Twin theaters even have the capacity to play the same film at staggered times and can be considered a single theater in licensing agreements. This larger aggregate seating capacity of two auditoriums can be a positive factor in securing motion pictures. Another licensing problem particular to a multiplex is whether a bid made during negotiations for a given auditorium of a multi-auditorium theater, once accepted, can be followed by the exhibition of the picture on another screen of the multiplex. A multiplex exhibitor cannot, however, secure a picture for a larger auditorium and then play the film in a smaller theater. A government memorandum filed in December 1979 stated that combining the seating capacity of several screens is permitted where the combined seating capacity does not exceed the seating capacity of the largest single-auditorium theater.[158]

In some bid requests, the distributor reserves the right to expand an existing run at a later date. Therefore an exhibitor bids one of a limited number of theaters playing the picture, and the distributor can add other theaters later without recourse from the exhibitor.[159]

Wide-release patterns are increasing expenses. More prints are needed and more house nuts need to be paid as the film is opened over a greater area of the country. In the 1980s when blind-bidding was increasingly outlawed, distributors devised a means of securing a certain amount of the box office grosses. In the bid letters they began to specify a minimum per capita requirement, meaning that the distributor's share must be at least a specific amount per adult and per child. This is not considered price-fixing since the exhibitor is free to charge any permutation of prices.[160]

If the exhibitor contracts for a "locked booking," the exhibitor must open the picture on the specific date, regardless of how well the current film may be doing. A "three-week corridor" refers to the fact that another picture will be coming to that theater in three weeks. If an exhibitor has contracted to play a film for four weeks yet it generates minimal attendance, the distributor may allow the exhibitor to terminate its run. At these times, a second-run film or an independent may be played as a last resort. If an exhibitor plays a picture for a fewer number of weeks than licensed for, he must pay 75 percent of the last week's grosses for each week the film is not exhibited. Yet this figure is probably minimal because if the film was successful, the exhibitor would still be showing it.[161]

Bids include a request for a holdover figure, or a minimum box office gross at which the exhibitor will continue to play the picture beyond the contracted playing time. For example, if in the sixth week of the engagement of the picture the gross receipts equal or exceed the holdover figure, the engagement shall continue for one week after the minimum run for a seventh week. Similarly, for each week after the seventh week of the engagement that the gross receipts equal or exceed the holdover figure, the engagement shall continue for one additional week. An exhibitor who bids a lower holdover figure, thereby agreeing to continue to play the picture at a lower box office gross, presents a better offer from the distributor's point of view.[162] Since the difference in box office on a film can be as much as 20 percent between playing top-quality theaters versus mediocre theaters, powerful exhibitors can demand higher box office figures for a film to be held over. Because of this, many films are thrown out of theaters that would have continued playing them in the past.[163]

Film buyers analyze bids based on a "gut feel," the track record of those involved in the production, the type of picture, comparable pictures to be released at the same time, how badly the picture is needed, whether one's ego necessitates having a big picture to show, the size of the promised advertising campaign, and their cash available for the guarantees. Booking strategy requires thought of what the opposition will bid. One may let others make large bids and win and then negotiate for the balance of pictures. To distributors all theaters are not equal. Location, number and quality of seats, its grossing history, sound and projection equipment, age, whether it is a single or multiple house, and whether it is a circuit house or an independent are all factors in selecting the "best" bid. When roadshow films were popular, the rest rooms became of great concern as they were crowded at intermissions. Bids came to be awarded to exhibitors based on the number and attractiveness of the toilets they had.[164]

Independent and less powerful exhibitors claim that bidding is not always conducted fairly. Some major circuits employ people to clandestinely procure screenplays of future films for which they will bid. Since they have the opportunity to evaluate the screenplay, such exhibitors have an unfair advantage.[165]

Exhibitors claim that favored exhibitors are given "five o'clock looks" or are told the highest bid after the bidding has ended, enabling them to win. In the Quad Cinema antitrust suit in New York Federal Court, Bernard L.

Goldberg, vice president of Golden Theater Management Corp. which operates the Greenwich Village fourplex, claimed distributors had given competitors "five o'clock looks" at his bids which enabled them to match or top his theater's bids, often a considerable time after the filing deadlines. He cited several instances where his bid had been the only one submitted on time, yet he still did not secure the film.[166]

In situations where no competition exists for a picture because only one exhibitor exists in an area or because there is no interest in a particular picture, the picture is not bid. The distributor and exhibitor can make a deal for the rental terms. If the film does not gross enough to cover the exhibitor's expenses, the terms may be "reviewed" or reduced, unless the contract specifies the picture is not subject to any adjustment or review. In a bid situation, the contract is supposedly binding in every way.[167] The adjustment evolved because in the past, the powerful distributors imposed such excessive terms that the exhibitors retaliated.[168] When the studios owned the theaters, the percentage of gross receipts remitted was not an issue. The majors insured mutually agreeable terms between one company's distribution arm and another's theatrical chain. After the divorcement of exhibition from production and distribution, the rental percentage assumed greater importance. To aid theaters, the sliding scale was instituted. The percentage due to a distributor could vary from week to week depending upon the week's gross receipts. The divorcement shifted power from the producers and distributors to the exhibitors. The "look," "wink," or "blink" was a modification of the sliding scale favoring the theater owner. The exhibitor would review the gross and decide whether it warranted him a sufficient amount of income. If he believed the rental was too high, renegotiation ensued.[169] For example, an exhibitor may agree to pay 60 percent of the gross with a "look." If the gross did not meet his standards, the terms would be lowered to a new agreed upon percentage. Terms are usually lowered 10 to 25 percent. Alterations are also made by comparison to previous grosses on similar movies. Distributors have such records of transactions from other distribution companies' grosses.[170] Yet if a film is extremely successful, it would be rare for an exhibitor to pay more than contracted for.

Distributors have tolerated these adjustments because they do not want to sue the exhibitors and create enemies. Years of antitrust litigation have discouraged distributors from joining together to enforce contracts. Attorney Michael F. Mayer wrote that when he was representing a distributor, he was told by the defense lawyer for an exhibitor that it was now a "custom of the trade" to reduce rentals from that which was contracted for. This exhibitor claimed the distributor had no right to sue him. In bid situations contract terms legally must be firm. In these cases, adjustments are infrequent. This unilateral reduction of rentals by exhibitors cheats not only the distributor but the producer as well.[171]

As bidding increases, "looks" are becoming less common. Distributors have recently begun inserting "no review" provisions in contracts. When "no review" provisions exist, a distributor may promise more flexibility on an upcoming picture. Mayer finds far fewer adjustments of rental terms on major films. When a film is bid competitively, changing the terms once the highest bid is accepted would be a breach of faith and law. The majors are so strong now that even where there is no bidding they are strong enough to insist on the terms agreed upon rather than the historical precedent of making adjustments. Yet the "look" or modification of terms is still common practice for most minor distributors and occasionally by the majors.[172]

Loew's Theatres had paid a one million dollar advance for *The Great Gatsby* in four New York Theaters on a 90/10 distributor/exhibitor split. The house nuts of the four theaters was $57,000. In the first six weeks, Paramount received only $217,429 in rentals for the New York engagement. It seemed unlikely Loew's would recoup their advance. Paramount was not legally bound to return it, yet they said they would return a reasonable percentage to ensure the studio would have the theaters in the future.[173] On the other hand, for *Jaws* Universal offered very stringent terms without the possibility for review. In March 1975 Universal sneak previewed *Jaws* in Dallas. From this, all were certain the picture would be a hit. Universal was asking for $100,000 guarantees in many houses that had never grossed that much in a run of any film, in addition to a minimum twelve-week playing time. Furthermore, Universal wanted justification for every house expense. The contracts also stipulated that no possibility of adjustments or return of advances or guarantees would be made should the film fail. They decided to saturate *Jaws* in a wide release of at least 400 theaters in the United States and Canada, instead of the 125–150 theater release pattern that was then usual.[174] Fortunately for the exhibitors, the picture was a success.

Exhibition contracts specifically define the terms of a picture's engagements and reduce the risk for the party with the greater bargaining power. Though the distributor or exhibitor might try to extract as much as he possibly can out of each license, without regard for the other party, his long term success ultimately is linked to the other party's success. Distribution and exhibition, though highly suspicious of the motives and practices of the other, need each other for their own survival.

Future of Exhibition

While some fear the extinction of theatrical exhibition, a few chains of theaters are extremely powerful and are becoming stronger. Alan Hirschfield, chairman of Twentieth Century-Fox, noted that if the majors could own theaters again, the pictures could be released more carefully. Since screen availability would be planned, a picture could build an audience and current marketing costs could be reduced to half the cost of saturation releases. He also believes the price of theater admissions should be based on the product, with distributors being able to set the admission price.[175]

On 27 February 1980 Loew's Theatres was permitted to produce and distribute as well as exhibit films. Since the Consent Decrees, approximately eight hundred private actions have been filed alleging antitrust violations of distribution and exhibition. The majority have concerned alleged vertical conspiracies between distributors and exhibitors, discriminating against other exhibitors. A few concerned horizontal distributor conspiracies and monopolistic practices by distributors which affect all exhibitors.[176]

Since the Reagan administration took over, the Consent Decrees have been up for review. In 1983 Robert Hutte, president of the five-thousand-screen NITE, urged stricter enforcement of the Consent Decrees. He said, "For the past thirty years, regardless of the political coloring of the Justice Department, the distributors have been able to control the enforcement" of the Consent Decrees. He stated that in all but one of approximately 1,600 cases alleging Consent Decree violations, major studios or major circuits have prevailed. The one exception was the 1978 case in which Twentieth Century-Fox pleaded no contest and paid a $25,000 fine on charges of block-booking *Star Wars* with *The Other Side of Midnight*. Hutte believes the Consent Decrees need to be retained as a "deterrent to distributors" even though they "have never really been enforced." Hutte fears that if the decrees are not upheld, the distributors will resume involvement in exhibition, leading to domination of the exhibition field.[177]

Debates over the future of theatrical exhibition itself range on the continuum from theaters remaining the same and as numerous to their entire extinction. More likely, theater exhibition will evolve to accommodate new technological discoveries for theatrical exhibition as well as those in home entertainment. New innovations strive to eliminate deterrents of going to the theater.

An experiment with the admission price has proven an effective tool to generate theater attendance. In Japan, "Eiga No Hi" (Movie Day) has existed for about a quarter of a century to honor Edison's pioneering work in the cinema and to remind people to patronize the theaters. In 1981 participating theaters halved admission prices on that day. Tokyo theaters registered a fourfold increase in attendance and a poll found that 78 percent of filmgoers favored a continuation of once-a-year discounts. In 1982, two more Movie Days were added, and in 1983 a Movie Day was created every four months. A general admission ticket in Japan in 1983 was $6.32. Theater owners view these days as a method of encouraging the development of the moviegoing habit.[178]

Exhibitors are actively trying to modernize their theaters to create more unique experiences for their patrons. Paramount Pictures allocated $300,000 to employ the Theater Alignment Program of the Sprocket Systems subsidiary of Lucasfilm to upgrade the quality of 70mm sound and projection for the two releases that opened in 1,300 or more situations, *Indiana Jones and the Temple of Doom* and *Star Trek III: The Search for Spock*. Paramount is the first distributor spending money to help exhibitors do what it has been prodding them to do: promote better 70mm presentation.[179] Paramount released 170 70mm prints of *Indiana Jones and the Temple of Doom,* which was a new record. A two-hour 70mm print costs $10,000. This price is down from the $14,000 per print price tag of *Return of the Jedi* and the $16,000 cost in 1981.[180] It may prove to be a wise investment to enhance the theatrical presentation of a picture to maintain the number of present theater-goers and to attract others.

At the 1904 St. Louis Exposition, scenic tours were introduced that consisted of a narrow room decorated to resemble the interior of a railroad car. Motion pictures of scenic wonders were shown at one end. When the room was full, train noises and train movements were created as the onrushing pictures were watched.[181] This attempted to provide tactile stimuli in addition to the visual and aural stimuli. Attempts are still being made to add another dimension to the movie experience. Exposition films are generally films of the future. They include experimental, grandiose, technological marvels, multiscreen and large screen formats, and can include audience involvement. The Epcot Center, a permanent world's fair, has more exhibition films and formats than any other single project.[182]

Entrepreneurs Alan Weber and John Harris in Monterey, California, believed there was still an audience that would enjoy attending films in a luxurious theater. They created The Dream Theater that opened in 1975 to play a mixture of first-run and art films. Other attractions included quality food and a variety of seating, including loveseats designed for two people.[183] People are still seeking the theater for an entertainment in itself. In addition to the artificial stimuli that the theater provides, it also allows for social contact with others. Such an experience cannot be duplicated in the home environment.

It is generally believed that the growth of home entertainment will ultimately eliminate sub-runs. Small theaters cannot afford to pay for new equipment and remain competitive. With less time elapsing between theatrical exhibition and a film's appearance in the ancillary markets, it is becoming increasingly more necessary to get a film out as quickly as possible.

The impact of the ancillary markets is evident in England. Because of television, British cinema audiences were reduced from twenty million people a week in 1955 to less than ten million people a week by 1960. The number today is less than two million per week. Some believe home video will replace theaters as the major film viewing medium.[184] In 1956 Trueman T. Rembusch, former president of Allied States Association of Motion Picture Exhibitors, which represented thousands of independent exhibitors, claimed, "The film companies are endeavoring to change the industry 'from a mass to a class-entertainment medium' in accord with the expressed philosophy of Samuel Goldwyn that, 'Fewer pictures and fewer theaters will make a greater motion-picture industry.'"[185]

Exhibitor James Edwards is not frightened about the future of theaters. "People will still want to go out and enjoy themselves.... Look at the restaurant business. Lots of them are packed—even though there's a kitchen in every private home."[186] Anthropologist Hortense Powdermaker said:

> Modern man is lonely, desperately in need of personal relationships. He goes to the movies, and for two hours he has the illusion of close, intimate, personal contact with exciting and beautiful people. His loneliness is briefly assuaged.[187]

A psychological experience takes place in the theater that is unique and cannot be replicated in the home environment. Even if the physical accoutrements of the theatrical experience, such as the large screen, superior sound, darkness, and lack of disruptions can be simulated, the gestalt involving the presence of strangers, the size and magnitude of the theater, and particularly the unfamiliar environment that demands full attention to the film when compared with the home create a unique reaction within the viewer.

7

Foreign and Ancillary Markets

The ancillary markets encompass all means of exploiting a motion picture other than theatrical exhibition. Because the domestic theatrical market's domination has been waning, most pictures depend upon the ancillary markets to make a profit or at least to recoup the cost of production.

Table 7-1.   Major Markets

	1978	1982	1984
Domestic	51%	41%	40%
Foreign	30%	17%	16%
Pay TV	2%	18%	19%
Network TV	13%	8%	6%
Syndication	4%	7%	7%
Home Video	0%	9%	12%

(Reprinted with permission of Paul Kagan Associates, Inc. Copyright 1986 Paul Kagan Associates, Inc.)

Until recently, the foreign market provided the greatest source of additional revenue and security to the producers.

The Foreign Market

The European filmmakers, in their desire to appeal to the cultured class, had generally sought to make films in direct competition with the stage. In America, however, showmen gave the common man what he wanted to see, what he could understand, and what he could afford. American filmmakers found a means of communicating with the audience by entertaining on an emotional level instead of merely trying to educate people by appeals to the intellect, and found that their films were appreciated all over the world. The American film would quickly grow to compete with and finally dominate the world market.

By 1910, the international trade in motion pictures had been established. The Europeans were selling film at the competitive price of twelve cents a foot. Denmark contributed several somber dramas, Italy contributed one-reel spectacles based on history or the Bible, and Germany exported Oskar Messter's risqué comedies. The French film, however, dominated the screens of the world during the first decade of the century.[1]

For years, the upper classes of European nations avoided the cinema. They preferred the opera and stage. Yet in 1912, English and German traders noticed that American merchandise was gradually taking over their control of the market. They discovered American films showed merchandise in the motion pictures that audiences wanted and preferred. Since more than 90 percent of movies shown in foreign countries were American, this influence was great. The Europeans decided to produce pictures to compete, yet the films were not publicly accepted. Propaganda against American films was prevalent. The morals of Hollywood were attacked and American industrialists were accused of attempting to control international commerce through subtle advertising of merchandise in motion pictures. However, these attempts at reducing the popularity of American films proved futile.[2] The First World War shut down motion picture production in Europe in 1914, further enabling the American product to take over. War wages in America allowed people to spend money on movies, which also accelerated the growth of the industry.[3]

The United States has always maintained a liberal policy on the importation of foreign films. However, other countries enacted various methods of protecting their own films. Foreign countries feared the public would not tolerate the complete ban of American films. They therefore instituted laws to benefit their own film industries.

The screen quota system requires that a theater reserve an established portion of the theater's screen time for their domestic films. It may demand that a percentage of the theater's films be domestic or that a specific number of weeks per unit of time measurement be devoted to domestic films. This system allows films to be imported, but then they must compete for the limited screen time available. Restrictions on the number of films that could be imported are also made.[4]

Americans were forced to buy their share of foreign films in order to obtain licenses to distribute their own productions. It was believed that when these foreign films would be shown in America, foreign merchandise would be advertised. It was also thought that by placing tariffs on American films, the cost of export would be too high for any films other than the very best to be exhibited in a foreign country.[5]

In 1914 America supplied one-half of the movie production in the world. By 1917, nearly all the motion pictures produced in the world were from the

United States. Increased profits, costs, and further expansion encouraged ruthless competition. The industry had become a large-scale operation, dependent on a larger global mass market.[6] Between 1925 and 1926, motion picture revenue had generated $1.25 billion. This increased growth was far greater than could have been anticipated.[7] But it was the postwar years that allowed films to attain world dominance. With the United States possessing half of the theaters in the world and American films usually being amortized at home, the pictures could be rented very cheaply abroad. Foreign productions could not compete with these reasonable quality films.[8] Robert Sklar wrote, "In practice, during the interwar years, American pictures as a whole did no better than break even at the domestic box office. But with production costs already covered, every ticket sold outside the United States, less overseas distribution costs, produced profit."[9]

From 1926 to 1928, foreign revenue represented 25 to 40 percent of the total earnings of a film. The average American film received approximately half of its foreign revenue from England. From 1925 to 1927 American producers had an almost complete monopoly of the English market. From 1928 to 1929, the government leaders in Germany and France began a movement to impose heavier deterrents to the importation of American pictures. They organized a European "bloc" against American films. Their goal was to impede American producers with tariff regulations and restrictions. English, French, German, Scandinavian, and Italian distributors agreed to distribute each other's product. France then demanded that America establish a "film bank" with $10 million to lend to French producers. The American producers, represented by the Hays Organization, refused to comply. Since the French continued their demands, the Americans closed their exchanges in France and stopped exporting films to them. The French theater owners, however, protested to their government, as they knew audiences would dwindle without American films. In a few months, France abandoned its program and restored American films to their previous position.[10]

The effects of World War II were felt by 1944, when the foreign market had been reduced to essentially the British Empire and Latin America. During World War II, production capital in foreign countries was scarce. Protective measures developed during the 1920s and 1930s were abandoned. Because many markets were closed during the war, a large number of unplayed films were stored up for release abroad.[11]

In 1945, the MPAA's former Foreign Department became the Motion Picture Export Association of America (MPEAA). The MPEAA was organized as a legal cartel under the Webb-Pomerene Export Trade Act of 1918. The aim was to stimulate exporting by small and medium-sized firms. The act allowed competitors to cooperate in foreign trade by forming export associations that could have been considered illegal under the Sherman Antitrust Act of 1890 and the Clayton Antitrust Act of 1914. This exemption allowed companies to combine for fixing prices and for allocating customers in foreign markets. The MPEAA was able to act as the sole export sales agent for the companies, to set prices and terms of trade for the films, and to arrange the distribution abroad. By allowing the majors to unify legally, competition among the American companies overseas that might have proved detrimental for the American market was alleviated. The MPEAA performed services of expanding markets, keeping open existing markets, expediting transfers of income to the United States, reducing restrictions on American films through negotiation, disseminating information about market conditions to members, and negotiating film import agreements and rental terms. The MPEAA maintains headquarters in the United States, with an extensive network abroad in key film markets.[12]

During World War II, foreign governments passed currency restrictions that froze earnings generated by American companies. It was still preferable to obtain a share of the money and give up the rest than to refuse to export films and get nothing. By 1950, the overseas market took on greater importance than ever before and often determined whether the film would be profitable or would take a loss. In the 1950s, approximately 40 percent of all theatrical revenue came from the foreign market.[13] After the divorcement of the studios from their theaters and with the growth of television, the studios, no longer having a secure outlet, began producing fewer films. With fewer films produced in the United States, distributors sought out foreign films from England, France, Sweden, Italy, and Japan that could be acquired cheaply enough to render distributing them profitable.

In the early 1950s, Walter Reade established Continental Distributing to acquire foreign films for his theater in New York City. They then began distributing the imports to other theaters. Requiring a steady flow of product led Continental to begin investing in foreign film production.[14]

During the 1950s American investment increased in European films in an attempt to take over the small European markets. This also necessitated that the films be exploited in the United States. England, France, and Italy tried to establish their own distribution chains in America, but American distributors were able to maintain a monopoly in the United States while simultaneously strengthening their worldwide distribution networks. Therefore, foreign films could only profitably enter the American market by means of American companies.[15]

In England, the Rank Organization, believing the United States tried to discourage importation of English films in particular, announced in 1957 that they were establishing Rank Film Distributors of America to penetrate the United States market while evading American companies. Even though in two years they had set up ten offices and had licensed theaters in key cities, they had to go out of business. They found there was not enough audience support and they lacked the power of domestic distributors.[16]

Foreign governments instituted production subsidies to aid their domestic filmmakers. However, foreign subsidiaries of American companies were able to conform to the stipulations and qualify. They therefore had access to European subsidies and benefitted from programs designed to encourage European film production. In an attempt to appeal to the foreign market, to reduce production costs, and to create greater realism, many films began to shoot on location in foreign countries. Even though countries frequently restricted profits of films from being taken out of the country, they encouraged American producers to make their films in their country with that blocked currency. This factor further enticed production overseas. By the early 1960s, approximately 53 percent of all theatrical revenue was generated from foreign rentals.[17]

The foreign market has always been depended upon to supply a significant percentage of worldwide theatrical rentals, which in 1983 reached a new high of $2.1 billion.[18] Though the U.S. majors are estimated to be responsible for at least 80 percent of the Canadian film distribution market, Canadian rentals are included in the domestic rentals.[19]

For selling, the territorial order of importance descends from Japan, Italy, Germany, France, Spain, United Kingdom, Australia, Argentina, Sweden, to Mexico. The greatest annual earnings, however, descend from Germany, France, Japan, the United Kingdom, Spain, Italy, Australia, Mexico, Brazil, Argentina, to Sweden.[20] But in 1983, Japan provided the greatest revenue of any country, more than $114 million.[21]

Robert Myers divides the world market into forty principal areas covering 120 countries. He finds that problems specifically related to the foreign market include language, taxes, monopolies, playing time obligations, censorship, local printing, currency fluctuations, cassette piracy, and changing release patterns.[22]

While each territory has a specific value and potential, international markets suffer radical changes because of politics and economics. The foreign market goes up when the dollar is weak and it goes down when the dollar is strong, regardless of the same number of people in the theaters.[23] Consequently, while the total amount of revenue from specific foreign markets may appear high, the percentage of total film rentals may actually have decreased. Sudy Coy of Orion Pictures International claims that diminishing returns from the foreign market are largely due to the devaluation of currency and declining theatrical attendance. She claims while foreign revenue accounted for 50 percent of theatrical billings four years ago, foreign revenue accounted for only 35 percent in 1983.[24]

Some believe that U.S. companies exported too many money-losing movies. Foreign buyers became wary and thus reduced the amount of money they would pay for films. Others believe the market is suffering from too much product. The distributors, only interested in making money, have been able to convince buyers to purchase their pictures, regardless of the content. Latin American distributor Edward Sarlui stated, "We bring in an essentially worthless piece of film and we bring dollars out. Nobody knows what value to place on an unreleased film. It's a feeling."[25]

Overseas, there is no bidding for pictures. There are also fewer theater circuits. In most countries, a few exhibition circuits exist and if they do not pick up a film, it may not be released at all. As the foreign theatrical market declines, it is becoming more unpredictable, as 20 percent of the pictures earn 80 percent of the business.[26] Michael Solomon, chairman of Telepictures Corp., which distributes independent television product, claims that out of seventy foreign markets, 10 percent bring in 90 percent of all income.[27]

In the television market, foreign countries have been successful in controlling the importation of U.S. product. An organization's ability to sell a picture to foreign television markets is often a function of the country's laws. Most of Europe has state-run television. In Japan, which has state and private commercial television stations, only 3 percent of its entire programming can be imported.[28] Robert Myers stated that cassette sales in the United Kingdom exceed the box office gross, and Sweden's video income is greater than the box office revenue.[29] This switch in markets has created an insecure climate in many foreign countries.

The European Economic Community investigation charged U.S. distributors with crowding out European films from their own marketplace by block-booking and blind-bidding. MPEAA President Jack Valenti denied the practices, which would be a violation of the European Common Market rules safeguarding competition. Valenti questioned how it is possible to blind-bid after the pictures are in general release in the United States.[30]

The majors each used to have their own foreign branches overseas. For example, MGM alone used to have 101 foreign offices.[31] United Artists had 66 offices in 37 countries and 44 subdistributors in 22 countries.[32] They realized that greater efficiency could be gained by consolidating their operations. Paramount and Universal formed one joint company, Cinema International Corporation (CIC), to streamline their overseas operations. They are the world's largest film distributor, netting about 35 percent of American global theatrical revenues. In 1973, CIC picked up MGM and Disney territories. In 1981, they broadened into United International Pictures (UIP) to handle overseas distribution for Universal, Paramount, and MGM/UA.[33] Warner Bros. and Columbia have combined offices or have established local partnerships.[34] Twentieth Century-Fox is closing its foreign branches to use local distributors in major markets.[35] It is estimated that UIP gets at least 60 percent of its revenues from Europe, with France, Italy, Spain, and the United Kingdom contributing two-thirds of that amount.[36] UIP expects $400 million in rentals in 1983 from the approximately thirty-five features they will handle. UIP, operating in approximately forty countries, is successful because of the interaction between their sales and marketing departments and because they have strong films to handle.[37]

Producers selling their films in foreign territories may choose a major distributor to ensure an already existing exhibition network. The major may grant the producer consultation rights in marketing and may grant limits on the amount to be spent on marketing. They will charge most producers a 40 percent distribution fee for all foreign territories; those in the United Kingdom will be charged a 35 percent fee.[38] They also cross-collateralize all markets, which means that they use the total rental of all territories against the total expenses in all territories to calculate the net profit.

The majors can pick up films for overseas distribution with no intention of a domestic release. A picture acquired by a major for foreign distribution has to compete with their own product, which was financed by their company. The majors therefore have a greater vested interest in the success of their own productions.[39]

Some majors and independent domestic distributors give foreign independent distributing companies the rights to distribute their films in many territories. Foreign independent distributors are often preferred because they do not cross-collateralize one territory with another. If huge rentals are earned in one locale, they will not be offset by the losses in other countries. Many also offer a 50/50 split with all costs off-the-top.

In comparison to the majors' personnel who are often relocated executives or recently transferred from one territory to another, the independent distributors are local people with a sense of their market's mentality. Subdistributors are often important producers in their own territories and are influential with exhibitors.[40]

The outright sale of a film to a foreign distributor avoids supervision difficulties and the overhead of maintaining an operation. It is most used when a single film is distributed by a small company in the United States, with the producer retaining worldwide rights.[41]

The "institutional independent" is a company which produces a yearly lineup of films and can afford its own foreign distribution organization. The large independent sales organization has strong financial backing and can pay an overall advance guarantee to help a film get made. Smaller sales organizations with little capital may be as effective if they have dedicated people working for the film. A good film that is not too important to a large company may be better handled by a smaller company.[42]

Independent American distributors frequently distribute their films abroad through locally owned film exchanges in the various countries or territories. Their distribution deals are usually on a percentage basis similar to the deals an independent would make with a subdistributor domestically. Generally, the local distributor advances costs which are recouped from gross revenues to be shared 50/50. The local distributor, having a financial stake in the film, consequently has a vested interest in increasing box office revenues. If the American distributor advances costs, the foreign distributor only receives 30 to 35 percent of the rentals.[43] A filmmaker may be content to know that the foreign distributor is only receiving a 30 percent fee, yet if his incentive to market the picture is diminished, the filmmaker's profits will be diminished accordingly.

Recently, foreign sales agents, also known as foreign distributors or producer's representatives, have emerged as a liaison between independent producers and independent distributors abroad. It is their job to place a picture in as many theaters as possible in the county in which the distributor operates. Foreign sales agents receive a 10 to 25 percent commission, depending on their services and investment. Independent foreign sales companies make up the core of film market participants. These companies buy films for Europe, Latin America, Japan, Australia, the Far East, and Africa. Most did not exist more than five years ago. Hollywood's domination as a production center and the deterioration of foreign local film industries created the need for the formation of these new companies. Investors and independent producers were convinced they could get more money by controlling the foreign sales themselves via foreign sales agents. The foreign sales field was easy to break into. With one or two pictures to represent, preferably action-adventure, one was in business. Yet many foreign sales firms soon discovered they would have "to cause" films to be made to maintain an inventory for distribution abroad. In some instances, investments are made in productions in return for foreign sales rights. Foreign sales companies have become intrigued by the potential of cable and pay-television, and are forming divisions to sell the films they control in these new markets.[44]

In 1977 Mark Damon founded Producers Sales Organization (PSO), an international distribution and marketing company with a staff of seventy. Damon believes it is more advantageous for a producer to sell foreign territories independently than to allow a major to take 40 percent off-the-top and out of the remaining 60 percent to recoup prints, ads, and guarantees.[45]

Many companies use film markets as a primary source of selling pictures and may take a flat commission or a percentage for acquiring a certain amount in guarantees or advances. Generally, they receive 10 to 20 percent of the gross income for negotiating the deal. Terms are usually for five, ten, or fifteen years, with rights then reverting back to the producer. At the film markets they make arrangements with foreign distributors to release the picture by a certain date and to set minimum and maximum amounts for prints and advertising.

Foreign sales agents personally accompany a producer or filmmaker to festivals. Howard Goldfarb of Goldfarb Distributors finds their costs for festivals run between $50,000 and $75,000. When they take on a picture to distribute, they take on the responsibility to get it to the market. Goldfarb's foreign distribution deals generally secure 20 percent on signature of the deal with the balance due on delivery, within sixty to ninety days. Goldfarb will allow delay of payment and delivery if the distributor does not have available theaters in which to play the picture. Six months to one year after delivery, Goldfarb is lucky to receive 20 percent of the return. By eighteen months to two years, Goldfarb will have received 90 to 95 percent of what is owed to him.[46]

Wolf Schmidt, president of Kodiak Films, distributed domestically and was involved in foreign sales for twelve years. However, since domestic distribution became so expensive because of advertising costs and, therefore, dangerous for independents, Kodiak began to concentrate on foreign sales exclusively. To ensure a flow of product, they are involving themselves more in actual production.[47] Schmidt advises filmmakers to bring their pictures to them for consultation before they are completed. He believes he can make suggestions about what to include in the picture to enhance saleability. They are willing to finance reshooting or recasting if given the opportunity.[48]

It is often advisable not to attain pre-sales if one predicts a picture will be a huge grosser. If one leases a film in foreign territories using pre-sales, local distributors generally demand a 50 percent distribution fee. Yet there is no cross-collateralization and the producer may request consultation on marketing. If one leases the film without securing pre-sales, the foreign distributors ask only a 20 percent distribution fee. There is still no cross-collateralization and one can obtain adequate marketing control based on the potential of the film. Those who pre-buy do so to make money. Since they risk buying before seeing the finished product they expect a greater return for that risk. Producers generally use foreign pre-sales to minimize the downside risk and interest paid. Attorney Raymond L. Asher claims that if one pre-sells a film for more than the negative cost, the risk on how the film performs at the box office is minimized. Since guarantees are payable when the film is delivered, the producer has cash while waiting for box office receipts to come in, which can be used to pay off loans and halt interest.[49]

Patrick Wachsberger, a partner in J and M Sales, a foreign sales agency, believes the best time to pre-sell a movie is just before starting principal photography. It is then that expectation is high if it is believed the picture will actually be made. If the film is finished and is good, one can secure a much better deal; if it is bad, the producer will get little or nothing. To produce a $5 million film, J and M is able to secure 40 to 50 percent of the cost from pre-sales. He finds that Germany and Japan alone generally contribute 20 to 30 percent of the foreign market.[50]

It is crucial to select the right local distributor, one who is equipped to recommend a proper local title for the film, to suggest advertising, and to oversee the release schedule.[51] Generally, a film that grosses $1 million at the foreign box office returns approximately $200,000 to the film's owners. The remainder is exhausted by advertising expenses, the theaters, and subdistributors.[52]

The amount to be spent on prints and ads is increasingly being negotiated with distributors. If distributors spend too excessively it ultimately comes out of the producer's share. Yet the foreign distributors must have some freedom in the advertising of a picture. Every country has trade papers and magazines, along with general circulation publications, in which advertisements may be placed. One must also ensure that posters and other advertising accessories are delivered to foreign distributors to promote the picture. Individual ad campaigns must be created specifically for different countries with varying sensibilities.

The collection of foreign revenue is often difficult because of currency controls, screen quotas, and theater admission tax, in addition to unscrupulousness.[53] Distribution contract disputes often favor the local people.[54] Other abuses include double-billing a producer's film with a picture owned by the subdistributor, or giving more favorable terms for the subdistributor's film. Some subdistributors own theaters and distribute films in their theaters on their own unfair terms.[55]

Independents, in particular, have problems with accounting and financial returns. Unlike the majors that have a staff dedicated to such matters, the independents do not, and must obtain box office results and trade papers to see how much a picture has earned. Auditors and accounting firms can be employed to travel in the foreign marketplace to ensure accuracy in the reporting of rentals.

The foreign market offers hope to independents who may not have secured domestic distribution. Michael J. Solomon, chairman of Telepictures Corp., which distributes independent television product, finds that the international market is unlike the U.S. market. A greater variety of pictures is accepted, and he finds that foreign distributors and exhibitors are stunned by the general tendency in the United States to believe that "the only good picture is a film that makes money."[56] For example, Toho, a major distributor/exhibitor in Japan, paid a $700,000 advance for *My Tutor,* an independent picture that received little acclaim domestically.[57] *Piranha,* a small independent film, grossed $14 million in the foreign market.[58]

The foreign market has proven a valuable outlet for pictures that are not readily accepted in the United States. Although the foreign theatrical market is shrinking, it is being balanced by the foreign video and cable markets. Foreign buyers for American product often want and need a greater variety than can be theatrically exhibited in the United States. This prospect offers hope for the independent filmmaker and distributor and allows motion pictures to be a truly universal means of communication.

Ancillary Markets

Ancillary markets are very important to the independent filmmaker and distributor, as they often provide a significant percentage of a picture's total revenue. A few hundred thousand dollars or even a few million dollars may be insignificant to the major distributors; however, to an independent it can mean profit and the ability to produce or distribute additional pictures. The growth in strength and number of ancillary markets has begun to change the nature of the traditional distribution of a motion picture.

Since ancillary revenues usually depend upon a film's theatrical exposure, the distributor may open the film in markets where he expects to lose money. This exposure will, however, attract attention to the film and ensure a more lucrative ancillary sale. Theater exhibitors are very concerned about the shortening of "windows," or the length of time allotted between each market's release. They fear that if pictures are released too quickly to the other markets, the theatrical revenue will be threatened. Beginning in 1982, ancillary outlets began financing and controlling the production of their own features. These made for television movies and films made for pay television can be released theatrically overseas.

Many exhibitors fear pay television will lead to their demise. Ron Lesser believes that first-run theaters will remain the initial exhibition point, but that second and third runs will be eliminated. The films will be sold to cable instead, resulting in fewer theaters.[59]

It is not only the exhibitors who fear loss of market dominance. The major distributors also fear that the markets they do not control will become the major markets. George Lucas said:

> I've been saying for a long time that Hollywood is dead. That doesn't mean the film industry is dead. But for one region to dominate is dead, although it will take ten or fifteen years to have that visible. The filmmaker hasn't figured out that he doesn't need the agents and the studio executives. What is Hollywood? An antiquated, out-of-date distribution apparatus, a monopoly, a system designed to exploit the filmmaker. The system is collapsing because of new technologies. The movie companies are structured inefficiently. In good times, it doesn't show. But they won't be able to survive the bad times.[60]

Alan J. Hirschfield, chairman of Twentieth Century-Fox, noted:

> Despite the fact that our industry possesses the unique ability to produce the software...we're beset with problems of extraordinary costs, extraordinary risk and wholly inadequate return for our efforts and investments, both for ourselves and our creative partners.... It appears evident that we're looking at a profitless prosperity.[61]

Hirschfield's negative projection of the future, however, concerns the position of the motion picture studio. There is little evidence of a dwindling audience. With approximately twenty million homes equipped with pay cable in 1983, 395 new features were produced and released. Box office revenue rose 37 percent in actual dollars over the past three years. The box office gross of 1983 was $3.766 billion, or 9 percent higher than in 1982. Fifty-one to 52 percent of the box office gross remained with exhibitors. Admissions have risen more than 17 percent during the past three years, with nearly two billion tickets sold, more than has been sold in the past twenty-two years.[62] *Indiana Jones and the Temple of Doom* recorded the biggest six-day gross in motion picture history, more than $42 million, and a single-day gross record of $9.3 million.[63]

Hollywood's lowest point was in 1973 when only fourteen million people went to the movies weekly, compared to forty-four million weekly in 1946. However, hits like *The Godfather, The Exorcist, Jaws,* and *Star Wars* revived apathetic audiences.[64] In the 1980s films have grossed more than ever imagined possible. It demonstrates that a film that moves the audience will be viewed, enjoyed, and viewed again.

Regardless of how society changes, people still respond emotionally to human issues. Filmmakers repeatedly resort to old stories. Remakes of old films are considered a secure investment because the film has already proven itself at the box office. Producers of remakes attempt to improve on the original and make them contemporary for audiences who were too young to have seen or remembered them. Not everyone, however, has lost faith in the theatrical market. Though the growth of ancillary markets has reduced the reissue of films not all have been released to these other markets. In addition to the repertory circuit, approximately sixty films were reissued in 1983, more than the fifty-five in 1982. Walt Disney's Buena Vista Distribution rereleases their pictures in approximately six-to-seven year cycles. *Fantasia,* an exception, is selectively released as an event. Their one to two annual reissues meet seasonal needs. *Snow White and the Seven Dwarfs,* a 1937 animated feature, made $14.5 million in domestic rentals in 1983 and was surpassed by only twenty-seven new pictures released in 1983. Buena Vista believes their reissues are successful because of the exhibition of prints in excellent condition and new marketing campaigns designed especially for contemporary audiences. They generally rerelease eight hundred or more prints for a summer launch and at least one thousand prints for a Christmas release, requiring $5 million to $8 million. They do not believe that television exposure necessarily reduces a film's theatrical potential. Both *Alice in Wonderland* and *Dumbo* have had television exposure prior to effective reissues. Universal, with Steven Spielberg's approval, has committed not to sell *E.T. The Extra-Terrestrial* to any other media before a theatrical reissue. They believe the short-term revenues will not prove to be as great as what will be generated in the long term.[65]

A demonstration of the need to adapt to the changing marketplace was made by Walt Disney Pictures. They unveiled Touchstone Films, a new division to produce more mature movies than the stereotypic Disney product. Its first film, *Splash,* opened to great success on 9 March 1984.

While creating new opportunities, the new distribution technologies upset the balance of power in the motion picture industry. Different markets in different countries and in the United States are at varying stages of development.

Filmed entertainment is appearing in more places than in just the theater. A desire for additional sources of filmed entertainment is evident by the growth of the videogame industry, which increasingly incorporates the latest technology. Games now contain live-action film footage and animation sequences combined for interactive play. Another new invention which uses motion pictures is the video jukebox now being operated commercially. Because of prohibitive costs, there are still only approximately one thousand in operation.[66]

Movie bars have been created where a person can eat and drink while watching a picture.[67] Another market that provides revenue from a motion picture includes exhibiton in airplanes. In-flight movies began in 1961 and have become the first window for films after theatrical release. Films are shown in-flight ninety days after release for generally eighty-five dollars per flight.[68] The three major distribution companies of these films are Avicom, Transcom, and Inflight. Transcom, serving sixty airlines, had film rentals in 1973 of close to $150,000 and in 1983 of more than $15 million. Eastern Airlines uses an anonymous film reviewer who rates films on a scale of one to ten on how the film is expected to play. The reviews are combined with age demographics of the flight's passengers. Films are often edited by the producers to flight lengths and are run on Super 8 or video equipment.[69]

Other important markets include the Armed Services, the educational market, merchandising, publications, music publishing, and soundtrack. Though these individual markets may not supply great revenue for a particular film, they allow a motion picture to reach a wider audience. The newer markets, however, offer the possibility for revenue that can exceed theatrical rentals. The main areas of growing importance are television, pay cable, and home video. Instead of distributors and exhibitors trying to eliminate the competition, it can be viewed positively if the success in other markets increases the overall audience. Leo A. Handel wrote that a positive correlation exists between media and that different communications media stimulate interest in each other.[70]

Network Television

Historically, television is blamed for the reduction in the moviegoing habit. Television continues to command the audiences and ultimately influences what people expect from motion pictures. Samuel Goldwyn wrote, "It is a certainty that people will be unwilling to pay to see poor pictures when they can stay home and see something which is, at least, no worse."[71] In the introduction of *Fast Forward,* Les Brown wrote:

> A book that sells 30,000 copies thanks to the praise of critics is a hit; a play that is SRO for a season in a 1,000-seat house is a smash. But a television show with a prime-time audience of 20 million viewers is a failure, even though that single night's audience is sufficient to fill a fair-sized Broadway theater to capacity every performance, for forty years.
>
> Moreover, television doesn't need reviews, as the other art forms do, to help it amass an audience. Television generates its own audience just by being television. People watch in predictable numbers every time period of the week, regardless of what is being shown.[72]

The National Association of Broadcasters released a study that found viewer attitudes toward television are "overwhelmingly negative" and almost a total reversal of six years ago when opinion was favorable. People felt dissatisfied, less entertained, were less impressed with it technically, and believed it to be a negative social influence. Yet audiences have not dwindled but have actually increased.[73]

The Nielsen Television Index, which continually provides estimates of television viewing and nationally sponsored network program audiences, found that women view television more than men, older men and women view more than younger age groups, and younger children view more than older children and teenagers. It also showed that situation comedies attract the largest prime time overall audiences.[74]

After initial resistance, the motion picture industry adapted to television's entertainment force in the world. Studios realized television's demand for product and began relying on television for an additional source of revenue. This outlet, however, dwindled when the purchase costs became so high that the networks realized they could produce their own movies-of-the-week for less. Instead of spending up to $10 million for several airings of a blockbuster, they could produce a movie for a few million dollars, often with greater audience interest. Frank J. Moreno, president of the Frank Moreno Company, states that whereas one out of ten pictures once was able to secure a network sale, now only one out of twenty-five does so.[75] Syndication is now a bigger market for films than the network sale. Syndicators often use "the ribbon," or a general theme, to package nine to twelve pictures together for a sale.

Television has used marketing research as a tool in decision making. The TVQ, a statistical procedure for rating television personalities and programs, is conducted by Marketing Evaluations to assess the popularity of network programming and to give a rating for performers based on likability and familiarity to members of households who fill out TVQ questionnaires. They claim 90 percent of their clients are from New York-based advertising agencies. Subscribers to the service pay up to $8,000 a year for the "performer Q," published annually, and the quarterly "progamming Q." Three different surveys are conducted and include 5,400 people responding to the questionnaires from 3,750 households. The Screen Actors Guild, as well as minority groups, are against this system. They find that the surveys themselves are restrictive in not including a wide range of people. They also believe that since casting decisions are often based on these statistics, their talent and opportunity are also restricted. Motion picture producers have also employed such surveys to assist in casting selection.[76]

Television also employs research in testing new completed programs, and each season numerous television programs or "pilots" are made of scripts. After millions of dollars are spent on producing the shows, they are tested and most are never aired. The cost, often in excess of $1 million for one never aired pilot, could easily finance an independent theatrical feature. This system is an example of the belief in the inability to test elements prior to a script being realized on film or tape. Because of the even greater cost of major motion pictures, they cannot so easily be abandoned. Since so much has been invested, there is a need to release the picture to justify the expense.

The networks' share of the total viewing audience has decreased from 91 percent in 1978–79 to 81 percent for 1982–83. Pay-television now commands 7 percent of the audience. Of those watching non-network programming, 39 percent watched pay-television. Since the networks have been losing a share of the audience to pay-television, they are considering bidding to acquire feature films again because they believe it is the feature film that attracts audiences to pay-television.[77]

Pay-Television

Ralph Lee Smith observed that history was marked in May 1980 when the National Cable Television Association convention opened in Dallas. Innumerable people who were not directly involved in the cable industry from all fields were drawn to the convention by a sense that "something momentous was happening in America." Smith wrote:

> It was clear that America was on the threshold of becoming a "wired nation," that in the next few years homes and offices all across the country would be equipped for cable television, the rapidly expanding technology that creates dozens of new channels in each community, foreseeably as many as, or more than, fifty.[78]

Pay-television is an outgrowth of cable television, first designed to transmit better commercial television signals to homes in areas of poor reception. This was first accomplished by use of a community antenna that picked up signals from nearby metropolitan areas and transmitted them to the subscribers' sets over a coaxial cable. Programs came to be imported from commercial television stations outside the community's normal viewing area. Since cable channels required government approval for hookup, the government also required them to provide facilities for local productions as well as transmission. In essence, the government required these distributors to also produce product. In the early 1970s the reduction in the amount of federal regulation of the cable companies and the communications satellite technology that made possible simultaneous delivery of programming to cable operators throughout the country contributed to cable television's growth. Prior to satellite's introduction, a few pay-television programs were transmitted on a local basis. Local operators, generally charging from seven to ten dollars for the basic cable service, found they could double their income by providing an additional pay-television service. Home Box Office was a pioneer in providing films shown over local cable systems. Finally, when HBO began using a satellite in 1975 and created a nationwide network, its sales expanded immensely. While cable is the dominant mode of transmission of home video to the subscriber, pay-television programming can be delivered by microwave, by scrambling a broadcast signal and using a decoder, or by a satellite in conjunction with a dish antenna aimed at the satellite.[79]

In the last five years, the most dramatic change in the economics of the business has been the growth of sales to and revenue from pay-cable and home video markets. The percentage of total revenues contributed by worldwide theatrical film rentals dropped from 81.6 percent to 58.8 percent, and for the first time domestic film rentals constituted less than 50 percent of the total revenue share. During this time, pay-cable television fees rose from 1.4 percent to 17.4 percent. Home video royalties had grown from being virtually nonexistent to 8 percent of all revenues. The new ancillary markets represent 25 percent of total film revenues, which is approximately the reduction in global theatrical rentals. Network revenue dropped from 13.1 percent to 8.7 percent in the same five-year period, making it the first time in more than a decade when network license fees constituted less than 10 percent of the total gross income.[80]

The first year pay-television appeared on studio balance sheets was in 1978 when it accounted for 2 percent of all film revenues. It has since increased by more than 900 percent, representing nearly 20 percent of the revenue produced by each feature.[81]

Pay-television offers movies to people in their own home, free of commercials and censorship. A film can be presented uninterrupted and unedited. Producers sell films to pay-television based on the number of subscribers. If a producer's film is distributed by a studio, the theatrical losses are cross-collateralized with pay-television revenue, in addition to other markets. A filmmaker may opt to make a direct deal with pay-television. Selling the pay-television rights, however, may reduce the chances of securing a favorable distribution deal and may eliminate the possibility completely. The pay-television "window," or the amount of time that must elapse after theatrical exhibition prior to television exhibition, is approximately nine months to one year and is decreasing.

Pay-television middlemen have established themselves as the motion picture distributors to cable households.[82] Many pay-television channels have proliferated and many have gone bankrupt. Yet Home Box Office remains strong with two-thirds of the nation's pay-cable market. They have been and continue to be experimental long-range thinkers in the industry.

In 1971 New York cable television pioneer Charles F. Dolan founded Sterling Communications, which was later acquired by Time, Inc. He envisioned a combination of films and sports delivered by microwave to be offered as an optional channel by cable operators to their subscribers. In 1972 Dolan hired Gerald M. Levin, a lawyer, to draw up the plan to secure rights to programming. Levin coined the name Home Box Office (HBO) and served as chief executive from 1973, when Dolan left, until 1979. Levin believes four early decisions were critical to HBO's success. They decided to provide a steady flow of entertainment on a subscription basis instead of charging for viewing individual events. Programming would consist of more than just movies. They fostered a sentiment of partnership with cable-television operators by asking them to affiliate with HBO instead of HBO merely licensing channels from the operators. This included allowing operators to keep half of all subscriber fees. And they decided to become a national network, using microwave transmission as early as 1975.[83] In 1975 HBO leased an RCA satellite and initiated the first national pay network to cable systems.[84]

In 1978 HBO began a series of strategic moves. They spent more than $35 million to license more than one hundred films even though they had only 1.5 million subscribers. In 1980, when they realized subscribers would pay for more than one service, they launched Cinemax as a sister service to offer foreign and art films.[85] In 1981, HBO spent $133 million on movie payments, surpassing the largest chains, General Cinema and United Artists, for the first time. In 1982, they instituted "pre-buys" or paying for the rights to exhibit a film before it is theatrically distributed. These pre-buy deals involved license fee guarantees of generally 25 percent of a film's negative cost. Though Paramount, Universal, and Warner Bros. threatened that they would not handle any picture whose pay rights were pre-sold, it was too late. By November 1981, HBO had struck a limited-exclusivity deal with Columbia Pictures. In February 1982, by assisting Mike Medavoy to form Orion Pictures from Filmways for $10 million in cash, HBO secured equity in Orion and exclusivity on all the company's films.[86]

HBO cofounded Tri-Star on 30 November 1982, a movie-making venture which Columbia and CBS capitalized at $400 million. Tri-Star licensed to HBO the pay-TV rights to at least thirty-six films during its first four and one-half years. In March 1983, HBO also masterminded a $125 million film production limited partnership venture called "Silver Screen Partners," the first of a series of limited partnerships, using pay-TV guarantees to attract capital. HBO is granted approval of all films in exchange for a promise to buy the pay-TV rights and pay back investors if they do not break even on the film's production costs in five years.[87] E.F. Hutton's "Silver Screen I" attracted $83 million to distribution through Tri-Star.[88]

HBO now has complete control over the creation and distribution of their programming in the United States and is expanding into the foreign market. HBO and Showtime/The Movie Channel have become partners overseas in the British pay-cable Premiere venture, with Columbia, Twentieth Century-Fox, Warner Bros., and the British Goldcrest and Premiere's partner, Thorn EMI Screen Entertainment.[89]

As pay-television was slowly growing, HBO took the initiative of expanding their domain. After HBO had already gained considerable stability and was becoming more powerful, the studios and exhibitors finally began to take notice. Robert Selig, president of the 1900–screen Theatre Association of California, stated that HBO is "the devil within our industry. . . . it will so dominate the industry—and is so doing—and the source of supply that the very position of the theatres as the primary source of motion picture entertainment may be threatened."[90] The motion picture industry did not realize the potential of pay-TV until the late 1970s when they could not ignore how much money they were losing out on. In pay-television, the theatrical distributors keep less than 20 percent of the revenues. The cable operator, or exhibitor, gets approximately 50 percent of subscriber fees and the balance goes to the pay-TV network which functions as the distributor. Nearly a quarter of the nation's total, almost eighteen million homes, receive one or more pay channels.[91]

Though the motion picture industry has attacked HBO for its power, they are also accusing HBO of trying to decrease their dependency on the studio-produced motion picture. HBO is increasingly becoming more like the networks in their scheduling. They are emphasizing original weekly series to build viewer loyalty.[92] An HBO report revealed that some of its original programming scored far better with the subscribers than did theatrical motion pictures. Pay-TV networks believe that audiences are satisfied with the appearance of a schedule full of new programs. Two or three major programs or movies per month keep audience ratings and satisfaction scores at acceptable levels.[93]

The studios, believing they were being left out of their fair share of the pay-cable revenue, made several attempts to enter the competition. In 1980 the Justice Department sued the four studios which formed the pay-television service Premiere. The studios, claiming they would withhold their films from competitive services for nine months, lost on antitrust grounds.[94]

Paramount Pictures Corp. and MCA's Universal were involved in a joint venture of a merger of Showtime and The Movie Channel. The Justice Department voiced that it would sue to block the deal on antitrust grounds. The Justice Department, however, did approve the merger of Showtime and The Movie Channel, since only one motion picture company is involved. (The Movie Channel is co-owned by American Express and Warner Communications.)[95] This merger of the second largest (Showtime) and the third largest (The Movie Channel) pay-television services reduces the domination of HBO. Because of HBO's strength, it only has to pay approximately twenty cents per subscriber for the same film costing Showtime or The Movie Channel fifty cents per subscriber.[96] By combining efforts, Showtime and The Movie Channel not only hope to reduce costs but aim to improve their buying power. Films comprise three-fourths of most pay-television schedules.[97]

Arbitron Ratings claims 39 percent of the country's television homes are hooked up to cable.[98] A study by A.C. Nielsen Co. revealed that pay-cable penetration drops by almost 50 percent in households that have video cassette recorders. Such households frequently rent video cassettes. Pay-cable penetration was 42 percent in homes with recorders that did not rent video cassettes and only 23.8 percent in homes that did rent them.[99]

A study undertaken by RCA Corporation hypothesizes that by 1990, revenues from pay-television will rise to $16.3 billion, or three times what the theatrical box office is expected to be. Consumer spending for home video software will increase from $500 million to $6.2 billion during the next eight years. These predictions are ominous for those who have a greater share in box office receipts than in ancillary revenues. In an attempt to obtain the ancillary revenues more quickly and to avoid the diminuition in value of the film from pirating, a film will play for less time in theaters. Approximately three or four months after the first-run theatrical release, the film will be sold or rented to the public on video cassettes and video discs. Cable distributors are anxious to put the picture on pay-TV while the advertising for theatrical exhibition is still fresh. Because many foreign countries have little selection on television, the home video market is larger in these territories than in the United States. Some speculate that the home video market in these foreign territories will become the primary market. [100]

The major elements in pay-television agreements are when "the window" will commence and how long it will last. Other elements include whether rights are exclusive or non-exclusive, the number of exhibition days and the number of transmissions, and whether compensation is via flat fee or per subscriber. [101]

According to a survey conducted by Carmel-based Paul Kagan Associates, pay-TV networks in 1983 spent $805 million on programming, a 29 percent increase from the $623 million spent in 1982. Of the total spent in 1983, $594 million was spent for rights to broadcast motion pictures, a $100 million increase from 1982. Original programming costs were $211 million in 1983, up from $143 million in 1982. [102]

The cable industry, however, is trying to provide new and unique programming for their subscribers. For example, the Mood Channel offers such scenes as aquariums and fireplaces to affect feelings. Other programs are more intellectually stimulating. Cable-Satellite Public Affairs Network (C-Span) began televising sessions of the U.S. House of Representatives and has expanded to cover a range of official government activities.

New concepts in programming, regardless of the means of distribution, have been successful. Music Television (MTV) is a twenty-four-hour music video channel similar to a radio format that plays popular rock songs with a visual image included. When Warner Amex, a joint venture of Warner Communications and American Express, began MTV, they met with almost universal resistance. Even the music industry did not believe the concept would succeed. When MTV went on the air 1 August 1981, it was unable to secure time on key cable systems in New York and Los Angeles. They therefore designed a series of commercials in 1982 that featured rock stars urging listeners to demand MTV. The campaign was a huge success. At the end of the year, they were adding 750,000 homes a month. [103]

MTV originated on pay-cable and is now influencing the motion picture industry. The music segments or "videos" that are the staple of the channel have become so popular that they may serve as an added attraction in theaters or may even become a new entertainment in theaters. The videos exhibited on MTV have even had an indirect influence on the motion picture. With the goal of injecting into films what is perceived to be attractive to young audiences, many pictures have added these music and dance segments, often without relevance to the story. These pieces may be filmed with the goal of being exposed on MTV for advertising purposes. MTV programming, initially rejected as an idea that would not work, has proven to have affected all areas of the industry.

It was believed that foreign films and independent pictures would be a main element in cable programming. However, these films once again do not attract sufficient viewers to make it profitable. In their programming of pictures, however, when audience tastes were measured, pictures appealing to a wider audience took favor.[104]

Pay-per-View

Pay-per-view refers to a program that is transmitted to a home in return for payment for that specific show. Exhibitors fear that since pay-per-view could eliminate enormous marketing costs, studios will mercilessly turn to it without concern for the exhibitor's welfare. Producers claim the theatrical audience is different from the pay-per-view audience, and that pay-per-view is expanding the market and not reducing the theater-going audience. Though research backs up the belief that the pay-per-view audience is older and does not go out to movies, exhibitors still fear their market will dwindle. When cable or a system to receive pay-per-view is in more homes, the cost of production could be made back in one night. An enormous amount of money could be saved on interest and on the traditional means of distribution that require months and years to recoup revenues. Pay-per-view would allow studios to retain control over their films, as they could distribute it themselves and retain the profits instead of distributing it through a channel like HBO.

Alan J. Hirschfield, chairman of Twentieth Century-Fox, believes a pay-per-view movie will earn forty, eighty, or one hundred twenty million dollars in a single night. Also, these distributors of pay-per-view hope to retain 70 to 80 percent of the revenue compared to the approximately 40 percent return that theatrical distribution provides. In 1978, Columbia's *The Deep* was shown pay-per-view over ON-TV in Los Angeles. Of their twenty thousand subscribers, more than half paid three dollars to see it, even though it had already played for several months in theaters. In 1981, a Rolling Stones concert and the Sugar Ray Leonard/Thomas Hearns welterweight championship fight were aired as pay-per-view events. In September 1982,

Star Wars was the first movie shown nationally on pay-per-view. Even though it was released on video cassette and was playing as a reissue in theaters, approximately 30 percent of subscribers paid eight dollars to see it.[105]

Universal Pictures experimented with the $12 million theatrical version of *The Pirates of Penzance* by opening it simultaneously in selected theaters and as a pay-per-view telecast. Since exhibitors are adamantly opposed to pay-per-view, it could only be booked into smaller theaters. Only about 10 percent of the potential pay-per-view audience chose to view it, and the box office revenue was also very disappointing. This study, however, does not take into account that there may have been a very limited audience for this picture regardless of how it was released.

Pay-per-view offers a direct service to the people who want to see a film in one's own home. If proven to generate more revenue than it extracts from other markets, it will become an important additional source of income. Yet pay-per-view movies still have to be known by the public so they will pay to see them. Theatrical distribution has been the barometer of a film's worth in ancillary markets. However, research has discovered that some films that do poorly in the theaters are heavily viewed on cable. A disparate audience seems to exist with access to cable. David Londoner believes that pay-per-view will be successful when it can be employed on impulse.[106] If a viewer can pick a film merely by pushing a button and be billed later, Londoner believes it will be best positioned.

HBO already accepts pay-per-view and does not want to acquire pay-TV rights to a film later than three months after it is a pay-per-view event. The studios' research indicates that a pay-per-view event should be aired nine to twelve months before it is available in other outlets as incentive for subscribers to pay the higher fee required by their technology and marketing. The studios worry that pay-per-view may not be able to be tested appropriately since pay-per-view cannot now match the dollars offered by an HBO deal. HBO has also been acquiring rights to other markets, such as syndicated television and direct broadcast satellite.[107]

Direct broadcast satellite allows transmission of programming via satellite directly to subscribers equipped with a disk-shaped antenna on their roofs or nearby. It is predicted that films will be broadcast to theaters by satellite transmission within ten years. This would eliminate the physical needs for quantities of prints and related shipping.

Home Video

Home video refers to non-broadcast programming generally viewed on a television monitor. Video cassettes and video discs are the primary markets of home video. Pay-television appears to have become a more stagnant marketplace with revenue having reached a plateau, whereas home video is still experiencing a great growth. Producers are even acquiring all production funds from home video distributors and pictures are being produced exclusively for this expanding market.

The fastest growing market for independently produced pictures is home video. Producers can recoup as much as 25 percent of the budget for $8 million to $10 million pictures.[108] In the mid-seventies, pictures went from theaters to television where distributors received approximately $2.5 million from the networks per picture. Today, home video and pay-cable account for $4 million to $5 million per picture, while networks pay $2 million to $3 million per picture. Even though ten million homes with video cassette recorders account for 250 million tape rentals in the United States, distributors see only a portion of the revenues because of the sales to retailers. The $450 million license fees paid to producers in 1983 was only 18 percent of that industry's total revenues.[109]

A recent RCA Corp. study projected that theatrical revenues will reach only $5.6 billion by the end of the decade, while worldwide retail revenues of pre-recorded video cassettes and video discs will approach $10 billion. It is based on a forecast of a population of forty million video players in the United States and seventy million in the rest of the world by the end of the decade.[110] The study concluded, however, that both video and theatrical revenues would be less than pay-TV's projected $16.3 billion revenue in 1990.[111]

The rise of the video cassette market and cable television has reduced the art theater audience. People are now able to see pictures at their own convenience, have the security of knowing they will not miss a picture, and have access to rent it anytime they want.

A UCLA School of Management study based on the consumption habits of fourteen hundred video cassette recorder owners showed that one-third of them prefer to see films in theaters first, and generally see a picture within a month of theatrical release. Robert Klingensmith, Paramount Home Video's senior vice president in charge of video distribution, conducted a study which found 60 percent polled saying "they might buy the cassette of a movie that they had enjoyed in a theater if it were available for purchase." A subsequent UCLA study overseen by Klingensmith demonstrated that substantially reduced retail prices on cassettes would sharply enhance sales. He believes cassettes of feature films are a supplementary market and not an alternative to filmgoing.[112]

Paramount decided in 1983 to offer *Flashdance* cassettes for $39.95 the weekend after Labor Day while the film was still in theatrical release, playing on six hundred screens in its fifth month and still generating more than $3 million weekly at the box office. Contrary to fear that everyone would stop going to the film, business increased 10 percent over the Labor Day weekend.[113] *Flashdance* continued selling tickets even after it was sold on video cassette and disk in September. It proved that a spring picture does not have to be pushed aside by summer releases. It is also an example of the extraordinary amount of money that can be recouped outside theaters. *Flashdance* cost $9.5 million to produce and earned $36 million in film rentals in the United States and Canada. It is expected to bring in $27 million in non-theatrical revenues.[114] The advertising campaign for the video cassette even added to box office grosses. Klingensmith estimated that sales for video cassettes would have increased by a hundred thousand, worth $4 million in retail sales to theater owners, if *Flashdance* video cassettes had been available in theaters during its entire run.[115]

Raiders of the Lost Ark sold more than 545,000 cassettes for $39.95, totaling $21.7 million. The studio generally receives 60 percent of this gross. Each cassette costs eight to ten dollars to make, and the producer's cut is generally 20 percent of the studio's gross.[116]

The major elements of video cassette and video disk license agreements include the system for which the rights are granted. The term, the territory, and whether the compensation is to be advanced, guaranteed, or in the form of royalties, are delineated. Other factors to be considered include container charges, fluctuations in price, club operations, foreign sales, free goods, and promotional copies.[117]

European countries are finally beginning to establish pay-cable. Video cassettes and disks, however, are already big business. International sales in video cassettes are outpacing domestic sales. Terry Semel, President and Chief Operations Officer of Warner Bros., wrote, "Over the next year or two, cassette revenues overseas may equal, if not exceed, theatrical revenues." Studios have distributed cassettes in only about ten to twenty countries overseas. Since such a great potential exists in other countries with the lack of competition from pay cable and pay-television, studios are aggressively moving to get into as many countries as possible.[118]

A new move to turn theater lobbies into sales and rental marts for video cassettes of pictures has begun. The 150–screen San Francisco-based Syufy Enterprises circuit has agreed to sell cassettes of Paramount features. Since non-theater related outlets now monopolize the market, it may be wise for theater owners to stop opposing the video cassette industry. Attempts to sell video cassettes at theaters have failed in the past, but those tests are thought to have been premature. A rental operation would involve $35,000 to $40,000 per theater for a library of approximately seven hundred titles. Exhibitors are hesitant about making this investment.[119]

Ritter-Geller Communications is now testing video cassette rental in supermarkets. They believe markets are a prime location for sales and rentals because they offer the consumer the convenience of acquiring the tapes as part of a regular necessary errand.[120] The video rental dealers are analogous to the exchanges, only now the customer is the individual instead of the exhibitor.

In 1981 Maxwell's Video Store in Erie, Pennsylvania, began a nickelodeon business. They created twenty booths for rent at $5 apiece. Each could accommodate four people who could watch legitimate video cassettes on a television set while enjoying free popcorn. Their business was successful, grossing between $250,000 and $300,000 per year.[121]

New technologies and novel means of distribution have produced areas of controversy. The very function of a video tape recorder was questioned by the major distributors who believed that they were being unfairly eliminated from participation in repeat showings of recorded programs or by the showing of a tape to several people. The individual's right to use the material at one's own convenience was upheld by the "Fair Use" doctrine. The "Fair Use" doctrine states that "fair use is 'a privilege in others than the owners of a copyright to use the copyrighted material in a reasonable manner without his consent, notwithstanding the monopoly granted to the owner by the copyright.'"[122]

Cassettes are often rented hundreds of times for a few dollars, while the producers do not receive any share of this revenue. This is because of the First Sale Doctrine, whereby the distributor relinquishes all rights to the buyer or cassette retailer, who may resell the cassette or rent it over and over again. Therefore, the cost of the cassette to the retailer is greatly increased in an attempt to secure a portion of the rental money in advance. Unfortunately, this also prices the item beyond the reach of the people who may want to buy it.[123]

In 1976 Walt Disney Productions and Universal City Studios filed a copyright suit against the Sony Corp., manufacturer of the Betamax video recorder.[124] The Supreme Court ruled on 17 January 1984 that the practice of home video taping is not a violation of copyright laws. It ruled that "time shifting," the practice of taping shows for later viewing, is a fair use of the product. It also ruled that the manufacturers of video cassette recorders are not "contributory infringers." Sony, therefore, cannot be held legally responsible even if the Betamax recorder were being used in a way that violated copyright law. However, whether VCR owners may record shows transmitted over pay-cable television was left unclear.[125]

Because of the great number of recorders already owned and the increasing demand, the industry believes that it should be compensated for the use of its product. Jack Valenti proposed that a system to pay royalty fees on the purchase price of video recorders and blank tapes be instituted.[126]

Alan Cole-Ford, an analyst with Paul Kagan Associates, stated that in 1983 the six major studios earned more than $428 million by licensing their films to pay-TV services, while the three major commercial networks paid

$260 million in 1983 for feature films. The studios, however, made an estimated $820 million from their worldwide sales of pre-recorded video cassettes, accounting for 82 percent of the $1 billion business.[127] Because the market is so large, it is unlikely that companies will withhold their films from the air in opposition to the ruling.

When cassettes and inexpensive recording machines became available, piracy in the record business escalated. In the United States alone, between counterfeiting and piracy, more than $600 million a year is estimated being lost in the record business. The film industry is now facing a similar situation. Pirated video films are shown in public places abroad. In this situation, the tape is not paid for and box office revenue is lost since it is viewed for free.[128] In 1975 the MPAA launched an antipiracy drive. Since then, three hundred film and video piracy convictions have been reported. Globally, more than $1 billion dollars a year is lost to pirates.[129]

Unlikely offenders are being discovered. The MPAA has sued the state of Wisconsin for engaging in the illegal public showing of rented video cassettes to prison inmates.[130] The U.S. Air Force is allegedly engaging in video piracy by supporting duplication facilities which may be producing hundreds of thousands of illegal cassettes each year at its overseas bases. An Air Force spokesman claimed the copying was for private use only. The MPAA claims the Air Force is committing the violations of illegal duplication and illegal public performance by screening cassettes in an open area for a price. The Air Force claims it is not doing it for a profit motive.[131]

Alan Hirschfield believes exhibitors contribute to video cassette piracy because they demand a four to six month duration from theatrical exhibition to video. He finds that during that period, the pirates are selling video cassettes. He stated:

> If we can't get our proper share or proper price from exhibitors, then we will have to debut our movies on video cassettes all over the country on a rental basis with perhaps a pay-per-view showing to accompany it and just a few showcase theaters to validate them as films. We must evaluate this need for new distribution systems which are relevant to where audiences now see films—in the home.[132]

He claims piracy and the government's failure to protect copyrighted material is severely reducing the industry's potential profits. Though strongly opposed by theatrical exhibitors, he believes a solution is the shortening of windows to home video release to one month or less and the repeal of the First Sale Doctrine to enable distributors to recoup a greater share of cassette rental revenues.[133]

Exhibitors are angry over the unrestricted access by teens to R-rated features or video cassettes, which they are not permitted to see without parental accompaniment at theaters. Exhibitors complain that they lose teenaged patrons at the box office since they cannot get in, and lose money when the film is available on cassettes, where people see it at home. Exhibitors fear that even if theater standards are applied to video stores, 17-year-olds will buy or rent the tapes for younger teenagers. Currently, there is a general six-month window on theatrical release of R-rated features before they are marketed on video cassettes. Exhibitors want this window extended and threaten that they will not be responsible for policing ratings if no remedy is found to stop the video competition. Yet this could be worse for the industry in the future since communities depend upon the ratings and the accompanying enforcements.[134]

Theaters with limited audiences have booked subsequent run features only after the rental terms were reduced. However, with the growth of cassette sales and rentals and cable exhibition, to capture any audience left from the first run, exhibitors will have to book a film earlier and pay higher fees. Each of the new markets poses a threat to exhibitors and distributors who fear a portion of their audience will be lured away and who have not learned to adapt to stay in business.

Technological Future of Filmed Entertainment

As science advances, numerous attempts to create a more fulfilling viewing experience have been made. People have always looked ahead and imagined what technology would create. In 1907 the need for technological standardization of motion picture film was recognized. A consensus known as the Motion Picture Patents Agreement was reached to define 35mm width as the standard motion picture film. In 1916, the Society of Motion Picture Engineers, today known as the Society of Motion Picture and Television Engineers, was formed to aid and perpetuate technological standardization. After World War II the American Standards Association became the American National Standards Institute, and was created to act as a strong organization for voluntary national and international standardization.[135] During the Depression, the economic disaster facing the country did not adversely affect the motion picture industry. The momentary panacea was the introduction of sound. When Warner Bros. was on the verge of bankruptcy in 1926, they invested in the Vitaphone process and introduced *Don Juan* with synchronized musical accompaniment. In 1927, they presented *The Jazz Singer* with synchronized speech. Attendance grew from sixty million paid admissions per week in 1927 to more than a hundred million in 1929.[136] Films have usually had some sort of sound accompaniment, whether it was music used to drown out projector noise or to create an emotional atmosphere. Early showmen hired "barkers," who were commentators who attempted synchronized speech with the film. They were replaced when subtitles entered the picture. Pianos and orchestras soon became commonplace. The large film companies prepared musical scores and cue sheets specifically for distribution with their films.[137] Loew's scheme, which he called Humanova, involved placing actors behind the motion picture screen to speak the dialogue in the film.[138]

To ensure a monopoly in sound, American Electrical Industries bought up the patents on competing sound systems in the United States and abroad. They then entered into trade agreements with the firms that would not sell. They were able to acquire world control and hastily began marketing their equipment to European studios and theaters. Sound on film was rapidly standardized all over the world.[139]

After the novelty of sound wore off and became accepted as commonplace, audiences began to dwindle. Even with reduced admission prices, games like Screeno, Banko, and Bingo, and the addition of double features to lure the audience back, weekly attendance dropped to sixty million in 1932 and 1933. The studios, expecting the theater attendance levels to remain constant, had overextended themselves financially. Their heavy investments in studio equipment, the costs of converting to sound, mortgage payments, and heavy interest on loans all added to their financial troubles.[140] The motion picture industry lost $83 million in 1932 and $40 million in 1933.[141]

The motion picture industry picked up at the end of the 1930s. By 1942, most people not in the military were making money and able to spend part of it on movies.[142] The demand for films in military centers offset the decline in foreign revenue. As the war drew nearer and, subsequently, during the war, the government needed films to explain the world situation to the nation. With the aim of reaching the widest audience, the government turned to Hollywood filmmakers to meet the demand that could not be filled by documentarians alone. The war was glamorized by the stars and by the execution of the productions. One recruiting film produced by MGM, released a few weeks prior to Pearl Harbor, even depicted sailors playing guitars while girls danced on the beach at Waikiki.[143]

In 1946, the first full peacetime year, American movies reached the highest level of attendance. However, the motion picture industry was met with great challenges that would alter the structure of the business. In addition to the breakup of the studio structure, television began its commercial expansion in 1948. By the end of the 1950s, 90 percent of the homes in the United States had television sets.[144] Instead of adapting to television by producing product for it, the studios continued to fight it. Finally, the studios were no longer able to resist the tempting prices and began selling their films and film libraries to television.

Hollywood could not compete with television, yet it continued a futile attempt to find a new method of luring audiences back to theaters.

Throughout the history of motion pictures, entrepreneurs have always been searching for new gimmicks to attract an audience. Color became of the greatest importance in the 1950s as a weapon to compete with television. Color, however, was not a new invention. Many of the earliest short films in France had been handpainted to add color. By the time Herbert Kalmus had perfected his Technicolor process, sound had just arrived and distracted from his discovery.[145] When color was widely brought out, audiences generally accepted it but were not going to give up television because of it. Hollywood needed to create an event that could not be experienced at home on television. The three-dimensional process as a gimmick was revived in the 1950s, but excitement for it quickly waned.

The small size of the television screen led Hollywood to revive the wide screen which had been in existence since the beginning of motion pictures. The Lumières even employed it in 1900. Yet business was so good then that theater owners did not need a gimmick to attract customers. Lorenzo Del Riccio introduced Magnascope in 1924, utilizing a screen four times the normal size for the purpose of blowing up certain climactic scenes.[146]

Experiments in different sizes proved costly for the exhibitors who had to keep purchasing new equipment to adapt their theaters for particular films. In 1929, several major studios had brought out the wide screen; however, the excitement with sound dominated. The big screens also emphasized the graininess of prints and washed out the image. The stock market crash made it difficult for exhibitors to continue to invest in new systems. In 1931, the Technicians Branch of the Academy of Motion Picture Arts and Sciences, in conjunction with the director and producer branches, met to discuss standardizing screen shape. Exhibitors were assured that no further attempts to change screen size would be made.[147]

In an attempt to offer the theater audience what television could not, the wide screen craze resurfaced in the 1950s. The artistic structure of films was altered as directors and cameramen had to adjust to the new space. Initially, directors regressed to theatrical patterns, using the camera literally and unimaginatively to record action. The films lost impact and production slumped. George Stevens stated, "Unless we come to our senses, we'll end up with a magnificently huge screen, no picture, and no audience."[148]

The giant picture sought to simulate vision by employing more width than height. The exhibitors now welcomed this new addition that could greater involve the viewer psychologically in the filmic experience. The phrase "Cinerama does to you!" was employed in the advertising to attract audiences to the experience of viewing a wide screen motion picture.[149]

Indecision about standardizing the screen continued. Systems like Cinerama were too costly, with $75,000 needed to equip a theater. CinemaScope was very adaptable. A lens could be clamped onto a conventional projector at a cost to the exhibitor of about $20,000. To encourage the sale of this process, Twentieth Century-Fox leased cameras and lenses to rival studios to assure exhibitors that there would be a continuous flow of product. By the end of 1958, CinemaScope had become standard equipment in virtually every theater in the United States and in the larger theaters around the world. [150]

Paramount, however, refused to go along with CinemaScope and introduced VistaVision, which required theaters to purchase an additional lens for their projector. This, too, was widely accepted. But, when they tried to distribute 70mm VistaVision prints the theater owners refused. Despite theater owners' resistance to extra wide screens, Mike Todd successfully leased theaters to exhibit *Oklahoma!*, which utilized his 65/70mm Todd-AO process. [151] Today, exhibitors are still faced with the prospect of costly 70mm equipment and new sound systems.

Distributors view 70mm prints as a marketing tool. They serve to lure the audience to a film by creating the feeling of an event. Fourteen percent of the total theaters showing *Indiana Jones and the Temple of Doom* screened 70mm prints, which accounted for 30 percent of the overall business. The other theaters, however, might have had a significantly lower seating capacity, and audiences might have attended the same theaters regardless of the print size. However, 70mm prints are increasingly being used as an added attraction. [152]

A new Super 8 projection system and lens capable of theatrical use without transfer to 16mm or 35mm is a reality. The Super-Vision lens enlarges the image of an 8mm print ten to fifteen hundred times without loss of clarity or definition. [153] This system is expected to be used in miniplex theaters. It will also allow for movies made in 8mm to be available for viewing by a wider audience. Sony has created a system that projects three-quarter-inch video cassette tapes in Cinemascope, 35mm, 16mm, or television screen size. Sony claims the new tape, called "Cine-Matic" videotape, will retain most of the resolution of film while conventional film-to-video conversion only reproduces 70 percent of the original picture. Sony finds its new system almost piracy-proof and plans to install these video theaters in shopping centers in Japan. [154] Making use of space, Japan has begun to use shopping mall parking lots to exhibit feature films. Though drive-ins have not existed in Japan, they are now created with portable screens and projection equipment and audio signals are fed through the car radio for sound. [155]

Motion has always been a novelty to man. When film was first shown to crowds, people screamed at the presumed reality of a train coming toward them. Audiences soon became used to this and wanted a new thrill. New attempts to create more intense responses to motion are constantly being experimented with. To create a greater perception of reality on the screen, Douglas Trumbull's Showscan process involves shooting 65mm film at sixty frames per second and projecting the image at that speed on a curved screen. Four specially built one-hundred-seat theaters have been built in pizza parlors to test market this new process.[156] Though the results have received favorable reactions, the cost of wide implementation of the process is still prohibitive.

Attempts have been made to improve the quality of the picture itself and the theatrical environment. New technology offers improved film with a greater dynamic range, jumbo screen formats, varying aspect ratios, computer generated images, more complex visual effects, improved sound, more complex technical and animated inventions, and theater enhancements to embellish the experience of theatrical exhibition. The studios once had departments for technological experimentation. However, little research is funded by studios today because in the near term, it does not produce profits. With instability of jobs, executives are usually not at one studio long enough to implement such projects and reap the rewards of the potential results.

Experiments involving viewer participation are being made. Choice-A-Rama was developed with faculty members of the Massachusetts Institute of Technology. A remote-control applause meter is mounted alongside the screen and registers audience response to questions posed at four intervals. The inventors believe they are on the verge of interactive film. Tests in a small town in Massachusetts established audience preference for violence over peace, bad taste over good, and sex over culture.[157]

Changes in motion picture presentation in the theater were derived from experiments and developments of earlier years that were never in general use. Dormant inventions were revived in an attempt to recapture a dwindling audience. Inventions such as sound, color, and the wide screen that were incorporated into the drama of the film have survived.

As pay-television increasingly offers viewers a greater variety of programming, theatrical exhibitors are also experimenting with the theater environment itself and with the methods of presentation. To enhance the theater-going experience, the interior of theaters must be renovated or created to make them an attraction for going to the movies, instead of serving as a deterrent. Opinions differ concerning what constitutes ideal conditions for viewing a film. Some believe a viewer should be isolated, whereas others believe the communal audience experience is preferable. The surroundings can also affect the perceptions of the movie. Stan VanDerBeek introduced Cine Naps, a multimedia event called a "dream theater." The audience was invited to watch films and nap, while being surrounded with an endless stream of visual and aural images. Afterwards, analyses were supposedly made to determine whether the experience stimulated any common dream content.[158]

A film exploits senses of sight and hearing to stir up our emotions. When one is immersed in the filmic experience, one's biological clock ceases to dominate, as the psychological clock takes over. The viewer is able to put aside the mundane elements of life as filmic devices alter his conception of time. In a dark room without extraneous stimuli, the viewer can fully concentrate on the visible stimuli. This sensory experience can then begin to overtake the intellectual, rational process.

Each viewer, with a unique experience, will read a film according to his own frame of reference. The spectator is not a tabula rasa upon which the film leaves its imprint. The viewer brings all of his past experiences to the viewing and actively perceives the visual stimuli. For example, when people are given a Rorschach test, they see elements that define their experience. However, familiar elements in society condition people, resulting in the commonalities often found between individuals' responses on various tests. Perceptual commonalities are quite culturally oriented. On a more universal scale, Carl Jung spoke of the "collective unconscious," or psychological characteristics inherited from mankind. A filmmaker must be conscious of the range of emotions he will arouse in the particular audience and whether the images will elicit the intended response. Only then can the communication be effective.

Many people in the motion picture industry are fearful of change. They imagine that their area of expertise will be replaced or eliminated. Though the technology advances rapidly, the content remains within people's creative minds. Frank E. Rosenfelt stated, "Hardware becomes obsolete.... Software increases in value."[159]

The independent filmmaker often has a desire to make a film by his own rules. It is these people who experiment with elements of film, which when refined, eventually influence the theatrical feature. When motion picture equipment became accessible to more people with the introduction of 16mm and 8mm film, experimentation increased. Abstract animation and the graphic film first grew in continental Europe, flourished in London, then was transplanted across the ocean to the United States and Canada.[160]

Graphic film's history is a progression of increased experimentation with subject matter, tools, and viewer response. A film can be the medium for conveying a dramatic story or to express elements of the filmmaker's subconscious. The filmmaker's tools are no longer restricted to props, actors, or paint. The physical world is viewed through a different perspective.

Filmmakers' goals include the conveyance of information, emotionally involving the viewer in a dramatic story, arousing the sensual being, and the transcendance of conscious reality. Filmmakers may seek new methods of expressing their experience and can even strive for new experiences to be derived from their creations. Intrinsic elements of the graphic film include motion, light, color, space, and time. These elements may not be consciously considered if the narrative is the sole focus of the film. However, in the graphic film, the expressive role is dominant.

The graphic filmmaker is involved in experimentation with ideas and levels of consciousness. Anything that may aid in this quest is voraciously exploited. Concomitant with the graphic film's history has been the progression of increased technological advancements. This has ultimately been reflected in the methods of creating the graphic film and in the film experience itself. Graphic elements are no longer valued solely for narrative functions. New uses may be found for old techniques along with the development of unique techniques for the new expressive goal.

Reaction against the graphic film stems from people being conditioned by dramatic films. Having experienced "film" as a dramatic or educational medium, people expect a certain form and are disappointed when it is not delivered. They do not like the unfamiliar and not knowing how to react, they respond defensively. One's consciousness may be at the level of arduously struggling to give a logical dramatic meaning to what one sees. If this is not possible, the viewer may become very frustrated. During his process of trying to make the imagery conform to his reality, the viewer is missing the filmic experience. Expectations need to be changed to allow for full appreciation of the film. Exposure to graphic films at an early age is preferable so minds remain open to varying perspectives. Only after exposure to a variety of films can one begin to discriminate between elements.

Graphic films attempt to go further than the reality of the physical world. They often aim to transcend to the emotional, spiritual, primitive, and subconscious level. It can be a new means of expression, not intellectual understanding, but emotional and spiritual. These films need to be appreciated as an end. Barriers such as length need to be removed as such film is art and not subject to quantitative measurement. The aesthetics and emotions aroused serve as judge.

Charles Csuri, creator of computer-generated films, believes that in time "the artist will sit down and think about an image, and then a computer will translate his brain impulses into that picture."[161] David Prince wrote, "This augmentation of the human intellect is a product of man-computer synergism, a partnership between the man and the computer, combining the best qualities of each to form a capability of great power."[162] Kepes wrote that art and science are in a symbiotic relationship and that each grows stronger when nourished by the other.[163] Gene Youngblood, author of *Expanded Cinema*, believes a need exists for a "new aesthetic discipline" which requires an artist competent in technology and the arts.[164]

One needs the technological knowledge to transform one's ideas into a reality; yet, the artistic thought needs to be there initially. All aspects of the computer's functioning must be programmed. Due to speed and the ability to assess and subsequently modify programs, it may appear to act unpredictably and thus produce the unexpected. Only in this respect can the computer enter the realm of contributing to the artist's work. It merely suggests syntheses that one may or may not accept. [165] Jasia Reichardt linked foreigners, computers, and poets by the idea that they all make unexpected linguistic associations. [166] Art can be created that can not be physically created by man. Yet man is needed to inspire the process. Technology cannot be an artist itself, for its very existence depends upon the human factor.

The use of new technology in art is part of our scientifically oriented society. Images of inhumanity are generally equated with machines. The technical aspect of the computer is thought to be analogous to the creation of the monster by Frankenstein. Though people fear technology will grow on its own, it can be exploited as an extension of the human element. Man cannot cease investigating and thinking. Experiments in film can inspire emotion and novel thought leading to new creations to expand the realm of motion pictures. Article 19 of the United Nations' 1948 Universal Declaration of Human Rights states:

> Everyone has the right to freedom of opinion and expression; this right includes freedom to hold opinions without interference and to seek, receive and impart information and ideas through any media regardless of frontiers. [167]

8

The Distribution Agreement

Distribution agreements are used by distributors to license a picture from a producer. Bargaining power is all important in securing the most favorable deal. One must be knowledgeable of the methods of allocating costs, recouping expenses, and paying profit participants. If one is unaware of the intricacies of the deal, one might claim the distributor is cheating him if a picture grosses $50 million and is still not generating profits. If a producer who does not expect to receive profits is only working for a salary, he may care little about the terms of the distribution contract, allowing the deal to favor the distributor. Attorney Kenneth Ziffren believes that more money is made or lost deciding when to negotiate a distribution deal than at any other time. The deals are increasingly made before the picture is viewed. If a producer cannot secure a distribution deal, there is no assurance one will receive any revenue from other markets.[1] Ziffren wrote, "What looks good on paper may not work in the real world. . . . It is in the interest of both sides to capitalize on the avarice of the other and deals so structured stand a much better chance of working."[2] Howard Koch believes making a picture without a distribution deal is extremely risky. If distribution is secured after the picture is made, he believes the deal will be poor. If the majors put up prints and advertising costs and that is all that is recouped, the producer will get nothing. Ned Tannen equated a lack of access to distribution with playing Russian Roulette with six loaded cylinders. He believes one will inevitably lose because the distributors have their own unreleasable pictures and certainly do not need more from independents.[3]

There are innumerable variations on these deals. A particularly advantageous deal for the producer may reduce the incentive for the distributor to make the film profitable. The producer has little to say about the deal the distributor makes with the exhibitor, unless he distributes his own picture. The method of allocating costs and profits can provide significantly different results to the producer. A filmmaker must first understand how the box office gross is divided between the exhibitor and distributor because it is the rentals received by the distributor upon which all expenses and profits are calculated.

By 1920, pre-release showings provided the majors with an indication of what the rental terms should be. Because independent exhibitors tried to reduce the figures, it was therefore wiser for the majors to acquire more accurate information from the theaters they owned. Film rentals as a percent of box office by the end of World War I were between 15 and 20 percent.[4] Between 1949 and 1952, distributor rentals were approximately 20 to 25 percent of the box office gross. By the beginning of the sixties, distributors were earning 30 to 35 percent of the box office dollars.[5] The figure increased to nearly 45 percent in the late seventies.[6] Film distributors' percent share of domestic theatrical film box office was 38 percent in 1983, down from 42 percent in 1982 and 1981, and 46 percent in 1980.[7] It is generally believed that 40 to 45 percent of the domestic box office gross is received by the distributor. NATO, however, claims that 54 percent is the average.[8] Independents average a recoupment of only 35 percent, with foreign or art films lucky to receive that much.[9]

The most successful films, however, can earn between 60 to 65 percent of the box office, eventually ending their runs at less than 40 percent film rental.[10] Minimum floors allow for this increase. A floor is the minimum, agreed-upon percentage of the box office receipts that the exhibitor will pay to the distributor regardless of whether the house nut has been recouped. On first-run exhibitions, the 90/10 over-the-house expense deal and the straight percentage deal are combined so that the distributor receives as his share of the gross receipts the higher sum between a 90/10 house expense deal and a direct percentage of the gross receipts computed on a weekly basis. In a 90/10 deal, the house nut is deducted from the gross before remitting 90 percent of the overage to the distributor as a film rental. Where minimum floors exist, for example, in a 90/10 deal with a floor of 70, the exhibitor pays whichever is greater: 90 percent of the gross after deducting the house nut or 70 percent of the gross. If 70 percent of the gross is larger, the exhibitor must pay the nut out of the remaining 30 percent. Floors usually change weekly, with a 70 percent floor the first week, 60 percent the second week, 50 percent the third week, and a 40 percent floor for the balance of the run.

Some exhibitors are even offering lower floors to win bids. For example, if the box office gross is $10,000 and the nut is $3,500, the exhibitor would pay the distributor 90 percent of $6,500 or $5,850. Ten percent of $650 would be kept by the exhibitor. Yet with a floor of 70, 70 percent of the total $10,000 is $7,000 which is greater than the $5,850 rental on a 90/10 deal. The exhibitor, therefore, pays the higher amount, or $7,000, to the distributor and loses $500 of the nut, which is usually made up by the concession sales.

Rentals in excess of the guarantee paid by the exhibitor are referred to as "overages." The distributor is not paid until the earnings of the picture exceed the guarantee. The shared advertising expenses are paid in the same percentage as film rental earned. For example, if the gross if $25,000 and the nut is $4,000, the net is $21,000. Ninety percent of $21,000 is $18,900. The true net becomes $18,900 as a percentage of $25,000 or 75.6 percent. The distributor pays 75.6 percent of the advertising costs that week, not 90 percent, and the exhibitor pays 24.4 percent.

A few houses in Los Angeles and New York have strict 90/10 deals with no floors. They, however, have a large house nut.[11] Before the distributor receives 90 percent, the exhibitor retains 100 percent until he recovers his house nut. If he paid for advertising, he will next deduct 90 percent of that cost. The advantage of this deal over four-walling is that one is not liable for the house nut should the picture not even generate sufficient revenue to cover it. However, clauses exist that oblige one to pay the house nut. This deal, therefore, becomes a four-wall arrangement where the distributor is only eligible for 90 percent of the profits instead of 100 percent, while maintaining 100 percent of the risk.

The blockbuster era has seen the growth of the 90/10 formula, once reserved for first-run theaters in a few cities.[12] Exhibitors reportedly put up more than $33 million in guarantees for *Indiana Jones and the Temple of Doom*. It had practically covered its negative costs, $27 million, and its initial releasing costs, $7 million to $8 million, before it was released. With a strong opening and a split of 90/10 percent, overall profitability would be higher than the average percent of box office gross most pictures command. *E.T. The Extra-Terrestrial,* for example, was able to give producers an estimated 53 to 54 percent of the gross.[13]

The large multiple bookings also helped generate huge opening week grosses, the initial weeks being when the distributor receives the greatest percentage of the box office. When minimum guarantees were demanded, exhibitors began offering more in bids to secure a picture. For example, *The Empire Strikes Back* received $32 million in guarantees even though there was no mention of guarantees in Twentieth Century-Fox's bid letter.[14] *Return of the Jedi* set a new opening and single day gross with $6,219,629 from 1,002 theaters in its first twenty-four hours on a Wednesday. Its $6,027 per theater average was another high, with grosses aided by some theaters remaining open for twenty-four hours. Twentieth Century-Fox, the distributor, had given all exhibitors the extended hours option; however, only approximately fifteen screens acted on it.[15] *Return of the Jedi* entered the top five films of all time in just seven weeks after release with $127 million in domestic rentals. Since the distributor's share is highest in the opening weeks, Twentieth Century-Fox has amassed nearly 75 percent of the box office in rentals.[16]

Sliding scales are another means of calculating film rentals. One method divides the seven-day week into ten units, based upon traditional grossing capacities of the various days of the week. Sunday is rated as one to two units, Monday through Thursday is one unit each day, Friday is two units, and Saturday is two to three units. Playing a film on Friday and Saturday alone usually means getting 40 to 50 percent of the week's business.[17] If a week's gross is $2,000, the per unit gross is $2,000 divided by ten units, or $200. A distributor/exhibitor contract may stipulate that if the per unit gross is between $120 and $130, the exhibitor will pay 25 percent of that gross, whereas if the per unit gross is $130 to $140, the exhibitor will pay 27.5 percent of the total gross.[18]

In addition to understanding the distributor/exhibitor rental agreement, a filmmaker also needs to know what to expect from the producer/distributor contract. One must read the contract carefully and hunt for definitions of terms that may have differing meanings. "Net profits" and "gross receipts," for example, have varying definitions in distribution contracts. Most deals between a producer and distributor involve theatrical distribution terms of more than ten years and can run the length of copyright of the picture.[19]

One must first understand what the distribution expenses are, as they will be deducted from the rental received from the exhibitors. Mike Medavoy listed the order of recoupment of costs as being (1) distribution fee, (2) prints and advertising, (3) negative cost, (4) interest, (5) all forms of taxes, foreign and domestic, (6) MPAA dues, (7) theater checking, and (8) deferments. He stated the general rule to break even is, therefore, that three and one-half to four times the negative cost must be taken in at the box office.[20]

The distribution fee covers studio overhead which includes the distributor soliciting play dates, booking the picture, and collecting the rentals. If one were distributing one's own picture, one might have difficulty in collecting rentals and might end up paying an agency 50 percent to enforce collection.[21]

Distribution expenses include release prints and all laboratory and sound work, shipping and delivery charges, shorter length versions, foreign and television versions, retitling, recutting, redubbing, securing and registering copyrights, advertising, publicity and exploitation, censorship fees, insurance, royalties and license fees for music or copyright, license and permit fees to secure entry, licensing and exhibition in any country, taxes and the cost of contesting taxes, checking any exhibition, use or performance of the picture, trade association dues, attorney's fees for preventing or obtaining relief from infringement of copyright or for unauthorized exhibition and distribution, fees to government agencies, labor organizations or collective bargaining agents to facilitate distribution and exhibition, and subdistribution fees.[22]

Distribution fees that the majors charge are as follows: United States, 30 percent; Canada and the United Kingdom, 35 percent; and the rest of the world, 40 percent.[23] While a 25 percent fee for syndication sales is common, a 10 percent distribution fee is usual for network sales.[24] Revenue from trailers and advertising accessories is not included in gross film rentals. A distribution fee of 10 percent of the net is generally charged for miscellaneous sources of revenue, such as music, phonograph, merchandising, 16mm non-theatrical rights, and books.[25] When deals include "off-the-top" deductions, they are deducted from gross receipts taken ahead of the distribution fee. Though prints and advertising are common, any expense can be negotiated to be deducted first, making it an off-the-top deduction.

Foreign gross receipts are generally defined as "the actual United States dollars received in the United States." This prevents a participant from claiming his commission on any foreign receipts which are blocked or frozen. The distributor never receives the full foreign gross receipts because of the distribution fee foreign subsidiaries charge to cover the expenses of operation.[26] Subdistributors or sales representatives abroad charge 10 to 25 percent to sell a picture in foreign territories. In some areas, exhibitors have deals with subdistributors, which are locked territorial monopolies. One must be careful not to let subdistributors and the major distributor both charge distribution fees for the same service.[27]

Independent distributors or state's righters contract for franchises to distribute movies on a state-by-state or territory-by-territory basis. These franchise holders receive commissions ranging from 10 to 50 percent of the film rental collected from each play date. They are individual entrepreneurs who may represent one to a dozen independent producing and distributing companies.[28] In most cases, the distribution fees charged represent the total fee of the distributor and the subdistributor. Some companies charge a greater distribution fee when they use a subdistributor. It can be agreed upon contractually for a company using a subdistributor that the distributor's and the subdistributor's fee not exceed a certain amount.[29]

Richard Lederer stated that the studio's main interest is protecting their 30 percent distribution fee, which is taken off-the-top, when only approximately 17.5 percent is actually needed to run the company.[30] Attorney Peter Dekom believes that the average studio nut for distribution of a picture is closer to 10 percent of the collected film rentals. Dekom said that studios are in the business of making distribution fees, which is from where their profit comes. Dekom finds the usual distribution deal inherently unfair because studios first recoup their distribution fee, which is profit, and then recoup their costs before the investors are involved. Dekom is utilizing a deal whereby investments are first recouped and then, after break-even, the deal reverts to the normal model allowing the distributor to charge the 30 percent distribution fee and the 25 percent distribution costs, with 50 percent of the remainder going to the creative side and 50 percent to the investment side.[31]

Historically, the distribution fee has been non-negotiable. However, due to the recently high grossing pictures, producers have successfully negotiated a sliding scale for distribution fees: for example, a fee of 30 percent for the first $20 million of domestic theatrical rentals; a fee of 25 percent for the next $20 million; and a fee of 20 percent when rentals exceed $40 million.[32] The independent production entity of Zupnik-Curtis Enterprises has arranged to pay for the approximately $6 million cost for prints and advertising on their *Dreamscape* in exchange for a 17.5 percent fee from Twentieth Century-Fox, reduced from the usual 30 percent. Since Zupnik would ultimately pay for prints and advertising anyway, he believes it to be a wise gamble.[33]

NATO does not find these 90/10 deals with high floors profitable. Since they must commit so much money to attract a blockbuster and give up most of the rentals, exhibitors may recoup greater revenue with a smaller film. Given a choice of a small film with a 50–50 split, an average film with a 70–30 split, and a blockbuster with a 90–10 split, an exhibitor may opt for the smaller film. With the 50–50 split, he has to sell 20 percent as many admissions as he would with the 90–10 split to make an equal profit.[34]

In New York, showcasing involves fifty to sixty-five theaters. A distributor has to generally make a settlement with the exhibitors for 25 percent if the gross is $300,000 or less. If a film generates $400,000 to $450,000, one can receive a 30 percent settlement. When it hits $500,000, one can secure 40 percent; if it reaches $600–700,000, one can get 45 percent; and if more than $800,000 is earned, a 50 percent settlement can be achieved. If it goes over $1 million, one can receive 60 to 70 percent depending upon who one is. Therefore, one must be sure advertising costs are less than what can be earned.[35]

A deal frequently offered independent filmmakers is a small percentage of the distributor's net, a 50-50 split of the advertising and no advance.[36] Many profit participants complain that a large grossing picture does not provide them any revenue. For example, a picture with a box office gross of $50 million, with negative costs of $10 million, advertising, prints, and interest costs of $7.5 million, distribution fees at 30 percent of $25 million amounting to $7.5 million, and a 50-50 split between distributor and exhibitor amounting to $25 million for the exhibitor would leave a net of zero from theatrical distribution. This picture, therefore, breaks even at $50 million.

The majors seek the preferred position of first negotiation/last refusal in regard to subsidiary rights and remake rights. If the producer sells other rights, the major can insist upon holdback periods before the rights in question are exercised. By selling these markets on an individual basis, cross-collateralization, which is the weighing of all profits and losses against each other in all markets, is avoided. This method, however, may also leave some areas unexploited.[37]

The gross of a picture on a weekly basis is only significant when the number of theaters it played in and the amount spent on advertising to achieve the gross are known. A distributor and exhibitor enter into cooperative advertising usually to provide for greater expenditure of advertising than the theater's usual commitment. The exhibitor generally deducts the distributor's portion of the cost of the cooperative advertising. Producers seldom benefit as it creates the situation in which the distribution fee is charged on the net film rental.[38] Jerry Tokofsky of Zupnik-Curtis Enterprises claims that for a picture to qualify as an "A" film for Home Box Office the minimum advertising budget must be $3.2 million.[39] Independents generally request from the distributor a guarantee that they will spend a minimum agreed-upon amount on prints and ads. This is particularly important if no advance is given, for if the picture is not succeeding, the distributor has no incentive to continue playing the picture.

Distribution agreements vary greatly as the producers and distributors aim to make their concerns paramount. Nevertheless, the deals are generally of three types with specific emphases. The distribution fee deal, or net deal, is the traditional method whereby the distributor takes a fee of generally 30 percent, recoups prints and ad costs both from the gross film rental, and then gives the balance to the producer. In a gross percentage deal, the independent producer receives a percentage, often 30 percent, of the gross film rental from the first dollar, and the distributor retains the remainder to recoup prints, ads, and fees. In an adjusted gross deal, the first dollar goes for distribution expenses and the rest is split on an equal basis.

For example, a picture earns $10 million in film rental while the marketing costs amount to $5 million. In the distribution fee deal, the distributor takes $3 million and costs are recouped out of the $7 million, with $2 million left for the producer. In the gross percentage deal, the independent producer receives $3 million, costs are recouped out of the $7 million, leaving $2 million for the distributor. In an adjusted gross deal, the $5 million is first recouped to pay the expenses, and then the remaining $5 million is split, with $2.5 million going to the producer, and $2.5 million going to the distributor.

Another example demonstrates that an independent producer receives less in a gross receipts deal if the picture is very successful. If, however, the picture is unsuccessful, the gross percentage deal protects the downside. Consider an example in which a picture earns $30 million in film rental, with $10 million in marketing costs. In a straight distribution fee deal, the distribution fee is $9 million and the $10 million costs are recouped, leaving

$11 million for the independent producer. If a gross percentage deal is used, the independent receives $9 million. The adjusted gross deal gives $10 million to the independent producer and distributor.

The independent producer receives the most from a gross percentage deal if a film is unsuccessful. It protects the downside. Gross percentage deals were rare ten years ago but are now common.

An increasingly common deal is one in which the independent producer holds onto ancillary rights while coming up with $3 million to $4 million for distribution costs and just using the service of a distributor as a booker. The distributor has no financial risk, yet does not have great incentive for his effort when he could be distributing a picture in which he has a significant financial interest. Distributors want the possibility of making a lot of money, not merely security against losses.

Ed Colarik claims 40 percent of all pictures have gross deals.[40] In the "gross deal" or "adjusted gross deal," the producer does not share from the first dollar. The first item deducted from every dollar is cooperative advertising. The amount left, called "adjusted gross receipts" or "gross receipts," is divided 70 percent to the distributor and 30 percent to the producer. All distribution costs are covered by the distributor's share. Producers find this deal advantageous because there is less chance of erroneous distribution charges. Since the heavy advertising costs are paid by the distributor, they will more likely control the costs and spending.[41] Advances are not given with the first dollar gross deal. A typical deal is one in which the independent receives 30 percent of the distributor's gross receipts until a multiple of print and advertising expenditures has been reached, generally two to three times the prints and advertising costs, and then the independent's share escalates upwards in plateaus of, for example, one to three million dollars, until the independent is retaining 65 percent of the distributor's gross and the distributor retains the remainder.

If the distributors have the bargaining power, they take limited, off-the-top deductions from the gross receipts before paying the independent its 30 percent. They also take an overhead allowance of 10 percent, or create a cross-collateralization or "eat-in" protection for themselves by crossing revenues of the independent in other media or territories with domestic theatrical gross in order to ensure the recoupment of costs.[42] This deal is made assuming no rights are sold and that there is no minimum advertising required.

If an independent wants an advance, the modified or adjusted gross deal is appropriate. The distributor is entitled to recoup a multiple of the advance and then continue to recoup distribution costs off-the-top and split the remainder with the independent. The independent's share of the gross rises with the success of the film. The independent, therefore, gets a return on the film by the advance and the major tries to get back the advance and its distribution costs before sharing further revenues with the independent.[43]

In a first dollar gross deal with an "eat-in," gross receipts are split 70 percent to the distributor and 30 percent to the producer until gross receipts equal 2.5 times the defined distribution expenses. Thereafter, the gross receipts are split 50-50. However, if after distribution expenses are recouped the distributor does not earn a minimum distribution fee of 22.5 percent of the gross receipts, the distributor can recoup from the producer's share of gross receipts to make up the difference. The distributor's "eat-in" cannot exceed the producer's share of gross receipts. This deal is beneficial for the distributors because they are assured of cost recoupment and are guaranteed a 22.5 percent fee. This deal is made when all rights are not available to the distributor and the distributor is only able to recoup revenue from the theatrical and network markets. It also benefits the distributors because after they earn their costs and fees, the remainder is split 50-50. Therefore, the distribution fee after break even is 50 percent of the gross.

In a net deal with non-recoupable advance, the producer receives the non-returnable advance against 100 percent of the net profits on the straight distribution deal, equivalent to 30 percent of the first $5 million of gross receipts and 35 percent on all gross receipts in excess thereof. The producer's downside is protected while the distributor is motivated by greed to promote the picture. The outright sale is used in small territories where independents cannot get a fair share of remittances, e.g., Burma, India, Cyprus, and Eastern Europe.[44]

The costs off-the-top deal is the most frequently used arrangement in the independent world. All costs are recovered and the remaining balance is divided usually 60 percent to the producer and 40 percent to the distributor, or it is split 50-50. Out of the 60 or 50 percent, the subdistributor recovers the minimum guarantee. The more costs deducted off-the-top, the less benefit to the producer. A bad deal is in which the distributor takes all costs off-the-top and then splits 50-50. If the film does badly one receives nothing, and if it is a hit one gives away 50 percent. A "guarantee" arrangement is one in which the distributor agrees to pay a given sum, for example, $2 million in two years. It is, in fact, an advance which is paid at a later date. Before it is paid, the distributor attempts to make his money back. In this deal, one must be aware of the terms on which the guarantee will be paid. A contract which states that a "first-class film" must be delivered leaves the distributor an out.[45]

Depending upon the negative cost of the picture, the higher the gross the more favorable is the adjusted gross deal to the distributor. The higher the gross, the more the net deal favors the producer.[46] The independent's downside risk is usually better protected with a first dollar gross deal. The upside, however, is maximized in the straight distribution deal. Conversely, if the major has the first dollar gross deal, it has a better upside but more risk; yet, with a straight distribution deal, its downside is more limited but its upside is also limited to only its distribution fee.[47] If a producer is confident a film will succeed, a net deal is preferable. If one wants to pay back investors, an advance protects the downside, entitling the distributor to a greater share at the back end. Though the risk/reward ratio must be considered, the distributor must remain motivated or he may choose to emphasize his efforts on another picture in which his profit share is greater. A better negotiated deal for the producer, therefore, may in effect be less profitable if the overall rentals are not maximized.

Those with interest in a film's revenue are often suspicious of how rentals are allocated for covering expenses and for providing profits. Because of misunderstanding the rental contract or because of the existence of dubious accounting methods, questions arise. The accounting firm of Laventhol and Horwath conducted the "Survey of Motion Picture Producers' Concerns and Attitudes." Forty percent of more than a hundred respondents revealed box office reports from domestic distributors were reasonably accurate, while an equal number of producers said the reports were substantially understated. In regard to reports from foreign distributors, 40 percent said that numbers were substantially understated, 28 percent believed they were accurate, and 32 percent did not respond.[48]

Initially, one must be aware of when rentals are paid. Typically, the managing partner believes 60 percent of domestic rentals are received in the year in which the film is exhibited and 40 percent in the second year. Foreign theatrical revenues are generally received 40 percent in the first year, 50 percent in the second year, and 10 percent in the third year. Pay and cable license revenues are generally received in the second and third years. Network television rentals are generally received 65 percent in the third year, 25 percent in the fourth year, and 10 percent in the fifth. Syndicated domestic television rentals are generally distributed evenly in the fourth and fifth years. Because of rapid technological changes, the revenue sources and timeliness of payment are being altered.[49]

One accounting procedure uses the periodic-table-computation method that amortizes film costs based upon tables prepared from the historic revenue patterns of a large group of films with similar distribution patterns. These revenue patterns are assumed to provide a reasonable guide to the experience of succeeding groups of films produced and distributed under similar conditions. The periodic-table-computation method is ordinarily used only to amortize that portion of film costs relating to film rights licensed to movie theaters. The tables should be reviewed regularly and updated whenever revenue patterns change significantly.[50] Laventhol and Horwath frequently performs investigative auditing for profit participants. Though they find occasional clerical errors due to the volume of transactions, more often the profit participant was not aware of what would be charged against profits, even though it was in the contract.[51] The "moving" or "rolling break-even" does not allow for a precise point in time or dollars when costs are fully paid.

Since distribution charges are constantly being incurred, confusion often results because the break-even point keeps on escalating.

The amount of money that is returned to participants in a picture can depend upon the accounting definitions, methods of computation used to determine costs and profits, and the order in which the calculations are performed. For example, four methods are used for the financial reporting of revenue from the licensing of films. By the contract method, the total revenue is recognized at the date the report is executed. By the billing method, revenue is recognized as the installment payments become due. In the delivery method, revenue is recognized at the date the prints are delivered to the licensee. And in the deferral or apportionment method, revenue is spread evenly over the period of the license. The method used will be a factor in the timeliness of payment and interest accrued.[52]

If one believes an error has been made in calculating profits, one needs to have the option of checking these figures. The rights of investigation should be carefully defined in the contract.

Benjamin W. Solomon advises that the distribution contract should state that during the first eighteen months of the release of a picture, a report will be issued monthly. After the eighteen months, he finds quarterly statements are generally adequate and that reports are most helpful if given on a county-by-county basis. Auditors are usually permitted to examine all reports submitted to the home office by sub-licensees. Solomon believes that this, too, should be stated in the distribution agreement and that it is also valuable to include a provision allowing auditors to interview employees in connection with the reports submitted. He also advises that one state in the contract which books and records may be examined. Solomon believes the auditor should have access to all exhibition contracts, all theater box office reports, shipping sheets, the gross receipts of pictures sharing a double bill with the film, all bills and checks for charges made against the picture, original reports from subsidiaries and licensees, documents pertaining to the transfer of foreign currency, contracts with advertising agencies and distributors of trailers, contracts for merchandise tie-ins, and all books and records pertaining to the business of the motion picture. Solomon advises that these specifics must be enumerated in the agreement.[53]

One needs to investigate the distributor/exhibitor contracts. For example, there are exchanges in the country known as "double-feature" territories where most theaters play a double bill. Sometimes the films are from the same distributor, but not necessarily. Even if they are, two producers are generally involved, with varying rental agreements. One feature may be rented on a percentage and the other on a flat fee.[54] When films are sold to television, a distributor will often sell many as a package for a lump sum. It is important to know the method of allocating this revenue to the individual pictures.[55]

One must be aware of exhibitor deductions specific to certain states. Twenty states do not levy admission taxes on filmgoers. Yet communities in those twenty states have imposed local taxes. Pomona, a southern California suburb, has the largest admissions tax of 10 percent. Berkeley, Fresno, and Chico, all in California, levy a 5 percent admission tax. Only New York, Connecticut, and Hawaii have film rental sales tax. Connecticut's, at 7 percent, is the highest.[56]

A filmmaker must be knowledgeable about the agreement between the distributor and exhibitor, as well as understand the details of the producer and distributor contract. The means of allocating profits on both levels will ultimately affect the producer's profit, but more importantly, it can be the difference between a commercially successful picture and a commercially mediocre or unsuccessful picture. The creation of a successful picture can ensure not only that the picture is widely seen but that the filmmaker will have the opportunity to make another film.

9

The Major Distributors

Even though it is possible to continue making low-budget independent films, people generally strive to produce or direct a major studio picture. The independent film is therefore often used as a career stepping-stone. The major studio film ostensibly grants the filmmaker prestige and an abundance of resources. However, the power envisioned may be quite limiting. Since vast amounts of revenue are involved in the production of a film, numerous limits may be placed on the imagined freedom that money can buy. Even though the budgets are larger, service charges are concomitantly increased. However, filmmakers generally strive to make a studio film since they generally can attract the greatest audience. Making a studio picture also puts one in contact with the powerful people in the industry. Such associations could ensure future employment. In *Indecent Exposure,* Aaron Stern, a psychiatrist and film producer, stated:

> The motion-picture industry has been aptly compared to "thousands of people fighting each other in the open sea to get to a lifeboat that seats only ten to fifteen." Each film studio represents a lifeboat that might produce ten to fifteen pictures.[1]

Naive filmmakers often strive for their first opportunity to make a picture with the majors. Productions at a studio are not always as idyllic as imagined. Mike Medavoy, executive vice president of Orion Pictures, stated that the six phases of studio film production are (1) wild enthusiasm, (2) disillusionment, (3) panic, (4) search for the guilty, (5) punish the innocent, and (6) reward the non-involved.[2]

The majors have distribution networks that function to get a film played in the most theaters for the maximum number of people. The major distributors are considered to be Columbia, Metro–Goldwyn-Mayer (MGM)/United Artists (UA), Paramount, Twentieth Century-Fox, Universal, and Warner Bros. Tri-Star Pictures, Orion, and Disney's Buena Vista are also in this league. Cannon Films, an independent, has been producing and releasing as many pictures as the majors. MGM left the distribution business and was releasing the pictures it financed through UA.

Instead of the general 30 to 35 percent distribution fee, UA distributed MGM's product for 22.5 percent of gross rentals, with UA advancing all print and advertising costs.[3] MGM since purchased UA, forming one company, MGM/UA Entertainment.

Tri-Star Pictures, formed in November 1982 by CBS, HBO and Columbia Pictures, announced it would be a major distributor with its own sales, marketing, advertising, and branch managers.[4] It was capitalized at $1 billion, with $200 million invested by each partner and a $400 million credit line established through several banks. HBO licensed all films produced or acquired by Tri-Star during its first four-and-a-half years of business. Columbia originally was to distribute the pictures but Tri-Star set up their own releasing organization, though they reportedly pay Columbia a distribution fee of 12 percent of film rentals for use of their accounting and billing systems.[5]

When the majors threatened to enter the pay-television business, HBO was anxious to secure reliable sources of programming. HBO's arrangement with Columbia proved costly. HBO is obligated to pay 25 percent of the production costs of Columbia's films and also pay additional fees based on each picture's box office performance. HBO also agreed to purchase the pay-television rights to three or four Columbia films each year on an exclusive basis at a price nearly one-third of the film rentals. *Ghostbusters* is costing HBO $37.5 million for these exclusive rights. Such costly arrangements will expire in several years.[6] Since Tri-Star is a partnership of Columbia, CBS and HBO, it has many assets and means of recouping its investment. Columbia wants to expand its production; CBS wants to build up its supply of pictures for network use; and HBO needs films to air on an exclusive basis. They have succeeded in establishing a production and distribution division simultaneously. Their first picture, *The Natural,* grossed $48 million in the United States and Canada. Their next feature, *The Muppets Take Manhattan,* grossed $26 million; however, their subsequent films, *Where the Boys Are* and *Meatballs II,* were failures.[7]

A major distribution company needs a flow of product to maintain active relationships with exhibitors. Since they need approximately ten to twelve pictures per year, they can produce half and pick up the rest. Alan Ladd, Jr., resigned as president of Twentieth Century-Fox in 1979 to head The Ladd Company. He told the *Los Angeles Herald Examiner:*

> When you are involved in a major company like this (Fox), you really must supply a minimum of 12 pictures a year. You have an enormous overhead, you have 3,000 employees, and you have to produce a product flow of one picture a month, hopefully more. An independent may do one picture, three, four, five, whatever. Also, at a studio, you'd like to think that everything you did was what you want to do, but that doesn't always happen to be true. You have to feed a distribution system. You just can't sit back and say, "There are only five films that I like this year, and that's all we'll make." The company would go broke very quickly.[8]

Table 9-1. Releases by the Majors

Total Majors	In-House	Pickups	Classics	Total Releases
1984*	59	61	28	148
1983	58	73	31	162
1982	63	52	22	137
1981	55	58	4	117
1980	76	40	1	117

* 1984 films completed, in progress, and set to roll through November 1983.
(Source: "Majors' Releases In-House vs. Outside Acquisitions," *Daily Variety,* 6 October 1983, 14)

Since the studios no longer need to release more than fifteen pictures a year, the top talents vie for these few opportunities. Since major successes have proven quite unpredictable, the studios try to minimize their risk by employing people associated with recent successes. Because of their need for elements to provide evidence that the odds favor a success, the studios actively seek associations with the stars. Comedians Richard Pryor, Eddie Murphy, and Michael Keaton have signed individual contracts with the majors that involve their making five films each. This resembles the old system where actors were under contract to a particular studio. The banks, however, realize the unpredictability of a picture's success. Al Howe of Bank of America stated, "If I discover that one of my men believes he knows which film will make money and which will lose...I say he has 'gone Hollywood' and I fire him!"[9] To further reduce risk, the majors are picking up more product. These films can be either completely or partially financed by others. If the majors provide a negative pickup, they at least save on the interest of the money by not having to pay until the picture is delivered. They may also secure cheaper product, often non-union, which they themselves could not produce. Completed pictures offer them the safest bet, as they can be seen before they are purchased.

The majors produced less than half of their schedules "in-house" for their 1984 releases. Table 9-1 provides an enumeration of the types of productions released by the majors from 1980 to 1984.

In an attempt to be safe, material already proven successful in other markets or pictures that have proven successful in the past become possibilities for theatrical distribution. In recent years, Buena Vista, the distribution arm of Walt Disney Productions, has mostly distributed reissues of their classics. As can be observed in table 9-2, the majors rely on alternative material as well as original for their total releases.

The studios are very cautious about their selection of pictures they choose to release, and often rely on the weekly network series as their bread and butter.[10] Alan Hirschfield believes movies are overly emphasized in

Table 9-2.   Majors' Releases Classified by Source

	1981	1982	1983	1984*
Sequels and Series	9	11	16	12
Remakes	8	9	7	11
Other Adaptations	31	39	37	34
Originals	63	57	68	73
Total	111	116	128	130

*Majors' productions in progress through December 1983 for 1984 release, including acquisitions.
(Source: "Majors' Releases, Classified by Source," *Daily Variety,* 7 December 1983, 2)

Hollywood. He noted, "I have this same problem with Marvin Davis, he comes in here and wants to talk about movies. . . . There's not a single studio in town that could survive with movies alone." Studios generate income from television productions and then syndications.[11]

Though the precise value of film libraries is difficult to measure, they are valuable assets worth millions. MGM/UA's is the largest with an estimated 4,459 films having an estimated value of $733 million. MCA/Universal has approximately 2,000 films worth an estimated $367 million; Columbia has 1,800 films worth $330 million; Warner Bros. has 1,800 films worth $330 million; Twentieth Century-Fox has 1,000 films worth $183 million; Paramount has 720 films worth $132 million; Orion has six hundred films worth $110 million; and Disney has one hundred sixty-nine films worth $500 million.[12]

In the motion picture field, the studios are mainly a distribution system and financier of pictures. Distribution is, however, a costly proposition. In 1973, MGM closed its distribution offices around the country and drastically reduced production to four pictures a year. At the end of the seventies, Kirk Kerkorian, who had acquired controlling interest of MGM in 1969, realized the increasing value of the ancillary markets and decided to make more pictures again. Kerkorian acquired the indebted United Artists, which had no production facilities, but did have a library of 2,500 features. UA also had the distribution arm that MGM had been using to distribute its films since 1973.[13]

The importance of distribution is evident in the recent selection of studio heads. In 1983, five of the seven major studios were headed by distribution-trained executives. In December 1982, Robert Rehme, former chief of distribution and marketing for Universal, became head of Universal Studios. In January 1983, Frank Mancuso, previously president of Paramount Distribution, became president of the motion picture division at Paramount Pictures. In February 1983, Frank Yablans, who had worked in distribution at Warners, Disney, Filmways and Paramount, became head of MGM/UA.

Table 9-3.   Average Film Negative Costs

Year	Negative Costs
1978	5.7 million
1979	8.7 million
1980	9.4 million
1981	10.4 million
1982	11.6 million
1983	12.5 million

(Reprinted with permission of Paul Kagan Associates, Inc. Copyright 1986. Paul Kagan Associates, Inc.)

Terry Semel, former chief of distribution at Warner Bros., became its president. Norman Levy had been head of distribution at Columbia Pictures before becoming vice chairman and head of distribution at Twentieth Century-Fox, with responsibilities far exceeding distribution.[14] Alfred Hitchock said, "Distribution is a freemasonry like the kitchens of a restaurant. They have deep dark secrets. I have never yet been able to discover how much it costs to distribute a film."[15] While many may not know the exact cost of distributing a picture, the majors have to face increasing costs when launching a picture. Therefore, extreme caution is necessary. Tom Gray, senior vice president of Raymond Chow's Golden Harvest Group, stated:

> There's no way to make money on a film that costs between $5 million and $8 million—you need a big picture to make big deals. So you either make something for between $1 million and $3 million and get out cheaply, or for between $15 million and $50 million and ask for the sky.[16]

Table 9-3 illustrates the steady increases in production costs that the majors have incurred. This "blockbuster" mentality has created a dearth of medium-budgeted pictures. Greater concentration is given to either pictures heavily emphasizing special effects or adult pictures that are expensive because of the stars involved. In 1984, the films of the majors' total release schedule consisted of 25 percent, with budgets of $14 million or more. The majors had heavy financing from outside investors to cover this risk.[17]

There is extreme interest in reducing the costs of producing a picture. Production costs are so high that states even strive to attract location productions, while offering cost-conscious producers an added bonus. Arkansas instituted a policy of offering a 5 percent rebate after $1 million or more is spent in the state.[18]

For the last five years, Paramount Pictures has had pre-tax operating earnings of approximately $70 million annually, making the studio one of the strongest profit producers for Gulf and Western Industries, its parent company. When Barry Diller took over in 1974, he implemented an emphasis on reducing costs. Paramount's pictures are made with fewer stars and production costs average $8.5 million, compared to the average of $11 million. They are, therefore, able to produce more pictures a year, averaging fifteen, and can increase their chances of producing a hit. Paramount spends less on marketing than some competitors. Furthermore, they avoid national television advertising in favor of local television spots, which they believe are most effective.[19]

Paramount produces pictures on the "advocacy system." Since an executive has to believe that a project will become a hit and must commit to it, Paramount may be slow in accepting a project. Paramount professes to believe in paying little to new talent because they will work for a "labor of love" and because it is less of a financial risk than paying $5 million to a potentially failing star or director.[20] In 1981, because of an impending directors' strike and a shortage of finished productions, Paramount decided to produce seven low-budget films, costing between $4 million and $8 million. One of the seven was *An Officer and a Gentleman,* which earned a domestic gross of $125 million. Paramount President Michael Eisner had accurately predicted one of the seven would be a hit, one a great failure, and the rest in-between.[21]

Independent producers often complain about the studio overhead charges attached to the pictures with which they are connected. Part of studio overhead covers high executive salaries. For example, in 1982 at MGM/UA, ten executives were each paid $250,000 or more a year, with David Begelman making $450,000. The studios also pay the overhead of "in-house" producers, amounting to $200,000 to $500,000 a year each. MGM/UA had twelve such producers.[22]

Ned Tannen stated that in 1980 Universal had 110 properties in development that they later cut to twenty-four, no longer able to afford to write off $5 million to $8 million a year in development costs. Mike Medavoy stated that in 1980 Warner Bros. had $5 million to $10 million in development for 125 scripts, out of which they produced four. This would no longer be possible as they now seek completed packages.[23] Agencies package or put together several elements such as the script, director, producer, and stars. These packages are then shopped to the majors. If a studio wants the project, more time and energy is saved than if they only had an idea for a film or a screenplay since the deals are already put together. This arrangement allows agents to wield great power.

Though it is believed by almost all before production that a picture will be a hit, it is never a certainty. Paramount claimed to have $18 million in commitments from exhibitors, $6 million in guarantees, and $12.6 million in

Table 9-4.   Major Studio Releases

Year	Releases	Year	Releases
1974	140	1979	118
1975	108	1980	133
1976	117	1981	142
1977	100	1982	149
1978	101	1983	159

(Reprinted with permission of Paul Kagan Associates, Inc. Copyright 1986 Paul Kagan Associates, Inc.)

advances for *The Great Gatsby*. It opened in 370 theaters in 1974 and after three months in release had earned only $9.5 million in rentals.[24] Though the producers, distributors, and exhibitors believed in the picture, it did not prove successful. Within twenty-four hours after a picture opens, its success can be predicted. Fifteen to 25 percent of the total box office grosses are earned in the first seven days of release by typical studio films.[25]

Because of the costs involved in a motion picture's release, a distributor may acquire another picture that is similar to his picture to keep it from being competitive. This protects the distributor's greater interest in his own picture.[26]

In 1974, the average picture cost was $2.5 million, marketing costs were $1 million, the average admission price was $1.89, and concession items of a Coke and popcorn amounted to a quarter. By 1984, the average motion picture production costs had grown to $12 million, the average marketing costs had reached $7 million, the average admission price had grown to slightly more than three dollars, and a Coke and popcorn had escalated to $1.50. Alan Hirschfield pointed out that in the past ten years, ticket prices have risen only 65 percent while concessions have risen 500 percent. He believes pictures are used by exhibitors to lure people to their theaters to sell them concession items. He said, "It is extraordinary that we are in the only business that cannot price its product based on its costs." Hirschfield referred to the "arcane consent decree" as "a disgrace and about as relevant to our business today as silent films." If studios could own theaters "we could clearly ensure . . . that the most modern aspect in a theater was not the concession stand, but its screen."[27]

The majors have remained powerful, with independent companies attempting to succeed but more often failing. The new pay-television market granted the opportunity for HBO to become powerful enough to establish itself in one field of distribution and move laterally into the theatrical market via Tri-Star. HBO now has complete control over the creation, distribution, and exhibition of their programming. Paul Kagan Associates finds that

HBO's voracious appetite for movies, requiring 150 to 175 new titles each year, has been a factor in the rise in productivity in the industry.[28]

Hirschfield believes the majors lost control of the cable market because they are like dinosaurs carrying around a big tail. He stressed that change is necessary for the studios' survival, as he believes the ancillary markets will soon be known as the primary markets. Hirschfield does not find the cost of production too severe, but believes productivity needs to increase. To keep costs down, he advises increased emphasis on the story and not the cast, as demonstrated by George Lucas' and Steven Spielberg's successes. Hirschfield believes the elimination of the Consent Decree would solve the escalating marketing costs which he believes are out of control. An alliance with a chain or owning theaters could keep costs down by allowing a slower roll-out of product and by allowing a film to find an audience. Though one studio could not supply theaters completely, an alliance with 150 theaters in top markets could afford the luxury of performing tests and letting a picture play for more than a few weeks.[29]

The majors remain the most powerful distributors and are increasing their number of releases by acquiring pickups. They have the relationships with exhibitors to play in the best theaters and the resources to coordinate a national release. The power of the majors in conjunction with their prestige makes the majors the first choice for most filmmakers. The majors can ensure that a great number of people will have the opportunity to see a picture. The majors, however, will usually impose limitations on the filmmaker. The filmmaker is not free to create whatever he wants even though he may have all the resources necessary to implement his vision. A studio executive, a committee, or research results may alter the script, decide who will star in the picture, select the crew, and even dictate the style of the film. In post-production, the editing, music, and sound track may still be dictated by these powers. Because the majors offer less freedom, a filmmaker with financing might prefer an independent distributor who will not subject his influence upon the picture. Once a filmmaker earns enough power, he may be able to command terms from the majors that would provide all of the resources but none of the limitations. Then, the majors can serve as an effective means to communicate a filmmaker's vision to the greatest number of people.

Limited-Market Distributors and Theaters

While motion pictures were evolving into common entertainment, an interest in alternate forms of film other than the commercial feature was growing. In Europe, the concept of cinema as art appeared early and developed in conjunction with the concept of cinema as business, whereas in the United States, movies were products produced in factories.[1] In 1907, Film d'Art was formed in France to introduce the general cinema audiences to the great artists of the French national theater. The earliest successes starred Sarah Bernhardt in recreations of her stage roles.[2] Increasingly, more avant-garde films were being made. Because the films were different and often incomprehensible by literal standards, they were often rejected by masses of people as being odd. The filmmakers making art films did not respect the taste of the general moviegoing audience. These two extreme positions developed into factions that still exist.

In 1950 Perry Miller began the Film Advisory Center, with Robert Flaherty as chairman, to encourage the importation of art films. By getting art and film authorities involved and holding screenings, they were able to stimulate interest in a variety of films. They provided distributors with advisers on adapting such films for the American market and assisted in organizing special film festivals. The First American Art Film Festival, held in Woodstock, New York, in 1951 was attended by distributors, exhibitors, artists, and critics.[3]

Cinema 16 was organized by Amos Vogel in 1947 as America's largest and most successful film society.[4] Initial programs consisted of social documentaries, controversial adult films, experimental films, international classics, and medical psychiatric film studies. Cinema 16 described itself as "the Off-Broadway of the cinema...."[5]

In 1952, Twentieth Century-Fox became impressed by the size and enthusiastic reception of the art film movement, and produced a series of seven art shorts for general distribution. The series included films on Botticelli, Vermeer, Degas, Renoir, and Raphael, all photographed in European galleries. To make the subjects more popular, stories were devised for each. These contrived scenarios destroyed the films for the art house audiences and were rejected by the mass market as being too "highbrow."[6]

After the war, a film society movement had grown in the United States. Art theaters had sprung up to meet the demand. In 1946 there were approximately twelve of these theaters, with half in New York. They grew in number to 450, with additional theaters willing to play outstanding foreign successes. During these same years, box office attendance fell from an estimated ninety million per week to an average of forty-five million a week. In addition to blaming television, people also cited film societies for the loss of interest in Hollywood films.[7]

Because the judgment of which films to distribute is still the distributors', in 1960, Jonas Mekas and others created the New American Cinema Group. One of their objectives was to discover new means of production and distribution. In 1962, they created their own film distribution center, the Film-Makers' Cooperative. They introduced six radical principles: the cooperative would distribute every film submitted; the cooperative would be governed by the filmmakers themselves; the filmmakers would remain the owners of the film and sign no contracts with the cooperative; all rentals, except 25 percent to run the cooperative, would go to the filmmakers; all films would be treated equal; and the filmmakers' income/expense balance sheets would be kept by the secretary, with copies sent to the filmmaker. They realized that any inclusion of aesthetics would create impasses. In 1967 to 1968, they created a commercial branch of the cooperative, the Film-Makers' Distribution Center, which would promote films thought to be capable of doing well in commercial theaters. They discovered that in order to succeed, they had to succumb to the techniques they disdained. Amos Vogel wrote:

> The genuine avant-garde film and the genuine formal narrative film by their very natures are noncommercial and appeal to limited audiences only. To succeed with such films commercially one needs to embrace not only the commercial distribution methods but also, eventually, the content, the styles, the formulas of the commercial film.[8]

The Whitney Museum carried on the Cinema 16 film society. In 1970, David Bienstock showed independent films of all concerns, yet was denounced by Jonas Mekas, its founder. Mekas proudly announced to be concerned with "only about five percent" of all independent and underground cinema, which represent the minimal, structural works of the cinema.[9]

It is apparent that varying standards exist about which films deserve to be exhibited. Since most films have an audience, the problem is in making them accessible to those who want to view them. These pictures, too, can be divided into those that are commercial and those that are too esoteric for even minimal release.

After World War II, the Walter Reade Organization was a leader in distributing foreign films in the United States. Their films included those of Jacques Tati and English comedies from the Rank Organization. They invested 25 to 50 percent of the total budget in exchange for the same percentage of profit and the western hemisphere distribution rights for 35 percent of rentals.[10]

Independent distributors used to be the sole importers of these pictures. When the majors realized that they could earn a profit distributing sexy foreign films in the fifties, they began to distribute these pictures, lost a great deal of money, and reduced this emphasis. The market, therefore, reverted back to the independents. Once again, the independents began to achieve great success with a few of these pictures.

Until 1973, Ingmar Bergman pictures had been distributed by the majors for a maximum gross of $350,000 for any one picture. *Cries and Whispers* was the first Bergman picture distributed by an independent, New World, and earned a theatrical rental of more than $2.5 million.[11]

Though *I Am Curious Yellow* earned $9 million, the highest rental of a foreign film, the average successful foreign film rental is between $1.5 million and $2.5 million.[12] A picture distributed by the majors needs to earn at least $10 million in rentals. Because it is usually impossible to generate this amount with foreign films, the classics divisions were created by the majors to employ cheaper and more limited methods of getting these pictures to the public. The majors realized once again that a market for these pictures does exist and have again begun to take over the market. Almost all major companies have a classics division, originally created for foreign quota reasons. Companies could not take all the money out of a country that their films earned, and began putting those funds into production and distribution of foreign product. When the majors realized that independents were earning profits from pictures they had rejected, they became interested. The studios had divisions to handle their classic films in their libraries for release to television or specialized theaters. By the end of the 1970s, the new film markets had expanded. A great need arose for product for pay-television, video cassettes and video discs. The potential of these markets was first realized in 1979 by Nathaniel Kwit, the former head of UA Classics.[13]

Kwit was vice president of the division that booked theatrical dates for UA's library of films. He wanted to get the subdivision into first-run distribution, and acquired Truffaut's *The Last Metro* for $125,000 by persuading Truffaut that UA Classics would combine its name with a passion for thrift and concern for the product. UA Classics began acquiring films for a low price, often without an advance to the producer, approaching the deal as partners. Their standard deal is a split of profits 50-50, with the costs coming off-the-top. They keep the advertising costs low and do not take a distribution fee. Kwit opened *The Last Metro* in New York for only $22,000 and generated $86,029 the first week, a house record.[14]

John Sayles' *Return of the Secaucus Seven,* made for $60,000, and *Lianna,* made for around $350,000, were released by UA Classics and earned approximately $2 million each. Since half of the ticket sales were in New York theaters, UA Classics is considering making a direct deal with particular exhibitors.[15]

The executives of the classics divisions believed autonomy from the studio was necessary for success. Sam Kitt, former head of UA Classics, attributed the demise of autonomy to the sales managers. He stated:

> The general sales fellow who handles the commercial films is going to be fighting for his product line. He's going to get extraordinarily jealous about the amount of publicity the classics films are getting and either kill off the division or bring it within his organization.[16]

In 1981, Orion Pictures Corp. established Orion Classics headed by executives from what had been UA Classics, to be run as an autonomous division of the parent company.[17] Their most successful picture, *Diva,* earned more than $7 million at the box office, running for fifty-two weeks in New York. Orion Classics spends between $200,000 and $250,000 to release a picture, with New York accounting for $100,000 of that alone.[18]

Orion Classics, already acquiring and investing in the production of small films abroad, also hopes to produce American films for the market.[19] William Bernstein of Orion claims they opened their classics division to establish relationships with new filmmakers who may make a more commercial picture in the future and because the possibility exists that one film may find a large audience. Though the percentage earned against their investment is adequate, it is insignificant compared to that of the parent company.[20]

Twentieth Century-Fox's International Classics opened in June 1982. It was renamed Fox Specialized Films, and then renamed TLC Films (for Tender Loving Care). After the release of *Eating Raoul, Piaf,* and *Threshold,* Fox Classics gradually took over more advertising and publicity duties from the studio's publicity department. They found it easier to do because they were more intimately involved with the films and filmmakers. By February 1984, Fox Classics began reorganizing. TLC Films department creates the advertising and sets the release date and pattern. The picture is then given to the domestic distribution department.[21]

While Fox International Classics believes they can offer the independent producer all the advantages of specialized treatment, they also offer the possibility of a mass release through their parent company should the film prove successful. Paul Bartel, the filmmaker of *Eating Raoul,* finds the studio's classics divisions "a godsend," because he does not believe independents can match the manpower and clout of the majors. Fox Classics successfully distributed his *Eating Raoul* in partnership with Quartet Films, the New York-based independent.[22]

Triumph Films, formed in March 1982 as a joint venture between Columbia Pictures and France's Gaumont, the leading European distributor and exhibitor, will have the right of first refusal for domestic distribution of Gaumont's titles.[23] While most specialty distributors believe these films must be marketed in a unique manner, Triumph Films believes that if a film is marketed in the same way as Columbia releases its pictures, the audience potential could be expanded. They produced and released *Das Boot* in 1982, which lost money for them. Gaumont in December 1983 was displeased with the large amount of money Columbia was spending to market Triumph's films, making it too difficult for pictures to break even. Though Columbia did not agree, they mutually decided to reduce spending to keep the company going.[24]

Though Triumph Films handles Columbia's current specialized films, Columbia Pictures Classics, in existence for a decade, handles the pictures already domestically released by Columbia. They hold large retrospectives and supply their classics to art houses. They also sublease 16mm prints to subdistributors who rent to schools, institutions, and individuals.[25]

Universal Classics had been one of the most active and heavily financed classics operations among the majors.[26] It was opened in May 1982 and has released *Napoleon, Moonlighting,* and *La Traviata.* They have even invested in the production of *Under the Volcano.*[27] Universal Classics' advertising budget is generally in the $30,000 to $50,000 range to launch a picture on one screen. Radio and television are not used. Jim Katz, head of Universal Classics, claims the goal of any Classics picture is to break out and cross over to reach a broader audience. He maintains that a cooperative relationship exists between Classics and the larger organization. They are able to take advantage of the larger company's resources when the picture warrants it.[28]

When Universal Classics released eight unsuccessful pictures in a row, the major chains wanted their old successful pictures back. The chains preferred to play a rerelease of a blockbuster than an art film. When Universal realized this, they stopped actively looking for films at festivals. Their classics division will now distribute existing films from the Universal library. If they do handle a specialized film, it will play through the studio's regular distribution system.[29]

Paramount Pictures and Warner Bros. were the only studios who did not create separate entities to handle specialized pictures.[30] Warner Bros. Film Classics, created in 1979, concentrated on Warner titles released since 1950, as their films prior to that were sold to United Artists. Their division serves repertory theaters and midnight movie theaters with their releases, but not with acquisitions specially for such release. Warners is enjoying success with midnight movies such as *The Rocky Horror Picture Show, The Song Remains the Same, The Exorcist, Road Warrior,* and *A Clockwork Orange.* To further keep costs down, the shipping charges are paid by the exhibitors, while the artwork is generally chosen from the already created campaigns.[31]

Embassy Pictures reissued *The Ruling Class* with a $100,000 expected loss for prints and advertising. Their sole purpose was the enhancement of the film's value for cable and video. To their surprise, it made money.[32]

When the majors and other companies entered the market, they escalated the costs for everyone. It is difficult for independents to compete because the majors can offer more money up front. By 1983, severe competition for independent pictures existed. The independent film distributors such as Almi Pictures, Cinecom, the Sam Goldwyn Co., Spectra Films, and Quartet Films had formerly been the only ones interested in the pictures. They found they could not compete financially with the major studios. Almi's Ben Barenholtz stated, "What the classics divisions did manage to do is hike up the prices on films to the point where they're not economical to distribute...." Since they had to bid against one another, the prices the studios paid to secure the films soared.[33]

Ben Barenholtz discovered *Cousin, Cousine,* and acquired it for $55,000. It grossed $10 million, earning Libra Films more than $3 million in rentals. Since the majors have entered the competition for select foreign films, the acquisition price has ranged up to $1 million for *Fanny and Alexander.* The expenditure can be justified. UA Classics acquired François Truffaut's *The Last Metro* for $125,000, spent $250,000 on prints and advertising, and earned rentals of $2.5 million. The prices, however, have been escalating. A French agent even requested $250,000 for the next Eric Rohmer film that had no script but was synopsized as "sorta like his *Pauline at the Beach,* but in the snow."[34]

Dan Talbot of New Yorker Films had acquired *The Marriage of Maria Braun* for $25,000 when it was a buyer's market. Though Talbot has acquired three hundred titles in eighteen years, he cannot afford to pay $250,000 for a picture. Talbot claims the classics divisions are not independents who put up their own money but are merely employees spending the studio's money.[35] He finds high prices are now paid for obscure or second-rate films. Talbot does find that the competition for product forces distributors to look closer at less obvious pictures for distribution. He, for example, found success with *My Dinner with André* and *Chan Is Missing,* which might not have been distributed in a less competitive market.[36]

A problem exists with the majors' acquisition of these pictures. If the films open to a limited box office, they will pull the picture out of release immediately. An independent specialized in the market might be more content at a smaller profit, allowing the film to play for more time. Skip Kamm, a buyer and booker for a thirteen-screen independent Western Amusement circuit, finds a dearth of product for his art houses despite additional imports by the majors. He believes they sell their pictures to the circuits with multiple screens, regardless of the effect on the picture.[37] Jeff Down, a specialized film promoter and distributor for *The Stunt Man, Hearts and Minds, Northern Lights,* and *A Little Romance,* said:

> I found out that studios really don't know how to sell a film if it's not a formula sell. If it's anything Richard Rush said—the studios are set up to sell Fords and not Ferraris—they cannot deal with anything that isn't the thing. They also, because of the whole economic set up of the studios, have not learned other ways of communication that aren't money ways....[38]

The classics divisions soon discovered that the pay-television channels had little interest in buying such specialized pictures. HBO film buyer Steve Sheffer stated:

> Some are wonderful, but they have limited value in relation to a service such as HBO. Our philosophy is to run films with the largest broad appeal.

Sheffer claims they pay for a film based on the theatrical film rental earned.[39]

This renewed interest in the theatrical market has steadily increased the number of independent films released in New York. However, the market is still very limited. For example, distributors have learned that pictures do not do well without critical acclaim. New York accounts for 35 percent of an art picture's total revenues, compared to accounting for 10 percent of Hollywood product. An anonymous executive listed the impact of New York critics on the success of a picture in descending order: Vincent Canby, Gene Siskel and Roger Ebert, David Denby, *Time* and *Newsweek,* Andrew Sarris, and Pauline Kael, and found Rex Reed and Kathleen Carroll's reviews of no significance.[40] Unable to compete with the majors, the independents that once relied upon this product had to find alternative films to exhibit or go out of business. However, as before, repeated experience with cost exceeding revenue will reduce the majors desire to dominate this market by mere expenditures. A refinement of their techniques is necessary for survival.

Exhibitors themselves are just as actively involved in the distribution of limited-market films to the public, by dealing directly with filmmakers or foreign distributors. They often are the ones to actively seek the right to exhibit these pictures, instead of distributors seeking them out. Limited-market theaters or second- and subsequent-run theaters generally play the product of the larger theater chains after they have exploited the pictures. Art houses, also called revival or repertory houses, are generally independent theaters that play a specialized product and are financially negligible in terms of overall exhibition revenue. Since the late seventies, many independent second-run houses have resorted to playing art or old films for survival. In Manhattan alone in the last decade, the number of revival houses has tripled.[41]

Low-grossing theaters or limited-market theaters comprise 15 to 20 percent of all screens.[42] The number of theaters playing art product is expanding in certain areas. No longer are New York, San Francisco, Chicago, Boston, and Los Angeles the sole markets. Washington, D.C., Baltimore, Detroit, Houston, Florida, and New Mexico are included. While some large chains are now experimenting with a few of these films to fill up their multiplexes, art theater owners have been the ones to keep these films alive. Major independents in the foreign import market include Continental, owned by the Walter Reade exhibition chain, and Cinema 5, the parent company of Rugoff Theatres. Since they have their own affiliated chain of art houses, they are assured of an outlet for their pictures.[43] In the mid-1960s Don Rugoff organized Cinema 5, where Frances Speilman worked as general sales manager. After quitting in 1979 she organized First Run Features in 1980 to assist a group of eight filmmakers in the distribution of mostly 16mm and documentary pictures. Though a challenge, she found increasingly more exhibitors, including big circuits, willing to give the pictures a try.[44] She claims there are four hundred bookers around the country who play her pictures in their theaters.[45]

New Day Films, created in 1972, is a cooperative for the distribution of feminist films run by the filmmakers themselves. All share the costs of promotion and divide up the work, with the revenue earned from a film going directly to the filmmaker. New Day originally had three films to distribute. Each time a picture is accepted for release, a new filmmaker is admitted into the group.[46]

Film cooperatives were created as avenues of distribution for filmmakers who wanted to produce unconventional films and still maintain control over their work. Initially, they were clubs of filmmakers seeking to evade commercial distribution. Since all films were accepted, they ultimately had thousands of pictures to deal with.[47] Some filmmakers who tried self-distribution found "self-destruction" a more appropriate title. "Distribution is, in many ways, a dreary, non-creative, paperridden, full-time job and not something likely to be done successfully by a person primarily interested in making films."[48] Filmmakers with this attitude felt a need to get together and organize a more efficient means of distributing their work.

Two major co-ops are the Film-Makers' Cooperative in New York City and the Canyon Cinema Cooperative in Sausalito, California. Both were organized in the sixties in response to distributors' refusal to look at experimental shorts. They offer physical distribution facilities at minimal cost; however, since they accept all films, a filmmaker must still promote his film for it to be recognized. The Film-Maker's Cooperative in New York is open to any filmmaker. The filmmaker sets the rental fee and receives 75 percent of each film rental. The co-op receives the 25 percent rental fee but owns no rights. Canyon Cinema Cooperative in Sausalito is a non-profit organization that accepts all films, including those shot in 16mm and 8mm. They charge a 40 percent rental fee for their services.[49]

For exposure, filmmakers may showcase their film at an institution. A filmmaker, however, has to be aware of the fact that this may deter a distributor from picking up the film if these screenings cut into the theatrical run in any major cities.

An independent feature can gain exposure by being screened at the "New American Filmmakers" series at the Whitney Museum of American Art or at the Film Forum. Both are in New York, where critical and audience acclaim is valuable. A film is run for one to two weeks for a rental fee in proportion to the film's length. The Pacific Film Archive in Berkeley usually offers a guarantee against 50 percent of the box office. These screenings may provide important connections to other screenings, distributors, and festivals on the West Coast. Honorariums, good press coverage, and connections to festivals can be obtained by a screening at the American Film Institute Theater in Washington, D.C.[50]

The Association of Independent Video and Filmmakers was created to develop methods of self-help by providing information and moral support about distribution, exhibition, and all aspects of film production.[51] Whereas film societies generally existed to exhibit films, Media Arts Centers have been created as non-profit institutions that exhibit films, conduct lectures, teach, and provide newsletters for their patrons.[52]

New York's Film Forum is devoted to showing unreviewed American and foreign films that have never been seen on television or the commercial circuit. The non-profit theater is a full-time, year-round, autonomous movie house in the United States that is devoted to independent films. An independent can open a film there, pay advertising costs, and hope to secure engagements elsewhere.[53]

Other organizations have been created that truly cater to the limited market. The Pasadena Filmforum was founded by Terry Cannon in 1975 to exhibit experimental films. Averaging only forty to fifty people at their weekly screenings, they provide an atmosphere which facilitates discussion.[54]

Filmmakers, finding it impossible to get their films distributed or exhibited, have bought their own theaters. For example, Lionel Rogosin, distraught that no distributor would take his film, *Come Back, Africa,* and having no place to exhibit it, opened the Bleecker Street Cinema in New York.[55] Similarly, Daniel Talbot, a film critic, was frustrated that certain foreign films were not being exhibited. He opened the New Yorker theater in the sixties. When he found the audience too limited, he moved into distribution of films to schools and community audiences, using other people's theaters for exhibition.[56] In 1969, his experiment with a one-dollar admission to expose audiences to these films proved a financial fiasco. Talbot believes "the New York audience has the worst taste in the world."[57]

If a filmmaker can convince an exhibitor that the film will draw a sizable audience, it may be possible to exhibit a film at a commercial theater when it is regularly closed. The power of an individual exhibitor and audience demand is most evident in the phenomenon of the "midnight movie." A few unique films have played at select theaters at midnight across the country for years. They are films that are events in themselves, that people attend over and over again. With virtually no paid advertising, the audience finds the film by the power of word of mouth. The habit of going to midnight movies came out of the 1960s' revolution in late-night entertainment. These films were organized around special events such as concerts, Halloween, and film marathons. In 1967 Mike Getz organized a network of seventeen theaters across the country to showcase experimental films of independent filmmakers that had practically no outlet. Although thought to be a deviation from regular exhibition hours, by 1972 an estimated $35 million a year was collected just at midnight exhibitions. Midnight screenings allowed films that would not obtain theatrical release to be seen, and gave theater owners the opportunity to make extra money with minimal advertising. Midnight movies are now an established part of exhibition. In 1982 from six hundred to one thousand theaters nationwide were running regularly scheduled midnight movies on weekends.[58]

El Topo, the first midnight film, initially had Cannon Productions as its American distributor. After Cannon edited out thirty minutes of sex and violence, making it incomprehensible, Cannon then shelved it. Ben Barenholtz, owner of the Elgin Theater in New York, decided to test if he could open an unreviewed film based on word of mouth. He successfully opened *El Topo* in 1970 as an event and a curiosity item.[59]

George Romero showed *Night of the Living Dead* to American International Pictures, who liked it but wanted him to make the ending more upbeat and to insert sex scenes. When Romero rejected their offer, the Walter Reade Organization decided to distribute the picture under the Continental Films label for their drive-in circuit. It premiered in 1968 and is reported to have made more than $30 million worldwide for the $114,000 production costs.[60]

The Harder They Come was completed in 1972 for about $150,000. This Jamaican feature gained prominence at the Venice Film Festival and Filmex.

New World Pictures secured it for distribution. Since their advertising campaign, treating the film as black exploitation, was not working, the director was allowed to distribute the film himself if he paid the advertising costs. Realizing the attraction was the reggae music, he turned it into a success in Boston and then at other midnight showings.[61]

Reefer Madness, released in 1936 under the original title of *Tell Your Children and/or The Burning Question,* was rereleased in the mid-1970s. It was originally produced to assist passage of a law making marijuana illegal in 1937, and was rediscovered in the 1970s by the lobby for marijuana, the National Organization for the Reform of Marijuana Law. The new, cult-oriented distributor, New Line Cinema, recognized *Reefer Madness*'s economic potential. Prior to 1972, the midnight movies were limited to specific cities and theaters. *Reefer Madness* made the college midnight movie circuit a viable and lucrative network.[62]

Pink Flamingos, the first real blockbuster hit, cost $12,000 to make and had grossed more than $5 million by the end of 1980, mostly at midnight shows. After it premiered at the 1971 Baltimore Film Festival, New Line Cinema picked it up but did not have success with it. Finally, at the urging of John Waters, the filmmaker, New Line showed it at a midnight screening in New York in 1973. It played once a week for eight years at the Nu Art in Los Angeles. By 1975 it had grossed almost $3.5 million.[63]

The successful play *The Rocky Horror Picture Show* made into a film for $1 million was released by Twentieth Century-Fox in September 1975 but met with failure. As an experiment, it was opened as a midnight movie—not accepted studio marketing strategy. People began going to *The Rocky Horror Picture Show* dressed in costume and began participating in the film. Fox charged exhibitors 80 percent of gross receipts; advertising was less than five hundred dollars a year; and the annual gross was $5 million. If a theater did not pay the high rental, Fox had a long list of theaters waiting for the picture. In 1976, *The Rocky Horror Picture Show* began its more than six-year midnight run to more than five thousand people each week in more than two hundred theaters in the nation. By the end of 1979, it was in more than 230 theaters every Friday and Saturday, grossing over $250,000 per week.[64]

In 1977 *Eraserhead* premiered at the Los Angeles Film Exposition, and more than half the audience walked out during the first half hour. Ben Barenholtz, who had a new distribution firm, Libra Films, and was making money on *Cousin, Cousine,* agreed to distribute it. After the audience found it on the midnight circuit, it was viewed as a classic. *Harold and Maude* opened in 1972 and Paramount believed they had a $1.5 million bomb. Slowly, repertory theaters in college towns began playing it for long runs.[65]

United Artists had picked up the French *King of Hearts* for domestic distribution and received mediocre reviews. Even in art houses, it did not catch on and disappeared. Yet in 1971 it began playing in Cambridge where it ran twice a night for almost seven years. In Seattle, theater owner Randy Finley noticed it sold out every time it played. Believing it had great potential and that United Artists did not know how to market it, Finley convinced them to sell him exclusive theatrical domestic distribution rights. *King of Hearts* was playing for $50 to $75 a showing before Finley took it over. By the end of four years, his Specialty Films had brought in more than $1 million. Major distributors, thus, have a policy of not selling the rights to any film to anyone.[66]

Midnight movies were discovered by the audience, with relatively no advertising costs. People went repeatedly to the same movie to participate in the ritualistic community experience created by the audience. These films did not succeed as first runs but were long lasting successes playing at midnight. The films created an event, with the viewer functioning as active participant and not merely as a passive observer.

The exhibitors took chances and allowed the midnight movie to become an event. Exhibitors have been experimenting with other screenings. New York City has fifteen theaters catering to seven specific ethnic groups: Spanish, Chinese, Japanese, Indian, Russian, Italian, and Greek. To stay in business, many exhibitors also act as distributors, showcasing the films in their New York theaters and then renting the pictures to other parts of the United States. Films are also four-walled: for example, occasionally once a month by a Japanese distributor, and on Sundays by an exhibitor playing an Italian film.[67] Laemmle Theatres, also catering to select audiences, has begun programs on Saturday and Sunday mornings. They have exhibited a Shakespeare festival, a psychology series, a British film series, and an Ingmar Bergman retrospective.

Zoetrope experimented with roadshowing. Francis Coppola presented a multiscreen version of Abel Gance's 1927 *Napoleon* at Manhattan's six-thousand-seat Radio City Music Hall. A live orchestra played a score composed and conducted by Carmine Coppola. In eight showings it grossed $800,000.[68]

Regardless of the new programs being offered to audiences, exhibitors are still quite fearful of a shrinking market. In Europe, art house patronage has declined by 75 percent in the last ten years.[69] The small art theaters were known in the trade as "sure-seaters" because empty seats always existed.[70] Exhibitors are worried that this name will again become appropriate.

NATO devised a pilot film rental plan to aid in the survival of limited-market theaters that gross less than $75,000 a year. Low rentals and exclusion from cooperative advertising are offered.[71] NATO, however, is convinced that multiplexing is more important than special film rental terms from distributors. Since few of these theaters could afford twinning, the

Department of Housing and Urban Development is offering loans for such construction of up to $50,000 at 6.5 percent to 7.0 percent interest over a five-year period.[72]

A popular picture can play twelve thousand dates, of which five thousand theaters have incomes so small that they do not merit a percentage agreement. It is, therefore, rented for a flat price.[73] Art films, even if well received, only gross $15,000 to $20,000 in a medium-sized theater per week. The film is probably in no more than one such theater in six or eight cities at a time.[74]

Laemmle Theatres, which operates fourteen screens in the Los Angeles area, does not blind-bid because the possible loss would be too great. When they find that their competition has booked itself up by bidding, they are then free to negotiate for whatever other pictures become available. Laemmle wrote that small foreign films may secure rentals of 25 to 50 percent, using a sliding scale, with advertising shared on a 50-50 basis. The scale graduates upward as the gross increases. Laemmle does not regard concession sales as a significant profit center, but more as a convenience to the customer.[75] Even small exhibitors must pay a $75 to $100 guarantee for costs of shipping against 35 percent of the box office. If the minimum were not a guarantee, distributors would lose most of the time.[76]

Since the amount of money involved in these films is so limited, even the number and condition of prints become an issue. Since striking a new print is costly, UA Classics struck a print only after Landmark Theatres assured them they would book Sam Pekinpah's *Ride the High Country* for enough days to cover the $1,300 print cost.[77]

Many exhibitors still base their releases on the word of New York critics and will not premiere a foreign film before it is first exposed in New York. The influence of New York, however, is not felt as greatly in Seattle.

Though Seattle ranks between seventeenth and nineteenth among American cities in box office grosses, it is among the top five cities for specialized films. With a population of just over one million, one-third of its thirty-six theaters are devoted to specialized product. Fred Roos, the co-producer of Francis Coppola's films since *The Godfather, Part II*, claims that every Zoetrope film he has been involved with has been tested in Seattle. Screenings of a picture in various stages of progress provide them with important feedback.[78]

Randy Finley, who co-owns fourteen theaters, is attributed with the growth of the specialized moviegoing audience in the area. He believes the success is partly due to the fact that Seattle is controlled by the local film critics instead of the national press. He makes sure the critics see the film ahead of time and fights back if he believes a film received an undeserved, unfavorable review. To generate word of mouth, Finley admits the first one thousand people to a film for free. He believes this has a greater impact than other advertising of the same cost. To make the *King of Hearts* a success, Finley employed radio promotion and shouted advertisements at the University of Washington to attract attention.[79] Seattle audiences attended local showings of *The Stunt Man* and *The Black Stallion* when national distributors were prepared to give up on the pictures.[80] Seattle is established as having a unique and sophisticated audience.

While there is evidence of a decreasing total number of limited-market theaters, there is also evidence of growth of these theaters in select areas. Laemmle believes the new denomination of the art market by the majors is healthy. There is more product coming over, and more American independent films that do not qualify for major distribution are getting shown. Laemmle, however, notices a tendency for some of the majors' classics units to discourage the participation of the exhibitor in the promotion of the films. Whereas the independents used to look to Laemmle for expert advice, he is now viewed as a nuisance to the majors.[81]

Landmark Theatres operates thirty-two repertory theaters nationwide. Though the studios' classics divisions wanted them to share in million-dollar advertising campaigns, Landmark believes they, not the classics divisions, have the expertise in advertising such films by the use of in-house promotions, calendars, and mailings to special interest groups.[82] Although additional advertising might increase the audience, it is too grave a risk for them to take. If a distributor misjudges the gross the picture will generate, the loss of revenue on a picture might condition a distributor or exhibitor not to take the risk again on a foreign film, and instead play it safe with exploitation product.

Bob Langer, who runs a revival house in Manhattan and one in Los Angeles, claims the films that do well in one place do poorly in the other. He finds science fiction and action films do well in California. In New York, artistic and foreign films are more popular. Figuring out what to book where is a major gamble in itself.[83]

More second-run houses are turning to revival or repertory theaters out of desperation. Yet a limited audience exists for these movies that are constantly cycled between these theaters in a given area. Landmark President Steve Gilula said, "A repertory program is often considered as a policy of last resort—God's gift to losing theaters." Landmark has had revival theaters longer than anyone in the country. Gilula states location is of prime importance, though the market is changing so rapidly that there is no guarantee of success. The films shown are now easily seen on cable. Gilula claims their audience does not consist of as many teenagers and college kids as before and is therefore dwindling. They are trying new programs such as rock music and laser shows.[84]

Gary Meyer, vice president of the Landmark theater chain, noted, "The cassettes have made the biggest impact. We thought that they would appeal mainly to an upscale audience that doesn't go to the movies much anyway. That was the case when it first started, but not now." Since pictures are released on video cassettes so soon after first-run theatrical release, their audience is further diminished. Their theater in Berkeley has the highest daily average gross of any theater in the city on a yearly basis. Meyer, however, claims that specialized theaters have a larger overhead than commercial theaters. Featuring two different pictures a day and creating calendars and special programs augments costs. Meyer finds that the old dependable pictures such as *King of Hearts* and *Harold and Maude* are played out. They also need to find new midnight movies, as even *The Rocky Horror Picture Show* audience is dwindling.[85]

Douglas Edwards, a non-profit exhibitor of independent films, commented on the filmmakers: "Frequently their integrity is greater than their achievement." The general sales manager of New Yorker Films, Jeff Lipsky, said:

> Though some of these films look as good or better than Hollywood films, a lot of them get short shrift because they're called independent films and get lumped together with a lot of things that shouldn't be seen by anybody.... If I were an independent filmmaker, I'd take a hard, critical look at my film, and if it lacked quality, drop it.[86]

Yet if one believes in the value of a film, it is to the advantage of many people that exhibition is sought and secured. Film societies and film cooperatives serve to aid filmmakers in getting their esoteric work to the public while providing the service of entertainment and education for audiences. A tenacious filmmaker has innumerable places whence to seek financing and distribution of his film. And if these established sources prove fruitless, he still can create a new means of attracting funds and exhibiting his film. Film societies, cooperatives, and independent theaters were created to fulfill the interest in films as art and to support experimentation in motion pictures.

11

Independent Distributors

Independent distributors have the same goals as do the majors. They aim to offer a picture to the largest audience to generate the greatest profit. The independents, however, are very diverse, ranging from one-person operations to large companies that are similar in structure to the majors. While the large organizations must produce profits, the independents that are merely one-person operations may have the sole aim of distributing their own pictures, which no one else will handle, or they may believe they can secure a greater profit by marketing the pictures themselves.

By gaining the rights to only one film, a person can enter the distribution business. There are approximately fifty to a hundred independent distributors, depending on economic conditions. Since they are financially limited, there is a high rate of mortality.

As can be seen in table 11-1, the percentage of independent pictures rated by the MPAA peaked in 1977 with 70.4 percent, while their share of total films rated has since dwindled to under 50 percent. Regardless of commanding such a percentage of the films rated, their percentage of the box office revenue is 10 to 15 percent. The majors' new classics divisions have redistributed the films from the independents to the majors.

Regardless of their percentage of the market, independents have always existed. Independents have served to nurture talent, giving directors, producers, and actors their first job opportunities. Independents have also developed many of the innovative themes that have entered the mainstream of the business. For example, *Halloween*'s success led to fifteen to twenty-five major releases in the horror genre. The success of *Eat My Dust* and *Grand-Theft Auto*, released in the mid-1970s, is considered to have been a forerunner of television shows such as the "Dukes of Hazzard." Successful films showing women in jeopardy, such as *Big Bad Mama*, had an impact in demonstrating that audiences were willing to watch programs with women in central activist roles such as "Charlie's Angels." *Harper Valley PTA*, an independently produced and distributed film, led to other pictures based on songs.[1]

Table 11-1.   Independent Production, 1970–1983*

12 Months Ending May 31	Indie** Sources	All*** Sources	Indie Share
1970	133	410	32.4%
1971	246	505	48.7%
1972	239	490	48.8%
1973	294	542	54.2%
1974	357	557	64.1%
1975	292	449	65.0%
1976	312	462	67.5%
1977	299	425	70.4%
1978	225	343	65.6%
1979	189	337	56.1%
1980	205	342	59.9%
1981	171	312	54.8%
1982	192	349	55.0%
1983	154	315	48.9%

*Based on indie-made features which received MPAA film ratings.
**Excludes production for major companies by affiliated indie units and films acquired via negative pickup and other deals at various stages of production. However, includes many films later acquired for release by MPAA and other prominent distributors.
***Includes films from indies plus MPAA, Walt Disney Prods., Orion (Filmways/AIP) and their affiliates.
(Source: MPAA data, updated and arranged by *Daily Variety,* "15-Year Indie Production Pulse," *Daily Variety,* 13 June 1983, 18.)

Most companies that handle a few pictures for distribution realize the pictures have been turned down by most of the other distributors by the time they have the chance to acquire them. Therefore, they usually begin to produce their own pictures. Lee Beaupre wrote that searching for commercial, independent pictures is "a long, frustrating tour through more cinematic garbage than most people know exists—a fact to which I can attest after one year of such fruitless wading while working for Levitt-Pickman Film Corp."[2]

Companies with independent distribution networks can afford to make exploitation films. If it appears that a picture will make money, they can ask for a large acquisition price from a major by using self-distribution as the threatened alternative. The independent without a distribution network, however, is in a weak bargaining position unless he can get distributors bidding against one another.[3]

Individuals who form their own distribution company, often because they have made a film that no one else would handle, may take on other films for release. A filmmaker must be wary of these companies, with little to lose and only profit to be gained. They often have little experience in distribution and may destroy a film's potential success. They can easily file for bankruptcy without concern for the films they have acquired. Since independents are not diversified, a few failures can gravely affect the company.

Table 11-2.   U.S. Releases

	1982	1983	1984*
Majors' Distribution	116	124	143–150
Majors' Classics Divisions	20	33	34
Foreign "Art" Imports	56	60	87
Other Indie Distribution	137	140	155
Total Mainstream Releases	329	357	419
Kung Fu—Martial Arts	29	13	10
Hardcore Pornography	93	101	95
Total New Releases**	451	471	524

*Total films announced for release by distributors thus far; kung fu and porno estimated at just under last year's levels.
**Does not include reissues or foreign-language films imported for ethnic circuit only. Also excluded are shelved films (MPAA rated, but unreleased to date, and not yet assigned a 1984 opening slot, numbering thirty-three and forty-seven titles in 1982 and 1983 respectively).
(Source: "Films Newly Released in U.S.," *Variety*, 7 March 1984, 414.)

The "B" picture that became popular in the mid-1930s when distributors believed double features would lure audiences back into the theaters, took from seven days to three weeks to make.[4] These pictures that evolved into the independently produced films must keep improving their quality as the majors elevate their production value. Low-budget filmmakers often claim that their budgets are larger than they really are and that their shooting schedules are longer than they really are to imply greater quality. Because of the effects-oriented commercial films the majors offer, the standards of expectation have been raised. Pictures are rapidly pushed through theatrical exhibition to home video and pay-cable. An increasing number of pictures bypass a national release in theaters, evading New York completely. Many more pictures are being released regionally.

Increased costs of promoting and advertising pictures have hurt independents. A one-hundred theater break in New York once cost $20,000 in advertising to earn $1,000 a theater in film rental and generated a profit of $70,000. Today one must spend more than $100,000 to be competitive with the majors and must play the film more than one week to make a profit.[5] Ed Colarik, president of International Marketing Consultants, believes finding the "handle," the one marketable strength of a film, is the single most important talent independent distribution has. Colarik also suggests testing the film in small towns at midnight showings, and then regionally convincing exhibitors to book it. Since word spreads among exhibitors, he suggests sticking to one rental policy.[6]

Many films are produced without publicity to avoid imitation, union problems, and location difficulties. Thus, they lose much valuable publicity that the majors generate prior to advertising. Among exhibitors, the independents are second priority to the powerful majors. An independent may have a $6 million ad campaign scheduled for an opening of a picture around the country in June, and will be unable to book a theater in New York until August.[7] The independents can therefore rely on certain theaters that cannot command the product from the majors. These theaters, however, are generally low grossing. Also, it might be unwise to open a picture in direct competition with the best pictures of the year.

Independent distributors of all sizes employ subdistributors because they generally cannot maintain their own exchanges. Subdistributors or state's righters can be individual entrepreneurs who represent eight to ten companies within a given city.

A number of independents who distribute through subdistributors become active only when they find a suitable picture. It is often a picture that they are financially involved with or one that has been rejected by the majors. They generally can book directly with theaters in their own territory.

Distributors may also acquire pictures strictly for the ancillary markets. Independent American distributors distribute their films in foreign territories through locally owned exchanges in the various countries or territories. The distribution deal is generally on a percentage basis similar to a domestic subdistribution agreement. When the local company puts up prints and ads, revenues are shared 50-50. When the American distributor advances costs, local participation declines to 30 to 35 percent of the distributor's share.[8]

For domestic releases, independent distributors generally start with only a few prints, from ten to twenty-five, and test market the film in several regions to make sure it is not merely a one-region success. One hundred prints can usually handle a picture that grosses $1 million at the box office. Each time a successful picture plays, it generates $5,000 to $10,000 a theater.[9] A picture can be distributed on this theater-by-theater basis. Many subdistributors have to survive on a subsistence level until a major hit revives them. Because of this, many are accused of holding onto cash for too long, needing it to pay their debts.

The majors are now acquiring and producing what was once independent product. For example, *Alien* was initially intended as a low-budget exploitation picture that ultimately became a high-budget Twentieth Century-Fox film. The producer of *Friday the 13th* was in the distribution business and initially intended the picture to be distributed independently. Paramount acquired and profitably distributed the picture. Paramount, however, took away an opportunity that would have gone to an independent.[10]

Independents are increasingly investing in larger budgeted general appeal pictures. For example, *The Muppet Movie* and *Battle Beyond the Stars* have been extremely successful. The availability of private investors willing to gamble on films allows for production outside the studio system.[11]

Artista Films found it necessary to enter production to maintain a product line to distribute. President Lou George stated, "It became a matter of survival.... We were practically forced into production. It is vital for the independent distributor." They produced *Surf II* in 1983 when no *Surf I* existed, and mainly handle action-adventure pictures "because that's what the foreign market likes. Action films always have a market."[12]

In the 1960s and early 1970s, many theaters would distribute independent films on a first-run basis. Theaters also existed that distributed major and independent product on a subsequent sub-run basis. Independent distribution patterns would be to play seventy-five to one hundred theaters in a major city and make a profit from a one-week run. The independent would then release it in a second run and make an additional profit. Today, these tracks for consistent sub-run release no longer exist.[13] Independently distributed pictures still account for a small amount of the hundreds of millions of dollars paid for pay-television licenses. Independents also receive less of a fee even if it is a success by a major's standards. Since the pay-television channels are becoming more secure about a supply of films from the majors, they are becoming increasingly tougher on the independents. President of HBO Film Licensing Steve Scheffer claims that 35 to 40 percent of their annual lineup of approximately 180 new titles introduced on HBO and Cinemax are independent. Showtime/TMC finds about 15 percent of their product to be acquisitions from independents.[14]

The future is bleak for independent distributors without major resources and who rely on independent subdistributors, particularly since subdistributors are vanishing. Independents with their own exchanges can generate enough rental to pay marketing costs and to secure product. These major independents can generate film rental in a year of $10 million to $50 million each. They can diversify their product to occasionally compete with the majors and can distribute pictures that would be unprofitable for the majors to distribute.[15]

Independent distributors may appear as financial failures in business, yet generate enough profit for one person to survive. Ed Colarik has had two independent distribution companies and claims to have personally sold to every chain in the country. Colarik distributed *Love and Sex Italian Style,* an Italian sex comedy, which played in art houses and generated $400,000 in film rental, with $75,000 spent on prints and ads. With a 50/50 split, the distributor and producer shared $325,000. Though these numbers are relatively miniscule, the cash can be significant to those involved.[16] Independents have survived and will survive by distributing pictures that the majors find unprofitable to handle, while only competing with the majors occasionally with their most commercial product. For a major to find a picture acceptable, it must be able to generate millions of dollars in rentals. To a small company, a rental a fraction of this size can be enormous.

Ken Wlaschin, artistic director of Filmex, believes an American independent feature movement began at the end of the seventies when

Northern Lights won the first Golden Camera Award for best first film at Cannes. He hopes that in another ten years a distribution setup of a hundred theaters, though not of one chain, will show these pictures. If such a system existed, a distributor could easily coordinate a wide release. Wlaschin defines an exploitational film as one made with the intention to make money, while a personal independent film is made because the filmmaker has a passion to make it and will find a market afterwards if one exists.[17] Regardless, films are still judged by some standard criteria and certain pictures are therefore excluded.

Though the United States Government does not directly sponsor filmmaking, many sources of funding exist to provide filmmakers with capital. Grants from the National Endowment for the Arts, the Corporation for Public Broadcasting, and innumerable private companies are providing millions of dollars for production each year. Although the different organizations have their own restrictions regarding form and content, their very existence demonstrates an awareness of the need to fund filmmakers, in addition to a realization of the value of the films that are produced. Independents can acquire grants from governmental organizations and private companies, yet one's proposal still must meet their standards. Instead of sex or violence as criteria, a film must concern the humanities for a National Endowment of the Arts grant. Because a picture may not meet any distributor's standards, a filmmaker may have to distribute the film himself if he is so inclined. When one cannot secure distribution and does not want to handle the picture oneself, one has the option of selling it outright.

Ken Hartford began Cinevid in 1981 with an ad in the Hollywood trade papers offering to "buy your picture sight unseen." He was soon the owner of 220 films, which he successfully sold at MIFED to distributors who wanted to fill their broadcast time or to create video cassettes. Hartford said, "We only sell them in packages. Usually when you sell a motion picture, you do a press kit, hold a screening, and so on. We sell them like potatoes, so many to a bag." He claims it is the artwork that sells the films for which he charges a flat fee.[18] Hartford buys the rights to approximately 140 pictures a year and sells them internationally, admitting that the pictures he sells are of low quality. He does not even view most of the films he buys. Hartford claims, "If it's an action movie, a thriller, a horror picture, we buy it sight unseen. If it's some kinda drama, some picture with a lot of dialogue, we might want to look at it first to make sure it's not all talk." They then change the title and create artwork for the picture. Since the films are mostly sold in cassette form to foreign markets, Hartford leaves off the title so the local distributor can create the title in his own language. Hartford claims to see less than 10 percent of the pictures. The artists do their work from a synopsis they read. Yet the picture may still not have been seen by anybody. He stated:

What difference does it make? The beauty is, the guy buys his cassette, he takes it home, it's his. He's got a real movie there. It's got action, it's got adventure. If he doesn't like it, that's his problem. He bought it sight unseen. Just like we did. [19]

To these buyers, the film is treated as a product only, and not anyone's creation of passion and meaning.

If the filmmaker does not wish to distribute his picture himself or to sell it outright, there are various independent distributors that could handle the picture. While numerous distributors may exist at any one time, only a few have survived for more than a few years or to distribute more than a few films. American International Pictures was the most successful independent, employing unique production, marketing and distribution techniques.

American International Pictures

Low-budget pictures had been the "B" pictures in the pre-television era and provided theater chains with second features at a fixed rate. [20] When such pictures were no longer provided by the majors, other companies were able to supply the still existent demand. American International Pictures (AIP) was created in 1954 as an independent company specializing in "B" movies and action films. Though most predicted that only the big pictures would survive because of television, Samuel Z. Arkoff and James H. Nicholson believed that exhibitors would still need such pictures. They believed if they made them economical enough and yet distinct enough from television, their pictures would be successful. Arkoff, an attorney, partnered with Hank McCune in the first film network series on NBC-TV, "The Hank McCune Show," and Nicholson, an exhibitor who owned theaters in Los Angeles and had been a distributor of Universal Pictures reissues, formed American Releasing Corporation. [21]

Roger Corman had made a picture for $66,000 called *The Fast and the Furious,* which Republic wanted. Nicholson, however, persuaded Corman to give him thirty days in which to use the picture as bait to raise $90,000 from state's rights distributors against production of another five pictures to go with it. Arkoff and Nicholson succeeded and began their new company. They initially aimed to distribute only, but it became apparent that production was necessary to ensure the right kind of picture to distribute. Arkoff, with his production experience, and Nicholson, with his advertising and merchandising expertise and ability to think up appropriate movie titles, decided to produce. To them, the title of the picture was of primary importance, with the story created to match the title. Their initial name was Golden State Productions, under which they produced *Apache Woman.* American Releasing Corporation became known as American International Pictures a year later. [22]

Arkoff and Nicholson each contributed $3,000 to set up their distribution company. They accumulated $25,000 in salary deferments, $35,000 in advances from subdistributors, $25,000 in advances from the film lab with the lab work itself deferred, and $10,000 in advances from foreign distributors. Sufficient to make inexpensive pictures, approximately one hundred were made by these means.[23]

They realized that the small theaters needed product because these independent exhibitors could not secure the major films. They also believed they could make money by supplying the country's drive-in theaters with less expensive features that could be changed twice a week. Roger Corman made *The Beast with 1,000,000 Eyes* in eight days for $35,000. The production budgets of the other pictures ranged from $50,000 to $150,000. If a picture was one day over its ten-day shooting schedule or $1,000 over budget, Arkoff would threaten to, and occasionally would, tear pages out of the script. By 1959, their double bills were being imitated and the public began to sense that if two pictures were advertised with splashy ads, poor quality was indicated. They decided to make pictures in color and with $400,000 budgets. For eight pictures, Arkoff and Nicholson chose public domain Edgar Allan Poe stories and employed great horror stars who were underpriced.[24] With these sensationalistic films catering to younger audiences, Parent Teacher Associations across America were outraged. Roger Corman's Edgar Allan Poe stories, however, earned respect, as they induced adolescents to read Poe's books. Libraries and schools became part of his sales force.[25]

Theater owners generally booked an "A" picture and a "B" picture, usually of different genres to lure moviegoers of varying tastes to their theaters. The producer of the "B" picture received little of the box office revenue. AIP employed a new idea of playing a double bill of two pictures of the same genre. Their first experiment with two science fiction pictures, *The Day the World Ended* and *The Phantom from 10,000 Leagues,* was a success. AIP had rented the films together on a percentage basis, refusing to split them to eliminate the possibility that they would be sold at flat second-feature prices.[26]

This success set the pattern for their operations. They sought to anticipate trends in popular taste and then to move on to a new trend before it became old. They were successful with motorcycle sagas, beach pictures, youth films, and science fiction pictures.

When the majors tried to produce such pictures, they were not profitable because of the films' large overheads. AIP also created a new level of importance around drive-in theaters that seemed to thrive on action, science fiction, and horror pictures. AIP geared much of its advertising and promotion to multiple drive-in openings. Finally, the drive-ins were supplied with new product, as were first-run theaters.[27] At the beginning, AIP's pictures were usually shot in less than twelve days, budgeted between $75,000 and $150,000, and were made in black and white.[28] AIP's aim was to release select films through select distributors for a specialized audience.[29]

When the double bills ended in the late fifties, the company turned to more ambitious product.[30] In the sixties, AIP realized a new second feature was unnecessary.[31] When Annette Funicello's exclusive contract with Disney lapsed, AIP decided to make beach party pictures starring her. Arkoff stated, "We never showed parents... the Peter Pan syndrome. No responsible adults. No school. No church...." After a few years their films reflected more anger. Arkoff claims his pictures in the sixties mirrored teenagers' attitude progression from high-spirited to rebellious.[32] The youth-oriented motorcycle picture *Easy Rider* (1969) started as an AIP project. After discord with Arkoff, Bob Rafelson and Bert Schneider took it to Columbia, where the picture grossed $20 million.[33]

While the majors were losing half a billion dollars between 1969 and 1974, AIP was making a profit. During those years, the studios had produced two dozen films that could not capture the youth market as had AIP's *The Trip, The Wild Angels,* and *Wild in the Streets.* AIP has had success in creating new trends and mixing old genres to create new ones. His *Blacula* combined horror and black films. *I Was a Teen-age Frankenstein* combined youth and horror genres.[34]

Nicholson wrote that the first question they ask before they buy a story or have one written is "will it sell?" They believed excitement, action, and different themes or formulas that work were necessary.[35] Arkoff has relied upon listening to what young people wanted to see, instead of relying upon his own opinions. "No matter how good I think I am, after a certain age you don't react the same," he stated.[36] Arkoff would visit Cannes annually to keep contacts alive with international buyers and sellers and to "smell out the scene."[37] He noted:

> I look upon my movies as being merchandise, just as Woolworth's has a line of merchandise. The fact that many of my acquaintances wouldn't buy Woolworth's merchandise doesn't keep it from being perfectly good merchandise. Many people in this business feel that merchandise not aimed at them must be shoddy. They wouldn't feel that way about overshoes.[38]

Arkoff commented, "We are a merchandising company. That may sound inelegant."[39] The marketing of pictures has always been of top priority for AIP. They often employed movie publicity schemes. For example, *Blacula* audiences were offered bay leaves as protection against the black vampire.[40] AIP employed a frog jumping contest in a hundred cities for the release of *Frogs.*[41]

Arkoff stated, "We never pretended to be arty. We are realistic and practical. We are cost conscious, but we are not penny pinchers. We spend where spending will increase revenue. . . . We have had profits every year of our existence."[42] On the twenty-fifth anniversary of AIP, New York's Museum of Modern Art honored AIP for its history of "distinctive and innovative cinema." Arkoff commented, "I suppose time can dignify anything. . . ." In her essay "Trash, Art and the Movies," Pauline Kael

> wondered if the company's crude opportunism wasn't really the key to its box-office appeal. From *I Was a Teen-age Werewolf* through the beach parties to *Wild in the Streets* and *The Savage Seven,* American International Pictures has sold a cheap commodity, which in its lack of artistry and its blatant and sometimes funny way of delivering action serves to remind us that one of the great appeals of movies is that we don't have to take them too seriously. . . . At some basic level (audiences) like the pictures to be cheaply done, they enjoy the crudeness; it's a breather. . . a vacation from proper behavior and good taste and required responses.

The Museum of Modern Art's curator, Adrienne Mancia, believed the tribute to AIP was warranted because "AIP films very much reflect or anticipate moods in the popular culture of America, especially during the '50s and '60s. . . . More than any studio, AIP was really feeling the pulse and tempo of what was happening among a broad section of the population."[43]

Arkoff was always a maverick in the industry. He referred to the creative people in the industry as "barnacles." "As time has gone by, layers of barnacles have encrusted the picture-making process."[44] Now, actors, directors, and writers all want profits, and to be included in the control.

Arkoff allowed new talent to learn and grow. Many producers and directors who became famous started at AIP. They include Francis Ford Coppola (*Dementia 13*), Woody Allen (*What's Up Tiger Lily?*), Martin Scorsese (*Boxcar Bertha*), John Milius (*Dillinger*), Ralph Bakshi (*Heavy Traffic*), Tom Laughlin (*Born Losers*), Vincent Minnelli (*A Matter of Time*), Richard Rush (*Hell's Angels on Wheels*), and Brian De Palma (*Sisters*). The rising stars that appeared in their pictures include Jack Nicholson, Peter Fonda, Michael Landon, Richard Dreyfuss, Richard Pryor, Robert De Niro, Charles Bronson, Candy Clark, Bruce Dern, Connie Stevens, Don Rickles, Fabian, Cher, David Carradine, Mike Curb, and Dennis Hopper. These directors also used established stars such as Vincent Price, Peter Lorre, Ray Milland, Basil Rathbone, and Christopher Lee.[45]

Few independent distributors can have sales staffs around the country as the majors do. Arkoff said that when AIP began and made only four or five pictures a year, their franchise holders handled other pictures too. Gradually, as AIP grew, the franchises became exclusive AIP distributors and needed AIP's consent to take on another's product. AIP was then able to take them over.[46] Arkoff believed many pictures were successful partially because of AIP's twenty-eight exchanges.[47] AIP had exchanges all over the United States and released pictures worldwide. Approximately five hundred pictures were released in their first twenty-five years, having grossed at the box office in excess of $1.5 billion.[48]

AIP was a master at cutting all costs. They shot on location and procured as many elements as possible for free. When Arkoff felt greater competition from television movies, however, he decided to increase spending. At the end of the 1970s, costs had risen and their films were no longer satisfying their audiences.[49]Though their domestic film rentals had been down for several years, 1978 was the first time in AIP's history that the company showed a financial loss. Increasing production and marketing costs, elimination of tax shelter financing, and their belief in rising audience tastes contributed to their situation. As the majors chose to make higher-budgeted pictures and the small independents made the exploitation films, AIP was in the middle. AIP gradually made more expensive pictures. *The Amityville Horror* cost more than $5 million. AIP became involved in international cofinancing deals for blockbusters like the $11 million war adventure *Force 10 from Navarone*. The $16 million *Meteor*, an attempt to cash in on the disaster trend, was a failure. Their release of *Matilda, The Norseman, Our Winning Season, The Private Files of J. Edgar Hoover,* and *California Dreaming* failed to find an audience. Their one success of the summer, *Love at First Bite,* was produced by Mel Simon Productions and was merely distributed by AIP.[50]

Arkoff sold his company to Filmways in March 1979 for approximately $25 million. That summer *Love at First Bite* earned AIP more than $18 million in rentals and *The Amityville Horror* generated $35 million in rentals.[51] *The Amityville Horror* proved to be the third greatest grossing picture to be released by a non-major, surpassed only by *The Graduate* (Joseph E. Levine) and *Mary Poppins* (Walt Disney).[52]

Filmways tried to become an instant major and even released Arkoff, who had remained as chairman and chief executive officer of a subsidiary. Nearly every Filmways picture was a failure. In February 1982, a movie production company founded in 1978 by former United Artists executives purchased Filmways for $26 million and renamed it Orion.[53] Orion has since attempted to join the major distribution status. Their high-budget pictures have little resemblance to pictures made under Arkoff's leadership.

AIP's success was guided by Arkoff, who was able to discover or predict what audiences wanted to see and then was able to supply the product. He offered audiences new ideas, new talent, and a new means of presentation. AIP distributed sixty-four pictures earning more than $1 million in domestic rentals from 1970 until it was acquired by Filmways, which had six such releases. AIP was the dominant independent distributor of the 1970s.

Avco Embassy

Embassy Pictures was formed in 1967 by Joseph Levine, the producer, who sold it in 1974 to the Avco Corporation. Avco Embassy was a financial services company initially keeping its film subsidiary to distribute but not finance motion pictures.[54] It specialized in merchandising films from independent producers. They offered ad testing and a territory-by-territory sales approach, while handling a limit of twelve to fifteen pictures per year. They claimed to have an unlimited amount of money to merchandise films, while offering the situation whereby independent producers would not be competing for attention with in-house financed pictures. They also claimed to offer a better deal because their operating costs were less than the majors.[55]

They realized their strength was in the operation of exchanges. President William E. Chaikin claimed, "Cutting exchanges can be penny wise and pound foolish—what does it cost? $60–70,000 a year per branch?"[56] In 1976, Avco decided to give their sixteen branch offices, the largest number of any independent distribution company, greater autonomy than ever before to stimulate creative sales thinking and problem solving on the local level. Believing a direct correlation existed between the success of a film and the degree of cooperation between sales and advertising prior to the setting of play dates, they were striving for greater integration and coordination between sales and advertising departments. Avco consulted the advertising department not only in regard to expenditures but also to the timing and location of openings.[57]

In 1978, Robert Rehme entered as vice president in charge of marketing. After he initiated investing small amounts in production, he was quickly promoted to president. He implemented a means of minimizing risks and maximizing profits. To finance pictures, Avco secured outside investors to cover their portion. Once their share was recouped, they rolled the money over into a new investment. They were thus able to increase production from five or six pictures in 1977–78 to fifteen in 1981. The revenues had quadrupled in three years, allowing more money for production. *The Fog* cost less than $1.5 million and grossed $30 million; *The Howling* cost $1.7 million and grossed more than $20 million; *Scanners, Prom Night,* and *Phantasm* cost less than $5 million a picture and grossed around $15 million each. Rehme believed consistency of policy was necessary. He believed they had to deliver commercial pictures made basically for North American audiences because with few exceptions, pictures that do well domestically succeed elsewhere. Rehme picked up films, believing he had to give exhibitors more than one horror film every month for a balanced flow of product. Rehme claimed Avco gave producers the freedom to execute their movie, and consulted with them regarding the selling of the picture. Avco, however, retained the right of approval over script, director, producer and principal stars, while encouraging "team work."[58]

The most ambitious year for Avco Embassy was 1981, with a release slate of fifteen pictures representing an aggregate production total cost of $80 million.[59] Rehme claimed to be making "bread and butter pictures" instead of taking chances. However, he intended on expanding the scope of their standard low-budget action-adventure and horror pictures.[60]

Another success that year, *Time Bandits,* had been rejected for domestic distribution by the majors and was picked up by Avco Embassy. Avco agreed to take only a 17 percent distribution fee instead of the usual 30 percent. It became a success with more than $17 million in domestic rentals.[61]

Avco Embassy secured 5 percent of the theatrical film rentals in the domestic market in 1981. By employing self-generated exploitation productions and independent pickups, they were able to generate more than $61 million in film rentals.[62]

Avco Embassy firmly believed in the power of publicity. Whereas the majors emphasized the Los Angeles and New York press, Avco found no market too small. Roving publicists were sent to areas not covered by their offices. Though they performed audience tests, Rehme found no substitute to being in the audience in person.[63]

After Avco's successful year, Jerry Perenchio and Norman Lear purchased Avco Embassy Pictures for approximately $26 million.[64] Perenchio and Lear intended to steer away from exploitation pictures in favor of more serious films.[65]

Zapped proved to be their greatest money-maker thus far, generating more than $6 million in domestic rentals. Their other successes, *Vice Squad, The Seduction, Paradise,* and *The Soldier,* also proved to be of the exploitation genre. Only the children's picture *Savannah Smiles* proved to be a commercial success and fit the type of picture they claimed they would emphasize.

Avco Embassy had proved successful with exploitation films not offered by the majors. Their emphasis on marketing techniques designed for the smaller film proved successful for their thirty-six pictures that earned domestic rentals of more than $1 million since 1970. When Avco was bought out and became Embassy, the owners wanted to streamline the operation, reduce the number of exchanges, and become involved in more artistic product. Though seven of their pictures have already earned more than $1 million in domestic rentals, it remains to be seen if they can gain as much commercial power in independent distribution as Avco once commanded.

New World Pictures

After Roger Corman's *Gas-s-s-s* (1970) and *Von Richtofen and Brown* (1971) were recut by AIP and United Artists, respectively, Corman decided to start his own distribution company.[66] In 1970, Corman formed New World, which was composed of two companies: New World Productions to produce the films, and New World Pictures to distribute New World Productions' product and acquisitions.[67] In New World's first year, eleven out of eleven pictures were box office successes.[68] Corman continued to make a profit each year.

In the beginning, New World released films primarily to the drive-ins until the majors invaded the market.[69] Corman then decided to deal with commercial and art films, while avoiding the middle picture. New World specialized in soft-core sex, action, horror, and foreign product.[70]

While the domestic gross potential of a commercial picture was believed to be unlimited, New World believed the domestic gross for art pictures to be between $1 million and $3.5 million.[71]

The Story of Adele H., directed by François Truffaut, was distributed by New World. Without a distributor, it had premiered as the closing entry at the New York Film Festival. For $75,000, Corman then secured the distribution rights, ordered one hundred prints, and budgeted advertising at $100,000. With rentals of more than $2.5 million, New World made a profit. The film was booked without securing advances or guarantees from exhibitors and no bids were taken since no competition existed. The picture opened in one theater. New World paid for all advertising and received 75 percent of the first week's gross, 50 percent of the second week's gross, and 35 percent of the subsequent weeks. Because of the New York performance and positive critical reviews, New World subsequently commanded rental terms of a 50 percent split of the box office gross with cooperative newspaper advertising split similarly. The lead actress' Academy Award nomination enabled New World to secure additional bookings. However, once she did not win, the nomination's publicity value was no longer effective. The average run for a film outside New York is two to three weeks in a dozen cities, and mostly only one week in others, according to Robert Rehme of New World. *The Story of Adele H.* had played fewer than one thousand play dates in a year of release.[72]

New World's in-house productions usually began with an idea of Corman's. After having it evaluated for box office potential domestically, overseas, and for television, he would then try to pre-finance the picture.[73] New World relied on the trailer to sell the picture, with all else being secondary. If sufficient footage to produce an effective trailer did not exist, trailers were created with new footage shot specifically for this purpose or were made from scenes clipped from another movie.[74]

Piranha was presented in script form to New World with half of the financing, $500,000, secured by United Artists, who wanted the picture to be produced by New World Productions. New World financed the other half of the negative cost in exchange for distribution rights in the United States and Canada, while United Artists secured the distribution rights for all other territories. For United Artists, the picture has generated approximately $10 million in gross film revenue and for New World has grossed about $4 million. *Piranha* was opened in July 1978 in hundreds of theaters, with television advertising. The five hundred prints have played 4,300 play dates. [75]

New World owns ten domestic branches: Los Angeles, New York, Atlanta, Dallas, New Orleans, Chicago, Detroit, Washington, Memphis, and Oklahoma. Their first foreign office opened in Canada in 1978, their second in the United Kingdom in 1979. In other domestic areas, their product is handled by subdistributors. Generally, the standard domestic theatrical distribution fee of 30 percent is divided between the regional branch and the national distributor. The subdistribution fee is also 15 to 20 percent. New World occasionally raises the incentive to branches, regarded as independent businesses, by offering a 22.5 percent fee if an older picture's gross reaches a certain amount. New World also rewards branch managers with a profit participation if certain goals are reached. The New World exchanges book the pictures, yet the distribution strategy, term approvals, and advertising allotments come from the home office in Los Angeles. [76]

Similar to the majors, New World averages 30 percent of the expected gross spent on cooperative advertising. The more a picture grosses, the lower is this percentage. For example, if 30 percent is spent on the first $1 million, only 25 percent of the gross may be spent for the second $1 million. [77] Corman claims that studios generally charge up to five times higher for advertising and publicity than independents. The independents have lower overhead and generally charge a few points less than studios as a distribution fee. He believes that a medium-budgeted picture that can generate $5 million to $10 million in rentals is better serviced by an independent as it is important to them while only of minor significance to a major. [78]

Corman claims the advantage of smaller distributors is that their costs are less and they can be more efficient. The break-even point of a picture distributed by an independent is about double the negative cost. He finds the advantage the majors possess is their power to book theaters sight unseen. [79] New World also saves money on interest by quickly releasing pictures. New World cannot afford the time required to screen pictures for exhibitors' bidding. [80]

Roger Corman claims to have shot *The Little Shop of Horrors* in two days and one night and *The Raven* in fifteen days. Though today there is better equipment, faster film, and perfect studio-controlled conditions, the number of days it takes to shoot a picture is often sixty to seventy. Believing pre-planning is the key to efficiency, in his early career Corman regularly produced pictures in less than fifteen days on budgets under $200,000. Corman, however, advises always being open to new ideas. Similarly, he does considerable market research, yet ultimately exercises his own judgment.[81] At New World, he was able to control the directors of his films. He said, "Anyone who can operate a lathe drill can direct a movie."[82]

Corman decided to sell New World because he felt the market was changing. He said, "It's very difficult to persuade an audience to pay money to see a $1,000,000 film when they can pay the same amount of money to see a $20,000,000 to $30,000,000 film, or they can see a $2,000,000 Movie of the Week on television for nothing."[83]

Corman was required to gamble more of his own money to compete for playing time and to attain the same profits. In 1982 New World made twelve $2 million pictures and earned only 30 percent on each of them, not as much as in previous years.[84] Corman sold New World in 1983, with its library of 110 films and ten-branch distribution arm, to three lawyers for $16.5 million.[85]

Robert Rehme, who is attributed with being responsible for Avco Embassy's success, became the president of New World. He said, "We're gonna make hit pictures, high-concept pictures." The term "high-concept" became popular in the early seventies among television executives. A "high-concept" picture is easily described in ten words or less and does not require a star. The idea is the main attraction, and is able to be conveyed easily in fifteen-to thirty-second television advertisements or in printed advertisements. The old exploitation pictures fit the mold of this euphemism.[86]

Harry Evans Sloan, one of the new owners of New World, claims it is necessary for their budgets to increase because a picture without stars is unable to be sold to the networks. Though Corman's pictures were successful in the theatrical market, Sloan estimates that only two or three of the approximately one hundred pictures released in the past ten years have had network sales. New World plans to make pictures for half the cost of the majors' pictures. They believe a $10 million production must gross $25 million to break even. This is estimated to have a 2 percent chance of success. They therefore claim that the $5 million film grossing $12.5 million gives it a 20 to 25 percent chance to be profitable and is more secure.[87] It is estimated that in 1981, New World Pictures' domestic theatrical revenue represented a 1 to 1.2 percent share of the marketplace. The new New World strives for a 6 percent share. They intend to produce pictures they believe will sell internationally.[88] The new owners of New World signed with the Directors Guild of America, something Roger Corman had never done.[89]

The new owners of New World found that the low-budget pictures of the Corman era had low ancillary value. New World has decided to concentrate on modestly budgeted pictures to improve their ancillary value as well as their theatrical worth. The new New World distributed sixteen pictures in their first year. Four were Corman films for which New World was serving as a subdistributor; the rest were pickups except for *Angel,* their own production. They have decided not to distribute pictures if they cannot secure all domestic rights. They believe in releasing pictures cautiously. For example, opening a picture with ten prints and advertising campaigns of less than $50,000 is not uncommon for them. If the picture develops an audience, the release is broadened. If it is unsuccessful, it is pulled from theatrical release and exploited in the ancillary markets. New World has also refused to enter bidding against the majors for a picture.[90]

New World plans to produce eight to twelve pictures annually, with budgets from $2 million to $7 million, while acquiring five or six films a year from independents.[91] They have found action-adventure is the easiest to sell, while the victim who obtains revenge is also a secure investment.[92]

With Roger Corman's knowledge of the market, use of new talent, and directed marketing skills, New World remained a stable company. The new New World is further attempting to increase its strength in the marketplace.

Crown International

Crown International Pictures was founded in 1959 by Newton P. (Red) Jacobs. It is now identified with Marilyn and Mark Tenser, his daughter and son-in-law. Crown became active in production in 1970 and has been involved in production on an estimated twenty-five to thirty films to date. Its breakthrough picture was *The Pom Pom Girls* in the late 1970s and since then has been specializing in upbeat youth comedies. Mark Tenser, president, who succeeded Jacobs in 1974, estimates that their theatrical revenues are down to 60 percent of their overall take, compared to 70 to 80 percent at the end of the seventies. They now receive 30 percent of all revenue from the foreign market.[93]

Tenser believes Crown "owes its success to creative innovation and careful planning. And, we always keep in mind that an independent in today's marketplace has to be on top of the trends."[94]

Crown, a producer and distributor with a foreign sales arm, produces two or three low-budget, youth-oriented films annually. Crown generally acquires six films a year on a pick-up deal or a straight distribution deal. They handle their own advertising and market testing. Because of the escalating cost, they have decreased their television expenses 20 to 30 percent.[95]

They are able to handle West Coast distribution themselves and use subdistributors throughout the rest of the country. Since they are self-sufficient in financing, they do not need to obtain pre-sales.[96] Crown finds it is most advantageous financially to license films to home video individually after completion.[97] Taking a great risk, the marketing campaign for *My Tutor* was $3 million in television buys alone.[98] The picture earned more than $7 million in domestic rentals.[99] Because of Crown's success with *My Tutor* they have been able to accelerate their production plans. They also foresee coproduction possibilities in the future.[100]

Crown International Pictures, which celebrated its twenty-fifth anniversary in 1984, produced and then released *Tomboy* with their first wide break in the company's history. Because of increased advertising and promotion costs and the shortening of the window on theatrical release due to ancillary markets, they chose the wide break.[101] Tenser stated "We like to entertain. . . . We still think upbeat films are where we're at."[102] He believes gambling is necessary in the film business to allow new ideas, new talent, and new marketing concepts to prosper.[103]

Crown has had sixteen pictures that earned more than $1 million in domestic rentals from 1970 to 1983. They attribute their success to building slowly from their breakthrough picture, *The Pom Pom Girls*. Their cautiousness has bought them stability and a library of approximately two hundred pictures.[104]

Film Ventures

Film Ventures had thirteen releases that earned more than $1 million in rentals in the seventies and early eighties. Ed Montoro of Atlanta, Georgia, became involved in distribution after he wrote, produced, directed, and edited *Getting into Heaven*. Montoro established Film Ventures International in 1971 in Atlanta and bought the Italian-made *Boot Hill* for $40,000, which grossed more than $1 million. He then produced *Grizzly*, which grossed more than $8 million, and *Day of the Animals*, which earned more than $4 million.[105] His company's growth resulted from success with *They Call Me Bruce*, which generated a more than $16 million box office rental, and *The House on Sorority Row* with more than $10 million, while *Incubus* had domestic grosses of more than $15 million and *Vigilante* more than $6 million.[106]

Film Ventures tests the advertising campaigns for each picture as individual openings. They begin with three markets and fewer than twenty prints. For advertising primarily on television and in the papers, they may spend $8,000 in Norfolk, $4,000 to $7,000 in Fresno, and $6,000 to $10,000 in Las Vegas. Montoro opened *The House on Sorority Row* in 300 theaters and opened *Vigilante* with 250 prints. They had already proven in their tests that the pictures could make a profit.[107] Film Ventures' *Kill or Be Killed* was initially weak, but was bolstered by large television buys.[108]

Film Ventures uses Cannes to acquire worldwide distribution rights to pictures they will sell. They had planned on releasing *Mutant* with a wide spring break, yet decided to wait until the fall. Because of the numerous releases by the majors in May and June, they were unable to obtain open-ended bookings. Instead of playing the film for a few weeks, they decided to wait until the summer product was exhausted.[109]

Montoro has produced ten pictures. Since he finds the number of suppliers is dwindling, he believes exhibitors should give the independent better terms instead of penalizing them for not supplying a larger amount.[110]

Film Ventures has a staff composed of former AIP employees. They have a sales manager, branch managers, accountants, and specialists who monitor the number and location of their release prints. They rarely use subdistributors; when they do, they are people with whom they have a franchise agreement so they know what they are doing at all times. Montoro negotiates directly with the theater chains. Montoro said, "The chains make or break a company like ours. They may have 850 screens apiece, and you have to talk to only one guy to get on all of those 850 screens. It's just what the majors do." Montoro has thought of going to other independents to set up a distribution company to serve them all. But plans fall apart when the topic of who the boss will be is discussed. Montoro claims "We were, and in many ways we still are, a marketing company." They pick up films and market them, having turned to production to control the kind and quality of at least half of the films they distribute.[111]

American Cinema

American Cinema wanted to compete with the majors by making large-budgeted pictures. They intended to use the credibility of the executives to attract filmmakers while offering creative freedom, even director's final cut if the picture was delivered within budget and on time.[112]

American Cinema's most successful pictures have been the Chuck Norris martial arts films. They claimed their *Charlie Chan and the Curse of the Dragon Queen* reflected their willingness to make more than mere exploitation.[113]

American Cinema used a market-by-market release approach. For *Good Guys Wear Black,* they determined the number of karate enthusiasts in a city, advertised in karate studios, and staged karate demonstrations.[114] Believing in expensive television campaigns, their *Good Guys Wear Black* in 1978 was their initial success, followed by *A Force of One* and *Silent Scream,* one of the biggest independent releases of the spring in which it was released. Critics did not find it wise for them to spend $5 million to $6 million on *The Octagon* since it was predicted to have a limited audience. Although such actions have been lethal for other companies, their gamble paid off.[115] However, after six years of business, American Cinema went into bankruptcy in January 1982, with more than $57 million in debts.[116] They had succeeded with kung fu, horror, and action pictures, but then dismissed key personnel who knew the marketplace.[117] This, along with taking on projects that proved to be uncommercial, was too grave for the company to withstand.

Jensen Farley

Jensen Farley began its domestic distribution operation in 1981 with the release of *Private Lessons,* which was made for $2.1 million and completed in 1980. Its producers showed the picture to the majors, and even though they offered to pay the cost of prints and advertising, their request for distribution was rejected by all. R. Ben Efraim believed the picture needed a young audience for its humor to be appreciated, whereas the executives watched the picture privately. Only Mike Ridges, who handled special marketing projects at Universal, believed the picture could generate $6 million in rentals. Although Universal had passed on the project, Ridges, who had originated Sunn Classic Pictures, left Universal to start his own company. He and Neil Wise, another Sunn Classic distribution executive, formed ADI Marketing Inc. and agreed to test *Private Lessons.* When it tested greater than predicted, they realized it was too large for ADI to handle. Ridges brought the picture to Raylan Jensen and Clair Farley, former distribution heads at Sunn Classic.[118] *Private Lessons* opened on a regional basis, having grossed nearly $7 million by the time it had covered a fourth of the country. It earned more than $30 million in the United States and Canada.[119]

The Salt Lake City-based Jensen Farley decided to handle foreign sales in-house instead of using an established foreign sales organization. They were at the 1983 American Film Market with seven new pictures in the $2 million to $6 million dollar range and nineteen from the Taft International library.[120] However, Jensen Farley Pictures, two years old in 1983, was alleged to be $9 million to $12 million in the red. Jensen and Farley were planning to commit $1 million to $5 million of their own money to aid the situation.[121] Though operations were suspended supposedly to remedy the situation, Jensen Farley Pictures filed for bankruptcy in 1983 in Utah Federal Bankruptcy Court.

Jensen Farley had proved that a picture that is thought to be unreleasable needs to be tested to verify the opinion. Though they found initial success with *Private Lessons,* and with ten other pictures that earned more than $1 million each in domestic rentals in only two years, it appears they had overextended their financial limits.

Motion Picture Marketing

John Chambliss founded Motion Picture Marketing in 1978 and since then has acquired and distributed nearly thirty features.[122] He bought old films that had been released unsuccessfully, created new titles and campaigns for them, and then re-released them. *Dracula's Great Love* was retitled *Cemetery Girls, Eager Beavers* was changed to *Swinging Barmaids,* and *Cries in the Night* was changed to *Funeral Home.* All were financially successful.[123] Motion Picture Marketing picked up *Vampire Playgirls,* which turned out to be the biggest grossing picture in Salt Lake City in late May and early June of 1980, except for *The Empire Strikes Back.* The titles prove intriguing to exhibitors looking for independent product.[124]

Chambliss was tired of distributing pictures "there's always something wrong with." Chambliss, therefore, became an executive producer of Billy Fine's *Savage Streets,* a $1 million production which he distributed. Although they have released *Mausoleum, Gates of Hell,* and *Concrete Jungle,* Chambliss claims he will upgrade the caliber of his pictures, with less emphasis upon the horror genre.[125] Motion Picture Marketing's first in-house production was *Final Exam,* in 1981.[126] Chambliss claims they have never lost money on a picture. The day *Final Exam* opened domestically, they already had their negative costs covered from exhibitor guarantees. They attribute their success to being in constant contact with exhibitors, believing exhibitors do know what pleases their audience.[127]

Michael Mahern, partner in Motion Picture Marketing, has suggested that the majors should create an old "B" picture unit. He stated:

> Five percent of the market is up for grabs. You're talking about a market that's fairly reliable, without big hits or big flops. You have to realize that few films in this area will do over $10,000,000 in rentals, but it's a market that's existed for a long time. AIP used to fill it, then Avco Embassy. The hole may not be too noticeable now, but the vacancy should really be apparent by 1983. There will be a lot of opportunities.[128]

Motion Picture Marketing has found success with ten releases that earned more than $1 million in rentals. They realistically assess the audience and meet the demand.

New Line and Bryanston

New Line has steadily released a variety of pictures, often taking considerable risks. In 1973, John Waters' *Pink Flamingos,* made for $12,000, became a midnight movie classic. His $300,000 *Polyester* featured "Odorama." Each member of the audience received a scratch and sniff card containing aromas to be smelled at cued times during the film. The picture opened in multiple runs throughout the country, including twenty-two theaters in the Los Angeles area and grossed more than $2 million in the United States.[129] New Line has distributed all of John Waters' films.

New Line Cinema allows the producer or director to work with them on the advertising campaign if they believe the concept is sound.[130] To advertise *The Evil Dead,* New Line Cinema stressed, "The producers recommend that no one under seventeen be allowed to see *The Evil Dead.*" Their ad in *Variety* stated, "Sorry, Vincent Canby, that you had to stand in line."[131]

New Line seeks to acquire product because of the great amount of money that can be made from distribution. They claim art films were never intended to be a central focus of their operation. Releasing two hundred to three hundred prints of a broad-based entertainment picture can generate more cash than most art films. They do not believe the net from art films can support production. New Line, in an attempt to broaden their annual output to nearly two dozen pictures, has restructured their company so domestic markets would be supplied by two sides. New Line Distribution Inc. is set up to handle twelve mass market pictures a year, six pickups and six in-house productions. New Line Showcase was recently created to acquire, release, and market from eight to ten foreign or domestic independent "art" pictures a year, while New Line International will continue to handle films for the world market. To ensure their future, New Line believes they need to have a release schedule comparable to the majors.[132]

New Line is actively involved in production of pictures to ensure product to distribute. President Robert Shaye even takes the pictures they produce to the majors to secure a negative pickup. He said their production emphasis will be "to give a profitable outlet for people who don't want to simply be involved with studio development deals and studio lunches, but to people who really want to make movies."[133] If they do not make a deal with the majors, then they can distribute the picture themselves.

The course of events around the release of *The Texas Chainsaw Massacre* illustrates the need for filmmakers to carefully select the distribution company to handle their picture. *The Texas Chainsaw Massacre,* directed by Tobe Hooper, was filmed in 16mm in the summer of 1973 for $140,000 and was blown up to 35mm. When all of the majors and most of the independent distributors turned it down, Bryanston Distributors showed interest.[134]

Bryanston was a new company that had successfully released *Andy Warhol's Frankenstein* and *Return of the Dragon.* Bryanston gave the filmmakers and investors in *The Texas Chainsaw Massacre* $225,000 up front and 35 percent of worldwide distribution profits. They were happy with Bryanston's distribution of the picture. In 1974, it opened in more than two hundred theaters across Texas. By 1975 it had earned more than $6 million in rentals, while the four quarterly financial reports sent to the investors from Bryanston reported "gross receipts" of only $1,082,422. After the investors recouped their money off-the-top with interest, and the lawyers and accountants were paid, only $8,100 remained to be split among the twenty filmmakers who had deferred their salaries in exchange for a percentage of the net. In 1975, the investors hired the accounting firm of Solomon and Finger to audit Bryanston's books. The president, Solomon Finger, recalled that the "attempted" audit of Bryanston "was as much of a horror story as the movie." After six months, Finger gave up because Bryanston was "unable to provide a picture-by-picture breakdown of film rentals billed." Bryanston was sued for breach of contract in 1976. However, they were already broke, with creditors after them. The investors decided to settle out of court in 1977. Bryanston agreed to pay them $400,000 for their share of profits and to relinquish control of the picture. The film, however, was in the hands of subdistributors, exhibitors, and film labs around the world, who claimed Bryanston owed them money and wanted the investors to settle the debt in exchange for the picture.[135]

Bryanston folded in 1976 when its president, Louis Peraino, was convicted on federal obscenity charges for the production and distribution of *Deep Throat*. In May 1976, a week before the investors filed suit against Bryanston, Peraino assigned the domestic rights of the picture to an independent distribution company in New York, Joseph Brenner Associates. For the film, Brenner paid off a $10,000 Bryanston debt to National Film Service. Brenner distributed the picture from 1976 until 1978, and received little profit.[136]

In 1981 New Line Cinema began a new campaign for *The Texas Chainsaw Massacre* (1974), put it back into wide release, and again found a large audience.[137] By 1981, seven years after its initial release, it earned $6 million domestically for New Line Cinema. In eight years it has grossed $50 million worldwide while generating revenue with reissues. Wizard Video purchased the video cassette rights for $200,000, the highest price ever paid for an independent film up until 1982.[138]

The ordeal involved in *The Texas Chainsaw Massacre* proved that regardless of circumstances, a picture liked by audiences can succeed. Though it was released eight years after Bryanston's release of it, New Line was able to succeed with it.

Associated Film Distribution

To avoid paying distribution fees, Associated Film Distribution (AFD) was formed by Lord (Lew) Grade to distribute films in the United States and Canada. Instead of exploiting markets that were not supplied by the majors, Lord Grade sought to create a full-scale distribution system from scratch and to produce the pictures to supply them. Grade had been a film producer and head of British television. When large-budgeted pictures he produced, such as *The Eagle Has Landed* (1978) for Columbia and *The Boys from Brazil* (1978) for Twentieth Century-Fox, failed at the box office, he was convinced it was because of distribution. He established AFD to handle his and EMI's, the British company, product in America.[139]

To finance his productions, Grade formed an alliance with Boston-based General Cinema Corp., the nation's largest chain. Grade believed volume production would win the loyalty of distributors.[140] AFD had trouble securing other theaters and even had to lease a theater in New York to assure themselves of a showcase.[141]

AFD was severely hurt by *Can't Stop the Music* and *Raise the Titanic* in 1980.[142] They blamed their failure on being denied access to the top theaters, while having to fight for secondary theaters. When only *The Muppet Movie* proved successful in 1981, AFD agreed to close its offices and distribute through Universal.

AFD's failure reveals that high rentals do not necessarily indicate commercial success. Though they had nine pictures that generated more than $73 million in domestic rentals in 1979 and 1980, this revenue was not great enough to cover the production, advertising, and distribution expenses.

Cannon

The Cannon Group was formed by Dennis Friedland and Christopher Dewey, who raised $50,000 to make *Inga,* a sexploitation film that grossed more than $4 million.[143] Cannon's goal was to produce a success and gain leverage to make nine more ambitious films. They began by doing business with local subdistributors. Even though the subdistributors stressed their own productions or those of their better customers, it was the only way Dewey and Friedland saw to start in the business without having more than $1 million in capitalization. They believed film companies lost money by setting up a sales force before having product.[144] To protect themselves, Cannon required exhibitors to remit gross receipts directly to them and not through the fifteen subdistributors they used. The subdistributor commission of 15 to 25 percent of gross receipts was then paid by Cannon.[145] In 1970 Cannon Films had a larger production schedule than any of the majors, with seven films in release and twelve scheduled for release within the year. Their average budget was $300,000 raised through limited partnerships on a film-by-film basis, with Cannon owning 50 percent of each project and controlling distribution. They even had a staff of twenty-five.[146]

Since the company's inception in 1966, outside financing of their sixteen in-house productions, four coproductions, and ten pickup productions has amounted to approximately $2.9 million. An estimated $7.6 million has been derived from distribution or sale of rights on the features. However, *Joe* accounted for 72 percent of the total, with rental at more than $5 million on a production cost of less than half a million dollars. *Joe* proved to be their only hit. [147]

The cousins Menahem Golan and Yoram Globus had produced more than forty pictures in Israel in sixteen years before buying controlling interest in Cannon (its stock had dropped to twenty cents a share). [148] Cannon was also $3 million to $4 million in debt. Golan and Globus both grew up on American films and realized the impact they had in the world market. It was apparent that the majors could easily have their films played overseas because they controlled the distribution, whereas independent theaters could not secure the sought-after American picture. Golan and Globus decided to bring high-quality pictures to independent distributors around the world. They also realized that a picture could now be sold in many markets and media. This led them on a search to acquire a library of pictures. Cannon had sixty negatives and they already had forty from Europe. With the belief that 30-year-old films could still be sold, their library has grown to 320. Golan believes the need for product is growing and even if Hollywood produces five times the number of pictures as last year, it will not meet the variety that multiplexes and cable demand. Golan stated:

> With such a need of product there was reason to change the philosophy that said that moviemaking is a risky business. If you know how to make a film and know how to license that film then there is no way you can lose money as long as the picture has a budget of $5 million or less. There is no risk.

They began to change the exploitation image of Cannon films by making a wide variety of pictures. To protect their downside, by the completion of principal photography, 85 percent of the costs have been covered by pre-sales. They are in profit by the time the picture opens. [149] "If you can't presell for enough money, you don't make the picture." Cannon is so successful with pre-sales because their pictures provide the sex, action, stars, and the right price for the buyers. Since their budgets have been low, it is easier for them to acquire sufficient pre-sales to cover their cost than if they were budgeted at $20 million. They do, however, slip in a picture occasionally, such as their $12 million *Sahara,* starring Brooke Shields. [150] They also make economical pictures quickly for a variety of tastes, with average negative costs of $4 million. After they successfully completed principal photography of the picture *Breakin',* they finished post-production in two months, and had it in distribution by MGM/UA the next month. [151]

Cannon strives to increase their reputation by making several high-budgeted films using big names. They believe that by elevating their image, they will attract better writers, directors, and stars to work for them. They therefore make the exploitation product concomitantly with more respectable films of higher commercial risk. [152]

In 1981, since Golan and Globus built their reputations on their ability to sell to independent distributors at Cannes, they refused to join the AFM because they would have had to forego Cannes. Instead, they attended both Cannes and the AFM. They set up a suite at the same hotel where the AFM was held and lured film buyers away from the AFM. [153] Golan claims they announce their production schedule at one market, show a promotional reel at the next market, and by the time the original market appears they have a completed picture. [154]

Golan claims that they go to MIFED to get the sense of the international market, which he believes American companies do not understand. While most companies have experienced a drop in the percentage of theatrical revenue from the foreign market, to 30 percent foreign and 70 percent domestic, Cannon claims theirs has remained 50-50. [155] Cannon prefers to sell their films to the foreign market on percentage deals instead of for a flat fee, believing trust can be built this way. [156]

Golan and Globus attribute their success to their skill in the foreign market. [157] Globus stated, "We figure if we could sell a black-and-white Hebrew-language movie in Japan and Taiwan, we could sell anything. . . . We can prove that any movie with a budget of less than $5 million can make money." [158] Golan also said, "We're a different breed, a different kind of company. . . . Cannon has filled a need in the foreign market for the independent distributor who couldn't get Hollywood product ten, five, or even three years ago." [159]

Cannon acquires theaters where it is difficult to sell their pictures. For example, because EMI and Rank controlled exhibition in the United Kingdom, Cannon was unable to get their films played. In 1982, when the Classic Cinema chain, Britain's third largest chain with 130 screens and sixty-seven theaters, was for sale, they bought it and brought it from losses to profit. Cannon now has distribution in England. They also are in exhibition for profit. Money comes directly from the theaters, and theatrical release doubles the money they can get for their films in television and video markets. [160] Cannon scheduled a production lineup of seventeen new features from 1983 to the first half of 1984, representing an investment of $130 million. Cannon also formed a television division to produce $40 million worth of programming. They have also picked up four films for domestic distribution. [161] Golan noted:

> Hollywood is a place where deals are made on tennis courts, at parties and in informal situations. So what's important is who you know and how you know him. Sometimes, even, it's not the quality of the film that matters so much as who is proposing it. If you don't know the right people in the right way it can be very difficult. And also it's a matter of style. We are film-makers. We get on with it and make movies. In Hollywood, 90% is talk and only 10% is making movies. It's not a style that suits us.

Golan said that when they arrived in Los Angeles, for the first two years their phone calls were not returned. But they established their credibility by making pictures. They found stars were willing to work for less if given challenging parts. It is their attorneys, afraid of failures, who advise them against it. [162]

Cinemation and Jerry Gross Organization

Jerry Gross' Cinemation successfully distributed six pictures from 1970 to 1974 which generated more than $1 million in domestic rentals.

In 1971, Melvin Van Peebles financed, produced, wrote, directed, composed the music for, and starred in *Sweet Sweetback's Baadasssss Song*. He also orchestrated the marketing, advertising, and distribution. The film grossed $10 million from a reported investment of $500,000. [163] Van Peebles believed a need existed for a picture about a black person who would triumph over white adversaries. The picture was showing at the Museum of Modern Art in New York when he made a distribution deal with Cinemation. Van Peebles futilely protested the "X" rating by the MPAA. When they refused to alter their decision, he advertised it as "rated X by an all-white jury." [164] The picture earned more than $4 million in domestic rentals in 1970.

Jerry Gross formed a new company, the Jerry Gross Organization. Released in 1979, *Penitentiary* was the first black-oriented picture in years to generate huge grosses. Such pictures in the early 1970s accumulated profits in the opening week or two, but then diminished quickly. *Penitentiary* had played continuously for half a year by reaching a wider audience. [165] It eventually earned $4 million in domestic rentals. *Penitentiary* was advertised with newspaper quotes such as "Realistic and gritty in a way *Rocky* never was." They also emphasized its more than $11 million gross. *Zombie,* with its more than $5 million gross, claimed, "We are going to eat you! *Zombie* . . . the dead are among us!" *The Boogey Man* was advertised as "The most terrifying nightmare of childhood is about to return!" For *Blood Beach,* the ad read "Just when you thought it was safe to go back in the water. . . . you can't even get across the beach!" Jerry Gross' *The Miss Nude America Contest* claimed, "The beauty contest you will never see on TV!"

Bobby Roth made a film in mid-1980, originally titled *Mystique* and financed by Mexican-based Televicine Internationel. Jerry Gross was to distribute the picture in the United States. Though the picture was a serious drama concerning mind control seminars for potential executives of an advertising agency, Gross aimed for the exploitation market. The title was changed to *Brainwash* and opened in small southern markets. The ad featured the lead actress, Yvette Mimieux, in a white jacket opened to expose a black bra. When this proved unmotivating, Gross then opened it in Miami with ads featuring a woman in an unbuttoned pajama top and the phrase, "No one could ever make me do that . . . or that." The film was released elsewhere under the name *The Naked Weekend*. Roth, the filmmaker, claims Gross was merely interested in a quick profit without regard for the picture's image or future. Televicine gave up on the picture after Gross had spent all the funds allocated for distribution in the United States. Roth screened the film for the Cineplex exhibition chain's Neil Blatt, who said, "I saw it as a thinking-person's movie." He agreed to give it a chance if Roth could devise a more sophisticated image. It opened as *Circle of Power,* translated from the title of the film's French release, with an ad showing a circle of empty chairs.[166]

Jerry Gross atempted to use his exploitation marketing skills with Roth's picture. It proved that even he could not move audiences to see the picture.

Atlantic Releasing

Atlantic Releasing, principally a distributor of art films, entered the production field with *Valley Girl,* thus shifting its emphasis from acquisitions to production. The success of *Valley Girl,* the growth of the classics divisions, and the limited appeal of independent product in ancillary markets were factors in its expansion of functions.[167] *Valley Girl* was produced for $3 million and earned $6.4 million in rentals.

Vice President Jonathan Dana said that in late 1982 it was "a field day for selling pictures...." He found that virtually any picture could be sold to pay-television. He claims buyers were paying $250,000 for rights that could have been acquired for $20,000. Foreign films were much more saleable before the research caught up with the marketplace.[168]

Atlantic Releasing had success with the foreign films *Madame Rosa* and *Montenegro* before entering the exploitation field. After their success with *Valley Girl,* they too plan on increasing the budgets and aiming for a broader audience.

Troma

The Troma team has been producing films since 1971 and distributing them since 1974. The Manhattan-based Troma has produced a picture a year and distributed several others. They make pictures for a specific audience that enjoys "youth-oriented, raunchy comedies." Troma was formed in 1974 by Lloyd Kaufman and Michael Herz. Kaufman in 1971 had coproduced, written, directed, edited, scored, starred in, and distributed *The Battle of Love's Return,* a satire which received favorable reviews. Kaufman and Herz have worked as production managers and handled location shooting for *Rocky, Saturday Night Fever, My Dinner with André,* and others. They believe this knowledge of production has been an advantage to them as distributors.[169]

Kaufman claims that though they do not have much money to pay people, "People look at working for us as a prestige thing. They talk about surviving Camp Troma."[170] Troma produced *Squeeze Play* for approximately $150,000 and it grossed $8 million outside metropolitan New York. United Artists then picked it up for distribution in the New York area. *Squeeze Play* was licensed to pay-television for $600,000.[171] Troma receives a lower split of the box office than the majors. Before they can even play in first-run theaters in major markets, their films have to play for months in smaller cities to build up a box office record. Only after *Squeeze Play* had played for eighteen months did it hit New York and Chicago.[172]

Troma does not pre-sell its rights and generates a large portion of its earnings from foreign licensing. They had feared that their films would be of low priority to the foreign financial companies, but discovered the foreign exhibitors were more interested in their films because they could purchase them for significantly less than the cost of a major studio release.[173]

Troma charges a 25 percent distribution fee after advertising and promotion is deducted. They have a reputation for honesty. When an investor puts up $50,000 or 10 percent of a picture's budget, that investor receives 10 percent of the net until break even. Then, the investor receives 5 percent of any profits. Kaufman claims $50,000 will double within four years unless the film is terrible.[174]

Though *Waitress* was made for $400,000, they expected to spend more than $3 million on prints and advertising. More than $125,000 was spent on the New York opening alone. Instead of their usual dozen prints, 250 prints were distributed region-by-region, relying heavily on local showmanship by exhibitors. They also hired one employee to travel around the country to assist in local promotional efforts.[175] They believe it makes economic sense to spend more on promoting a film than on producing it. They also believe the use of a gradual release pattern on a market-by-market basis is the most lucrative.[176]

Troma, Inc. places ads in industry publications using the slogan, "The Troma Aroma Is $$$!!" They have established Aquifilm to acquire pictures for Troma's distribution arm. The partners of Troma, Kaufman and Herz, own the building where they shoot their films and make their own commercials. Both partners produce or direct. Kaufman is the cameraman, "because on our films the kind of guys we could afford are hicks—no good," said Kaufman. They also use friends and relatives as actors.[177]

Troma hopes to start making higher budgeted pictures, in the $1 million to $2 million range, and to use stars. Hoping to strike it big, Kaufman stated, "We figure that if we keep on going in our slow, careful manner, the roulette wheel will stop on our number."[178]

Compass International

Compass International Pictures was established in 1976 as a distributor. It has since become involved in production, too. *Halloween,* made for $320,000, was rejected by all of the major distributors. Compass distributed the picture, which grossed $1.27 million by the sixteenth week of release. When it was re-released the following year, the box office revenue tripled. In the United States and Canada alone, it grossed more than $67 million, with a total worldwide gross in excess of $75 million.[179]

Moustapha Akkad, financier of the $300,000 *Halloween,* stated:

> But the key to it, the success of it, also, is that I had to control distribution. I formed a company for distribution and we distributed it ourselves, with a partnership with Irwin Yablans, and we made a company, and we distributed the picture. This way, we show money. And we show lots of money. But if we gave it to any major distributors, I don't think we'd see one single penny; and we had other experience to say that.[180]

Akkad described his experiences with major distributors:

> And everything is legal. You look at the books—and I'm talking from inside who experienced distribution—everything is legal, yet you are slammed with every kind of expenses and every kind of deals that you just legally can't do anything about it.[181]

Compass International, which made millions with *Halloween* in 1978, has decreased its distribution operations. Its *Fade to Black* was sold to American Cinema for domestic handling. President Irwin Yablans personally released *Hell Night* only because he did not receive adequate offers from others.[182]

Though John Carpenter and Debra Hill had succeeded with *Halloween* for Compass International, they chose to make *The Fog* for Avco. The larger motion picture company, Avco, afforded them sufficient funds in addition to total control.[183]

R. M. Films

Roger Ebert, film critic for the *Chicago Sun Times* and screenwriter for Russ Meyer's *Beyond the Valley of the Dolls,* wrote, "If there had been an auteur working in American commercial filmmaking during the sixties—a man totally in control of every aspect of his work—that had to be Meyer. It isn't so much that he operated his own camera as that he also carried it."[184]

Russ Meyer made pictures that rarely cost more than $250,000 and he rarely lost money. He had thirty successes and two failures of the sexploitation genre, which he wrote, directed, produced, edited, and shot with a crew rarely exceeding eight people.[185]

His first film, *The Immoral Mr. Teas,* was shot in 1959 in four days for $24,000. Financed by a San Francisco burlesque theater owner, the picture was the first authentic American nudie. Meyer imitated the popular nudist camp films imported from Europe. The film was limited to play in burlesque and marginal theaters and played in some college towns for nearly a year.[186]

Vixen was the first sexploitation picture to really break into the quality first-run markets. Meyer believes it is because it was the first such film designed for couples to attend. This satire grossed more than $6 million.[187] *Super Vixens,* made for $219,000, has grossed more than $16 million.[188]

Meyer shifted his emphasis from sex to violence in *Cherry, Harry and Raquel.* Meyer believed that since the majors had begun making more sexually free pictures and hardcore pornography was more abundant, his erotic films would no longer attract an audience.[189]

Meyer usually made between 75 and 125 prints and distributed all of his films himself. He either dealt with individual theaters or subdistributors who had small regional companies. The number of theaters open to Meyer dwindled because of the blockbuster mentality. He found exhibitors preferring big pictures for a broader audience over low-budget, specialized films. Meyer, therefore, opened a picture in one city at a time. For publicity, he appeared with an actress at the theater. If the picture was successful, theater owners elsewhere were less resistant to book his film.[190]

In *The Seven Minutes* and *Blacksnake,* Meyer deviated from the type of film he was associated with and found that audiences deserted him. Meyer even had four subdistributors invest in *Blacksnake.*[191] Even when he only slightly altered his format with *Up,* the audience was not there. Meyer is compelled to keep making what he thinks the audience is used to and wants. Since he does not have unlimited funds, such factors are of high priority to him.[192]

Meyer established ties with twenty-one subdistributors around the country who also represented other independently owned pictures.[193] David Baughn began the distribution company Scope III. In 1970 he joined Meyer to nationally distribute the X-rated *Vixen.* After two years, Baughn became a subdistributor in the thirteen western states. He learned "you cannot go out with one film in the market and expect to be treated with respect. You need a film waiting in the wings in order to make demands from an exhibitor, to make him both play and pay." Baughn believes an independent distributor can handle films with maximum budgets of $2 million. If they exceed that, he believes it is necessary to work on a national level like the majors.[194]

Meyer needed $38,000 in advertising costs to open *Beneath the Valley of the Ultra Vixens* in a major market. If the exhibitor could only supply a few thousand dollars in advertising, Meyer had to pay the balance. When he uses 90/10 deals, the 90 percent over the house expenses is split 75-25 between

Meyer and the subdistributor, 25 percent being the usual subdistribution fee, compared to the majors' 30 percent. Meyer rereleases his pictures on a percentage basis. Like the old AIP, he does not allow his films to play as a second feature with a major's film. His pictures made after 1969 command terms of 50 percent to 60 percent of the box office gross, with a 35 percent floor on the second week. He is gradually securing revenue from overseas, where before his films had been banned.[195]

Meyer finds that a picture can play in Lima, Ohio, and earn close to $4,000 in film rental while on the same weekend earn $300 in Chicago. Lima could be more successful because it has only one large drive-in, leaving youth little else to do. He finds that the majors often forget such lucrative areas. Meyer began to find competition when films from Denmark entered the market. Soon the inexpensive sexploitation picture was omnipresent. Meyer joined Twentieth Century-Fox because Richard Zanuck sensed the trend that more expensive sexy pictures could be successful. He made *Beyond the Valley of the Dolls* one of the five top-grossing pictures of 1970 for Fox.[196]

Roger Ebert categorized Meyer's pictures as early voyeuristic color comedies, the middle period of black-and-white Gothic-sadomasochistic melodramas, and finally, color sexual dramas. Meyer was able to survive by giving audiences the exploitation product they wanted. When he deviated from audience expectation, he met with failure. He therefore believes he cannot move into new areas. Yet it was Meyer who initially brought the sexploitation film into the market and showed audiences what they wanted to see. Where he once led the audiences, he now follows.[197]

Island Alive

Island Alive was created in 1983 by a producer who had no means of getting his film distributed. Island Records' Chris Blackwell, Alive Enterprises' Shep Gordon, and Carolyn Pfieffer, who headed a rock and roll management firm, produced a movie that distributors turned down. Island Alive was formed to distribute independent features by handling everything themselves. Intimately involved with each picture, they also handle the collection of film rental. Television advertising is not employed as it is too expensive. They have found coproductions are necessary to attain product; otherwise, the numerous studios' classics divisions secure the best product. Their general deal is costs off-the-top and 50 percent to the producer, while they retain 50 percent.[198]

Godfrey Reggio, who runs the Institute for Regional Education in New Mexico, a non-profit organization with the aim of using media in a progressive manner, had no film experience. He was determined to make *Koyaanisqatsi,* which ultimately cost more than $2 million.[199] *Koyaanisqatsi,* with its title from the Hopi word meaning "life out of balance," contained no actors or dialogue but was a series of images of nature and urban life. Deciding he wanted a more personal approach, Reggio backed out of an agreement for Columbia Pictures to release the picture through Triumph Films.[200] The Institute for Regional Education's director of distribution and promotion, Mel Laurence, said they wanted Island Alive to handle *Koyaanisqatsi* because they were oriented to the music business and utilized creative promotional devices. Island Alive planned for an eventual 300 to 350 domestic play dates, creating curiosity about the picture.[201] *Koyaanisqatsi* premiered at the Santa Fe Film Festival and was then shown in Telluride and New York.[202] The film won the "Francis Ford Coppola presents" endorsement at the 1982 New York Film Festival and had considerable exposure at international film festivals.[203] Island Alive averaged thirty-five working prints of *Koyaanisqatsi* in release.[204] *Koyaanisqatsi*, which opened in June 1983, has grossed $1.25 million as of January 1984 on fifty screens.[205]

Carey Brokaw, Island Alive's distribution and production head, believes that audiences' tastes are generally underestimated. "We think the public has an appetite for even more sophisticated entertainment than it's being offered," he said. Island Alive plans to produce and distribute three pictures a year and to acquire six to eight more to distribute. They are encouraged by the increasing business at art houses.[206] Island Alive realizes their limitations and plans to release through a major when they have a picture that merits a broad release of 250 prints or more.[207]

Additional Companies

Companies exist who either love exploitation films or enjoy the challenge of marketing such films. The best example of this type of company is the successful Motion Picture Marketing. Yet smaller versions of this model exist.

International Film Marketing claims to be an alternative to the independents. The 3-year-old company specializes in individualized handling by acting as a service outfit for the producer. The producers put up the money for prints and advertising in exchange for a reduced fee or they work together as a joint venture. President Roger Riddell claims, "We really act as a partner with the producer, rather than just taking the film away from him. . . ." They release pictures on a regional basis after careful test marketing and claim to do more promotions than other independents. They aim to handle four to six pictures per year. Their pictures include *Surf II—The End of the Trilogy*, *On Any Sunday II*, and *The Endless Summer*.[208] International Film Marketing is the distributor for the horror film *Sole Survivor*. Its advertising uses such elements as a mummified hand rising from a casket, even though that scene is not in the picture.[209]

Minnesota-based K-Tel was founded in 1962 by Philip Kives to sell household gadgets on television. Kives entered the record business in 1965 with the idea of licensing old hit singles in compilation albums backed by saturation advertising campaigns. Soon after it began, Kives was able to collect $4 million on his $7,500 initial investment. K-Tel expanded this marketing technique to films and had one successful release in 1975 with *Pardon My Blooper,* which earned $1.5 million in rentals.[210] While K-Tel was an expert in merchandising certain products, they were only able to succeed with one picture. Marketing techniques cannot always be generalized from one product to another.

Seymour Borde was not a filmmaker unable to secure distribution, but was a subdistributor who found he could not secure films to release. Seymour Borde and Associates is one of the many subdistributors left in Los Angeles. Borde claims the days of the subdistributor exclusively handling the product of others is gone. With the major distributors now into previously dominated independent territory, he must produce his own films. In 1978, Borde made his first film, *Summer Camp,* for $350,000 and grossed $6 million, allowing him to bankroll other films.[211]

Distribution companies were also formed to serve a major producer. For example, Lew Grade made a major attempt with AFD, yet failed. The television networks also attempted to enter the theatrical market. In the mid-sixties, Columbia Broadcasting System established a division to produce and distribute features. In 1967, its Cinema Center Films was formed for independent production companies.[212]

Similarly, Cinerama Releasing Corporation was the independent distributor for the American Broadcasting Company's features from 1970 to 1973, with eleven releases that earned more than $1 million in domestic rentals. They too, however, overextended themselves and had to go out of business.

A few independent distribution companies exist that specialize in art or quality product. New Yorker Films hopes their films are entertaining according to the definition, "the enjoyable occupation of the mind." They do not want their films to offer only an escape from reality but strive to "encourage sharper and deeper perceptions of both outer and inner realities." Their selection of pictures for their distribution collection has been guided by the belief expressed by Herbert Read:

> Only insofar as a society is rendered sensitive by the arts do ideas become accessible to it; if there are no images there are no ideas, and a civilization slowly but inevitably dies.

They want their world collection of films to educate people into feeling like members of a world community. They hope their films will create agreement, dissent, remembering, confrontation with the new and unfamiliar, and a new need to know more.[213]

Stony Island, a rock and jazz musical, was independently made for less than $380,000 by Andy Davis. When it was completed, Twentieth Century-Fox tested it and found it too arty for kids and too black for suburban art houses. No other studio would distribute the film. World Northal picked it up and placed it in ghetto and art houses during the summer. Davis was able to pay off two-thirds of his debts, and is being courted by the majors to make films about black kids and jazz.[214] World Northal had the expertise to release the picture to a select audience.

Many of these small companies exist that love films and work to get pictures seen. As businesses they must make a profit. Fortunately, a correlation exists between the number of people they move to see the picture and their profits.

Self-Made Distributors

Many independent distribution companies have been formed by filmmakers who did not intend to enter the distribution business. After making a film and discovering that no one would release their picture, their only recourse was to distribute it themselves. Many of these filmmakers employed methods used by other independent distributors.

Raphael D. Silver formed Midwest Film Productions in 1973 to produce *Hester Street,* written and directed by his wife, Joan Micklin Silver. They took the picture to the majors three times, and were rejected partially because the picture was in black and white.[215] When they could not secure distribution they decided to handle the film themselves.

Hester Street was made for $365,000 on a thirty-five-day shooting schedule. They contacted John Cassavetes, who was an independent distributor of his own films.[216] Cassavetes had opened his *A Woman under the Influence* in the rented Manhattan's Columbia I and II theaters himself, and was even able to secure advances from exhibitors.[217] The people who had helped distribute Cassavetes' *A Woman under the Influence* helped them launch their distribution company, Midwest Films. They negotiated the film on a theater-by-theater basis, with 90/10 deals, and even secured large guarantees and advances. It had taken a year from the time *Hester Street* was finished until it opened. It was ultimately shown in close to twelve hundred theaters in the United States and grossed more than $5 million. They made foreign deals for substantial guarantees against additional revenue if it was successful. Midwest found their lack of clout detrimental in distributing their *Between the Lines* (1976). Though they would book theaters for a particular day in advance, they would discover that theaters had dropped them or had them switched to another time. Since they had committed advertising dollars in proportion to the number of theaters booked, they frantically tried to maintain the same number of theaters for which they had allotted expenses. When confronted with exhibitors who would hold back payments, Midwest established a reputation for firmness by their willingness to sue for collections.[218]

The daughters of Joan Micklin and Rafael Silver produced *Old Enough.* Orion Classics acquired its domestic distribution rights from their production company, Midwest Films.[219] Midwest only distributed pictures out of necessity. They did not want to have to make films that would be assured distribution but made pictures they believed in. Distribution was a necessary function to get their work to the audiences. When they did not have to release a film, they chose not to.

Others who have decided to handle their pictures themselves included Wim Wenders. He decided to self-distribute *State of Things* when an American distributor who wanted to pick it up offered no advance or guarantee while being determined to spend $200,000 to launch it. Wenders realized he would be $200,000 in debt from the start. Instead, he decided to distribute it himself.[220]

George C. Scott independently financed *The Savage Is Loose* to be able to produce, direct, and star in the picture. Finding no company interested in dealing with him, Scott sold the picture outright to a 170–theater chain in Chicago for a flat fee and no percentage. He followed with other territorial deals, and finally reverted to the outright sale.[221]

Though Francis Coppola has never had trouble securing distribution of his pictures, his dissatisfaction with the majors has led him to seek alternative means of distribution. In 1974 Coppola acquired controlling interest in Cinema 5, the distribution company which also owned fifteen New York theaters.[222] Cinema 5 was an influential force in the import market. Coppola partially did it as a gesture to support its president, Donald Rugoff, against a threatened takeover by a powerful domestic exhibition chain. The possibility also existed that Coppola might distribute his own pictures through Cinema 5.[223] Coppola claimed to want to create an alternative for filmmakers. He assured all that it would remain a small, classy operation to ensure better exposure in its initial release. He said, "My motive has been to bypass the kinds of deals filmmakers have to make ... deals in which a filmmaker has to totally surrender ownership, final cut, any say in how a film is released, what the advertising is like, in order to get the dollars up front to make his movie."[224] Coppola furthered his quest by aiming to create his own studio. He purchased Hollywood General Studios in 1980, renamed it Zoetrope Studios, and hoped to create a repertory company to make high quality pictures. Coppola was not merely making pictures but was experimenting with new techniques to revolutionize filmmaking. In conjunction with using electronic techniques to modernize the industry, he wanted to recreate the old studio system.[225] Because of Zoetrope's heavy losses with *Hammett, One from the Heart,* and *The Escape Artist,* Coppola lost his studio. Though Zoetrope had successfully opened *Napoleon,* Universal Pictures took it over and released it with a pre-recorded sound track.

Mulberry Square

Joe Camp noted:

> Too many people in the motion picture industry today put the dollar sign first. Walt Disney never did this. He was first and foremost interested in putting a super piece of entertainment before the public. To involve an audience in his stories and to send them out feeling good. His philosophy was that if you do that well enough, the dollars will take care of themselves. That's my philosophy, too.[226]

Though Joe Camp was told movies about dogs would never sell, he made *Benji* anyway. Camp, who wrote, produced, and directed *Benji,* also raised money to create a distribution company. One of the majors had asked Camp to include obscene words so that it could be sold with a PG-rating. Though he would have had a distributor, he refused. Camp opened *Benji* 24 May 1974 in Dallas and played it during the summer mostly in Texas, Florida, and the Midwest. A couple of million dollars is believed to have been lost because of the inability to secure playing time. Some exhibitors who liked the picture could only book it for two weeks because of other commitments. The G-rated *Benji* grossed $45 million worldwide, though costing only $500,000 to produce and less than $2 million to promote.[227]

Disney features had been given special treatment by exhibitors. In Philadelphia, however, General Cinema abandoned its policy of not playing another family picture with Disney product because of *Benji's* track record. Camp claims it was the first time, at least in modern times, that the circuit has played two G-rated pictures day-and-date and in the same twin theaters. Camp also understood that Buena Vista, the distribution arm of Walt Disney, had a rule requiring that twins not play side-by-side with other family pictures. Because of its success in Detroit opposite *Bambi, Benji* opened nationally in June 1974 and began returning on a replay basis to pick up interrupted engagements on limited first runs in key situations.[228] United Artists Theatres warned Camp that *Benji* would do poorly in New York City since Disney pictures were not successful there.[229] Camp opened the film in a 450-seat theater in New York to find lines of children and adults. It broke the house box office record and continued its New York run for ten weeks.[230]

Camp said, "If the people don't like what we do, if it doesn't give them a moment or two of real uncompromised happiness, then we're not a success, regardless of how much money we make."[231]

Four-Walling

"Four-walling" is the term for renting of a theater's four walls for a specified amount of time. The exhibitor is paid the house nut and also retains all profits from the concession stand. The person renting the theater must supply all personnel, except for the concession workers, and pay for all advertising costs. For this, all of the box office gross is retained by the renter. The equivalent of film rentals in four-wall situations is determined by subtracting the flat theater rental fee from the total box office take. Exhibitors often rent theaters just to make money on the concessions.

Four-walling is often used by filmmakers who cannot secure distribution. By receiving the operating costs of the theater plus a profit, the exhibitor has nothing to risk or lose. This has proven to be a very successful means of earning rental for particular films. While the profits can be great, four-walling has also proven very costly and has contributed to the demise of many independents.

Four-wallers helped neighborhood theaters that suffered from a shortage of product. Theater owners gladly rented their houses for their operating costs and a guaranteed profit, instead of their having to pay guarantees to the majors for films that they might not have seen.[232] When exhibitors refused to book pictures on distributors' terms, the distributors four-walled theaters so the exhibitor had no risk. When these pictures proved profitable, the exhibitors did not like missing out on the revenue and claimed it a violation of the Consent Decree. They wanted NATO to take a stand against four-walling. After four-walling was believed to be a means of generating millions in rentals, many distributors tried it and failed. Four-walling lost its popularity, and was once again left for the few independents willing to take the risk to get their picture played.[233]

Norman Pader, public relations for NATO, stated that the four-wall companies "place great emphasis on scientific preliminary market surveys. They merchandise film like Procter and Gamble would merchandise a new bar of soap." These market studies and the accompanying advertising prove enormously expensive. The companies regularly spend three times the film's production costs on advertising to open a picture in a single market. Though they often spend more than the production cost on advertising, this ratio is extraordinarily high. The pictures are booked into many marginal theaters, the geographical boundaries of which are determined by the television umbrella and the reach of the television signals carrying the ads. Using costly saturation advertising, four-wallers rely on making money in a one- to two-week period.[234]

Four-wall rental figures are highly misleading because advertising costs are not deducted. Yet filmmakers use four-walling to earn huge rentals as proof to other exhibitors of their picture's drawing power. If one can demonstrate that a film broke the box office records for a particular theater, other exhibitors might risk booking the picture on a percentage deal. However, companies that specialize in four-walling do not aggressively advertise their grosses because exhibitors increase their rental demands when they see huge profits are being made from four-wall runs. While majors publicize high grosses to entice exhibitors to increase their bids, four-wallers minimize these figures to exhibitors to keep rentals down.[235]

In addition to being used as a test engagement, four-walling is also used for regionally produced films of a religious or educational nature. These pictures are booked into rented theaters, schools, and churches to stir community interest. After the screening, the picture is taken to another town.[236]

In the mid-sixties, several Utah men formed American National Enterprises to distribute a documentary entitled *Alaskan Safari*. After receiving very strong reaction in small towns, they created this prototypical distribution pattern. Their pictures were wildlife documentaries for their working-class family audience in the midwestern, southern, and western markets. Their market research studies discovered that print media advertising was ineffective though it was the standard method of promoting pictures. Television was deemed most effective, but was too costly for a limited release. They therefore began using region-by-region saturation bookings with heavy television buys on the least expensive independent stations to advertise the twenty to thirty theaters that they had rented.[237]

William Lynn, former executive vice president and director of marketing for American National, explained that three ad campaigns were normally prepared for each film. Isolated areas were used to test the ads on television, as one would test any product.[238]

American National believed in collecting box office cash immediately. They hired "checkers" in each theater who verified the first and last serial numbers of tickets sold for each performance. American National saved money by only striking a limited number of prints. They also booked theaters in the first three months of the year when theaters needed product and agreed to charge a moderate rental fee. The company thrived and refined its practices. Because of American National Enterprises' success, other companies were tempted to seek the benefits from four-walling.[239]

Alan Peterson, vice president of American National, stated, "It's a cyclical business by nature. We depend on a few months for revenue and we did not do well last fall." Peterson believes that there was too much competition and that the increased use of television by the majors diminished the uniqueness and effectiveness of the four-wallers' basic advertising approach. [240]

American National President Rip Coelson claims former employees who had aided in his development of the four-wall system left his company to successfully duplicate the technique, and are responsible for *Vanishing Wilderness, Chariots of the Gods?* and the reissue of *Billy Jack*. [241]

Arthur R. Dubs formed Pacific International Enterprises in the late sixties to distribute his first picture, *American Wilderness*. [242] When Dubs could not get a major to distribute his $50,000 picture, he four-walled it. Dubs has produced fourteen successful family pictures. His biggest grossing film, $50 million worldwide, was *Adventures of the Wilderness Family*, released in November 1975. [243]

Pacific International also employs heavy television saturation campaigns in conjunction with four-walling. They advertise their national booking team with offices in Oregon, Ohio, New Jersey, Georgia, Texas, New York, and Missouri while advertising themselves as "a universal force in family entertainment production and distribution." Dubs refuses to disclose the budgets of his pictures and the company's earnings. He has not used outside investments to finance his films. Though he was a successful four-waller, he abandoned the practice in the mid-seventies. [244]

Pacific International made *Mystery Mansion* in 1983. This family adventure, made for the regional theatrical market and produced by Arthur R. Dubs, wound up instead on video cassette, never having been exhibited theatrically. [245] Pacific International was one of the most successful four-wallers. They distributed ten pictures that collectively earned more than $70 million in rentals. These films are proving to have extended value in the growing ancillary markets.

Sunn Classic was another very successful four-waller, having released seven pictures that generated more than $94 million in rentals between the years 1973 and 1978. Sunn aimed for 3 percent of the total available audience. In the early seventies, they found their audience was not well educated or sophisticated, and not moviegoers. Their average patron did not attend movies more often than once every three months. The head of the four-wall household averaged 35 years of age, made $12,000 a year, and had two to three children. These families watched much television and were therefore prime receivers of advertising. Sunn had a plan to make sure a picture was "virtually foolproof." They used questionnaires to discover if people liked the script idea. Sunn screened the picture to determine what parts of the film would be effective for the ad campaign. The commercials were then shown to a group corresponding to their demographic profile. If this group did not respond positively, the ads were changed. The ads they decided to use were tested in the market, where a full ad campaign was run. Theater patrons were interviewed to ensure that the demographic profile corresponded to their predictions. Four days after the ad campaign was released, a testing bureau called viewers to check their response to the commercials. Sunn claimed that this procedure allowed them to predict the gross of any theater where the film was screened within fifty dollars. *The Life and Times of Grizzly Adams* was supposedly the true story of a man exiled in the wilderness who survived with the grizzly bear. They began the five-week shoot of this $300,000 picture in July 1974. By November 1974, the film had earned more than $2.1 million and was headed to a projected $20 million in domestic rentals.[246]

It is believed that Sunn four-walled too many times after audiences were aware that the sophisticated ad campaign would not deliver a comparable film. Sunn Classic was taken over by Taft Broadcasting.[247]

Four-walling can be a risky endeavor. Though several films appear to be quite similar, innumerable factors are involved in the ultimate success of each. Table 11-3 demonstrates the first two weeks of Pacific International's *Vanishing Wilderness,* American National's *Cry of the Wild,* and Sunn Classic's *Chariots of the Gods?* Sunn Classic did not make a cent from playing *Chariot of the Gods?* in 120 theaters in the New York market, but instead lost $250,000. Conversely, *Vanishing Wilderness* made $572,000 in two weeks for a 31 percent return of each theater's average fourteen-day gross of $17,000. *Cry of the Wild* generated 32 percent of each theater's average two-week gross of $14,200 for a net of $491,000.[248] When four-wallers fail, it is generally in large urban markets. Sunn's *Chariot of the Gods?* lost more than $200,000 in New York in one week, although the picture was ultimately successful.[249]

Minneapolis-based World Wide Pictures, an arm of the Billy Graham Crusade, is a non-profit movie company that uses four-walling to distribute one new picture approximately every eighteen months. They release a film only in the spring and fall, when they can best use their network of church contacts for promotion. They four-wall at least the first week of the run.[250]

Many filmmakers who were unable to secure distribution found no alternative to four-walling. *The Legend of Boggy Creek* was filmed in Arkansas on a $120,000 budget in 1972 by Charles B. Pierce, an advertising man. After Pierce produced the picture, he discovered that no distributor would even view it.[251] Pierce opened his picture in a rented five-hundred-seat theater in Texarkana, Arkansas. He called people he knew and invited them to see the picture. In three weeks he had grossed $55,000. Pierce, carrying ten prints of his film, then began to approach individual theaters. The picture made $45,000 in two weeks in Shreveport, Louisiana. Pierce then decided to have his picture distributed through Howco International Pictures, a small company in New Orleans. His picture has grossed $22 million.[252]

Table 11-3.   New York City Playoff Data—Three
Four-Wall Releases, 1973*

	Vanishing Wilderness	Cry of the Wild	Chariots of the Gods?
First Week			
Box Office Gross	$1,113,000	975,000	745,000
Number of Theaters	110	114	120
Total Theater Rentals	267,000	293,000	360,000
Advertising Costs	646,000	320,000	635,000
Net Profit (Loss)	200,000	362,000	(250,000)
Second Week			
Box Office Gross	756,000	550,000	—
Number of Theaters	110	97	—
Total Theater Rentals	267,000	231,000	—
Advertising Costs	117,000	190,000	—
Net Profit (Loss)	372,000	129,000	—

*First and second week figures indicated.
(Copyright © 1978 by the Film Society of Lincoln Center. Reprinted by permission from *Film Comment*, September/October 1978. Tables by Lee Beaupre.)

Tom Laughlin

Tom Laughlin is known as the maverick filmmaker who refused to accept the standard methods of operation in the motion picture industry. He boldly challenged the status quo, and to the surprise of most, was successful. His ideas that had been thought of as outlandish soon became the norm in the distribution of motion pictures. Laughlin and his wife, Delores Taylor, successfully wrote, produced, directed, starred in, and distributed *Billy Jack,* which earned more than $32 million in domestic film rentals, and *The Trial of Billy Jack,* which earned more than $28 million in domestic rentals. He was determined not to give up on his pictures. He finds it unjust that a studio executive who has never been personally involved in filmmaking has control over the fate of someone's work.[253]

Laughlin wrote and then starred in *The Born Losers* in 1967. The picture, distributed by American International Pictures, became the motorcycle cult film that introduced the Billy Jack character as the half-Indian, former Green Beret.[254]

Billy Jack, made for approximately $1 million in 1971, concerned the main character's struggle to protect the children at the interracial Freedom School against Establishment injustice. Twentieth Century-Fox had agreed to release *Billy Jack.* When Richard Zanuck of Fox demanded re-editing, Laughlin took the master sound tapes so that the film could not be released. Ultimately, for $100,000, Fox sold Laughlin back his film. Warner Bros. then secured distribution of *Billy Jack.*[255]

Leo Greenfield, head of sales at Warner Bros., believed *Billy Jack* was a poor movie and therefore booked it in drive-ins and "B" theaters.[256] In 1971, Laughlin objected to the handling of his film. In two years, it had earned $6 million in film rentals and Warner Bros. did not believe it could earn any more. Laughlin disagreed and "stole the master sound track and threatened to destroy it, unless he was given distribution rights."[257] *Billy Jack* was previewed in "ten theaters across the United States to the strongest preview response of any picture in recent history." Laughlin was therefore able to secure $2 million up front with a profit participation of 45 percent of the distributor's gross after actual break even was reached, with no further distribution fees allowed after the break-even point.[258]

Most people thought it was absurd for this actor to take on distribution, something with which he had no experience. Richard Kahn, senior vice president, worldwide marketing, Metro-Goldwyn-Mayer, wrote in 1979:

> It was on May 9, 1973, that the four-wall technique was first applied in the modern era to a film from a major studio-distributor. And if previous four-wall films had been of event stature, *Billy Jack* became an event that changed the face of the entire industry as much as the advent of sound almost a half century before.[259]

Four-walling was a 1930s distribution method that had been used in the 1960s by low-budget filmmakers. Before *Billy Jack,* no one had four-walled a "PG" film. Four-walling had only been used for films targeted at families who would enjoy outdoor nature films.[260] Four-walling for a wide audience was a novel experiment. It employed heavy television advertising unprecedented for a motion picture with general audience appeal. This necessitated the simultaneous leasing of theaters throughout the entire area of the television signal.[261]

With the financial support of Warner Bros., *Billy Jack* reopened in Los Angeles. They spent an unprecedented $250,000 on one week of advertising, and opened it in sixty-two theaters from Santa Barbara to Bakersfield to the Mexican border. The film became an event. At that time, *The Godfather* had the record for film rentals earned in one week, $925,000. Laughlin was able to generate $1,020,000 in a single week.[262] This led to another unprecedented $400,000 advertising expenditure to support a one-hundred-theater New York saturation. This, too, generated the largest first-week box office gross of $2 million.[263] This 2-year-old picture earned the studio an additional $90 million gross or $38 million in film rentals.[264]

Extensive use was made of television advertising directed to individual market segments. For example, the martial arts fan, the anti-Vietnam movement supporters, and the young romantic female were all individually targeted. It was the first application of basic marketing principles in the film business.[265] Electronic media amounted to more than 50 percent of their $3 million first week budget that included 169 local markets. Thirty-six thirty-second network spots and more than a dozen separate commercials to market the many elements of the film were created. Laughlin also used two hundred radio market areas, with 60-second spots of varying messages. Print advertising in college publications was in-depth, yet at a relatively modest cost.[266] Laughlin had retained his faith in the commercial appeal of his film. Instead of giving up and believing he was wrong, he fought to get his picture exposed to the greatest number of people. The theme song of *Billy Jack*, "One Tin Soldier," states, "Go ahead and hate your neighbor / Go ahead and cheat a friend / ... On the bloody morning after one tin soldier rides away...."[267]

Warner Bros. set up a four-walling unit which successfully rereleased *Jeremiah Johnson*.[268] In 1973, Metro-Goldwyn-Mayer imitated Laughlin's techniques for their *Westworld* release. Their "Operation Blitzkreig" opened the picture simultaneously in 125 Chicago theaters and 150 Detroit/Cleveland houses. Instead of renting the theaters outright, they negotiated rental terms of 50 to 60 percent of the gross. MGM spent $142,000 on television spots, $62,000 on radio spots, $10,000 on print advertising, $52,000 on personal appearance tours, and $150,000 on prints to launch the picture. *Westworld* grossed more than $2 million the first week in 275 theaters, for a net profit of nearly $700,000. Other studios began to copy the formula. Paramount reissued *Little Fauss and Big Halsy* while Universal experimented with *Breezy*. United Artists even hired Richard Moses, a former Taylor-Laughlin executive, to scan their film library for four-wall candidates. The majors found the huge cash expenditures to be highly risky. Concomitantly, theaters began inflating their "house nuts." In March 1974, NATO initiated an antitrust suit claiming that four-walling, when practiced by the majors, was a violation of the 1948 Consent Decree. Four-walling quickly lost its initial excitement for being able to generate huge profits in a short time.[269]

Laughlin had proven successful with four-walling yet chose not to continue the practice. Instead, he opted to form his own distribution company. Because of the success of the *Billy Jack* reissue, Laughlin was able to demand $8,000 to $10,000 cash advances per theater or he would not give exhibitors the sequel to *Billy Jack, The Trial of Billy Jack.* He had collected nearly $10 million before release of the picture.[270]

The Trial of Billy Jack was budgeted at $2.5 million, which Laughlin financed himself. In 1974 he opened a distribution company, Taylor-Laughlin, with a staff of one hundred. He hired former Under Secretary of Defense and former Litton Industries military specialist, John Rubel, as his chief financial officer to break down the country with a city-by-city analysis.[271]

Play dates for the film were selected by demographic charts. Part of the equation included age-group audience potential, market potential, video umbrella penetration, and more than four months of pre-testing the picture. It was previewed in rough cut, recut, previewed again, and recut again, to maximize the impact. In the first five days of release, with a $3 million advertising budget, *The Trial of Billy Jack* grossed more than $9 million in more than a thousand theaters, including 180 four-wall dates. Since the production cost $2.5 million, prints cost $1.3 million, and hosts at four-wall theaters and overhead added another $1 million, they were nearly able to recoup their costs in the first week.[272]

Believing conventional rental terms would prove more profitable, Taylor-Laughlin chose not to four-wall *The Trial of Billy Jack.* As shown in table 11-4, the more profitable "90/10 deal" gave 90 percent of the box office gross in excess of each theater's house nut to Taylor-Laughlin. They also secured a floor of 70 percent, stipulating that they would not receive less than 70 percent of the total box office gross for the first two weeks, not less than 60 percent for the next two weeks, and not less than 50 percent for the final week. The picture's grosses, however, dropped sharply. Had they four-walled the film, they would have missed out on $6,090,000 of revenue. Lee Beaupre believes the exhibitors probably renegotiated to give Taylor-Laughlin $12.5 million rather than $16.044 million. Laughlin still made several million more with the 90/10 deal than he would have had he four-walled the picture.[273]

By 1975, *The Trial of Billy Jack* had only earned $25 million in the first five weeks. Laughlin took the picture out of release and began the "Critics Contest." Warner Bros. advanced $600,000 for prizes to be given away for three hundred-word essays on why the critics are out of touch with audiences.[274]

In the advertisement, Laughlin stated:

Like the critics, many people running our industry often are out of touch with the American audiences for whom they are supposed to be making films. They are so unsure of how to market their product that they have created their own "Critic-Monsters" and have made them into superstars by quoting them in their ads and desperately seeking their favor. Yet, the only ones who really pay attention to the critics are other critics and the people in our industry, for the above facts overwhelmingly show (with the exception of certain Art films) that critics have no impact on what film audiences will go to see.

Table 11-4.   Paper Distribution Profits—*The Trial of Billy Jack*

	Box Office Gross	Number of Theaters	Total House Nuts	Profit (Loss)— "Four-Wall"	Profit— "90/10 Deal"
First Week	$11,015,000	1,109	$ 2,968,000	$ 8,047,000	$ 7,711,000
Second Week	$ 6,672,000	1,089	$ 3,076,000	$ 3,596,000	$ 4,670,000
Third Week	$ 3,089,000	1,038	$ 2,927,000	$ 162,000	$ 1,853,000
Fourth Week	$ 2,126,000	953	$ 2,685,000	($ 559,000)	$ 1,276,000
Fifth Week	$ 1,067,000	826	$ 2,359,000	($ 1,292,000)	$ 534,000
Five-Week Total	$23,969,000		$14,015,000	$ 9,954,000	$16,044,000

The advertisement also stated that "perhaps no pictures in history have proved more unpopular with the critics and distributors than *Billy Jack* and *The Trial of Billy Jack*. . . ."[275] The contest was unsuccessful, with only a few thousand essays submitted. The rerelease of *The Trial of Billy Jack* was also far less profitable than Laughlin expected.[276] He admitted to overruling all of his people on the hunch that the rerelease would draw a bigger audience than it did. He felt they were wrong, but discovered that, in fact, he was wrong.[277]

Prior to Laughlin's innovation of the wide release, a film would open in one or two theaters in major cities, then expand to two or three first-run houses, then to first-run neighborhood houses, and finally to neighborhood theaters and drive-ins. Although Laughlin's wide release pattern was innovative and successful for his film and could be for others, it would not ensure success. It led to a greater concentration on producing the blockbuster that could be opened simultaneously in more than a thousand theaters. It was faster to open a film wide and recoup the grosses quickly. But the smaller film with less mass appeal faded.[278]

In 1973, newspaper advertising accounted for 77 percent of the total $273 million industry expenditure. Television accounted for only 16 percent, with radio and other media amounting to 7 percent. Television advertising had almost doubled from 1973 to 1974 and accounted for 24 percent of the total.[279] The box office gross increased from $1.5 billion in 1973 to $1.9 billion in 1974. Twentieth Century-Fox successfully rereleased *The Poseidon Adventure* and saturated areas with *Dirty Mary, Crazy Larry*. They used traditional 90/10 exhibition rental agreements instead of four-walling arrangements. In 1975, Columbia successfully released Charles Bronson's *Breakout* with the largest number of prints ever used, 1,360, and the biggest single network advertising buy. Universal used similar techniques to market *Jaws*. Advertising expenses amounted to $380 million in 1975 while the box office gross grew to $2.1 billion. In 1976, advertising expenditures were $413 million and box office grosses were $2 billion. In 1977, advertising was $451 million and $2.4 billion was collected at the box office. In 1978, box office grosses were $2.7 billion with advertising expenses at $550 million. A greater percentage of box office grosses were being spent by distributors for advertising, but box office grosses were not increasing at the same rate as the increased advertising costs.[280]

Four-walling became unrealistically expensive because theater leases also increased, wrong pictures were selected for this method of distribution, and ineffective television advertising was common.[281] Laughlin had used the four-walling technique of taking over theaters to prove his film would attract an audience. By this method he was able to control the variables himself.

After a year of trial and error, *Walking Tall* turned out to be a success for Cinerama Releasing Corp. After *Billy Jack,* this was one of the few pictures that did not follow the established practice of opening in New York. *Walking Tall* was the story of a sheriff who was shot in the face in an ambush in which his wife was killed. The picture's ad campaign that opened in Los Angeles, Chicago, and Boston in 1973 stressed action and violence. Since the results were disappointing, the ads were changed to suggest greater violence, and this led to an even worse reaction. They noticed, however, that audiences were applauding at the end of the picture in places like Ogden, Utah. The ad campaign was revised to ask, "When was the last time you stood up and applauded a movie?" Cinerama Releasing also started booking it into smaller suburban theaters where the exhibitor could be persuaded to allow the picture to gain word of mouth. After this success, Cinerama Releasing booked the picture into a test run on the outskirts of Manhattan and then finally in Manhattan. Vincent Canby, therefore, had to examine "as much a phenomenon to be analyzed as a film to be reviewed." The producers believe if it had originally opened in New York, it would not have made any money. Because of its peculiar success elsewhere, the critics were compelled to view the film and wound up granting it favorable reviews. Cinerama Releasing then abandoned the idea of opening pictures in New York. They also learned to test market pictures before a general release. Since 1966, American National Enterprises has been producing wildlife and adventure films, and never has exhibited them in New York.[282] Though Laughlin did not initiate avoiding the costly New York release, he drew attention to the fact that a picture could succeed without it.

Laughlin received the Outstanding Showmanship Award at the 1976 Show-A-Rama where he presented the exhibitors with a new rental plan that would make the dollar amount of the guarantee dependent upon the grossing power of the house.[283] Laughlin wrote:

> Generally, the distribution system today is so insensitive to marketing techniques that it is unable to sell a picture to a specific demographic market at the retail level. It is callously indifferent to the advertising and promotional needs of the exhibitor . . . relying instead on techniques developed forty years ago; and it borders on criminal in the amounts of money it steals from producers of films in the form of incredibly high distribution expenses, fees and other unsubstantiated and unwarranted charges made against the cost of the picture and therefore against the filmmaker's share of the profits.[284]

Laughlin emerged with hopes of creating a distribution company or studio. In 1984, Laughlin printed full-page advertisements in *Daily Variety* relating to "If You Were Put in Charge of a Studio Today, What Changes Would You Make?"[285] Since the studios are burdened with overhead consisting of thousands of employees, union contracts, huge credit, the upkeep of offices and equipment, Laughlin wrote, "Who do we expect is going to pay for all this overhead—the failures? The studio system today is an economic dinosaur from a bygone era and a business climate that no longer exists."[286]

Laughlin finds the fatal mistake that has caused the demise of all such attempts to create a new studio is that they are organized solely for production. Without realizing their primary need to be profitable, they plunge their money directly into production. He believes it is imperative to control distribution to enable control over the cash flow.[287]

He also believes the autonomous production unit enables the development of new talent. Since there are many audiences in the country, to become a full supplier for exhibitors, he advises dividing the distribution company into three separate distribution entities. One would distribute high-culture films, another would distribute mainstream star pictures, and the third would distribute low-budget, Corman-AIP type of pictures which are still the backbone of the exhibition business. Talent could learn and grow on the low-budget films and then be elevated to work on higher budget and higher culture pictures.[288]

Laughlin is positive in believing the most successful studio can be created by hiring people with the demonstrated "nose for the audience" or the skill of choosing films that people want to see. He then believes it is possible to predict, with 60 percent accuracy, films that will succeed. Laughlin believes that because past studio heads were filmmakers and not deal makers, they knew what audiences wanted to see. Laughlin stresses that executives today are not chosen for their ability to make films, but are generally lawyers, agents, and bankers chosen to prudently manage the company's money. He believes Clint Eastwood, Robert Redford, Burt Reynolds, Sylvester Stallone, Jane Fonda, as well as Bergman and Fellini, have noses for their own particular audience as did Truffaut. He also believes George Lucas and Steven Spielberg have this ability to predict success. The first six pictures on the list of all-time grossing films are *E. T. The Extra-Terrestrial, Star Wars, Return of the Jedi, The Empire Strikes Back, Jaws,* and *Raiders of the Lost Ark,* all made by Lucas or Spielberg.[289]

After much investigation of commercially successful motion pictures, Laughlin discovered key ingredients that commonly are found in these pictures. If any of these criteria are sustained throughout a picture, he believes the audience will be emotionally moved. For example, he cites "superior position" as a most valuable ingredient. When the audience knows something is going to happen when the screen characters do not, the audience is in superior position. The second most important ingredient he found, almost always present in commercially successful pictures, is "undeserved misfortune." When something happens to a character on screen that results in the audience having fear or pity for that character, the audiences will be moved. Laughlin believes

> sex and gore are a direct result of the failure of many of our fine writers to know how to apply these emotion-evoking ingredients to quality work. The lowest kind of emotional response, horror, disgust, or revulsion, can always be evoked by seeing a woman hacked up or gratuitous sex, but these pictures exist not because audiences want them, but because of the lack in the good writers to know how to emotionally move us.

Laughlin believes if general audiences wanted pictures such as the "Chainsaw Massacres," they would be top-grossing pictures, instead of those that celebrate life, love, and the heroic quest. "The tragedy is that too often panderers better understand the need for emotions in film than the literate writers do."[290]

Laughlin has had in-depth experience with the production and business side of the industry. He claims to dislike distribution but finds it a necessity that he be involved in it to ensure a film reaches its audiences. Laughlin is a filmmaker who has dared to challenge the industry and will continue to fight to ensure that films reach their deserved audience. He has questioned the distribution practices that were considered the norm. Though he is primarily known for four-walling, this was a strategy he used only when it was necessary.

Four-walling decreased in the early 1980s. The television saturation market dried up as viewers grew tired of the same films and similar ad campaigns. The cost of assuming all distribution and advertising expenses prior to release was too great and could easily be greater than the grossing potential of the picture. Most independent companies could not survive for a few lean years and went out of business.

Four-walling, however, has allowed select films to reach an audience when they otherwise would not have. When its potential for success was realized, four-walling became a very popular distribution strategy, used not only by independents but also by the majors. The overzealous use of this saturation technique soon proved too costly and risky. Just as the success of a film cannot be predicted, one could not foresee which pictures would benefit from this strategy. Four-walling has since become unpopular and is, as before, employed infrequently by the independents. Four-walling still remains a viable practice for a determined and dedicated filmmaker who wants to test his film or show himself and others that his picture can succeed with an audience.

12

"Successful" Independent Films and Distributors

The films released by independent distributors from 1970 to 1983 that earned domestic rentals of $1 million or more provide insight into the business of independent distribution. They are deemed "successful" because they at least had the opportunity to be viewed. There is a general belief among less informed filmmakers that if distribution cannot be secured by a major, one can always find an independent to handle the picture. This, however, is rarely the case. The independent distributor that is in the position to release product other than his own is usually a company with a narrow range of strict requirements. Though these criteria may be different from those of the majors, the independent distributor is just as shrewdly aware of his market as is his competition. While the majors may aim for a wide audience, independents usually go after a very specific segment of the population, allowing for even less deviation from the formula picture.

While most independent distributors remain in business to release one picture or for at most a few years, the successful companies specialize in a few genres. It is within these genres that the independent will choose the elements that will allow him to exploit the marketing techniques necessary to guarantee a profitable investment in a picture. Therefore, a filmmaker needs to be aware of the audience for which his picture is being created. This audience includes those who pay to exhibit it as well as those who pay to view it. These independents often emphasize a particular genre such as horror or youth pictures, and seldom risk making a picture outside of the proven formula film. While a few distributors do exist who specialize in the "art" film, they too are very selective of the quality of the picture and its potential public appeal.

A filmmaker needs to be aware of the audience that will most likely respond to his picture, unless he is not financially responsible to others and merely wants to make a picture for himself or a select few. Realistic projections about how a picture will perform should be considered. General beliefs that numerous independent distributors desperately need any product

Table 12-1. Film Genres over Time and as a Percentage of Total

Genre	Number of Films in Each Genre over Total Time	Percentage of Total
Action	62	16.71
Adventure/Thriller	18	4.85
Comedy	55	14.82
Documentary	24	6.47
Drama	66	17.79
Horror	79	21.29
Science Fiction	12	3.23
Western	8	2.16
Youth	47	12.67
Total	371	

whatsoever are not realistic. With the high costs of a release, a distributor must believe he will make a profit or he will not handle the film. An altruistic distributor who will release a picture to enable the work to find an audience will generally be the filmmaker himself.

The 371 films that reported film rentals of $1 million and more from the United States and Canada from 1970 to 1983, as enumerated in "Champs among Bantamweights" (*Daily Variety,* 13 June 1983), were distributed by seventy-one independent companies. Of course, many other independent films have been made that did not make the list, including hardcore sex features. The $1 million in rentals, however, is a base amount because with advertising and production costs, very few films would be in profit with a $1 million rental, though the ancillary profits might be as great or greater. A rental of $1 million is also a low enough figure to enable companies to demonstrate their existence and success while still providing the ability to conceal profits, as they can easily claim other costs were not covered by this rental. These particular films are significant because they at least reached a significant segment of the audience and had the opportunity to be viewed. Investigation of these films and companies dispels many misconceptions while providing a clearer view of the reality of the independent distribution business.

Initially, this study of the 371 pictures reveals which genres have found success in the marketplace. For analysis, the 371 pictures were divided into nine genres: action, adventure/thriller, comedy, documentary, drama, horror, science fiction, western, and youth. Table 12-1 reveals the total number of films in each genre and what percent of the total number of films they command. The 371 films were further divided into the following twenty-four genres (table 12-2). The number and percent of films in these categories are shown in table 12-3. While the major distributors need to release at least

Table 12-2.   Film Subgenres

Action	Action Drama
	Black Action Drama
	Crime/Violence Drama
	Martial Arts Action Drama
Adventure/Thriller	Adventure
	Suspense Thriller
Comedy	Adult Comedy/Drama
	Adult Sex Comedy/Drama
	Foreign Comedy
	Satire/Spoof Comedy
Documentary	Documentary
	Docudrama
Drama	Drama/Melodrama
	Family Drama
	Foreign Drama
Horror	Psychological/Murder
	Monster
	Supernatural
	Science Fiction
	Nature
Science Fiction	
Western	
Youth	Comedy
	Drama

twelve pictures each year to keep their distribution arms operative, the independent distributor may be able to survive with less than one film per year. An example of the small, successful distributor was made evident by Joe Camp and his Mulberry Square Productions. With an average production of one film every other year, Camp's objective of making quality entertainment with the zeal of an impassioned artist rather than as a strict businessman sets him apart from many of the other producers and distributors and may account for part of his exceptional personal success. Other distributors with a similar philosophy are Midwest Film, Faces International Films, and Taylor-Laughlin. While Midwest and Faces contributed only one film each to the list of 371, their pictures were not of the exploitative nature marked by so many independent productions.

Table 12-3. Film Subgenres over Time and as a Percentage of Total

Total Films	Subgenres	Percentage of Total
14	Action Drama	3.77
11	Adult Comedy/Drama	2.97
15	Adult Sex Comedy	4.04
8	Adventure	2.16
17	Black Action Drama	4.58
17	Crime/Violence Drama	4.58
4	Docudrama	1.08
20	Documentary	5.39
37	Drama/Melodrama	9.97
13	Family Drama	3.50
4	Foreign Comedy	1.08
16	Foreign Drama	4.31
14	Martial Arts Drama	3.77
17	Monster Horror	4.58
7	Nature Horror	1.89
28	Psychological/Murder Horror	7.55
25	Satire/Spoof Comedy	6.74
9	Science Fiction Horror	2.53
12	Science Fiction	3.24
18	Supernatural Horror	4.85
10	Suspense/Thriller	2.70
8	Western	2.16
35	Youth Comedy	9.43
12	Youth Drama	3.24

Like Mulberry Square, Midwest Film is a company owned by filmmakers who produce, direct, and distribute their own product. Joan and Rafael Silver's Midwest, which released *Hester Street,* appears concerned primarily with making movies they distribute for the purpose of having their efforts presented to an audience instead of being mainly concerned with financial gain.

In the same vein as Midwest is John Cassavetes' Faces International Films. An independent filmmaker for many years, Cassavetes became an independent distributor with *A Woman under the Influence.* Financed by Cassavetes and stars Peter Falk and Gena Rowlands, they traveled across the United States promoting, marketing, and booking the film directly with exhibitors. The picture, like most of Cassavetes' films, is the vision of the total filmmaker.

Not entirely unlike Camp or the Silvers or Cassavetes is Tom Laughlin, who believes strongly in his pictures and will make them entirely on his own terms. Though the pictures of each of these people and their companies vary in success in terms of total rentals, the objective of each is the same: to make films in which artistic expression is not a secondary function to the profit motive.

It is not coincidental that their films fall into the same time period and genre. During 1974 and 1975 the greatest jump in theater-going habits over the entire time of this study was recorded, and 1975 produced the most dramas of any year (13). Whereas 1980 stands out as a blockbuster year for independents (more than $208 million in rentals), upon inspection, it is clear that more than twice the number of films made the list that year than either 1974 or 1975, but the average film rental per picture in 1980 is significantly less than in 1974. In fact, 1974 had the highest per-picture rental average, with the exception of 1979. Furthermore, the 1974 box office revenue for the entire motion picture industry jumped the greatest single yearly percentage since 1942.

In 1974 Taylor-Laughlin appeared with one film, *The Trial of Billy Jack,* which accounted for 21.9 percent of these rentals for the year. Mulberry Square released *Benji,* which earned $12 million in rentals, making up 10.45 percent of all rentals that year. Mulberry Square and Taylor-Laughlin, both film companies formed by the filmmaker, had the two most financially successful films of the year, other than AIP's reissue of Taylor-Laughlin's *Born Losers,* which generated $12.5 million in rentals. Following the success of 1974, the number of independent distributors with pictures that earned rentals over $1 million increased almost 60 percent in 1975, double the number since 1970 and 1971.

Another new distributor who made the list of "Champs Among Bantamweights" in 1974 was Levitt-Pickman with *The Groove Tube.* Like many of the other films so far discussed, *The Groove Tube* was produced, directed, and written by the filmmaker. Although not distributed by the filmmaker and not a drama, but a TV satire of the comedy genre, the picture fits well into this category. Before theatrical distribution, *The Groove Tube* ran for five years off-Broadway and in other legitimate theaters in U.S. cities as a "video monitor" venture. Financially successful, with domestic rentals of $9.42 million, it was only one of three comedies released in 1974. The other two were the successful adult sex comedy/dramas *Flesh Gordon* (Mammoth) and *The Nine Lives of Fritz the Cat* (AIP), whose combined rentals were still almost 25 percent lower than those of *The Groove Tube.*

Most noteworthy of the emergence of new distributors with new kinds of products in 1974 is the fact that the success of the year is directly attributable to personal films created with a significant vision and objective. The three films—*The Trial of Billy Jack, Benji,* and *The Groove Tube*—together a mere 14 percent of the total product, account for almost 40 percent of one of the most profitable years in domestic rentals.

Another company whose choice of pictures to distribute is based upon quality rather than exploitation is New Yorker. Their two contributions to the list are Fassbinder's *The Marriage of Maria Braun* and Louis Malle's *My Dinner with André. My Dinner with André* is a film that is remarkable because it involves a conversation between two men, and would only have been made by an independent. It should, therefore, be apparent that if a film is acquired for a small enough sum or made well on a low enough budget, there remains a possibility that distribution may be acquired and a filmmaker will have his vision communicated and the exhibitor and distributor will make a profit.

Another distributor that deserves recognition for having brought inexpensively acquired, quality product to the public is the Samuel Goldwyn Company. The Scottish-made *Gregory's Girl* (1982) was brought to this country after a strong critical and financial success in England. For a fresh and charming youth comedy in a year that was dominated by films of this genre, *Gregory's Girl* returned comparatively little.

Since the boom in 1974, 1982 was the last year before the total yearly rental for independents would again fall below the $100 million mark. The significance of this is accentuated by the fact that ticket prices had increased, and by 1983 the average rental per picture had fallen to 1972 levels. During 1982, 24.1 percent of all films were in the youth genre, second only to the most overall successful year for independents, 1979, when 31 percent of all films were of this description. The importance of the youth film to the independent distributors is demonstrated by observation of the number of films in this genre per year and their combined and average rentals. The genre was becoming a major factor in 1978, with five releases. However, the total and average rentals were well below 1976 levels when only three youth pictures made the list. It should be noted that Crown International's release of *The Pom Pom Girls* directly increased the figures for 1976 with rentals of $7,425,000. Although written, produced, and directed by Joseph Ruben, the picture was of basic exploitation quality with minimal plot. The picture was a collection of scenes containing sex, vandalism, and a total disregard of authority—ingredients implanted to draw a large audience to generate large box office receipts.

The figures for 1979 may be misleading as well if Associated Film Distribution's (AFD) *The Muppet Movie* is not taken into account. With $32 million in rentals, this film represents more than two-thirds of the total rentals of this genre for the year. *The Muppet Movie* stands out because of its high quality, G-rating, and proof that people will go to the theater to see what can be seen at home on television—the Muppets.

The remaining one-third of the youth pictures of 1979 should not be discounted as insignificant. With a total of eight other films, there were more releases of this genre than any other year during this time frame. Furthermore, in 1979 two distributors emerged whose main business is the exploitation of the youth film—Seymour Borde and Associates and Troma—with their first efforts, *Summer Camp* and *Squeeze Play*, respectively.

The distributors appear to be solely concerned with the business of film. William Kirksey, executive producer of *Squeeze Play,* made the change from retailing and real estate to film production with a budget of $300,000. With $4.6 million in rentals and a marginal marketing campaign, *Squeeze Play* proved a wise, low-risk, high-return venture for its producers. The $1.47 million from rentals of *Summer Camp* returned to Borde, himself a subdistributor in need of product, demonstrated that regardless of quality light teen sex can sell tickets. This element in conjunction with higher production value may sell even more tickets. Quality filmmaking for this youth market, without sex, or without an exploitative ad campaign, as in *Gregory's Girl,* does not draw the large targeted audience that constitutes the youth genre's patrons. It is not surprising that inferior product in this genre, with titles such as *Girls Who'll Do Anything* (1976) and *Pick-Up Summer* (1981), would bring rentals equal to or greater than *Gregory's Girl.*

It was also in 1979 that Motion Picture Marketing (MPM) found success with *Cemetery Girls* and *Sex Education.* These "successes" were followed by *Vampire Playgirls* (1980), *Eager Beavers* (1980), *Satan's Playthings* (1980), *Locker Room Girls* (1981), and *Classroom Teasers* (1981). The unique ability of guaranteeing success by acquiring films inexpensively and creating new titles paid off for MPM. Splitting their product between youth and horror genres, they added further proof that these are the two most secure categories in which to assure the greatest probability for success.

Another company with much the same philosophy as MPM is Jensen Farley, with the highest-grossing youth film of all time, *Private Lessons* (1981). It earned $11,985,296 in rentals. Referred to more accurately as teen sexploitation, this movie is an example of a film that no one else would distribute but which eventually attained great success. Subsequently, the majors quickly rushed to take advantage of this rediscovered market. The mass production of high-budget, well-crafted studio productions quickly ensued. Although many of the majors' youth films fared well by independent standards, and a few by any standards, it became obvious to the majors that the mass appeal necessary to garner the huge returns demanded by the studio shareholders were the exception rather than the rule.

Crown International's forte has been the fundamental exploitation of the teenage sex comedy. When Crown released *My Tutor* in 1983, it was clearly similar to the proven theme of Jensen Farley's *Private Lessons* (1981) and *Homework* (1982). With $8 million in rentals, *My Tutor* was their biggest success in six years, slightly above the figures of *The Pom Pom Girls.* For years, Crown has brought low-budget, lighthearted pictures to the theaters. Though cost-consciousness is a crucial determinant, quality production values and talent are never discounted below tolerant limits.

Another significant independent distributor is American International Pictures (AIP), the mini-major whose total number of releases accounted for 17.25 percent, with 15 percent of the total rentals. While Crown concentrated on the youth genre, AIP emphasized the action genre. Their last year, 1979, before they teamed with Filmways, who subsequently acquired them, was their most productive year in terms of rentals, with 37.3 percent of the total, or $63.6 million. AIP produced an average of 6.4 pictures from 1970 to 1979, with at least five films each year with domestic rentals of more than $1 million (except 1971, when they had only three). Their share of the total yearly rentals in this study was 20.8 percent, for a total of $218 million over the ten-year period. While AIP's greatest rentals were from the action genre, their single-greatest box office success came in 1979 with *The Amityville Horror,* returning rentals of $35 million. The film starred Rod Steiger, James Brolin, and Margot Kidder, and the story was taken from a best-selling novel. The salaries of these stars and the rights to the book were probably more than the budget of most independent films.

Enormous amounts of money alone cannot buy a success. *The Amityville Horror* was released prior to the peak of the horror trend, with Samuel Z. Arkoff once again demonstrating his ability to sense a new audience taste. This well-made picture satiated the public's increasing desire for this genre. While one might assume that the reason for its success was its high budget, this is dispelled by the release, also in 1979, of *Meteor.* A follower of the disaster film trend, *Meteor* was not a unique or original film but a vehicle to capitalize on other current successes. With a complex financial history involving, among others, Run Run Shaw and producers Sandy Howard and Gabriel Katzka, the film was a box office disaster. With rentals of approximately $4 million, the film would be considered a success by typical independents' standards; however, with production costs in the $16 million range, *Meteor* could not recoup its costs. Even with such stars as Sean Connery, Natalie Wood, Karl Malden, Brian Keith, Martin Landau, Trevor Howard, and Henry Fonda, the public stayed away from the film.

The horror genre makes up 21.3 percent of all of the pictures enumerated from 1970 to 1983 and is the number one genre, having generated 20.68 percent of all rentals. The seventy-nine films of the horror genre were released by twenty-eight companies. AIP clearly dominated with sixteen films. This genre, represented every year, was the major factor for success among independents in 1980. Out of the entire period of the study, 1980 earned more rentals, $208.35 million, from the most releases, forty-seven from eighteen companies. Of the forty-seven releases, eighteen were horror, making up 38.3 percent of the year's pictures. Many horror pictures were released in 1983, making up 33.3 percent of the year's pictures, while the low was reported for 1976 with only 6.9 percent. Because of the popularity of the horror genre, it was further divided into five categories (see table 12-4).

Table 12-4. Subgenres of Horror Films*

Category	Percentage of Genre
Psychological/Murder	35.40
Supernatural	22.80
Monster	21.50
Science Fiction	11.40
Nature	8.86

*Total horror genre—79 films comprising 21.3 percent of total pictures.

Some distributors believe that a market for horror films always exists. Therefore, if one were to make a horror picture, the film would more likely have a chance at securing distribution than if it were, for example, a western, which made up less than 2 percent of the total films. If a genre has proven to be successful at the box office, less risk is involved in the release of a picture of that genre. Investors and distributors have case histories to substantiate a decision to release a picture, whereas if one makes a unique film, the distributor has to risk failure of his own judgment.

Except for a few exceptions such as *The Exorcist* and the horror-adventure thrillers *Jaws* and *Jaws 2,* large-budgeted horror films have not been box office blockbusters. In 1982, sixty-one domestically released horror films generated a record $230 million in film rentals. More than 140 horror projects were publicly announced for 1982 filming, yet only forty-five were actually shot in the United States, Canada, and Britain during the year. A dozen or more are likely to have been shot without publicity. This represents a 50 percent drop in production from 1981, when 110 horror pictures were shot, or 1980 when eighty-four were produced. The reduction may be due to the excess from previous years, including those unreleased that were still circulating. Of the horror pictures released in 1982, thirty-seven were shot in 1981, six were filmed and distributed within 1982, fourteen were made in 1980, and four had been produced in the 1970s.[1]

Because of the glut of product and the waning interest in cheap violent films, most national and New York publications have ceased reviewing low-budget horror pictures. For example, *Horror Planet, Xtro,* and *The House on Sorority Row* were bypassed by the *New York Times* and other publications. *Piranha II* and Cannon's *Hospital Massacre,* also known as *X-Ray,* were distributed overseas only. Jensen Farley Pictures' *Wacko* and Almi Cinema 5's *The Creature Wasn't Nice* were not even released.[2]

In 1983 domestic film rental for horror films dropped more than 50 percent from the previous year. It was the lowest performance since 1976 and reduced the combined market share by science fiction and horror films to approximately one-third of all pictures' business. Of the fifty-one new horror releases in 1983, twenty-seven were shelved pictures filmed in 1981 or earlier.

These pictures are being used to fill in an exhibitor's schedules between bookings. When a horror film could be expected to deliver two good weeks of business, many of the new films are not even commanding one weekend. Only nineteen films earned at least $1 million in 1983 compared to thirty-one in 1982, twenty-two in 1981, and twenty-six in 1980. Horror film production has merely leveled off, with approximately thirty U.S. pictures per year.

Although the horror genre commanded both the highest percentage of the total rentals and returned the most money, the average rental for a horror movie fell below the overall mean. The documentary category, generally considered the least commercial, earned the highest mean of more than $5.5 million per picture. Furthermore, of the nine genres, horror only ranked fourth overall for the highest average rental per genre.

At the third AFM in 1983, more than 20 percent of the films exhibited were horror films. Yet the majority of the horror films were old, filmed in 1981 or before, and had already made the rounds at previous markets.[3] Since action-oriented exploitation films frequently do better overseas than domestically, international sales can be more lucrative to the smaller companies that specialize in these genres.[4] At the 1984 market, action films and comedies dominated, accounting for more than half of the pictures, with only 8 percent of the new pictures in the horror genre.[5]

It should be observed that AIP built its reputation for financial stability through the years by producing and distributing low-budget exploitation pictures. While their emphasis was on the action and horror categories, their films covered all genres, as they responded to changes in the audience tastes and guided them as well. It is significant that AIP released 58.8 percent of all the black action/dramas, with 59.3 percent of all rentals generated in this category, for a total of $20 million.

The highest-grossing film in this genre was *The Mack* (1971), released by Cinerama Releasing Corporation in conjunction with AIP, and returning $4.3 million in rentals. While the film is noted for its financial success, it is also remembered for its nearly all-black cast, which included Richard Pryor. The success of *The Mack* led to AIP's release of three other films, or 75 percent of the total of this category, in both 1973 and 1974. AIP was the only company to achieve success in this genre in 1976 and 1978. The only other distributor to consistently release black films was Jerry Gross, working first as a company named Cinemation, and then as the Jerry Gross Organization. His first release of Melvin Van Peebles' *Sweet Sweetback's Baadasssss Song* (1970) stands as a landmark film. Written, produced, directed, and edited by Van Peebles, who also starred in the movie and composed the music for it, the film was one of the few made by a black for a targeted black audience. With $4.1 million in rentals, this picture rates a close second to *The Mack* in financial success.

In 1979 *Penitentiary* was released by the Jerry Gross Organization. The film stands as a model for its quality filmmaking. Written, produced, and directed by Jamaa Fanaka, the picture was his third feature and proved once again that the cinema belongs to the filmmaker with a point of view and the ability to communicate it. Filmmakers often enjoy the fantasy that their picture will be a blockbuster. If this hope is diminished because of a certain genre's perceived box office limitations, such films will not be made.

A genre in which quality could be diminished in favor of a formula is the crime/violence drama. Many of these productions made solely to earn a profit turned out to be unique pictures. One of the earlier movies released by AIP under the auspices of Sam Arkoff was produced and directed by Roger Corman, a man who was to become a historic name among independent distributors and an innovator with few equals in the film business. The remarkable element of Corman's *Bloody Mama* (1970) was not the $1.5 million it returned in rentals, nor its poor reviews, but the people involved in the production. Shot by the then unknown cinematographer, John Alonzo, its actors included Shelley Winters, Robert De Niro, and Bruce Dern. Continuing with this same routine formula, AIP produced a string of these pictures with the hopes that one of them would become an enormous success. This occurred in 1974 with *Macon County Line*. Although the picture was not much different from the rest of AIP's crime films, the picture returned $9.1 million in rentals, more than the previous five films AIP released in this genre combined.

Bloody Mama set a precedent for what was to become a Corman trademark when he started his own company, New World Pictures. A man of many talents, Roger Corman entered the distribution field in 1972 with the importation of Ingmar Bergman's *Cries and Whispers*. Throughout the years of growth of New World, it was this diversity of character that established Corman as a leader in the film world. While *Cries and Whispers'* return of $3.5 million in rentals was more than any of his other later imports, Corman continued to bring foreign pictures into the lives of Americans interested in the works of such great directors as François Truffaut, Federico Fellini, Alain Resnais, as well as those of Bergman.

It would be misleading to think of Corman as only a lover of the "art" film whose sole purpose in film distribution was to share his appreciation of quality pictures with the public. Similar to many other independents whose main concentration of effort is in the exploitation market, New World specialized in low-budget pictures, made inexpensively and quickly. This, in fact, was the mark of a Corman picture. Consequently, New World never had a blockbuster, and only had four films out of thirty-four that generated more than $5 million in rentals. Their top-grossing film, *The Private Eyes* (1980), generated $8.1 million in rentals. This film and *Death Race 2000,* which earned $5.25 million in rentals, accounted for 15 percent of New World's total domestic rentals over the eleven years that they had pictures with more than $1 million dollars in rentals. Furthermore, both of these movies were in the genre that accounted for almost 15 percent of New World's total output of films— the satire/spoof comedy.

Although New World only received 6.2 percent of the total rentals of films, they were one of the most successful independent distributors in the world for many years. Their secret was inherent in their low overhead operation, with almost everyone working for minimal salaries. Whereas filmmakers and actors working for other independent producers and/or distributors felt they needed to be compensated immediately for fear they may never work again, at New World the employees believed that working on a Corman production was more like going to school than a job. Meeting and working with people that had similar interests and goals provided new opportunities for people to learn a craft.

The mini-major Avco Embassy is more like a major distributor than the smaller independents. Though their 1970 entries were typical exploitation pictures, the talent involved in the productions was of a generally higher caliber. This, however, is not what distinguishes Avco Embassy from the rest of the independents, but it is rather the financial backing that the company later came to possess.

Before Embassy became Avco Embassy, they released three pictures in 1970 that might easily have been mistaken as those of AIP or New World. *C.C. & Company* was the typical motorcycle movie made popular by *Easy Rider* the previous year, and whose forerunners were an AIP specialty. *Soldier Blue,* though a western, may have been produced to exploit the success of the violent *Wild Bunch* (1969). *Sunflower,* a Carlo Ponti production of a Vittorio De Sica film, was an import like so many quality pictures brought to domestic distribution by Roger Corman. While the combined rentals of these three films only totaled slightly more than $5 million, they represented 18.75 percent of the year's total for 12.9 percent of the rentals.

In 1971, Embassy released the film that would remain their most successful for ten years, *Carnal Knowledge.* The film starred two actresses from the previous year's successes, Ann-Margret from *C.C. & Company* and Candice Bergen from *Soldier Blue.* This Joseph E. Levine production of a Mike Nichols film written by Jules Feiffer and starring Jack Nicholson was up to the standards of major releases. Credit must be given to Embassy for having the distribution skills to get the picture to the audience. *Carnal Knowledge* received $12.4 million in rentals and alone accounted for 30 percent of the year's total.

Though Embassy did not have a film on the list in 1972, they returned in 1973 with another hit, *A Touch of Class* ($8.4 million). The film starred George Segal, Glenda Jackson, and Paul Sorvino, and further highlighted the ability of Levine to give the audience a picture it wanted. *A Touch of Class* and the Italian-western *Trinity Is Still My Name* (1973) were the last films that Embassy would distribute before selling out to Avco.

After the departure of Levine from the sale of Embassy, the new company, Avco Embassy, was to have their most successful years from 1979 to 1981 with the 1978 arrival of Robert Rehme and William Shields. With all the financial backing and experience in exploitation, distribution, and exhibition, Avco Embassy released such hits as *Escape from New York* (1981), *Take This Job and Shove It* (1981), *The Fog* (1980), *The Howling* (1980), *Phantasm* (1979), among others, and the most successful grossing film in the company's history, the 1981 release *Time Bandits* ($18.4 million). While there can be no doubt that the new management under Rehme was a significant factor in the company's turnaround, there is another important factor. In 1980, AIP, the most prolific independent, was in the transition of being acquired by Filmways and had only one picture that year that earned $1 million or more in rentals. Furthermore, by 1981, AFD, the company that dominated the field with eight releases in 1980, was no longer in business. With the disappearance of AIP and AFD, a void was left in the marketplace that needed to be filled. It is, therefore, not surprising to find that Avco Embassy contributed 12.77 percent of the 1980 product, for 18.1 percent of the total rentals, equaling $37.75 million, and 25 percent of all the successes in 1981, for a record 44.4 percent of the rentals, totaling $63 million. They accumulated the greatest rentals from the comedy, horror, and action genres.

A look at the yearly state of the successful independently distributed pictures reveals the power of a few stable independents and emphasizes the rapid demise of numerous companies that enter the business with one film. It can be seen that the independent distributors that have established themselves by proving stability over the years and by releasing a consistent flow of product are the ones considered mini-majors. These companies, AIP, Avco Embassy, New World, and Crown International, though owned or referred to under different names, continue to play an important role in the distribution of independent movies to date. Tables 12-5 through 12-8 attest to the significance of these powerful independents. These were the only companies that consistently released pictures throughout the entire time span. Other companies such as CRC with eleven releases from 1970 to 1973, Jensen Farley with ten releases, and AFD with nine pictures in two years, were very strong but could not endure the high costs of operation.

Table 12-5.   Distribution Statistics for AIP, 1970–1983

Year	Number of Films	Percentage of Total	Distributor's Total Rentals (In Millions)	Distributor's Percentage of Total Rentals
1970	5	31.25	6.27	16.0
1971	3	21.43	5.33	12.9
1972	5	26.32	9.75	19.0
1973	8	40.00	12.30	19.4
1974	7	33.33	31.84	27.8
1975	8	22.22	25.50	19.1
1976	8	27.59	23.90	21.6
1977	8	27.59	27.35	23.5
1978	7	28.00	12.20	12.1
1979	5	17.24	63.60	37.3
1980*	1	2.13	3.50	1.7
1981**				

*Picture made in conjunction with Filmways.
**Company acquired by Filmways.

Table 12-6.   Distribution Statistics for Avco Embassy, 1970–1983

Year	Number of Films	Percentage of Total	Distributor's Total Rentals (In Millions)	Distributor's Percentage of Total Rentals
1970	3	18.75	5.04	12.9
1971	2	14.29	13.56	33.0
1972	—	—	—	—
1973	2	10.00	10.50	16.5
1974	—	—	—	—
1975	—	—	—	—
1976	2	6.90	8.75	7.9
1977	5	17.24	13.74	11.8
1978	4	16.00	10.80	10.7
1979	3	10.35	8.95	5.2
1980	6	12.77	37.75	18.1
1981	9	25.00	63.07	44.4

Associated Film Distribution (AFD) is the perfect example of a company that entered the distribution business with a total neglect for the history of the independent, exploitation market. Their first and sole 1979 entry, *The Muppet Movie,* was one of the highest-grossing independent films of all time. A quality picture in a popular genre with a high budget, the $32 million it returned in rentals certainly made the investment in the film a wise one. AFD subsequently released eight films in 1980, or 17 percent of the year's product, accounting for 19.8 percent of the total rentals. While this may create the

Table 12-7.   Distribution Statistics for New World, 1970–1983

Year	Number of Films	Percentage of Total	Distributor's Total Rentals (In Millions)	Distributor's Percentage of Total Rentals
1972	1	5.26	3.5	6.8
1973	1	5.00	1.08	1.7
1974	—	—	—	—
1975	5	13.89	12.25	9.2
1976	4	13.79	13.00	11.8
1977	4	13.79	9.00	7.7
1978	2	8.00	4.90	4.8
1979	3	10.35	9.75	5.7
1980*	5	10.64	16.80	8.0
1981	2	5.56	3.50	2.5
1982	4	13.79	8.70	8.5
1983	2	9.52	4.20	7.0

*One additional film made in conjunction with Quartet.

Table 12-8.   Distribution Statistics for Crown International, 1970–1983

Year	Number of Films	Percentage of Total	Distributor's Total Rentals (In Millions)	Distributor's Percentage of Total Rentals
1974	2	9.52	2.40	2.1
1975	—	—	—	—
1976	1	3.45	7.43	6.7
1977	3	10.35	7.07	6.1
1978	2	8.00	5.25	5.2
1979	1	3.45	1.75	1.0
1980	3	6.38	8.50	4.1
1981	2	5.56	2.35	1.6
1982	1	3.45	2.70	2.6
1983	1	4.76	8.00	13.4

impression that AFD's disregard of the exploitation business and its approach to the independent distribution of studio-like pictures was a successful venture, it was not. Had AFD been able to acquire their films for the cost of the exploitation pictures of AIP or Crown International, they would have revolutionized the independent distribution business. Some of the major deviations from the distribution practices of the successful independents were AFD's high cost of acquisitions, marketing and advertising, and their choice of genres. Whereas most of the successful independents chose one, two, or three specific genres in which to concentrate their efforts, AFD released eight pictures in 1980 in seven different genres. While 1980 was the year with a

Table 12-9.   Independent Distribution Companies

Year	Total Companies	Percentage of Annual Total
1970	9	12.5
1971	9	12.5
1972	10	13.9
1973	11	15.3
1974	11	15.3
1975	18	25.0
1976	15	20.8
1977	11	15.3
1978	13	18.0
1979	17	23.6
1980	18	25.0
1981	19	26.4
1982	16	22.2
1983	12	16.7

record eighteen horror pictures with rentals of more than $1 million, AFD did not contribute a single picture to this genre. The strategy contributing to AFD's demise was in direct contrast to such companies as AIP, New World, and Crown International, whose philosophies are to concentrate their efforts either in genres that are popular or specialties of the given company, and to keep all costs at a minimum determined by cautious predictions of the limitations of each picture. And perhaps most important is that the enormous success of one film is a bonus that is an exception, not a rule to be expected from each film distributed. Though AFD blames their failure on the inability to secure the first-run theaters at the prime times, it would have been wise for any company to have had the foresight and taken the responsibility of investigating the exhibition system prior to such heavy expenditures. Blaming the system for their failure after the fact does not implicate exhibition, but instead demonstrates their failure to analyze the booking system or their inability to realistically accept it. Though AFD earned more than $73 million in domestic rentals from nine pictures in two years, it was not enough to secure their continued existence.

Though the independent distributors generally release approximately the same number of pictures as the majors do per year, they secure less than 15 percent of a year's overall box office revenue. Total rentals from 1970 to 1983 amounted to $1,453,087,145. This is approximately the amount that the majors earn yearly. While the majors have remained relatively stable and few independents have survived, the majority of companies do not have longevity. From 1970 to 1983, seventy-one independents distributed 371 pictures. During this time, there was an average of 13.5 different companies per year that had distributed films with rentals of more than $1 million. Of the seventy-one distribution companies investigated, twenty-nine, or 40.85 percent, handled only one film. Ten of these films were comedies, for 34.48 percent. Five companies handled youth films; four, documentaries; four, dramas; three, action; two, horror; and one, adventure/thriller.

Of the six distributors that released more than ten films, none had average per-picture rentals of more than $5 million. Of these companies, Avco Embassy had the greatest average of $4.78 million, while CRC had the least with $2.26 million. However, if the films CRC made in conjunction with AIP are considered, then Crown had the lowest per-picture average with $2.84 million. Of the dozen distributors with ten or fewer films, but more than five, less than half had average rentals greater than $5 million. Sunn Classic commanded the highest average with $13.5 million. The remaining 53 companies all had fewer than five films and their averages are often the same as their total rentals.

American Cinema was greatly successful with action pictures, yet went bankrupt by overspending. Releasing pictures from 1978 to 1981, American Cinema earned 3.58 percent of all rentals and had a per-film average of $5.2 million. They averaged 2.5 releases per year with 40 percent of their films in the action genre and 30 percent in the comedy category. Their most successful year was 1979 when their three pictures earned 12.9 percent of all rentals.

New companies such as MPM, with two releases a year since 1979, seem successful, yet must have the resources to cover the slow times and the foresight not to overextend themselves because of one huge success. Just because one makes an enormously successful picture does not mean it can be replicated or that the filmmaker is the sole reason for the success. When a picture has earned huge rentals, companies have hastily and drastically increased their budgets on subsequent films, only to find the audience was not there.

The four-waller Sunn Classic found enormous financial success, leading to their overconfidence, unawareness of the audience growing tired of their product, and their ultimate extinction. From 1973 to 1978, Sunn's seven releases earned 6.51 percent of all rentals, averaging $13.5 million per picture. Sunn's high per-picture average was created by a $24 million rental from *In Search of Noah's Ark* and their 1975 domination of the market with 28.77 percent of all rentals from *Grizzly Adams'* $21.895 million rental, *Mysterious Monsters* with a $10.960 million rental, and *Frontier Freemont*, with a $5.52 million rental. Sunn's films consisted mainly of documentaries, totaling 71.43 percent in the genre, with the remaining films in the drama category. Sunn was unaware that the audience was becoming bored with their similar releases and grew tired of the saturation advertising campaigns that promised more than they delivered. Sunn also faced the growing competition in the genre and particularly in their advertising strategy. Sunn did not adapt to the changes in the marketplace quickly enough to survive.

While a particular genre may be a substantial percentage of all pictures over total time, there are fluctuations in its yearly strength. This may be due to fewer pictures being produced of the genre or of distributors' foresight that the market would not support as many releases. A study of these selected films and companies reveals that very few independent distributors exist and that the mortality rate is high. Though an average of 13.5 distributors exist per year, only 5.4 companies release two or more pictures a year. The companies that release only one film are generally created to distribute one specific picture. A group of people will form a company for the production and distribution of one film. These companies, though they may appear as numerous outlets for product, are not viable distributors for a filmmaker because they generally only have resources relating to a particular motion picture. Even if they would like to release a filmmaker's picture, they probably could not. And if they did, the filmmaker would probably command a very poor deal and might be unhappy with a weak release. Companies that do release a few pictures per year also have financial limits on the pictures they can acquire. Since they generally produce a picture of their own, it will naturally be given first priority in the amount of money that will be allotted for advertising, and more effort would likely be expended in securing better theaters at more favorable times of the year. A further limitation to a filmmaker is that these companies generally specialize in a few genres that they know how to successfully exploit. Since these distributors have less capital than the majors, the costs of releasing a single picture are a substantially greater percentage of their overall worth. They are therefore less likely to risk the high advertising costs on a picture for which they are unsure an audience exists. If these companies make a wrong judgment, they are often forced out of business. Many companies have experienced success with one film and believed that they could simulate the results. They often gambled, overextended themselves, and discovered that they had lost millions of dollars. Therefore, the independents that have existed to release more than a few films are cautious and aware of the particular market with which they have had success. Unless a picture in a genre other than with which they are familiar is so obviously commercial, it is unlikely that an independent will handle it because the possibility of loss would far exceed their desire to gamble their entire business for the uncertain gain. A filmmaker also may not want a distributor with experience only in horror films to handle an "art" film.

The larger independents can gamble on releasing a variety of pictures because they have more resources and generally have their own distribution network or relationships with subdistributors. Like the majors, these independents must supply product to these outlets to maintain their power in the exhibition market. Although they generally produce pictures of their own, they actively pick up independent productions. It is these few companies that offer hope to a filmmaker in need of a distributor. However, they have no need for what they consider an uncommercial picture. Though they are independents, they often strive to compete with the majors and distribute pictures that simulate releases by the majors. Their standards of production are often higher than an independent filmmaker may be able to afford. These independents, however, have the resources and skills to successfully handle a picture made by an independent filmmaker. New World, for example, has a history of releasing foreign and domestic independent features. There are very few of these companies, and they still demand that a picture be commercially viable before they will expend any effort in a release.

It seems apparent that for a distribution company to have longevity, it must prudently keep costs to a minimum and continue to produce films. Over time this will also provide the company with the ability to book better theaters as the exhibitors come to expect product from them. When they can provide a flow of product that the exhibitors depend upon for a certain level of quality, they will wield more power. This cautious approach does not preclude the possibility of any one of these pictures becoming a blockbuster. If one does, however, it must be viewed as an isolated film that happened to have the appropriate elements in the right combinations at the right time. It is risky to believe that one can replicate this success and drastically increase future production budgets. Many filmmakers and distributors have hopes of gaining entry into the major leagues. Once they have earned a large rental from the success of one film, they pour this money into one other single picture. Unlike the majors, they do not have the financial backing to survive if the picture fails. They have gambled all of their earnings on one picture, often after years of frugal struggle.

Conclusion

A film is often idealistically viewed as being created as art by the writer and filmmaker, without regard for any external considerations, particularly financial. Many people with an intense love of motion pictures attend film schools to learn how to actualize their filmic vision. It soon becomes very apparent that if one wants to create motion pictures in "Hollywood," one needs to understand and accept the fact that filmmaking is a business.

"The criterion of the media world in the 1970s is 'form follows finances.'"[1] James Monaco further stated:

> Film used to be an industry: its aim was to make films first, money second.... Today, film is clearly a business.... If the accountants' analysis shows the profit margin is markedly greater if, say $10 million is spent on one blockbuster and its attendant publicity than it would be if spent on ten smaller films, then the blockbuster will be made, the smaller films won't. It's not that those smaller films wouldn't have made a profit. It's just that they wouldn't have made so great a profit.[2]

Since financial success is so important in the business, it is imperative that a film is distributed to maximize this potential.

Because of the fewer number of films released by the majors and their growing interest in the pictures aimed at a mass audience, the independent distributor offers hope to filmmakers. The majority of independent distributors, however, specialize in a few genres of the more exploitative nature. These companies serve the valuable function of offering practical experience to new filmmakers. The number of distributors who specialize in "art" or more serious films is small. However, because of the proven response at the box office and the voracious consumption of films in the new ancillary markets, the majors have begun classics divisions to acquire these art pictures and are even involved in their production.

A great variety of distributors exists on the continuum from those who specialize in handling classic films to companies who distribute low-quality product by employing dubious advertising methods. Many companies exist that have distributed only one picture, while the few stable companies have released hundreds. The companies that have the resources to release a picture and learn from failures are able to refine their methods. On subsequent releases, they are more adept at spending advertising dollars only when they will generate greater revenue than costs. The larger independent distributors are more aware of which theaters generate higher grosses and are able to secure the more desirable theaters because they can guarantee exhibitors a constant line of product.

It is imperative that the independent filmmaker choose the appropriate distributor for his particular picture. Whereas a knowledgeable distributor can practically ensure a picture is seen by a wide audience and earn relatively large rentals, a distributor inexperienced in the particular genre of a film could ensure that a commercial movie is hardly seen, resulting in minimal rentals. A filmmaker must investigate a company's history in terms of its age, employees, specialty, releases per year, which theaters and play dates the distributor can command, critical acclaim of their releases, prime means of advertising, and their profit/loss record.

Samuel Z. Arkoff stated, "There are more myths, illusions, and fictions behind the camera than in front of it."[3] Many people in the business find it necessary to distort facts either for personal reasons or as a matter of business practice.

A distributor may want to protect himself from added competition by concealing what he believes are his unique skills. Experienced distributors feel that years of working in the business served as their unique education and treat this experience as a coveted resource. Therefore, it may be difficult to gain in-depth information of value on these companies.

Producers, distributors, and exhibitors may exaggerate or lie about certain elements of a film and the extent of their involvement with a particular film. For example, a film with a production budget of $1 million may be advertised as a $4 million film in an attempt to assure distributors of a certain quality of production. If a film fails to generate the expected box office response, a distributor may mask his culpability by blaming the failure on the advertising campaign, the producer, the time of the film's release, an element in the film, or the film itself. Therefore, those employed in the field may feel it is to their advantage to evade the truth. Since the motion picture industry is a business of relationships, one can discover a person's or distributor's reputation. Though this might not be accurate, it can serve as a warning of a potentially dangerous involvement.

When the studios owned their own theaters, they were able to produce the pictures they wanted because they were assured of an outlet that they could control. With the divorcement of the studios from the theaters, and when audiences began to dwindle, motion pictures were soon made for a specific reason—to contain elements that would be attractive to the exhibitors and the public. Because of the uncertainty of exhibition, greater risk was involved in the production of a film. The financiers, who were the distributors, began to demand stricter controls on the pictures. The new ancillary markets, however, are destabilizing this concentrated power of the majors.

For most pictures, the domestic theatrical market is the prime source of revenue, with the foreign market contributing at times 50 percent of a film's total earnings. The home video market, however, is increasingly becoming a major factor in a picture's revenues and is having a greater influence upon a picture's release. Home Box Office easily dominates the pay-television market in the United States and has been contributing a great percentage of a film's budget in exchange for exhibition rights. They have begun to create programming strictly for their pay service. The video cassette market is increasing in all parts of the world and is even replacing the theatrical market in some countries. Cassette distributors, also in great need of product, are now beginning to produce films solely for their market. The length of time a picture plays in theatrical release is shortening as these ancillary markets acquire more power and demand a more prompt release in their area to capitalize on the advertising from the theatrical release. With the recent growth and demand for product from the ancillary markets, filmmakers are again beginning to be able to control the exhibition of their pictures. Increasingly, they are able to be responsible for the success or failure of their film.

Because of the rapid growth of the new markets, some filmmakers are avoiding the expense and risk of theatrical release and are having their pictures distributed in these ancillary markets alone. The value of the product, however, is still not as great as if first showcased in the theatrical market. The possibility, however, exists for a filmmaker to distribute his work himself to the individual markets.

Regardless of the various tests that can be employed in the prediction of the ultimate success of a picture, innumerable variables exist that render this goal impossible. A film that generates critical acclaim may not be responded to by audiences, while a picture deemed poor by reviewers may capture the passion of moviegoers. The strengths of an individual film must be assessed to reveal which elements, if any, are most marketable.

Neither the filmmaker nor the distributor can be certain how well a film will fare in the marketplace. But they can employ their knowledge to make intelligent predictions. In the end, a strong commitment to the film must be made by the filmmaker and the distributor. One must realize that the manner in which a picture is distributed is an intrinsic factor in the ultimate success of a film.

A viable alternative to seeking distribution is to distribute a picture oneself. Though this requires a great commitment of not only money but time, it has proven highly profitable for those tenacious enough to learn the business and then to physically implement the necessary practices. Because every picture is unique, no single method of distribution will always produce the same results. A particular means of distribution is particularly effective for a certain type of film. Though most filmmakers aim to make the best film they can with the resources available, the quality of a completed picture is often beneath expectation.

A picture may, in fact, be poor or distributors may not have the vision to see the possibilities in a unique film. In such cases, filmmakers with conviction have pursued distribution themselves. Most exhibitors are reluctant to play a picture without a distributor, and smaller theaters will not want to take the financial risk. Filmmakers have often resorted to four-walling to get their picture seen. Though it involves a great expense in advertising and theater rental, a positive public response can be all that is necessary to convince a distributor to handle the picture or at least other exhibitors to book the film.

Four-walling proved enormously successful for a few companies. These companies initially began because of a filmmaker's desire to have his film seen in a new segment of the market. Their novel techniques, however, continued to be employed to sell similar product. When their advertising offered exciting new stories and the films did not fulfill the promises, the audience's theater-going behavior was extinguished. The companies that have succeeded have not aimed only to extract the greatest amount of money from the audience with the same type of film, but have changed to create new trends or at least to adapt to others before the audience grew tired of their pictures.

If one has made a bad picture for little money and one merely wants to make as much profit as possible, it is wise to open the picture in one region with many prints and a great amount of advertising. With well-targeted ads, the audiences will be moved to view the picture, and several million dollars can be recouped in these one- to two-week releases. It is futile for the picture's run to be extended, as the audience attendance will drop off sharply once word of mouth spreads. However, if the picture was made cheaply enough, one can still profit by this regional distribution tactic. Many companies rely solely on this strategy. They acquire marginal pictures from desperate filmmakers for a minimal amount of money. After changing the title of the film to suit their tests, they release these pictures and earn a profit. The filmmaker rarely benefits financially in such instances because he was probably so desperate to recoup any money for his picture he probably sold all rights outright for a minimal sum.

Out of the nine different genres, horror comprised 21.3 percent of all the independent pictures that earned rentals of $1 million or more from 1970 to 1983. The psychological/murder horror was the most common type of horror film, making up 35.4 percent of five categories. With a picture in this proven genre, one could more easily secure distribution from an independent distributor. Even if the picture were of poor quality, it could be skillfully marketed to make a profit for the distributor.

An action picture is viewed by most distributors as the surest sale to foreign buyers. Over the years, foreign countries have maintained a voracious appetite for this genre. Since the majors produce high-budget action pictures, a marginal independent action feature may not be able to compete, and consequently will not be able to secure play dates domestically. A market, however, exists for such product overseas, both in their theatrical and video markets. If one has little hope of domestic success, it may be wiser to contract directly with a strong foreign sales agent and forego a domestic distributor who will demand worldwide rights and deplete profits by cross-collateralization of markets. If one has a picture that is unlikely to be successful domestically, one must take greater consideration of who the foreign distributor will be. If the domestic distributor is contractually obligated to a particular foreign distributor that may not be the best choice for handling the particular picture, or if the domestic distributor has minimal experience in the foreign market, the area of greatest potential for the picture to succeed in may be left dormant.

If one has produced a film for which the audience is unknown, the picture should be tested to find that audience. If and when the audience is found, the most effective release pattern must be decided upon. If one has a quality picture that the filmmaker believes will grow with positive word of mouth, the picture may be placed in an exclusive engagement and allowed to build an audience slowly. This often involves exhibitor commitment of having to endure several weeks of minimal grosses. An art exhibitor could afford such a chance during slow seasons or an exhibitor with a ten-screen multiplex might donate one screen to such experiments. Once the word spreads, the box office will grow and the film will then be able to secure bookings in other houses based on its positive results. The danger, however, is that if the picture remains at a constant minimal box office level and does not grow, the film will be taken out of release. Since exhibitors have a strong communications network, it will be even more difficult to secure bookings elsewhere after a proven failure. Therefore, the filmmaker may have limited his audience to a single screen in a single city, when he might have had the opportunity to orchestrate a wider release. At least in the latter case, more people would have had access to view the film, and the filmmaker's reputation might have subsequently been enhanced.

A decision must be made regarding whether to open the picture in New York and Los Angeles. Though these are the most lucrative and prestigious markets, they necessitate enormous advertising costs, almost ensuring a small picture to at best break even. The filmmaker may prefer to relinquish his profit for this exposure but also must face the possibility of securing negative reviews. Art house exhibitors in other parts of the country are less likely to play a film unfavorably reviewed in New York. Many exploitation distributors avoid these markets completely, finding audiences too sophisticated and advertising too costly. While the majors make their profit in the first runs of the major cities, these independents regularly exploit the more rural areas of the country.

If one has extreme confidence in a picture, it can be entered into film festivals to attain critical acclaim. Independent distributors of art films are heavily influenced by reviews. Therefore, if the picture is poorly received, the chances of securing distribution may be seriously diminished.

One must calculate the optimum time of the year to release one's particular picture. The Christmas/New Year week and the spring holiday, along with the months of June, July, and August have consistently averaged a greater percent of the U.S. population attending per week, while May, September, and October attract substantially less. Because of the huge number of people in the United States, there is a significant difference in box office gross between percentage points. If a certain percentage of the moviegoing population would choose to see one's film over others, then the greater the total population attending films at that time will mean a greater number of people will see the film. The crucial factors during these times are competition for the audience and for screens. Since all of the major films are released in these prime seasons, one's film will have to compete for theaters. Independent distributors cannot secure first-run houses during this time because they are booked up to a year in advance by the majors. An independent has a chance at this time only if a major film is unexpectedly a complete failure. If one's film is exploitational, it might be able to survive in such competitive times because the audience may not be satisfied by the majors' releases. One must know what films will be in competition against one's film at various times of the year. If one has an action picture and finds that in October few action pictures will be in release, it might be more profitable to go after a greater percentage of this considerably smaller October audience.

The amount of money spent on advertising is often the crucial difference between profit and loss. If too little is spent or is utilized in the wrong medium, the picture may not generate as much rental as it could. If too much is spent, the rentals will not cover the costs. By testing the film with various advertising campaigns, one can predict the size of the audience, budget the amount of advertising needed to reach the select number of people to generate the largest grosses, and spend less on advertising than will be recouped in rentals.

Numerous movies have cost up to $40 million to produce, were extravagantly marketed, and have earned only a few million dollars in rentals. Advertising might have been exposing elements that kept audiences away from the movie, or audiences might not have responded to the accumulation of elements such as the actors or plot. Yet there have always been films that are so strong that the audience finds the film regardless of the ineptitude of distribution.

The phenomenon of the midnight movies began without advertising. The select audience was able to locate the film, inform others, and generate millions of dollars in rentals. In other cases, for example with *Billy Jack* and *The Texas Chainsaw Massacre,* the initial distributor was able to secure a large audience for the picture. Believing an even huger, unexposed audience still existed, distributors rereleased these pictures years after the initial release and earned millions of dollars more. This demonstrates that though a picture is financially successful, it might still be able to tap millions of additional dollars. Up until recently, no one would have believed that motion pictures could gross more than $100 million. The behavior of repeat viewing was not as pronounced a factor in the past as it is today.

Market research cannot accurately predict the outcome of a film because the individual elements that are combined create a unique and unpredictable result. Although each individual element may be of highest quality and expertise, the creation might be less than desired. Even if the writer, director, producer, actors, and crew are inexperienced, they can create a successful picture far greater than the sum of the elements. Once it is completed, the picture can be tested and recut or retitled to augment its appeal to audiences. A filmmaker may have to decide whether he would rather have his work viewed intact by fewer people or change it to make it more accessible to a wider audience. A filmmaker needs to know for whom his picture is aimed and then strive to reach the greatest percentage of this audience.

Though filmmakers are the most necessary element in the motion picture industry, their ability to execute their craft is controlled by distributors. Filmmakers are generally employees of the distributors, and are therefore subject to the dictates of their employer. With knowledge, filmmakers could position themselves to hire distributors to work for their goals. Such a shift in power would enable filmmakers to control the content and destiny of their pictures. An independent filmmaker can continue to make any film he wants if he has a thorough understanding of the business of distribution. Without having to rely on the major distributors and his box office record, a filmmaker could be free to actualize his vision.

Filmmakers generally learn to distribute films the hard way after their film has been rejected for distribution by all of the major and independent companies. If a filmmaker studies the market before production, he will be able to budget costs to be lower than the minimum amount expected to be recouped. By this cautious practice, the filmmaker will be able to survive and continue making films.

The myth that numerous independent distributors exist who can distribute one's picture if rejected by the majors is erroneous. Though an average of 13.5 independent distributors release films which earn rentals of a million dollars or more per year, most of these pictures are their own productions or are of a genre in which they have expertise. Only an average of 5.4 of these independent distributors release two or more pictures per year. These are the larger and generally more stable companies; however, they control the production of most of the pictures and are very selective about the films they acquire.

A filmmaker must realize that a market does exist for most films. Though it may be quite limited, once found, the film can fulfill its function. If a filmmaker is aware of the factors involved in a film's distribution and has studied the release strategy used by distributors for films of a similar nature, he may be better able to predict which methods of distribution would be most effective for a particular type of film. A filmmaker who is committed to ensuring his picture has the opportunity to be viewed always has the option of distributing the picture himself, thereby creating his own independent distribution company.

The film industry was created by businessmen and showmen who performed all functions of producing, distributing, and exhibiting their product. When they were forced to relinquish part of their control, they realized that distribution was the key to economic power. They therefore chose to retain distribution and gave up exhibition. During this struggle for control of the channels of production, distribution, and exhibition of motion pictures, the movies evolved into a genuine art form and a truly commercial commodity as well.

Regardless of whether a filmmaker is interested in producing only art films or commercial product, it is wise to be realistically aware that the distribution of the motion picture can have a major effect upon the ultimate success of a film. The means of distributing a film can affect not only the commercial aspects but influence the critical success as well. Regardless of one's motives for producing a picture, one generally aims to have it viewed by the greatest number of people. Distribution practices can impede this goal or, if wisely executed, can be responsible for ensuring that the greatest potential of the picture is fully realized.

Appendix

Table A-1.   Champs among Bantamweights

Film Title (Domestic Distribution Company, Year of Release)	Total Rentals Reported as Received to Date
The Amityville Horror (AIP, 1979)	$35,000,000
The Muppet Movie (AFD, 1979)	32,000,000
The Trial of Billy Jack (Taylor-Laughlin, 1974)	24,000,000
In Search of Noah's Ark (Sunn, 1977)	24,000,000
Grizzly Adams (Sunn, 1975)	21,895,000
Love at First Bite (AIP, 1979)	20,600,000
Halloween (Compass Int., 1978)	18,500,000
Time Bandits (Avco Embassy, 1981)	18,415,921
Dressed to Kill (Filmways, 1980)	15,000,000
The Adventures of the Wilderness Family (Pacific Int., 1976)	14,872,000
The Jazz Singer (AFD, 1980)	13,000,000
Born Losers (AIP, 1974 reissue)	12,500,000
Chariots of the Gods? (Sunn, 1973)	12,460,000
Carnal Knowledge (Avco Embassy, 1971)	12,351,000
Benji (Mulberry Square, 1974)	12,000,000
Private Lessons (Jensen Farley, 1981)	11,985,296
Beyond and Back (Sunn, 1978)	11,702,000
Escape from New York (Avco Embassy, 1981)	11,000,000
The Fog (Avco Embassy, 1980)	11,000,000
The Sword and the Sorcerer (Group 1, 1982)	11,000,000
Mysterious Monsters (Sunn, 1975)	10,960,000
In Search of Historic Jesus (Sunn/Taft, 1980)	10,614,051
Caligula (Analysis, 1980)	10,000,000
Death Wish II (Filmways, 1982)	10,000,000
A Force of One (American Cinema, 1979)	9,980,000
The Octagon (American Cinema, 1980)	9,600,000
Joe (Cannon, 1970)	9,500,000
The Groove Tube (Levitt-Pickman, 1974)	9,420,000
Part 2 Walking Tall (AIP, 1975)	9,400,000
Willard (CRC/AIP, 1971)	9,300,000

Alice in Wonderland (General National, 1976)	9,100,000
Macon County Line (AIP, 1974)	9,100,000
Harper Valley PTA (April Fools, 1978)	8,550,000
Walking Tall (CRC/AIP, 1973)	8,500,000
A Touch of Class (Avco Embassy, 1973)	8,400,000
Good Guys Wear Black (American Cinema, 1978)	8,300,000
The Private Eyes (New World, 1980)	8,100,000
Across the Great Divide (Pacific Int., 1977)	8,076,000
The Bermuda Triangle (Sunn, 1978)	8,000,000
Blow Out (Filmways, 1981)	8,000,000
Silent Scream (American Cinema, 1979)	7,900,000
Challenge to Be Free (Pacific Int., 1975)	7,544,800
The Howling (Avco Embassy, 1980)	7,500,000
Hopscotch (Avco Embassy, 1980)	7,500,000
The Texas Chainsaw Massacre (Bryanston, 1974/ New Line, 1981)	7,452,000
The Pom Pom Girls (Crown Int., 1976)	7,425,000
The Vanishing Wilderness (Pacific Int., 1973)	7,395,542
Take This Job and Shove It (Avco Embassy, 1981)	7,300,000
Grizzly (Film Ventures, 1976)	7,272,000
Cherry, Harry and Raquel (RM, 1970)	7,250,000
Raise the Titanic (AFD, 1980)	7,200,000
Beyond the Door (Film Ventures, 1975)	7,122,644
Kentucky Fried Movie (UFD, 1977)	7,110,000
Kill and Kill Again (Film Ventures, 1981)	7,001,555
The Sailor Who Fell from Grace with the Sea (Avco Embassy, 1976)	7,000,000
They Call Me Bruce? (Film Ventures, 1983)	6,895,726
The Stewardesses (Sherpix, 1970)	6,878,450
Dawn of the Dead (UFD, 1979)	6,824,745
Kill or Be Killed (Film Ventures, 1980)	6,800,000
Phantasm (Avco Embassy, 1979)	6,800,000
Windwalker (Pacific Int., 1980)	6,437,000
Final Chapter: Walking Tall (AIP, 1977)	6,350,000
Zapped (Embassy, 1982)	6,347,980
Scanners (Avco Embassy, 1981)	6,253,860
A Woman under the Influence (Faces, 1975)	6,117,812
The Night the Lights Went Out in Georgia (Avco Embassy, 1981)	6,100,000
Prom Night (Avco Embassy, 1980)	6,000,000
An Eye for an Eye (Avco Embassy, 1981)	6,000,000
The Prize Fighter (New World, 1979)	6,000,000
Hangar 18 (Sunn/Taft, 1980)	5,759,931
The Last American Virgin (Cannon, 1982)	5,665,000
American Wilderness (Pacific Int., 1972)	5,663,966
Incubus (Film Ventures, 1982)	5,637,425
The Changeling (AFD, 1980)	5,600,000
The Wilderness Family, Part II (Pacific Int., 1978)	5,529,000
Frontier Freemont (Sunn, 1975)	5,520,000
Eat My Dust! (New World, 1976)	5,500,000

The Mirror Crack'd (AFD, 1980)	5,500,000
Frankenstein (Bryanston, 1974/Landmark, 1982)	5,400,000
Hawmps (Mulberry Square, 1976)	5,350,000
Late Great Planet Earth (Pacific Int., 1977)	5,251,000
Death Race 2000 (New World, 1975)	5,250,000
Vice Squad (Embassy, 1982)	5,200,000
Return of the Dragon (Bryanston, 1974)	5,200,000
Monty Python and the Holy Grail (Cinema 5, 1975)	5,170,000
Waitress (Troma, 1981)	5,150,000
Comin' at Ya (Filmways, 1981)	5,000,000
The Onion Field (Avco Embassy, 1977)	5,000,000
For the Love of Benji (Mulberry Square, 1977)	5,000,000
The Reincarnation of Peter Proud (CRC/AIP, 1975)	5,000,000
The Van (Crown Int., 1977)	5,000,000
Saturn 3 (AFD, 1980)	4,900,000
Mountain Family Robinson (Pacific Int., 1979)	4,807,000
The Legend of Boggy Creek (Howco, 1972)	4,800,000
Rabbit Test (Avco Embassy, 1978)	4,700,000
Fritz the Cat (Cinemation, 1972)	4,700,000
The Seduction (Embassy, 1982)	4,700,000
If You Could See What I Hear (Jensen-Farley, 1982)	4,689,636
Squeeze Play (Troma, 1979)	4,650,000
Maniac (Analysis, 1981)	4,500,000
Valley Girl (Atlantic, 1983)	4,500,000
Treasure of the Four Crowns (Cannon, 1983)	4,450,000
Tunnelvision (World Wide, 1976)	4,350,000
Wonder of It All (Pacific Int., 1974)	4,321,205
The Mack (CRC/AIP, 1972)	4,300,000
Flesh Gordon (Mammoth, 1974)	4,220,000
Force: Five (American Cinema, 1981)	4,200,000
Meteor (AIP, 1979)	4,200,000
The Bootlegger (Howco, 1974)	4,200,000
Dirt (American Cinema, 1979)	4,200,000
The Cassandra Crossing (Avco Embassy, 1977)	4,184,000
Sweet Sweetback's Baadasssss Song (Cinemation, 1970)	4,100,000
Homework (Jensen Farley, 1982)	4,047,994
Amin–The Rise and Fall (Twin Continental, 1983)	4,000,000
Galaxina (Crown Int., 1980)	4,000,000
The Exterminator (Avco Embassy, 1980)	4,000,000
Penitentiary (Jerry Gross Org., 1979)	4,000,000
Evel Knievel (Fanfare, 1971)	4,000,000
Futureworld (AIP, 1976)	4,000,000
The Town That Dreaded Sundown (AIP, 1976)	4,000,000
The Island of Dr. Moreau (AIP, 1977)	4,000,000
Highballin' (AIP, 1978)	4,000,000
Straw Dogs (CRC, 1972)	4,000,000
Lovers and Other Strangers (CRC, 1970)	4,000,000
Savannah Smiles (Embassy, 1982)	3,823,864
The House on Sorority Row (Film Ventures, 1982)	3,782,581

The Fifth Floor (Film Ventures, 1980)	3,775,000
One Dark Night (Comworld, 1983)	3,700,000
Tidal Wave (New World, 1976)	3,700,000
Cousin, Cousine (Libra/World Northal, 1976)	3,700,000
Timerider (Jensen Farley, 1983)	3,643,512
Battle beyond the Stars (New World, 1980)	3,600,000
The Great Scout and Cathouse Thursday (AIP, 1976)	3,600,000
Goin' All the Way (Saturn Int., 1981)	3,500,000
Mad Max (AIP/Filmways, 1980)	3,500,000
Carbon Copy (Avco Embassy, 1981)	3,500,000
Cries and Whispers (New World, 1972)	3,500,000
Watership Down (Avco Embassy, 1978)	3,500,000
Return to Macon County (AIP, 1975)	3,500,000
Breaker Morant (New World/Quartet, 1980)	3,500,000
The Last Unicorn (Jensen Farley, 1982)	3,436,053
The Concrete Jungle (Pentagon/MPM, 1982)	3,234,700
A Small Town in Texas (AIP, 1976)	3,200,000
I Never Promised You a Rose Garden (New World, 1977)	3,200,000
Force Ten from Navarone (AIP, 1978)	3,200,000
At the Earth's Core (AIP, 1976)	3,200,000
Spring Fever (Comworld, 1983)	3,100,000
The Boogens (Jensen Farley, 1981)	3,044,433
Coach (Crown Int., 1978)	3,000,000
Fear No Evil (Avco Embassy, 1981)	3,000,000
The Harrad Experiment (CRC, 1973)	3,000,000
The First Deadly Sin (Filmways, 1980)	3,000,000
Sorceress (New World, 1982)	3,000,000
The Man Who Fell to Earth (Cinema 5, 1976)	3,000,000
Give 'Em Hell Harry (Theatre TV, 1975)	3,000,000
Breaker Breaker (AIP, 1977)	3,000,000
The People That Time Forgot (AIP, 1977)	3,000,000
Shout at the Devil (AIP, 1977)	3,000,000
Tentacles (AIP, 1977)	3,000,000
The Nine Lives of Fritz the Cat (AIP, 1974)	3,000,000
Don't Go in the House (Film Ventures, 1980)	2,950,000
Piranha (New World, 1978)	2,900,000
The Day of the Animals (Film Ventures, 1977)	2,858,000
C.C. & Company (Avco Embassy, 1970)	2,804,000
Fade to Black (American Cinema, 1980)	2,800,000
My Brilliant Career (Analysis, 1980)	2,750,000
The Beach Girls (Crown Int., 1982)	2,700,000
Madame Rosa (Atlantic, 1978)	2,600,000
Cooley High (AIP, 1975)	2,600,000
Cinderella (Group 1, 1977)	2,600,000
Abby (AIP, 1975)	2,600,000
Jimmy the Kid (New World, 1982)	2,600,000
The Hearse (Crown Int., 1980)	2,500,000
Napoleon (Zoetrope, 1981 reissue)	2,500,000
The Cheerleaders (Cinemation, 1973)	2,500,000
Empire of the Ants (AIP, 1977)	2,500,000

A Matter of Time (AIP, 1976)	2,500,000
Slaughter (AIP, 1972)	2,500,000
Grand Theft Auto (New World, 1977)	2,500,000
The Land That Time Forgot (AIP, 1975)	2,500,000
Grey Eagle (AIP, 1977)	2,500,000
Jenny (CRC, 1970)	2,500,000
Foxy Brown (AIP, 1974)	2,460,000
J.D.'s Revenge (AIP, 1976)	2,400,000
Cheaper to Keep Her (American Cinema, 1981)	2,400,000
How to Beat the High Cost of Living (Filmways, 1980)	2,400,000
Seven Alone (Doty-Dayton, 1975)	2,391,446
Vigilante (Film Ventures, 1983)	2,389,524
Paradise (Embassy, 1982)	2,355,145
The Giant Spider Invasion (Group 1, 1975)	2,347,000
Ben (CRC, 1972)	2,300,000
Borderline (AFD, 1980)	2,300,000
Amarcord (New World, 1975)	2,300,000
Jackson County Jail (New World, 1976)	2,300,000
Heavy Traffic (AIP, 1973)	2,300,000
Crazy Mama (New World, 1975)	2,300,000
The Last House on the Left (AIP, 1972)	2,273,000
Against a Crooked Sky (Doty-Dayton, 1975)	2,273,000
Malibu Beach (Crown Int., 1978)	2,250,000
Star Crash (New World, 1979)	2,250,000
Ruby (Dimension, 1977)	2,233,128
Truck Turner (AIP, 1974)	2,230,000
Wuthering Heights (AIP, 1971)	2,200,000
The Teasers (Group 1, 1977)	2,200,000
Rabid (New World, 1977)	2,200,000
Saturday the 14th (New World, 1981)	2,200,000
The Soldier (Embassy, 1982)	2,169,074
Class of 1984 (UFD, 1982)	2,161,720
The Abductors (Brenner, 1972)	2,136,258
Trinity Is Still My Name (Avco Embassy, 1973)	2,100,000
Humanoids of the Deep (New World, 1980)	2,100,000
The Boogey Man (Jerry Gross Org., 1980)	2,100,000
The Children (World Northal, 1980)	2,100,000
Get Out Your Handkerchiefs (New Line, 1978)	2,086,000
Hester Street (Midwest, 1975)	2,055,497
Cornbread, Earl and Me (AIP, 1975)	2,020,000
Dillinger (AIP, 1973)	2,000,000
Blood Beach (Jerry Gross Org., 1981)	2,000,000
Personals (New World, 1983)	2,000,000
The Tin Drum (New World, 1980)	2,000,000
Coffy (AIP, 1973)	2,000,000
Don't Answer the Phone (Crown Int., 1980)	2,000,000
Autumn Sonata (New World, 1978)	2,000,000
California Dreaming (AIP, 1979)	2,000,000
Black Caesar (AIP, 1973)	2,000,000
Ginger (Brenner, 1971)	2,000,000
Girls in Trouble (Group 1, 1975)	2,000,000

Blacula (AIP, 1972)	1,980,000
Zombie (Jerry Gross Org., 1980)	1,925,000
The Seduction of Mimi (New Line, 1973)	1,921,000
Pink Flamingos (New Line, 1972)	1,900,000
Frogs (AIP, 1972)	1,900,000
The Gates of Hell (MPM, 1983)	1,897,350
Tales from the Crypt (CRC, 1972)	1,890,000
The McCulloughs (AIP, 1975)	1,876,000
Junior Bonner (CRC, 1972)	1,840,000
Dr. Phibes (AIP, 1971)	1,827,000
Timewalker (New World, 1982)	1,800,000
The Secret Policeman's Other Ball (Miramax, 1982)	1,800,000
Chomps (AIP, 1979)	1,800,000
The Master Gunfighter (Taylor-Laughlin, 1975)	1,800,000
The Devil's Rain (Bryanston, 1975)	1,800,000
The Rogue (Group 1, 1976)	1,800,000
My Dinner with André (New Yorker, 1981)	1,750,000
Swept Away (Cinema 5, 1976)	1,750,000
Van Nuys Blvd. (Crown Int., 1979)	1,750,000
Voyage of the Damned (Avco Embassy, 1976)	1,750,000
Death Ship (Avco Embassy, 1980)	1,750,000
Where Does It Hurt? (CRC, 1972)	1,700,000
The Domino Principle (Avco Embassy, 1977)	1,700,000
Bread and Chocolate (World Northal, 1979)	1,700,000
Parts: The Clonus Horror (Group 1, 1979)	1,680,000
The Godsend (Cannon, 1980)	1,650,000
Gimme Shelter (Cinema 5, 1970)	1,600,000
The Garden of the Finzi-Continis (Cinema 5, 1972)	1,590,000
The Streetfighter (New Line, 1974)	1,565,000
Hell Up in Harlem (AIP, 1974)	1,550,000
Bloody Mama (AIP, 1970)	1,542,000
Cross of Iron (Avco Embassy, 1977)	1,509,000
Return of the Streetfighter (New Line, 1974)	1,507,000
Let's Spend the Night Together (Embassy, 1983)	1,504,178
Horror Planet (Almi, 1983)	1,500,000
Charlie Chan and the Curse of the Dragon Queen (American Cinema, 1981)	1,500,000
Times Square (AFD, 1980)	1,500,000
Cannonball (New World, 1976)	1,500,000
The Kids Are Alright (New World, 1979)	1,500,000
The Manitou (Avco Embassy, 1978)	1,500,000
The Hellstrom Chronicle (Cinema 5, 1971)	1,500,000
Parasite (Avco Embassy, 1981)	1,500,000
Pardon My Blooper (K-Tel, 1975)	1,473,000
Summer Camp (Borde, 1979)	1,465,000
Exit the Dragon–Enter the Tiger (Dimension, 1976)	1,455,235
Reefer Madness (New Line, 1970 reissue)	1,443,000
Alone in the Dark (New Line, 1982)	1,441,000
The Hitchhikers (EVI, 1975)	1,425,000

Heartland (Levitt-Pickman, 1981)	1,400,000
Seven Beauties (Cinema 5, 1976)	1,400,000
Arnold (CRC, 1973)	1,400,000
Snakefist vs. the Dragon (21st Century, 1980)	1,400,000
H.O.T.S (Derio, 1979)	1,400,000
The Teacher (Crown Int., 1974)	1,400,000
Brother, Can You Spare a Dime? (Dimension, 1975)	1,400,000
The Chicken Chronicles (Avco Embassy, 1977)	1,350,000
Madman (Jensen Farley, 1982)	1,347,117
Mausoleum (MPM, 1983)	1,342,900
Vampire Playgirls (MPM, 1980)	1,320,000
Hell Night (Compass Int., 1981)	1,318,000
Cry of the Banshee (AIP, 1970)	1,306,000
Funeral Home (MPM, 1982)	1,301,700
The Black Godfather (Cinemation, 1974)	1,300,000
TNT Jackson (New World, 1975)	1,300,000
Count Yorga, Vampire (AIP, 1971)	1,300,000
Galaxy of Terror (New World, 1981)	1,300,000
Warlords of the 21st Century (New World, 1982)	1,300,000
Cathy's Curse (21st Century, 1980)	1,261,228
Joystick (Jensen Farley, 1983)	1,256,315
Hollywood High (Peter Perry, 1978)	1,251,000
Improper Channels (Crown Int., 1981)	1,250,000
Eager Beavers (MPM, 1980)	1,250,000
Pick up Summer (Film Ventures, 1981)	1,240,000
Goin' Coconuts (Osmond, 1978)	1,234,648
The Erotic Adventures of Zorro (EVI, 1975)	1,225,000
The Europeans (Levitt-Pickman, 1979)	1,220,000
It Happened in Hollywood (Screw, 1973)	1,220,000
Scream and Scream Again (AIP, 1970)	1,217,000
XTRO (New Line, 1983)	1,208,000
They Call Me Trinity (Avco Embassy, 1971)	1,208,000
Star (Comworld, 1983)	1,200,000
Bluebeard (CRC, 1972)	1,200,000
Inside Moves (AFD, 1980)	1,200,000
Cemetery Girls (MPM, 1979)	1,200,000
Gums (Analysis, 1976)	1,200,000
Detroit 9000 (General Film, 1973)	1,200,000
On Any Sunday (Cinema V, 1971)	1,200,000
Soldier Blue (Avco Embassy, 1970)	1,200,000
A Bullet for Pretty Boy (AIP, 1970)	1,171,000
Lunch Wagon (Borde, 1981)	1,170,000
In Praise of Older Women (Avco Embassy, 1979)	1,150,000
Graduation Day (IFI/Scope III, 1980)	1,150,000
Locker Room Girls (MPM, 1981)	1,150,000
Polyester (New Line, 1981)	1,120,000
Stuck on You (Troma, 1982)	1,105,000
The Marriage of Maria Braun (New Yorker, 1979)	1,100,000
Sex Education (MPM, 1979)	1,100,000
Grimm's Fairy Tales for Adults (Cinemation, 1971)	1,100,000

Boxcar Bertha (AIP, 1972)	1,100,000
The High Country (Crown Int., 1981)	1,100,000
High Risk (American Cinema, 1981)	1,100,000
Dolemite (Dimension, 1975)	1,100,000
The Story of Adele H. (New World, 1975)	1,100,000
Moonshine County Express (New World, 1977)	1,100,000
Stingray (Avco Embassy, 1978)	1,100,000
Cry Uncle (Cambist, 1971)	1,083,000
The Student Teachers (New World, 1973)	1,078,000
Classroom Teasers (MPM, 1981)	1,075,000
Satan's Playthings (MPM, 1980)	1,060,000
Quadrophenia (World Northal, 1979)	1,050,000
Crater Lake Monster (Crown Int., 1977)	1,050,000
Sunflower (Avco Embassy, 1970)	1,038,000
The Dunwich Horror (AIP, 1970)	1,035,000
Girls Who'll Do Anything (Group 1, 1976)	1,035,000
Land of the Minotaur (Crown Int., 1977)	1,020,000
The Evil Dead (New Line, 1983)	1,010,000
Curtains (Jensen Farley, 1983)	1,000,000
Gregory's Girl (Goldwyn, 1982)	1,000,000
One Down Two to Go (Almi, 1982)	1,000,000
Mon Oncle d'Amerique (New World, 1980)	1,000,000
Candy Tangerine Man (Moonstone, 1975)	1,000,000
Montenegro (Atlantic, 1981)	1,000,000
The House That Dripped Blood (CRC, 1971)	1,000,000
Circle of Iron (Avco Embassy, 1979)	1,000,000
Food of the Gods (AIP, 1976)	1,000,000
Jennifer (AIP, 1978)	1,000,000
Here Come the Tigers (AIP, 1978)	1,000,000
The Norseman (AIP, 1978)	1,000,000
Our Winning Season (AIP, 1978)	1,000,000
Youngblood (AIP, 1978)	1,000,000
Johnny Firecloud (EVI, 1975)	1,000,000
Sheba Baby (AIP,. 1975)	1,000,000
Police Women (Crown Int., 1974)	1,000,000
Golden Needles (AIP, 1974)	1,000,000
Black Mama, White Mama (AIP, 1973)	1,000,000
Sisters (AIP, 1973)	1,000,000
Scream, Blacula, Scream (AIP, 1973)	1,000,000
Slaughter's Big Rip-Off (AIP, 1973)	1,000,000
Poor White Trash Part II (Borack, 1976)	1,000,000
Johnny Got His Gun (Cinemation, 1971)*	1,000,000

*In addition to *Daily Variety's* list, the following films have been included in this study:

My Tutor (Crown Int., 1983)	8,000,000
The Great White (Film Ventures Int., 1982)	3,000,000
Chained Heat (Jensen Farley, 1983)	3,000,000
Screwballs (New World, 1983)	2,200,000

Rental champions from independent distribution companies reported rentals of $1 million and more for the United States and Canada, for the period of 1970 to June 1983.
(Source: *Daily Variety*, 13 June 1983, pp. 18, 25, 64, 86, 88, 92, 98, 108.)

Table A-2. Yearly Breakdown of Independently Distributed Films*

Year	Number of Films	Percent of Total Films	Average Rental per Year	Total Rentals per Year
1970	16	4.31	2,448,715.93	39,179,450
1971	14	3.77	2,933,500.00	41,069,000
1972	19	5.12	2,698,590.74	51,273,224
1973	20	5.39	3,173,727.10	63,474,542
1974	21	5.66	5,467,866.90	114,825,205
1975	36	9.70	3,704,616.64	133,566,199
1976	29	7.82	3,805,490.86	110,359,235
1977	29	7.82	4,016,935.45	116,491,128
1978	25	6.74	4,036,105.92	100,902,648
1979	29	7.82	5,873,336.03	70,326,745
1980	47	12.67	4,433,025.74	208,352,210
1981	36	9.70	3,945,112.92	142,024,065
1982	29	7.82	3,505,034.10	101,645,989
1983	21	5.66	2,847,050.24	59,797,505
Total	371			

*Earned rentals of $1 million or more, 1970–1983.

Table A-3. Breakdown by Genre of the Independently Distributed Films*,**

Genre	Total Rental per Genre over Total Time	Average Rental per Genre over Total Time	Percent of Total Rental per Genre
Action	208,946,992	3,531,403.10	15.07
Adventure/Thriller	65,428,074	3,634,893.00	4.50
Comedy	255,439,097	4,644,347.22	17.58
Documentary	133,714,942	5,571,455.92	9.20
Drama	255,081,039	3,864,864.23	17.55
Horror	300,553,111	3,804,469.76	20.68
Science Fiction	34,573,512	2,881,126.00	2.38
Western	29,134,000	3,641,750.00	2.00
Youth	160,216,378	3,408,859.11	11.03

*Earned rentals of $1 million or more, 1970–1983.
**Total rentals over total time $1,453,087,145.00.

Table A-4. "Successful" Independent Distribution Companies*

Associated Film Distribution (AFD)

The Muppet Movie	1979	$32,000,000
The Jazz Singer	1980	13,000,000
Raise the Titanic	1980	7,200,000
The Changeling	1980	5,600,000
The Mirror Crack'd	1980	5,500,000
Saturn 3	1980	4,900,000
Borderline	1980	2,300,000
Times Square	1980	1,500,000
Inside Moves	1980	1,200,000

American International Pictures (AIP)

The Amityville Horror	1979	$35,000,000
Love at First Bite	1979	20,600,000
Born Losers (Reissue)	1974	12,500,000
Part 2 Walking Tall	1975	9,400,000
Macon County Line	1974	9,100,000
The Final Chapter: Walking Tall	1977	6,350,000
Meteor	1979	4,200,000
Futureworld	1976	4,000,000
The Town That Dreaded Sundown	1976	4,000,000
The Island of Dr. Moreau	1977	4,000,000
Highballin'	1978	4,000,000
The Great Scout and Cathouse Thursday	1976	3,600,000
Return to Macon County	1975	3,500,000
A Small Town in Texas	1976	3,200,000
Force Ten from Navarone	1978	3,200,000
At the Earth's Core	1976	3,200,000
Breaker Breaker	1977	3,000,000
The People That Time Forgot	1977	3,000,000
Shout at the Devil	1977	3,000,000
Tentacles	1977	3,000,000
The Nine Lives of Fritz the Cat	1974	3,000,000
Cooley High	1975	2,600,000
Abby	1975	2,600,000
Empire of the Ants	1977	2,500,000
A Matter of Time	1976	2,500,000
Slaughter	1972	2,500,000
The Land That Time Forgot	1975	2,500,000
Grey Eagle	1977	2,500,000
Foxy Brown	1974	2,460,000

*Companies which distributed films that earned rentals in the United States and Canada of $1 million or more from 1970 to 1983.

J.D.'s Revenge	1976	2,400,000
Heavy Traffic	1973	2,300,000
The Last House on the Left	1972	2,273,000
Truck Turner	1974	2,230,000
Wuthering Heights	1971	2,200,000
Cornbread, Earl and Me	1975	2,020,000
Dillinger	1973	2,000,000
Coffy	1973	2,000,000
California Dreaming	1979	2,000,000
Black Caesar	1973	2,000,000
Blacula	1972	1,980,000
Frogs	1972	1,900,000
The McCulloughs	1975	1,876,000
Dr. Phibes	1971	1,827,000
C.H.O.M.P.S.	1979	1,800,000
Hell up in Harlem	1974	1,550,000
Bloody Mama	1970	1,542,000
Cry of the Banshee	1970	1,306,000
Count Yorga, Vampire	1971	1,300,000
Scream and Scream Again	1970	1,217,000
A Bullet for Pretty Boy	1970	1,171,000
Box Car Bertha	1972	1,100,000
The Dunwich Horror	1970	1,035,000
Food of the Gods	1976	1,000,000
Jennifer	1978	1,000,000
Here Come the Tigers	1978	1,000,000
The Norsemen	1978	1,000,000
Our Winning Season	1978	1,000,000
Youngblood	1978	1,000,000
Sheba Baby	1975	1,000,000
Golden Needles	1974	1,000,000
Black Mama, White Mama	1973	1,000,000
Sisters	1973	1,000,000
Scream, Blacula, Scream	1973	1,000,000
Slaughter's Big Rip-Off	1973	1,000,000

AIP/Filmways

Mad Max	1980	$ 3,500,000

Almi

Horror Planet	1983	$ 1,500,000
One Down Two to Go	1982	1,000,000

American Cinema

A Force of One	1979	$ 9,980,000
The Octagon	1980	9,600,000
Good Guys Wear Black	1978	8,300,000
Silent Scream	1979	7,900,000

Force: Five	1981	4,200,000
Dirt	1979	4,200,000
Fade to Black	1980	2,800,000
Cheaper to Keep Her	1981	2,400,000
Charlie Chan and the Curse of the Dragon Queen	1981	1,500,000
High Risk	1981	1,100,000

Analysis

Caligula	1980	$10,000,000
Maniac	1981	4,500,000
My Brilliant Career	1980	2,750,000
Gums	1976	1,200,000

April Fools

Harper Valley PTA	1978	$ 8,550,000

Atlantic

Valley Girl	1983	$ 4,500,000
Madame Rosa	1978	2,600,000
Montenegro	1981	1,000,000

Avco Embassy

Time Bandits	1981	$18,415,921
Carnal Knowledge	1971	12,351,000
Escape from New York	1981	11,000,000
The Fog	1980	11,000,000
A Touch of Class	1973	8,400,000
The Howling	1980	7,500,000
Hopscotch	1980	7,500,000
Take This Job and Shove It	1981	7,300,000
The Sailor Who Fell from Grace with The Sea	1975	7,000,000
Phantasm	1979	6,800,000
Scanners	1981	6,253,860
The Night the Lights Went out in Georgia	1981	6,100,000
Prom Night	1980	6,000,000
An Eye for an Eye	1981	6,000,000
The Onion Field	1977	5,000,000
Rabbit Test	1978	4,700,000
The Cassandra Crossing	1977	4,184,000
The Exterminator	1980	4,000,000
Carbon Copy	1981	3,500,000
Watership Down	1978	3,500,000
Fear No Evil	1981	3,000,000

C.C. & Company	1970	2,804,000
Trinity Is Still My Name	1973	2,100,000
Death Ship	1980	1,750,000
Voyage of the Damned	1976	1,750,000
The Domino Principle	1977	1,700,000
Cross of Iron	1977	1,509,000
The Manitou	1978	1,500,000
Parasite	1981	1,500,000
The Chicken Chronicles	1977	1,350,000
They Call Me Trinity	1971	1,208,000
Soldier Blue	1970	1,200,000
In Praise of Older Women	1979	1,150,000
Stingray	1978	1,100,000
Sunflower	1970	1,038,000
Circle of Iron	1979	1,000,000

Borack

Poor White Trash Part II	1976	$ 1,000,000

Borde

Summer Camp	1979	$ 1,465,000
Lunch Wagon	1981	1,170,000

Brenner

The Abductors	1972	$2,136,258
Ginger	1971	2,000,000

Bryanston

The Texas Chainsaw Massacre (Bryanston, 1974/New Line, 1981)		$ 7,452,000
Frankenstein (Bryanston, 1974/Landmark, 1982)		5,400,000
Return of the Dragon	1974	5,200,000
The Devil's Rain	1975	1,800,000

Cambist

Cry Uncle	1971	$ 1,083,000

Cannon Films

Joe	1970	$ 9,500,000
The Last American Virgin	1982	5,665,000
Treasure of the Four Crowns	1983	4,450,000
The Godsend	1980	1,650,000

Cinerama Releasing Corp. (CRC)

Straw Dogs	1972	$ 4,000,000
Lovers and Other Strangers	1970	4,000,000
The Harrad Experiment	1973	3,000,000
Jenny	1970	2,500,000
Ben	1972	2,300,000
Tales from the Crypt	1972	1,890,000
Junior Bonner	1972	1,840,000
Where Does It Hurt?	1972	1,700,000
Arnold	1973	1,400,000
Bluebeard	1972	1,200,000
The House That Dripped Blood	1971	1,000,000

CRC/AIP

Willard	1971	$ 9,300,000
Walking Tall	1973	8,500,000
The Reincarnation of Peter Proud	1975	5,000,000
The Mack	1972	4,300,000

Cinema 5

Monty Python and the Holy Grail	1975	$ 5,170,000
The Man Who Fell to Earth	1976	3,000,000
Swept Away	1976	1,750,000
Gimme Shelter	1970	1,600,000
The Garden of the Finzi-Continis	1972	1,590,000
The Hellstrom Chronicle	1971	1,500,000
Seven Beauties	1976	1,400,000
On Any Sunday	1971	1,200,000

Cinemation

Fritz the Cat	1972	$ 4,700,000
Sweet Sweetback's Baadasssss Song	1970	4,100,000
The Cheerleaders	1973	2,500,000
The Black Godfather	1974	1,300,000
Grimm's Fairy Tales for Adults	1971	1,100,000
Johnny Got His Gun	1971	1,000,000

Compass International

Halloween	1978	$18,500,000
Hell Night	1981	1,318,000

Comworld

One Dark Night	1983	$ 3,700,000
Spring Fever	1983	3,100,000
Ator	1983	1,200,000

Crown International

My Tutor	1983	$ 8,000,000
The Pom Pom Girls	1977	7,425,000
The Van	1977	5,000,000
Galaxina	1980	4,000,000
Coach	1978	3,000,000
The Beach Girls	1982	2,700,000
The Hearse	1980	2,500,000
Malibu Beach	1978	2,250,000
Don't Answer the Phone	1980	2,000,000
Van Nuys Blvd.	1979	1,750,000
The Teacher	1974	1,400,000
Improper Channels	1981	1,250,000
The High Country	1981	1,100,000
Crater Lake Monster	1977	1,050,000
Land of the Minotaur	1977	1,020,000
Police Women	1974	1,000,000

Derio

H.O.T.S.	1979	$ 1,400,000

Dimension

Ruby	1977	$ 2,233,128
Exit the Dragon-Enter the Tiger	1976	1,455,235
Brother, Can You Spare a Dime?	1975	1,400,000
Dolemite	1975	1,100,000

Doty-Dayton

Seven Alone	1975	$ 2,391,446
Against a Crooked Sky	1975	2,273,000

Embassy

Zapped	1982	$ 6,347,980
Vice Squad	1982	5,200,000
The Seduction	1982	4,700,000
Savannah Smiles	1982	3,823,864
Paradise	1982	2,355,145
The Soldier	1982	2,169,074
Let's Spend the Night Together	1983	1,504,178

EVI

The Hitchhikers	1975	$ 1,425,000
The Erotic Adventures of Zorro	1975	1,225,000
Johnny Firecloud	1975	1,000,000

Faces

A Woman under the Influence	1975	$ 6,117,812

Fanfare

Evel Knievel	1971	$ 4,000,000

Film Ventures

Grizzly	1976	$ 7,272,000
Beyond the Door	1975	7,122,644
Kill and Kill Again	1981	7,001,555
They Call Me Bruce?	1983	6,895,726
Kill or Be Killed	1980	6,800,000
Incubus	1982	5,637,425
The House on Sorority Row	1982	3,782,581
The Fifth Floor	1980	3,775,000
The Great White	1982	3,000,000
Don't Go in the House	1980	2,950,000
The Day of the Animals	1977	2,858,000
Vigilante	1983	2,389,524
Pick up Summer	1981	1,240,000

Filmways

Dressed to Kill	1980	$15,000,000
Death Wish II	1982	10,000,000
Blow Out	1981	8,000,000
Comin' at Ya	1981	5,000,000
The First Deadly Sin	1980	3,000,000
How to Beat the High Cost of Living	1980	2,400,000

General Film

Detroit 9000	1973	$ 1,200,000

General National

Alice in Wonderland	1976	$ 9,100,000

Goldwyn

Gregory's Girl	1982	$ 1,000,000

Group 1

The Sword and the Sorcerer	1982	$11,000,000
Cinderella	1977	2,600,000
The Giant Spider Invasion	1975	2,347,000

The Teasers	1977	2,200,000
Girls in Trouble	1975	2,000,000
The Rogue	1976	1,800,000
Parts: The Clonus Horror	1979	1,680,000
Girls Who'll Do Anything	1976	1,035,000

Howco

The Legend of Boggy Creek	1972	$ 4,800,000
The Bootlegger	1974	4,200,000

IFI/Scope III

Graduation Day	1980	$ 1,150,000

Jensen Farley

Private Lessons	1981	$11,985,296
If You Could See What I Hear	1982	4,689,636
Homework	1982	4,047,994
Timerider	1983	3,643,512
The Last Unicorn	1982	3,436,053
The Boogens	1981	3,044,433
Chained Heat	1983	3,000,000
Madman	1982	1,347,117
Joystick	1983	1,256,315
Curtains	1983	1,000,000

Jerry Gross Organization

Penitentiary	1979	$ 4,000,000
The Boogey Man	1980	2,100,000
Blood Beach	1981	2,000,000
Zombie	1980	1,925,000

K-Tel

Pardon My Blooper	1975	$ 1,473,000

Landmark

Frankenstein (Bryanston, 1974/ Landmark, 1982)		$ 5,400,000

Levitt-Pickman

The Groove Tube	1974	$ 9,420,000
Heartland	1981	1,400,000
The Europeans	1979	1,220,000

Libra/World Northal

Cousin Cousine	1976	$ 3,700,000

Mammoth

Flesh Gordon	1974	$ 4,220,000

Midwest

Hester Street	1975	$ 2,055,497

Miramax

The Secret Policeman's Other Ball	1982	$ 1,800,000

Moonstone

Candy Tangerine Man	1975	$ 1,000,000

MPM

The Gates of Hell	1983	$ 1,897,350
Mausoleum	1983	1,342,900
Vampire Playgirls	1980	1,320,000
Funeral Home	1982	1,301,700
Eager Beavers	1980	1,250,000
Cemetery Girls	1979	1,200,000
Locker Room Girls	1981	1,150,000
Sex Education	1979	1,100,000
Classroom Teasers	1981	1,075,000
Satan's Playthings	1980	1,060,000

Mulberry Square

Benji	1974	$12,000,000
Hawmps	1976	5,350,000
For the Love of Benji	1977	5,000,000

New Line

The Texas Chainsaw Massacre (Bryanston, 1974/New Line, 1981)		$ 7,452,000
Get out Your Handkerchiefs	1978	2,086,000
The Seduction of Mimi	1973	1,921,000
Pink Flamingos	1972	1,900,000
The Streetfighter	1974	1,565,000
Return of the Streetfighter	1974	1,507,000
Reefer Madness (Reissue)	1970	1,443,000

Alone in the Dark	1982	1,441,000
XTRO	1983	1,208,000
Polyester	1981	1,120,000
The Evil Dead	1983	1,010,000

New World

The Private Eyes	1980	$ 8,100,000
The Prize Fighter	1979	6,000,000
Eat My Dust!	1976	5,500,000
Death Race 2000	1975	5,250,000
Tidal Wave	1976	3,700,000
Battle beyond the Stars	1980	3,600,000
Cries and Whispers	1972	3,500,000
I Never Promised You a Rose Garden	1977	3,200,000
Sorceress	1982	3,000,000
Piranha	1978	2,900,000
Jimmy the Kid	1982	2,600,000
Grand Theft Auto	1977	2,500,000
Amarcord	1975	2,300,000
Crazy Mama	1975	2,300,000
Jackson County Jail	1976	2,300,000
Star Crash	1979	2,250,000
Rabid	1977	2,200,000
Saturday the 14th	1981	2,200,000
Screwballs	1983	2,200,000
Humanoids of the Deep	1980	2,100,000
Personals	1983	2,000,000
The Tin Drum	1980	2,000,000
Autumn Sonata	1978	2,000,000
Timewalker	1982	1,800,000
Cannonball	1976	1,500,000
The Kids Are Alright	1979	1,500,000
Warlords of the 21st Century	1982	1,300,000
TNT Jackson	1975	1,300,000
Galaxy of Terror	1981	1,300,000
The Story of Adele H.	1975	1,100,000
Moonshine County Express	1977	1,100,000
The Student Teachers	1973	1,078,000
Mon Oncle d'Amerique	1980	1,000,000

New World/Quartet

Breaker Morant	1980	$ 3,500,000

New Yorker

My Dinner with André	1981	$ 1,750,000
The Marriage of Maria Braun	1979	1,100,000

Osmond

Goin' Coconuts	1978	$ 1,234,648

Pacific International

The Adventures of the Wilderness Family	1976	$14,872,000
Across the Great Divide	1977	8,076,000
Challenge to Be Free	1975	7,544,800
The Vanishing Wilderness	1973	7,395,542
Windwalker	1980	6,437,000
American Wilderness	1972	5,663,966
The Wilderness Family, Part II	1978	5,529,000
Late Great Planet Earth	1977	5,251,000
Mountain Family Robinson	1979	4,807,000
Wonder of It All	1974	4,321,205

Pentagon/MPM

The Concrete Jungle	1982	$ 3,234,700

Peter Perry

Hollywood High	1978	$ 1,251,000

RM

Cherry, Harry & Raquel	1970	$ 7,250,000

Saturn International

Goin' All the Way	1981	$ 3,500,000

Screw

It Happened in Hollywood	1973	$ 1,220,000

Sherpix

The Stewardesses	1970	$ 6,878,450

Sunn Classic

In Search of Noah's Ark	1977	$24,000,000
Grizzly Adams	1975	21,895,000
Chariots of the Gods	1973	12,460,000
Beyond and Back	1978	11,702,000
Mysterious Monsters	1975	10,960,000
The Bermuda Triangle	1978	8,000,000
Frontier Freemont	1975	5,520,000

Sunn/Taft

In Search of Historic Jesus	1980	$10,614,051
Hangar 18	1980	5,759,931

Taylor-Laughlin

The Trial of Billy Jack	1974	$24,000,000
The Master Gunfighter	1975	1,800,000

Theatre TV

Give 'Em Hell Harry	1975	$ 3,000,000

Troma

Waitress	1981	$ 5,150,000
Squeeze Play	1979	4,650,000
Stuck on You	1982	1,105,000

21st Century

Snakefist Vs. the Dragon	1980	$ 1,400,000
Cathy's Curse	1980	1,261,228

Twin Continental

Amin-The Rise and Fall	1983	$ 4,000,000

United Film Distribution (UFD)

Kentucky Fried Movie	1977	$ 7,110,000
Dawn of the Dead	1979	6,824,745
Class of 1984	1982	2,161,720

World Northal

The Children	1980	$ 2,100,000
Bread and Chocolate	1979	1,700,000
Quadrophenia	1979	1,050,000

World Wide

Tunnelvision	1976	$ 4,350,000

Zoetrope

Napoleon (Reissue)	1981	$ 2,500,000

Notes

Chapter 1

1. Roy Madsen, *Animated Film Concepts, Methods, Uses* (New York: Interland Publishing, 1969), 3–4.

2. Ibid., 6.

3. Ibid., 7.

4. Jack C. Ellis, *A History of Film* (Englewood Cliffs, N.J.: Prentice-Hall, 1979), 15–17.

5. Kurt W. Marek [C.W. Ceram], *Archaeology of the Cinema* (New York: Harcourt Brace and World, 1965), 19.

6. Arthur Knight, *The Liveliest Art* (New York: New American Library, 1957), 15.

7. Marek, 82.

8. Roy Madsen, 8.

9. Peter Cowie, *Eighty Years of Cinema* (New York: A.S. Barnes and Company, 1977), 15.

10. Marek, 143.

11. George N. George, *The Communications Revolution: A History of Mass Media in the United States* (New York: Hastings House, 1977), 81.

12. Marek, 152.

13. Ibid., 83.

14. Gordon Hendricks, *Origins of the American Film* (New York: Arno Press and the New York Times, 1972), 14.

15. Knight, *The Liveliest Art* (1957), 17.

16. Lary May, *Screening out the Past* (New York: Oxford University Press, 1980), 22.

17. Marek, 84.

18. Robert Sklar, *Movie-Made America* (New York: Random House, 1975), 13.

19. Richard Schickel, *Movies: The History of an Art as an Institution* (New York: Basic Books, 1964), 15.

20. Gordon Hendricks, "The History of the Kinetoscope," in *The American Film Industry*, ed., Tino Balio (Madison: The University of Wisconsin Press, 1976), 39.

21. Schickel, 15.

22. Mae D. Huettig, *Economic Control of the Motion Picture Industry* (Philadelphia: University of Pennsylvania Press, 1944), 11–12.

23. Marek, 145.

24. Gordon, 79.

25. Balio, ed., 6.

26. Kenneth Macgowan, *Beyond the Screen* (New York: A Delacorte Press Book, 1965), 125.

27. Terry Ramsaye, "The Rise and Place of the Motion Picture," in *The Annals (The Motion Picture Industry)*, ed., Thorsten Sellin (Philadelphia: The American Academy of Political and Social Science, 1947), 2.

28. Richard Arthur Griffith, *The Movies* (New York: Simon and Schuster, 1957), 9.

29. Schickel, 22.

30. Ibid., 24.

31. Balio, ed., 17.

32. Ibid., 15.

33. Ibid.

34. U.S. Dept. of Commerce Bureau of the Census, *Wholesale Distribution Motion Picture Films* (Washington, D.C.: Government Printing Office, 1932), 9.

35. Ibid., 5–17.

36. Balio, ed., 14.

37. May, 35.

38. Sklar, 38.

39. May, 35.

40. Ellis, 92.

41. Sklar, 38.

42. May, 36.

43. Richard Griffith, Arthur Mayer, and Eileen Bowser, *The Movies* (New York: Simon and Schuster, 1977), 83.

44. Ave Pildas, *Movie Palaces* (New York: Clarkson N. Potter, 1980), 22.

45. Ibid., 16.

46. Ibid., 121.

47. Macgowan, 9.

48. Russell Merritt, "Nickelodeon Theaters 1905–1914: Building an Audience for the Movies," in *The American Film Industry*, 78.

49. Sklar, 31.

50. Merritt, 67.

51. May, 56.

52. Sklar, 36.

53. Balio, ed., 104.

54. Huettig, *Economic Control,* 15.

55. Ibid., 16.

56. Sklar, 40.

57. Ibid., 39.

58. Huettig, *Economic Control,* 18.

59. Balio, ed., 107.

60. Knight, *The Liveliest Art* (1957), 30.

61. Temporary National Economic Committee, *Investigation of Concentration of Economic Power, Monograph No. 43, The Motion Picture Industry—A Pattern of Control* (Washington, D.C.: Government Printing Office, 1941), 4.

62. Sklar, 40.

63. Knight, *The Liveliest Art* (1957), 30.

64. Terry Ramsaye, *A Million and One Nights* (New York: Simon and Schuster, 1964), 607.

65. Lee Beaupre, "How to Distribute a Film," *Film Comment,* July-August 1977, 45.

66. Huettig, *Economic Control,* 20.

67. Balio, ed., 109.

68. Huettig, *Economic Control,* 20.

69. James Monaco, *How to Read a Film* (New York: Oxford University Press, 1977), 201–2.

70. Balio, ed., 104.

71. Huettig, *Economic Control,* 17.

72. Balio, ed., 106.

73. Knight, *The Liveliest Art* (1957), 53.

74. Sklar, 145.

75. Huettig, *Economic Control,* 147–48.

76. Balio, ed., 220.

77. Knight, *The Liveliest Art* (1957), 53–54.

78. Lewis Jacobs, *The Rise of the American Film* (New York: Harcourt, Brace and Company, 1939), 84.

79. Macgowan, 184.

80. Knight, *The Liveliest Art* (1957), 30.

81. Huettig, *Economic Control,* 24–25.

82. Benjamin B. Hampton, *A History of the Movies* (New York: Covici Friede, 1931), 119.

83. Ibid., 122.

84. Ibid., 130–31.

85. Ibid., 147.

86. Ibid., 148–49, 160.

87. Ibid.

88. Ibid., 157–63.

89. Ibid., 163–66.

90. Balio, ed., 109.

91. Huettig, *Economic Control*, 30–31.

92. Hampton, 130–31.

93. Huettig, *Economic Control*, 30–31.

94. Sklar, 145.

95. Hampton, 147.

96. Ibid., 165, 167, 169.

97. Ibid., 150–51.

98. Huettig, *Economic Control*, 32.

99. Macgowan, 184.

100. Temporary National Economic Committee, 5.

101. Huettig, *Economic Control*, 33.

102. Ibid., 34.

103. John Baxter, *Hollywood in the Thirties* (New York: A.S. Barnes and Company, 1968), 11.

104. Howard T. Lewis, *The Motion Picture Industry* (New York: D. Van Nostrand Company, 1939), 17.

105. Huettig, *Economic Control*, 34.

106. Hampton, 254.

107. Ibid., 188–90, 255.

108. Huettig, *Economic Control*, 22–23.

109. Hampton, 252.

110. Ibid., 253.

111. Ibid.

112. Ibid.

113. Ibid., 188–90.

114. Mae D. Huettig, "The Motion Picture Industry Today," in *The American Film Industry*, 247.

115. Baxter, 11.

116. Gordon, 159.

117. U.S. Department of Commerce, 9.

118. Huettig, *Economic Control,* 17.

119. Ibid., 37.

120. Ibid., 144.

121. Ibid., 38.

122. Ibid., 145.

123. Ibid., 146.

124. Ibid., 147.

125. Ibid., 145.

126. Temporary National Economic Committee, 6.

127. Balio, ed., 116.

128. Ibid., 213.

129. Terry Ramsaye, *Vocational and Professional Monographs: The Motion Picture Industry* (Boston: Bellman Publishing Company, 1946), 8.

130. *The Public Relations of the Motion Picture Industry* (New York: Department of Research and Education, Federal Council of the Churches of Christ in America, 1931), 31–32.

131. Ibid., 34.

132. Ibid., 35.

133. Ibid., 41.

134. Ibid., 26.

135. Ibid., 44–47.

136. Temporary National Economic Committee, xii.

137. "What Blockbooking Does," *The Motion Picture Monthly,* December 1930, 9–10.

138. Huettig, *Economic Control,* 44.

139. Temporary National Economic Committee, 22.

140. "What Blockbooking Does," 10.

141. Sklar, 167–70.

142. Ibid.

143. Hearing before a Subcommittee of the Committee on Interstate and Foreign Commerce, House of Representatives, *Motion Picture Films,* 74th Cong. (Washington, D.C.: Government Printing Office, 1936), 420.

144. Ibid., 35.

145. Hearing before the Committee on Interstate and Foreign Commerce, House of Representatives, *Motion Picture Films,* 76th Cong., 3rd Sess., On S. 280 (Washington, D.C.: Government Printing Office, 1940), 7.

146. Mollie Gregory, *Making Films Your Business* (New York: Schocken Books, 1979), 134.

147. Temporary National Economic Committee, 73–74.

148. Huettig, "The Motion Picture Industry," 248.

149. Harry B. Swerdlow and Judianne Jaffe, "Current Antitrust Aspects of the Distribution/Exhibition Relationship," in *The Fifth Annual UCLA Entertainment Symposium, The Selling of Motion Pictures in the '80s: New Producer/Distributor/ Exhibitor Relationships,* eds., Peter J. Dekom, Michael I. Adler, David Ginsburg, and Michael H. Lauer (Los Angeles: The Regents of the University of California, 1980), 242.

150. Gary R. Edgerton, *American Film Exhibition and an Analysis of the Motion Picture Industry's Market Structure 1963–1980* (New York: Garland Publishing, 1983), 12.

151. *Daily Year Book* (1948), 61.

152. Michael Conant, *Antitrust in the Motion Picture Industry* (Berkeley: University of California Press, 1960), 45.

153. Balio, ed., 317.

154. Jimmy Lloyd Ball, "Distribution of Theatrical Motion Pictures: The History and Contemporary Practices of Independent Producers" (M.A. Thesis, University of Southern California, 1965), 76.

155. Balio, ed., 320.

156. Ibid., 318.

157. Arthur Knight, *The Liveliest Art* (New York: Macmillan, 1978), 244.

158. Ibid.

159. William Paul, "Hollywood Harakiri," *Film Comment,* March-April 1977, 42.

160. Knight, *The Liveliest Art* (1978), 242.

161. Sklar, 274.

162. Ibid.

163. Knight, *The Liveliest Art* (1978), 244–45.

164. Ibid.

165. Aljean Harmetz, *Rolling Breaks and Other Movie Business* (New York: Alfred P. Knopf, 1983), 175.

166. Knight, *The Liveliest Art* (1978), 246–48.

167. William Bernstein, "Financing and Supplying Filmed Product," in *The Growth and Financing of Filmed Entertainment,* eds., Nathan Adler and Larry Scherzer (New York: Arthur Young, 1983), 3.

168. Dale Pollock, "From Depths to Heights," *Daily Variety,* 30 October 1979, 30.

169. Seth Cagin and Philip Dray, *Hollywood Films of the Seventies* (New York: Harper and Row Publishers, 1984), 66.

170. Douglas Brode, *The Films of the Sixties* (Secaucus, N.J.: Citadel Press, 1980), 288.

171. Griffith, Mayer, and Bowser, 530.

172. Thomas M. Pryor, "Half Century Show Business Summary," *Daily Variety,* 25 October 1983, 15, 40, 44.

173. Stuart Byron, "The Industry," *Film Comment,* January-February 1980, 38–39.

174. Pollock, "From Depths to Heights," 24.

175. Axel Madsen, *The New Hollywood: American Movies in the '70s* (New York: Thomas Y. Crowell Company, 1975), 88.

176. Paul, 41.

177. Kathryn Harris, "Film Studios Threaten Retaliation Against States Banning Blind Bids," *Los Angeles Times,* 1 June 1981, part 4, 1.

178. Ibid., 3.

179. Edgerton, 84.

180. Lawrence Cohn, "Emerge Dominant Product Line for Exhibitors, 3 Nets, Syndie TV Cable, Homevid," *Daily Variety,* 7 July 1983, 15.

181. Michael Silverman, "Fox, Chairman Hirschfield Takes Aim at 'Profitless Production,'" *Daily Variety,* 19 April 1984, 10.

182. A.D. Murphy, "1983 Total Will Ring in at $3.69 Bil on Nearly Flat Ticket-Sales Base," *Daily Variety,* 10 January 1984, 1.

183. *"United States v. Columbia Pictures Industries et al.,"* in *The Financing and Distribution of Feature Motion Pictures* (New York: Benjamin N. Cardozo School of Law, American Bar Association Forum Committee on the Entertainment and Sports Industries, 17–18 March 1983), 361.

184. Stephen Taub, "Sunny Skies Ahead for the Old Dream Machine," *Financial World,* 15–31 July 1983, 47.

185. Aljean Harmetz, "Of '83 Movie Winners and Losers, 'Flashdance' Was Top Surprise," *The Register* (California), 20 January 1984, D11.

186. Steve Ginsberg, "Plenty of Variety among Hollywood Indie FilmMakers," *Daily Variety,* 13 June 1983, 16, 42, 46.

187. Lawrence Cohn, "Cutback in Majors' Prod'n Giving Indies Chance to Fill in Missing Spaces," *Daily Variety,* 5 May 1983, 19.

188. William A. Bluem and Jason E. Squire, *The Movie Business* (New York: Hastings House, 1972), 190.

189. Roger M. Reese, "The Sale, Marketing, and Distribution of a Motion Picture," Los Angeles, 26 February 1983.

190. Michael F. Mayer, "The Exhibition License," in *The Movie Business Book,* ed., Jason F. Squire (Englewood Cliffs, N.J.: Prentice-Hall, 1983), 340.

191. Deborah Caulfield, "Studio Head Warns of 'Profitless' Future," *Los Angeles Times,* 20 April 1984, part 6, 1, 6, 7.

192. Les Keyser, *Hollywood in the Seventies* (New York: A.S. Barnes and Company, 1981), 6.

193. Ibid.

194. Errol Cook, Lee Isgur, and David Londoner, "The Growth of the Entertainment Industry: The Analyst's Perspectives," in *The Growth and Financing of Filmed Entertainment*, 36.

195. Ibid., 37.

196. Ibid., 38.

197. Paul Kagan Associates, Inc., "Motion Picture Investments Seminar" (Los Angeles: 24 May 1984).

Chapter 2

1. Ramsaye, "The Rise and Place," 4.

2. Marjorie Rosen, *Popcorn Venus* (New York: Coward, McCann and Geoghegan, 1973), 26.

3. May, 41.

4. Sklar, 31.

5. *The Public Relations of the Motion Picture Industry*, 55, 63.

6. "Family Night," *The Motion Picture Monthly*, August 1930, 3-4.

7. David Curtis, *Experimental Cinema* (New York: Dell Publishing, 1971), 14, 44.

8. Ramsaye, "The Rise and Place," 8.

9. "Five Ways in Which Pictures Bring Goodwill among Nations," *The Motion Picture Monthly*, September 1930, 9.

10. Temporary National Economic Committee, 65.

11. Jack Valenti, "56 Eventful, Sometimes Stormy, Years of Film History," *Daily Variety*, 31 October 1978, 30.

12. Temporary National Economic Committee, 6.

13. Cobbett Steinberg, *Reel Facts: The Movie Book of Records* (New York: Vintage Books, 1978), 256.

14. *The Public Relations of the Motion Picture Industry*, 74.

15. Steinberg, 456.

16. Edwin Schallert, "The Parable of the Climbing Girl," in *The Movies on Trial*, ed., William J. Perlman (New York: Macmillan, 1936), 105.

17. Steinberg, 457, 491.

18. *A Code to Govern the Making of Motion Pictures* (New York: Motion Picture Association of America, 1955), 2.

19. Martin Quigley, "Importance of the Entertainment Film," in *The Annals (The Motion Picture Industry)*, 67.

20. *The Public Relations of the Motion Picture Industry*, 146.

21. Steinberg, 457.

22. Harmetz, *Rolling Breaks*, 93.

23. Steinberg, 458.

24. Ibid., 477.

25. Jack Valenti, "The Movie Rating System," in *The Movie Business Book*, 365, 367.

26. Harmetz, *Rolling Breaks*, 96.

27. Valenti, "The Movie Rating System," 368–69.

28. David Gritten, "The Battle to Avoid the 'X' Rating," *Los Angeles Herald Examiner*, 9 December 1983, D6.

29. Valenti, "The Movie Rating System," 368.

30. Gritten, D6.

31. Will Tusher, "Valenti Agrees to Exhibs' Demands to Provide More Explicit Info for Parents," *Daily Variety*, 27 January 1984, 1, 73.

32. Will Tusher, "First Change in MPAA Code in 16 Years Is Slated to Become Effective July 1," *Daily Variety*, 28 June 1984, 1, 18.

33. Will Tusher, "Exhibitors Are Not Required to Enforce Ratings," *Daily Variety*, 13 June 1984, 3–4.

34. Bruce A. Austin, "Do Movie Ratings Affect a Film's Performance at the Ticket Window?" *Boxoffice*, March 1983, 40.

35. Ibid., 44.

36. Jack Matthews, "An R for 'Scarface' Stings Panel," *USA Today*, 10 November 1983, D4.

37. Harmetz, *Rolling Breaks*, 91.

38. Keyser, 57.

39. "New World Pix: No 'Escape' Slight of Hand Is Planned," *Daily Variety*, 13 October 1983, 14.

40. Stephen Klain, "MPAA Files Fed Trademark Infringement over Rating Switch on 'Grave' Film," *Daily Variety*, 31 January 1984, 1, 22.

41. "Indian Censors Keep File Prints to Block Inserts," *Daily Variety*, 30 June 1983, 8.

42. "All the Ads Fit to Print," *Time*, 12 September 1977, 80.

43. *Technical Report of the Commission on Obscenity and Pornography: Volume III* (Washington, D.C.: Government Printing Office, 1971), 26.

44. *Joseph Burstyn, Inc. v. Wilson* (1952) 343 US 495, 96 L ed 1089, 72 S Ct 777.

45. *Gelling v. Texas* (1952) 343 US 960, 96 L ed 1359, 72 S Ct 1002.

46. *Technical Report*, 26.

47. Thomas R. Atkins, ed., *Sexuality in the Movies* (Bloomington: Indiana University Press, 1975), 93.

48. Shelley R. Stuart, *"Young v. American Mini Theatres, Inc.,"* *New England Law Review*, Fall 1976, 392, 414.

49. "Current Status of Obscenity Laws," *Intellect*, September 1977, 100.

50. "Statewide Obscenity Laws May Preempt Local Ordinances," *Daily Variety*, 2 May 1978, 42.

51. James Leslie McCary, *Human Sexuality* (New York: D. Van Nostrand Company, 1973), 387.

52. Lee Grant, "Shoot-out in Texas," *Los Angeles Times*, 25 December 1983, part 6, 22.

53. "All the Ads Fit to Print," 80.

54. Jonas Mekas, "Statement," *Film Comment*, Winter 1964, Z8.

Chapter 3

1. Ray Loynd, "'Bachelor Party' Wraps Shooting for 20th-Fox," *Daily Variety*, 15 November 1983, 12.

2. "Motion Pictures from Acquisition to Exhibition," American Film Institute Seminar (Los Angeles, 19 February 1983).

3. James Greenberg, "Continental's Prod'n Push Enhances Profile at AMFA," *Daily Variety*, 9 March 1984, 36.

4. "Motion Pictures from Acquisition to Exhibition."

5. William Thompson, "Traditional and Non-Traditional Methods of Financing Filmed Product: A Banker's Perspective," in *The Growth and Financing of Filmed Entertainment*, 10.

6. Ibid., 12.

7. Terry Semel,"Where Filmed Product Is Going," in *The Growth and Financing of Filmed Entertainment*, 51.

8. Robert Myers, "Foreign Distribution," in *The Fifth Annual UCLA Entertainment Symposium*, 161.

9. Peter W. Geiger, "Bankable Star Only a Myth," *Daily Variety*, 28 October 1980, 24, 26.

10. Huettig, *Economic Control*, 50.

11. Temporary National Economic Committee, 6.

12. U.S. Dept. of Commerce Bureau of the Census, 15.

13. Peter W. Geiger, "The Bank and Feature Financing," in *The Movie Business Book*, 108.

14. Bernstein, 4.

15. Ibid., 4–5.

16. Larry Scherzer, "An Accountant's Perspective," in *The Growth and Financing of Filmed Entertainment*, 20.

17. Bernstein, 5.

18. Joe Shapiro, "An Attorney's Perspective," in *The Growth and Financing of Filmed Entertainment*, 14.

19. David Pirie, ed., *Anatomy of the Movies* (New York: Macmillan, 1981), 13–14.

20. Bernstein, 5–6.

21. Ibid.

22. Michael Fink, ed., "Financial Adviser on Odds of Making Money in Movies," *Los Angeles Herald Examiner,* 8 December 1983, B11.

23. Bernstein, 6.

24. Diane Harris, "Want to Make a Movie?" *Financial World,* 15–31 July 1983, 50.

25. Cathy Taylor, "Investing in the Big Screen," *The Register* (California), 8 August 1983, C11–C12.

26. "Silver Screen Partners Prospectus" (New York: E.F. Hutton, 9 April 1983), 1.

27. Alex Ben Block, "It Looks Like a Movie Poster—But It's More of a Big Idea," *Los Angeles Herald Examiner,* 11 August 1983, A11.

28. Harris, "Want To Make A Movie?" 51.

29. Fink, ed., B11.

Chapter 4

1. Paul Rosenfield, "Getting the Real Dirt on Gossip," *Los Angeles Times,* 17 April 1983, part 6, 18.

2. Herbert Kosower, "A Study of an Independent Feature Film: 'You Don't Have Time'" (Ph.D. dissertation, University of Southern California, 1969), 88.

3. Richard Patterson, "'Chan Is Missing' Or How to Make a Successful Feature for $22,315.92," *American Cinematographer,* February 1983, 32–39.

4. John Hanson, "The Theatrical Self-Distribution of 'Northern Lights'," *Filmmakers Monthly,* October 1979, 19–24.

5. Vincent Canby, "The Power of the Times," in *The Cineaste Interviews on the Art and Politics of the Cinema,* eds., Dan Georgakas and Lenny Rubenstein (Chicago: Lake View Press, 1983), 295.

6. Roman Polanski, *Roman* (New York: William Morrow and Company, 1984), 440–42.

7. Steinberg, 416–17.

8. Axel Madsen, 125.

9. Don Ravaud, "Italian Festivals and Us," *Framework,* Summer 1983, 55.

10. "Florence Festival Back in Biz, Yanks Indies Monopolize Turf," *Daily Variety,* 28 July 1983, 2.

11. Axel Madsen, 125.

12. Amos Vogel, "More Apocalypse Now," *Film Comment,* May-June 1983, 76–77.

13. Edward Landler, "IFP Interview with Ken Wlaschin," *IFP West Newsletter,* September 1984, 2.

14. Ibid.

15. Canby, 282.

16. Clarke Taylor, "N.Y. Festival Spotlights U.S. Films," *Los Angeles Times,* 17 August 1983, part 6, 1.

17. Vern Perry, "The Man behind Filmex Gears Up for His Exposition's 12th Edition," *The Register* (California), 8 August 1983, C4.

18. Charles Champlin, "Wlaschin's World's Eye Filmex View," *Los Angeles Times*, 17 December 1983, part 6, 15.

19. Todd McCarthy, "Filmex Reports Solid B.O. for Its 1983 Unspooling," *Daily Variety*, 6 May 1983, 1, 11.

20. *18th Chicago International Film Festival* (Chicago: Illinois Department of Commerce and Community Affairs, Office of Tourism, 1982), 5.

21. William S. Bayer, *Breaking Through, Selling Out, Dropping Dead and Other Notes on Filmmaking* (New York: Macmillan, 1971), 92.

22. Deborah Caulfield, "Making It on Your Own in World of Filmmaking," *Los Angeles Times*, 21 January 1983, part 6, 1, 20.

23. Ron Epple, "Festivals: Independent Film-Makers Exposition," *Filmmakers Newsletter*, April 1974, 68.

24. Judith Trojan and Nadine Covert, eds., *16mm Distribution* (New York: Educational Film Library Association, 1977), 99.

25. Yanou Collart, "The Deauville Film Festival," *American Premiere*, November 1982, 33.

26. Trojan, 94.

27. Peter Cowie, ed., *International Film Guide 1983* (London: The Tantivy Press, 1982), 359.

28. "Cannes Winners over the Years," *Hollywood Reporter*, 3 May 1983, C-123.

29. Amos Vogel, "Independents," *Film Comment*, September-October 1978, 74.

30. "The Rules of the Game," *Hollywood Reporter*, 3 May 1983, C-131–32.

31. "Noncompetitive Screenings," *Hollywood Reporter*, 3 May 1983, C-136.

32. Austin Lamont, "Independents Day," *Film Comment*, November-December 1981, 71.

33. Mary Corliss, "Cannes Journal," *Film Comment*, September-October 1974, 2, 66.

34. Stephen Klain, "'Narayama' Pickup Parleys Underway," *Daily Variety*, 2 June 1983, 8.

35. Simon Perry, "Cannes, Festivals and the Movie Business," *Sight and Sound*, Autumn 1981, 228.

36. "Independent Companies Busy in and Outside of Hollywood," *Daily Variety*, 19 June 1980, 76.

37. Terry Ilott, "Films Good, Weather Bad, Business in between at 37th Cannes Festival," *Screen International*, 2–9 June 1984, 8.

38. Hy Hollinger, "AFM Surpasses Cannes, Milan As Trading Place," *Daily Variety*, 16 March 1984, 3, 46.

39. Roderick Mann, "82 Cannes Film Festival," *Los Angeles Times*, 25 May 1982, part 6, 4.

40. Ibid.

41. E.J. Dionne, Jr., "It's Business As Usual in Cannes," *Los Angeles Herald Examiner*, 14 May 1983, B4.

42. Hy Hollinger, "AFMA Members Reappraising Cannes Fest," *Daily Variety*, 20 May 1983, 16.

43. Lee Grant, "A New Film Market Where the Action Is," *Los Angeles Times*, 19 March 1981, part 6, 8.

44. Deborah Caulfield, "Sales Brisk at Second Film Market," *Los Angeles Times*, 5 April 1982, part 6, 4.

45. Grant, "A New Film Market," 8.

46. Andrew Vajna, "AFMA," *American Premiere*, November 1982, 16.

47. Grant, "A New Film Market," 1.

48. Hy Hollinger, "Goldman AFMA Prez; L.A. Mart in March," *Daily Variety*, 28 June 1983, 1, 19.

49. Teri Ritzer, "The Market," *Hollywood Reporter*, 24 March 1982, S3.

50. "Film Market Ends Its Run on Upbeat Note," *Daily Variety*, 14 March 1983, 21.

51. Hy Hollinger, "AFM Kicks Off as Hopes Soar," *Variety*, 2 March 1983, 166.

52. "Compass Int'l Finds Film Mart Price Too Steep," *Daily Variety*, 23 March 1981, 8.

53. Martin A. Grove, "Film Mart Will Sell Independent Pics," *Los Angeles Herald Examiner*, 18 March 1981, B5.

54. Ritzer, "The Market," S4.

55. Caulfield, "Sales Brisk," 4.

56. "Cannon Piggy-Back on L.A. Film Market to Sell Pix," *Daily Variety*, 23 March 1981, 20.

57. Deborah Caulfield, "Promoters, Purchasers and Porn," *Los Angeles Times*, 14 March 1983, part 6, 4.

58. Caulfield, "Sales Brisk," 4.

59. Michael Silverman, "AFMA Unveils International Arbitration Tribunal System," *Daily Variety*, 4 March 1983, 48.

60. Hy Hollinger, "Kodiak's Schmidt Thinks Too Many Sellers at AFMA," *Daily Variety*, 9 March 1984, 34, 37.

61. Hy Hollinger, "Deadbeats at Film Market," *Daily Variety*, 12 March 1984, 6.

62. Michael Goldman, "AFM Lets Hollywood's Films Be Offered Where They're Made: L.A.," *Hollywood Reporter*, 9 August 1983, S38.

63. Jack Searles, "Fright Movies Are Out, Big Pictures Are In," *Los Angeles Herald Examiner*, 9 March 1983, C3.

64. Lawrence Cohn, "AFMA's All-American Image Tarnished," *Daily Variety*, 23 March 1983, 4.

65. "Film Market Ends," 21.

66. Tina Daniell, "Majors Take Growing Interest in AFM as Both Buyers and Sellers," *Hollywood Reporter*, 1 March 1983, 3, 16.

67. "Film Market Ends," 21.

68. Ibid.

69. Searles, "Fright Movies," C3.

70. Daniell, 16.

71. "Film Market Ends," 21.

72. Michael London, "'Foreign Shoppers' Time at L.A. Movie Market," *Los Angeles Times,* 14 March 1984, part 6, 1.

73. B.J. Franklin, "AFMA Pride at Four-year Record of Achievement," *Screen International,* 10–17 March 1984, 8.

74. Hy Hollinger, "1984 Edition of Film Market Biggest in 4–Year History," *Daily Variety,* 7 March 1984, 22.

75. Andrew Kirtzman, "N.Y. Indie Distributors Propose to Dismantle Charter of the AFM," *Daily Variety,* 26 June 1984, 13.

76. Hedy Kleyweg, "MIFED '82," *Hollywood Reporter,* 12 October 1982, 34.

77. Colin Vaines, Terry Ilott, Anne Head, and Tina McFarling, "Largest MIFED Turnout, Business Only Average," *Screen International,* 19–26 November 1983, 8.

78. Tom Walden, "Germany," *Hollywood Reporter,* 12 October 1982, S65.

79. Hy Hollinger, "Fewer Buyers and Business Is Down but Cannes Fest Remains Major Showcase," *Daily Variety,* 23 May 1984, 12.

80. Hy Hollinger, "Despite All the Carping Cannes Still Potent Lure," *Daily Variety,* 9 May 1984, 16.

81. Cowie, ed., *International Film Guide,* 357.

82. "The American Independent Feature Market," *American Premiere,* November 1982, 24, 32.

83. "The Market: Five Years Progress," *The Independent Feature Project,* Winter 1984, 2.

84. Caulfield, "Promoters," 1.

85. "Porno Film Market Considered a Successful Event by Topper," *Daily Variety,* 11 March 1983, 38.

86. Ibid.

87. Caulfield, "Promoters," 4.

88. Raphael D. Silver, "Independent Distribution: Midwest Films," in *The Movie Business Book,* 293–300.

89. Gregory Goodell, *Independent Feature Film Production* (New York: St. Martin's Press, 1982), xviii.

90. Raphael D. Silver, 293–300.

Chapter 5

1. David Bergmann, "Giveaways Pitched in Good Times and Bad," *Daily Variety,* 19 August 1983, 12.

2. Steinberg, 400.

3. Knight, *The Liveliest Art* (1957), 108.

4. Steinberg, 400.

5. Sklar, 234.

6. May, 158.

7. Carl Laemmle, "The Business of Motion Pictures," in *The American Film Industry*, 153–168.

8. Chris Musun, "The Marketing of Motion Pictures" (D.B.A. dissertation, University of Southern California, 1969), 206–8.

9. Sklar, 234–36.

10. "Motion Pictures in Sound Condition," *The Motion Picture Monthly*, 1 December 1929, 2.

11. "Advertising Code for Motion Pictures," *The Motion Picture Monthly*, 1 July 1930, 3, 7.

12. Musun, 209–10.

13. Paul N. Lazarus, "50 Years Later: Marketing Name of Game," *Daily Variety*, 25 October 1983, 214.

14. Trueman T. Rembusch, *What the Public Wants to See* (Allied States Association of Motion Picture Exhibitors, 1949), 27.

15. John Waters, "Whatever Happened to Showmanship?" *American Film*, December 1983, 55.

16. Lazarus, "50 Years Later," 214.

17. Pirie, 96.

18. Pollock, "From Depths to Heights," 32.

19. Axel Madsen, 72.

20. Pirie, 98.

21. David Anthony Daly, "A Comparison of Exhibition and Distribution Patterns in Three Recent Feature Motion Pictures" (Ph.D dissertation, Southern Illinois University at Carbondale, 1978), 122.

22. Ibid., 49.

23. Thomas Simonet, "Market Research: Beyond the Fanny of the Cohn," *Film Comment*, January-February 1980, 68.

24. William Severini Kowinski, "The Malling of the Movies," *American Film*, September 1983, 53.

25. Gregg Kilday, "The Queue Factor," *The Movies*, September 1983, 77.

26. Aljean Harmetz, "Frank Yablans: MGM's 'Professional' Lion Tamer," *Los Angeles Herald Examiner*, 14 May 1983, B2.

27. "Future Shock in the Motion Picture Industry," UCLA Extension Course, 16 May 1983.

28. Helen Dudar, "All the Right Moves," *American Film*, March 1984, 39.

29. "Marketing Consultants Not Shy, but Find Low Profile Sits Best with Studios," *Daily Variety*, 13 July 1981, 68, 72.

30. Lee Grant, "The Annual Write of the Oscars," *Los Angeles Times,* 11 April 1983, part 6, 1.

31. Cook, Isgur, and Londoner, 40.

32. Michael London, " 'Betrayal': Showdown in the Commerce Corral," *Los Angeles Times,* 25 January 1984, part 6, 1.

33. Samuel Z. Arkoff, "Ninth Annual Publicists Guild Awards Luncheon Speech Transcript," (Beverly Wilshire Hotel, 7 April 1972), 2, 6–10.

34. Edwin Howard, "Why Films Silently Come, Quickly Go," *Journal of Producers Guild of America,* March 1972, 13.

35. Robert Evans, "The Producer," in *The Movie Business Book,* 18.

36. Robert Flaherty, "Nanook," in *The Emergence of Film Art,* ed., Lewis Jacobs (New York: Hopkinson and Blake, 1969), 220.

37. Peter Birge and Janet Maslin, "Getting Snuffed in Boston," *Film Comment,* May-June 1976, 35, 63.

38. Julian F. Myers, "Publicity Has Fallen into Disrepute in Hollywood, and As a Consequence Some $175 Mil Is Being Spent Needlessly in Advertising Pictures Every Year," *Daily Variety,* 28 October 1980, 30.

39. Stanley H. Durwood and Joel H. Resnick, "The Theatre Chain: American Multi-Cinema," in *The Movie Business Book,* 331.

40. "Marketing and Distribution in the Motion Picture Industry," UCLA Extension Course, 11 May 1983.

41. "Future Shock," 16 May 1983.

42. Frank J. Moreno and Paul S. Almond, "Life amongst the Giants," in *The Fifth Annual UCLA Entertainment Symposium,* 79–80.

43. Sheldon Tromberg, *Making Money, Making Movies: The Independent Movie-Makers' Handbook* (New York: New Viewpoints/Vision Books, 1980), 149–50.

44. David A. Lipton, "Advertising and Publicity," in *The Movie Business,* 227.

45. Dan Yakir, "Campaigns and Caveat," *Film Comment,* May-June 1980, 72.

46. Ibid.

47. Lawrence Cohn, "Middle-Range Films Bypassing Gotham," *Daily Variety,* 19 May 1983, 3.

48. Cohn, "Middle-Range Films," 3, 8.

49. David McClintick, *Indecent Exposure* (New York: William Morrow and Company, 1982), 111.

50. Cohn, "Middle-Range Films," 8.

51. Aljean Harmetz, "A Boon for 'Difficult' Movies," *Los Angeles Herald Examiner,* 28 October 1980, B6.

52. McClintick, 111.

53. Ball, 57.

54. David Lees and Stan Berkowitz, *The Movie Business: A Primer* (New York: Random House, 1978), 151.

55. Lipton, 230.

56. Tom Gilbert, "Exhibs Turn to Big-Screen Ads; Distribution Battle Anticipated," *Hollywood Reporter,* 9 July 1982, 1.

57. Ibid., 29.

58. Musun, 214.

59. Myron Meisel, "Seventh Annual Grosses Gloss," *Film Comment,* March-April 1982, 61.

60. Ralph E. Laine, "International PR beyond the Glitter," *American Premiere,* November 1982, 26.

61. Kyle Counts, "U.S. Foreign Sales Agents," *American Premiere,* November 1982, 26-28.

62. Don Carle Gillette, "Distribution Faces Drastic Overhaul," *The Journal of the Producers Guild of America,* December 1970, 17.

63. "Universal Moves to Bolster Its National Presence," *Daily Variety,* 18 November 1983, 1, 26.

64. David Chute, "The New World of Roger Corman," *Film Comment,* March-April 1982, 29.

65. Daly, 12.

66. Ephraim Katz, *The Film Encyclopedia* (New York: Thomas Y. Crowell, 1979), 4.

67. Lipton, 233.

68. Meisel, "Seventh Annual Grosses Gloss," 66.

69. Lees and Berkowitz, 144-46.

70. Harmetz, "A Boon," B6.

71. Aljean Harmetz, "Hollywood Pollsters Sneak Peek at Christmas Movie Earnings," *Los Angeles Herald Examiner,* 13 December 1983, B8.

72. Musun, 220-22.

73. Daly, 50.

74. Malcolm Vance, *The Movie Ad Book* (Minneapolis: Control Data Publishing, 1981), 9.

75. Arthur Lubow, "How to Read a Movie Ad," *Harpers,* June 1983, 15-17.

76. Ibid., 16-18.

77. "The Sale, Marketing and Distribution," 26 February 1983.

78. Dale Pollock, "Film Clips," *Los Angeles Times,* 2 May 1984, part 6, 4.

79. Richard Kahn, "Motion Picture Marketing," 266.

80. Lipton, 229.

81. Lazarus, "50 Years Later," 216.

82. Nancy Yoshihara, "Movie Ads Are a Big Hit with TV," *Los Angeles Times,* 25 August 1981, part 4, 5.

83. Byron Shapiro, "Marketing and Distribution," 11 May 1983.

84. David J. Leedy, *Motion Picture Distribution: An Accountant's Perspective* (Los Angeles: David J. Leedy, 1980), 27.

85. Mike Gerety, "Marketing and Distribution," 4 May 1983.

86. Daly, 116–24.

87. Pirie, 98.

88. Lees and Berkowitz, 153.

89. Dale Pollock, "Epic Promotion Fueled 'Gandhi's' Glory," *Los Angeles Times,* 21 April 1983, part 6, 1, 4.

90. Daly, 173.

91. Charles Powell, "Marketing and Distribution," 11 May 1983.

92. "Promo Name of the Game after All," *Daily Variety,* 7 June 1982, 54.

93. Aljean Harmetz, "Filmmakers Really Selling Product Now," *Los Angeles Herald Examiner,* 22 December 1983, C1, C9.

94. Aljean Harmetz, "Fox to Sell Rights to Plug Goods in Films," *New York Times,* 21 December 1983, C19.

95. Richard J. Pietschmann, "'And Maybe He Should Be Smoking a Virginia Slims . . . ,'" *Los Angeles Magazine,* October 1981, 172–79.

96. Ibid.

97. Stanford Blum, "Merchandising," in *The Movie Business Book,* 379–81.

98. Lees and Berkowitz, 155–58.

99. Blum, 380–83.

100. Lees and Berkowitz, 157.

101. Rembusch, 23.

102. Deborah Caulfield, "Studios and Art Films—The Heyday Is Over," *Los Angeles Times,* 22 April 1984, part 6, 17.

103. Leo A. Handel, *Hollywood Looks at Its Audience* (Urbana: The University of Illinois Press, 1950), 3.

104. Hampton, 351–52.

105. Handel, 4.

106. Beth Day, *This Was Hollywood* (New York: Doubleday and Company, 1960), 196.

107. Gilbert Seldes, *The Great Audience* (New York: The Viking Press, 1950), 217–21.

108. Handel, 46.

109. Seldes, 222.

110. Robert W. Chambers, "Need For Statistical Research," in *The Annals (The Motion Picture Industry),* 169.

111. Handel, 4.

112. Thomas Simonet, "Industry," *Film Comment*, January-February 1978, 72–73.

113. Handel, 5.

114. Paul F. Lazarsfeld, "Audience Research in the Movie Field," in *The Annals (The Motion Picture Industry)*, 160.

115. Handel, 4.

116. Chambers, 169.

117. Rembusch, 7–8.

118. Simonet, "Market Research," 66.

119. Seldes, 218–19.

120. William Goldman, *Adventures in the Screen Trade* (New York: Warner Books, 1983), 41.

121. Peter Boyer, "Risky Business," *American Film*, January-February 1984, 14.

122. Lee Grant, "The Private Diary of a Movie," *Los Angeles Times*, 24 July 1983, part 6, 1, 4–8.

123. Boyer, 77.

124. Simonet, "The Market," 66.

125. Harmetz, "Hollywood Pollsters," B8.

126. Boyer, 76.

127. "Blind Bidding Setback in Texas and Arkansas," *Daily Variety*, 30 March 1983, 22.

128. James Greenberg, "Exec Claims Mkt. Research Can Cut Risks in Showbiz," *Daily Variety*, 18 January 1984, 6.

129. Seldes, 224.

130. Bruce A. Austin, "Motivations for Movie Attendance," *Boxoffice*, October 1984, 13–16.

131. Jack Searles, "Rating the 'Quality' of TV Viewers," *Los Angeles Herald Examiner*, 25 April 1983, D3.

132. John Harrington, *The Rhetoric of Film* (New York: Holt, Rinehart and Winston, 1973), 154–55.

133. Gordon Stulberg, "The Establishment of a Film Company," in *The Movie Business*, 106.

Chapter 6

1. Edgerton, 67.

2. Ibid., 48.

3. Select U.S. Congress Senate Committee on Small Business, *Motion Picture Distribution Trade Practices—1956* (Washington, D.C.: Government Printing Office, 1956), 6.

4. Edgerton, 22.

5. Ibid., 46.

6. Ibid., 51–55.

7. Ibid., 91.

8. Ibid., 56–67.

9. Ball, 78.

10. Edgerton, 72.

11. Will Tusher, "No Shortage of Crises for Exhibition in '70s," *Daily Variety,* 30 October 1979, 90.

12. Edgerton, 85–86.

13. Will Tusher, "Exhib Leaders Thankful for Current Blessings but View Future with Nervous Optimism," *Daily Variety,* 31 October 1981, 46–48, 50.

14. Edgerton, 45, 52.

15. Ibid., 35–36.

16. Linda Grant and Robert E. Dallos, "General Cinema Hunt May Be Over," *Los Angeles Times,* 18 April 1983, part 4, 1–2.

17. Taub, 49.

18. Durwood and Resnick, 328.

19. Ibid., 329.

20. Ibid., 328–30.

21. Tusher, "Exhib Leaders Thankful," 46–58.

22. "Calif. National Champ in No. of Film Screens," *Daily Variety,* 21 November 1983, 1, 13.

23. Jim Robbins, "Exhibitors Heading for Big Boom in Screen Additions," *Daily Variety,* 8 December 1983, 3.

24. "22 New Screens on AMC Agenda for December," *Daily Variety,* 2 December 1983, 1.

25. Edgerton, 52–53.

26. Paul Richter, "Big Chains Find Edwards Formidable Foe," *Los Angeles Times,* 19 May 1981, part 4, A.

27. "Film 'Preempting' Surfaces In New York," *Daily Variety,* 6 April 1984, 10.

28. Jim Robbins, "Demand for Art Product Changing U.S. Exhibition," *Daily Variety,* 9 May 1984, 8.

29. Robbins, "Exhibitors Heading for Big Boom," 6.

30. David Lees, "The Secret Life of Henry Plitt," *Los Angeles Magazine,* January 1984, 94.

31. Lewis Beale, "50 Years Ago, on a Screen Far Away . . . ," *Los Angeles Times,* 5 June 1983, part 6, 5.

32. Ibid.

33. Ibid.

34. Toby Thompson, "The Twilight of the Drive-In," *American Film,* July-August 1983, 47.

35. Gerald Clarke, "Dark Cloud over the Drive-Ins," *Time,* 8 August 1983, 64.

36. Richard Klein, "'Passion Pits' of 50 Years Ago Now Family Oriented," *Daily Variety,* 13 June 1983, 90.

37. Louis Sahagun, "Drive In's Future Dims Across U.S.," *Los Angeles Times,* 22 August 1983, part 1, 3.

38. Ibid., 15.

39. Klein, "'Passion Pits'," 90.

40. Beale, 5.

41. Toby Thompson, 46.

42. Sahagun, 1.

43. Toby Thompson, 48.

44. Sahagun, 3.

45. Harris M. Plotkin, "Protolite Screen: Drive-In Breakthrough?" *Boxoffice,* March 1983, 64.

46. Toby Thompson, 48.

47. Sahagun, 3.

48. Toby Thompson, 49.

49. Sahagun, 15.

50. Toby Thompson, 46.

51. Ibid., 49.

52. Klein, "'Passion Pits'," 90.

53. Plotkin, 65.

54. Ibid., 64.

55. Ibid., 65.

56. Klein, "'Passion Pits'," 90.

57. Moreno and Almond, 71–72.

58. Ibid., 75.

59. Will Tusher, "Exhibs Suffer Major Change of Life, but Learning to Adjust," *Daily Variety,* 7 June 1982, 10, 61, 63–64.

60. Ibid.

61. Moreno and Almond, 73 75.

62. Sklar, 169.

63. Philip M. Lowe, "Refreshment Sales and Theatre Profits," in *The Movie Business Book,* 344–45.

64. Will Tusher, "Concessionaires Assn. Raises Members' Dues," *Daily Variety,* 3 January 1984, 1.

65. "Circuit Ends Price Cutting of Refreshments," *Daily Variety,* 20 September 1983, 3.

66. Edgerton, 55.

67. "The Motion Picture Industry," *Harvard Law Review*, March 1979, 1131.

68. "The Big Issue: Popcorn Prices," *Daily Variety*, 13 July 1981, 16.

69. Philip M. Lowe, 345.

70. Ibid., 348.

71. Tromberg, 169.

72. Will Tusher, "Noshers' Delight: 'Coke! Popcorn' Become Familiar Sounds in Film Theatres," *Daily Variety*, 25 October 1983, 154.

73. Philip M. Lowe, 349.

74. Swerdlow and Jaffe, 273.

75. Edgerton, 100–101.

76. Ibid., 102–5.

77. Tusher, "No Shortage of Crises," 40.

78. Jim Harwood, "Major Voice of California Exhibs Giving Up Pacific V.P. Stripes to Head Org," *Daily Variety*, 15 July 1983, 1, 33.

79. "Dispute over Exhib Unity Flares Anew," *Daily Variety*, 22 February 1984, 34.

80. Will Tusher, "NATO's Resnick Changes Stand on 'R' Pictures," *Daily Variety*, 22 February 1984, 1, 35.

81. "Overseas Circuits Sign Up with NATO," *Daily Variety*, 22 February 1984, 6.

82. "Feature-Film Clips on Sked at Show-A-Rama," *Daily Variety*, 31 January 1984, 14.

83. Will Tusher, "Six Majors Awarded 277G in Under-Reporting Suit against Indiana Exhib," *Daily Variety*, 5 October 1983, 1, 18.

84. Bayer, 86.

85. Gregory, 167.

86. "Tighter Columbia Credit Rules Reduce Bad Account Writeoffs," *Daily Variety*, 21 June 1983, 1, 13.

87. "NATO Concerned about Demands on Small Exhibs," *Daily Variety*, 30 March 1983, 1, 21.

88. Bayer, 84–85.

89. "Exhibs Told Employee Theft Is on the Rise," *Daily Variety*, 24 February 1984, 6.

90. Richter, C.

91. Bayer, 85.

92. Swerdlow and Jaffe, 248–49.

93. Ibid., 256–57.

94. "Film Clips," *Los Angeles Times*, 30 September 1983, part 6, 18.

95. Deborah Caulfield, "Battle of the Baldwin," *Los Angeles Times*, 20 November 1983, part 6, 1, 24–30.

96. "Complex in Baldwin Hills Sues Mann, WB Distrib'n," *Daily Variety,* 18 August 1983, 19, 23.

97. Max Bercutt, "Distrib-Exhib Deals Remain Complicated at Times Mysterious," *Daily Variety,* 24 January 1984, 11.

98. Sumner Redstone, "The Nature, Manner and Structure of Exhibition Arrangements," in *The Fifth Annual UCLA Entertainment Symposium,* 214–15.

99. "Theater Owners Work to Ban Blind Bidding," *Business Week,* 19 April 1978, 40.

100. Edgerton, 80.

101. Nat D. Fellman, "The Exhibitor," in *The Movie Business Book,* 319.

102. Lees and Berkowitz, 141.

103. Swerdlow and Jaffe, 254.

104. Harris, "Film Studios Threaten Retaliation, 3.

105. Moreno and Almond, 80.

106. Jim Robbins, "Wisconsin Anti-Blind Bidding Law Less Strict Than Sought," *Daily Variety,* 8 June 1984, 6.

107. Jim Robbins, "Ohio Statute on Blind Bidding Is Upheld on Appeal," *Daily Variety,* 7 June 1982, 4.

108. Will Tusher, "Strong Attempt to Outlaw Blind Bidding Defeated in Narrow Mississippi Vote," *Daily Variety,* 4 April 1984, 1, 20.

109. Will Tusher, "Court Rules Distribution Must Provide Sweeping Discovery in Penn. Case," *Daily Variety,* 20 January 1984, 62.

110. " 'Cruising' Spurs a Test of Booking Films Blind," *Business Week,* 3 March 1980, 26–27.

111. "Blind Bidding Setback," 1, 22.

112. "The Motion Picture Industry," 1128–47.

113. Jim Robbins, "Milwaukee Decision Hits UA Circuit, but Will Open Bidding; Distribs Are Happy," *Daily Variety,* 29 June 1983, 1, 14.

114. Swerdlow and Jaffe, 250.

115. Redstone, 232.

116. Swerdlow and Jaffe, 251.

117. Fred Kirby, "Quad Cinema Loses Its Anti-Trust Action over Splits; Appeal Planned," *Daily Variety,* 24 April 1984, 1.

118. Jim Robbins, "Quad Cinema Case Players React to Jury's Verdict," *Daily Variety,* 24 April 1984, 3, 14.

119. Jim Robbins, "Distrib-Defendants to Pay 325G-375G Each to Settle Quad's Anti-Trust Action," *Daily Variety,* 16 January 1984, 1, 42.

120. Frank Segers, "NATO Appeals Milwaukee Product-Splitting Decision," *Daily Variety,* 18 November 1983, 4.

121. Frank Segers, "Milwaukee Pix Splitting Finely Tuned," *Daily Variety,* 30 June 1983, 8.

122. Segers, "NATO Appeals," 6.

123. Will Tusher, "Pursuing National Policy That Practice Is Illegal under All Circumstances," *Daily Variety*, 24 January 1984, 1.

124. Robbins, "Milwaukee Decision," 14.

125. Edgerton, 81.

126. Robbins, "Milwaukee Decision," 14.

127. Richard Lederer, "Management: New Rules of the Game," in *The Movie Business Book*, 137.

128. Harmetz, *Rolling Breaks*, 220–22.

129. Dale Pollock, "Hot Time! Summer at the Box Office," *American Film*, June 1983, 12.

130. Ibid.

131. A.D. Murphy, "Domestic Film Box-Office Aims for New Dollar High during Holiday Period," *Daily Variety*, 17 April 1984, 1.

132. Musun, 49.

133. Ibid., 44–45.

134. Jack Searles, "Modest Movies Get the Elbow when Blockbusters Dominate U.S. Screens," *Los Angeles Herald Examiner*, 1 September 1982, B1.

135. "The Sale, Marketing and Distribution of a Motion Picture," 26 February 1983.

136. Bluem and Squire, 187.

137. Ball, 45.

138. Edgerton, 331.

139. Harmetz, "A Boon," B1.

140. Dale Pollock, "Summer Films: The Why of Those Red-Ink Blues," *Los Angeles Times*, 14 July 1983, part 6, 5.

141. "National Gross Service, Inc.," *Daily Variety*, 26 October 1982, 95.

142. Will Tusher, "NITE Prez Maps Strategy for Small-Town Theaters," *Daily Variety*, 13 December 1983, 6.

143. "Motion Picture Investments Seminar," 24 May 1984.

144. Will Tusher, "Not All Exhibs See Boom in Multiplexing As Good Omen," *Daily Variety*, 10 November 1983, 23.

145. "Marketing and Distribution," 18 May 1983.

146. Joseph F. Robertson, *Motion Picture Distribution Handbook* (Blue Ridge Summit, Pa.: Tab Books, 1981), 72.

147. Walter E. Hurst and William Storm Hale, *Motion Picture Distribution (Business and/or Racquet?!?)* (Los Angeles: Seven Arts Press, 1977), 2.

148. A.D. Murphy, "Film Rentals Move Westward Pic Industry Prominently Affected by Shift toward Coast; L.A. Top Exchange," *Daily Variety*, 8 August 1984, 1, 15.

149. Mayer, "The Exhibition License," 340.

150. Nat D. Fellman and Stanley H. Durwood, "The Exhibitors: Show and Teller Time," in *The Movie Business*, 217.

151. Harlan Jacobson, "Exhibition," *Film Comment*, January-February 1980, 39, 42.

152. Tad Danz, "Motion Pictures from Acquisition to Exhibition," 19 February 1983.

153. Richter, A, C.

154. Pirie, 94.

155. Howard Wilansky, "Marketing and Distribution," 18 May 1983.

156. Fellman, "The Exhibitor," 320.

157. Ed Colarik, "Marketing and Distribution," 25 May 1983.

158. Swerdlow and Jaffe, 258–69.

159. Fellman, "The Exhibitor," 320.

160. Ibid.

161. Andrew Rigrod, "Marketing and Distribution," 15 June 1983.

162. Fellman, "The Exhibitor," 318.

163. Robert Cort, "Advertising and Marketing of Theatrical Motion Pictures in the 1980s," in *The Fifth Annual UCLA Entertainment Symposium*, 140.

164. Howard Wilansky, "Marketing and Distribution," 18 May 1983.

165. Deborah Caulfield, " 'PSST, Buddy... Wanna See a Pre-Release Script?' " *Los Angeles Times*, 21 March 1983, part 6, 1.

166. " 'Five O'Clock Looks' Charged in Quad Cinema Anti-Trust Suit," *Daily Variety*, 28 February 1984, 1.

167. Fellman and Durwood, 219.

168. Mayer, "The Exhibition Contract," 212.

169. Beaupre, "How to Distribute a Film," 46.

170. Tromberg, 157.

171. Mayer, "The Exhibition Contract," 211–13.

172. Mayer, "The Exhibition License," 342.

173. Daly, 95.

174. Ibid., 119–21.

175. Silverman, "Fox Chairman Hirschfield," 10.

176. Swerdlow and Jaffe, 244–45.

177. Will Tusher, "NITE Prez Hutte Urges Strict Enforcement of Distrib Consent Decrees," *Daily Variety*, 13 December 1983, 1, 19.

178. "Japan Theatres Mull Ways to Recapture Their Auds," *Variety*, 4 May 1983, 335.

179. Will Tusher, "Paramount Allocates 300G to Back Up Its Call for Better Film Presentation," *Daily Variety,* 29 February 1984, 1.

180. Ibid., 17.

181. Bosley Crowther, *The Lion's Share* (New York: E.P. Dutton and Company, 1957), 27.

182. Marc Mancini, "Pictures at an Exposition," *Film Comment,* January-February 1983, 46.

183. David Linck, "A Real Exhibitor's Dream," *Boxoffice,* March 1983, 22.

184. Michael I. Rudell, *Behind the Scenes: Practical Entertainment Law* (New York: Law and Business/Harcourt Brace Jovanovich, 1984), 238.

185. *Motion-Picture Distribution Trade Practices—1956,* 12.

186. Richter, C.

187. Rodney Luther, "Television and the Future of Motion Picture Exhibition," *Hollywood Quarterly,* 1950–1951, 167.

Chapter 7

1. Knight, *The Liveliest Art* (1957), 28.

2. Hampton, 351–52.

3. Ramsaye, "The Rise and Place," 7–8.

4. Thomas H. Guback, *The International Film Industry* (Bloomington: Indiana University Press, 1969), 20.

5. Hampton, 357.

6. Temporary National Economic Committee, 5.

7. Hampton, 150.

8. Thomas Guback, "Hollywood's International Market," in *The American Film Industry,* 388.

9. Sklar, 216.

10. Ibid., 357–61.

11. Guback, "Hollywood's International Market," 394.

12. Ibid., 395.

13. Ibid., 397–403.

14. Guback, *The International Film Industry,* 73.

15. Guback, "Hollywood's International Market," 402.

16. Guback, *The International Film Industry,* 75.

17. Guback, "Hollywood's International Market," 400–403.

18. "'83 World Feature Rentals Reach New High," *Boxoffice,* October 1984, 28.

19. Sid Adilman, "Fox, Lamy to Argue Distrib'n Case," *Daily Variety,* 4 March 1983, 36.

20. Myers, "Foreign Distribution," 183.

21. "'83 World Feature Rentals," 28.

22. "The Financing and Distribution of Feature Motion Pictures," (New York: American Bar Association Forum Committee on the Entertainment and Sports Industries, Motion Picture Division Symposium, 18 March 1983).

23. Myers, "Foreign Distribution," 171.

24. Jim Robbins, "Offshore Ancillary Markets Boosting Indie Prospects," *Daily Variety*, 11 June 1984, 70.

25. Lees and Berkowitz, 126.

26. Hollinger, "1984 Edition," 1.

27. "Independent Film," 9 April 1983.

28. Joy Pereths, "High Profits from Low Budgets," 15 October 1983.

29. "The Financing and Distribution of Feature Motion Pictures," 18 March 1983.

30. Will Tusher, "Valenti Denies Euro Strategy for Monopoly," *Daily Variety*, 12 December 1983, 1, 16.

31. "60 Years of Revolution and Evolution in Film Biz," *Daily Variety*, 31 October 1978, 18.

32. Ibid., 26.

33. Sylvie Schneble and Tristine Rainer, "Financing and Foreign Distribution," in *The Movie Business Book*, 125.

34. Hy Hollinger, "Int'l Film Sales Reps Helped Make U.S. Pix Big Force Worldwide," *Daily Variety*, 26 October 1983, 6.

35. Schneble and Rainer, 125.

36. "Hard Dollar Puts Squeeze on Distribs' O'seas Coin," *Daily Variety*, 31 March 1983, 3.

37. Roger Watkins, "Five Staffers Are Due to Come on Board in Wake of High-Flying Releases," *Daily Variety*, 23 August 1983, 1, 18–19.

38. Joe Megel, "Foreign Presales: Can You Afford Them?" *American Premiere*, November 1982, 39.

39. Myers, "Foreign Distribution," 153.

40. Ibid., 157.

41. Michael F. Mayer, *The Film Industries* (New York: Hastings House, 1978), 77.

42. Myers, "Foreign Distribution," 170–71.

43. Mayer, *The Film Industries*, 76.

44. Hy Hollinger, "Foreign Marts Lure New Breed of Indie Sales Representatives," *Daily Variety*, 13 July 1981, 7, 99.

45. "Motion Pictures From Acquisition To Exhibition," 19 February 1983.

46. "Independent Film," 9 April 1983.

47. Ibid.

48. "Independent Companies Busy," 78.

49. Megel, 38.

50. "Independent Film," 9 April 1983.

51. Myers, "Foreign Distribution," 169.

52. Ellen Farley and William K. Knoedelseder, Jr., "A Tangled Web Clogs 'Chain Saw,'" *Los Angeles Times,* 12 September 1982, part 6, 4.

53. Mayer, *The Film Industries,* 77.

54. Myers, "Foreign Distribution," 164.

55. Mayer, *The Film Industries,* 72.

56. "Independent Film," 9 April 1983.

57. Howard Goldfarb, "Marketing and Distribution," 27 April 1983.

58. Myers, "Foreign Distribution," 172.

59. Adam Moss, "The Exhibition Game Ron Lesser on Owning the Theater near You," *Esquire,* July 1982, 98–99.

60. Aljean Harmetz, "Burden of Dreams George Lucas," *American Film,* June 1983, 36.

61. Caulfield, "Studio Head Warns," 1, 6.

62. "Valenti Urges Exhibs to Join Copyright Struggle," *Daily Variety,* 23 February 1984, 6.

63. "Digital Sound," *Los Angeles Times,* 30 May 1984, part 6, 6.

64. Harmetz, *Rolling Breaks,* 176.

65. Lawrence Cohn, "Buena Vista Finds the Film Rerelease Route to Be Paved with Gold," *Daily Variety,* 11 April 1984, 1, 11.

66. Ken Terry, "Bets Are Down on Future of Vid Jukebox," *Daily Variety,* 23 May 1984, 1, 11, 13.

67. "Now Playing: Sipping Cinemas," *Time,* 27 April 1981, 55.

68. Martin Marcus, "Marketing and Distribution," 1 June 1983.

69. Rod Granger, "Closeup," *Hollywood Reporter,* 6 August 1984, 2.

70. Handel, 155.

71. Samuel Goldwyn, "Hollywood in the Television Age," *Hollywood Quarterly,* 4 (1949–1950): 146.

72. Les Brown and Savannah Waring Walker, eds., *Fast Forward: The New Television and American Society* (Kansas City: Andrews and McKeel, 1983), 4–5.

73. Morry Roth, "NAB Survey Finds Negative Attitudes toward TV," *Daily Variety,* 12 April 1983, 1.

74. *1982 Nielsen Report on . . . Television* (Northbrook, Ill.: A.C. Nielsen Company, 1982), 8, 11.

75. "The Sale, Marketing and Distribution," 26 February 1983.

76. David Gritten, "The Controversial TVQ Ratings System," *Los Angeles Herald Examiner,* 5 January 1984, B1, B6.

77. Kathryn Harris, "Battle Looms for 1st Run of Films on TV," *Los Angeles Times*, 4 October 1983, part 4, 1.

78. Ralph Lee Smith, "Birth of a Wired Nation," in *Fast Forward*, 7–8.

79. *"United States v. Columbia Pictures Industries et al.,"* 358.

80. Bernstein, 7.

81. Paul Kagan, "A Primer on Pay TV," *Motion Picture Investor*, 30 April 1984, 1.

82. Peter Caranicas, "How Pay TV Got the Upper Hand," *Channels*, July-August 1983, 44.

83. Kathryn Harris, "HBO Takes Best Seat in the House while Rivals Still Wait in Line," *Los Angeles Times*, 5 June 1983, part 5, 3.

84. Lees and Berkowitz, 179.

85. Harris, "HBO Takes Best Seat," 3.

86. Kagan, 2–3.

87. Harris, "HBO Takes Best Seat," 3, 14.

88. Kagan, 2–3.

89. Tom Girard, "HBO and Showtime-TMC Become Partners Overseas in Premiere Cable Service," *Daily Variety*, 16 March 1984, 1, 47.

90. Will Tusher, "TAC Prez Bob Selig Terms HBO Threat to Theatrical Exhibition," *Daily Variety*, 1 September 1983, 2.

91. Peter Caranicas, "Hollywood Wakes Up and Smells the Coffee," *Channels*, July-August 1983, 44.

92. Tom Girard, "HBO Steps Up Weekly Series Emphasis," *Daily Variety*, 12 April 1984, 16.

93. David Crook, "Home Box Office Ratings Decrease 9% in One Year," *Los Angeles Times*, 6 March 1984, part 6, 1, 9.

94. Harris, "HBO Takes Best Seat," 1.

95. Kathryn Harris, "Movie Channel Forms Link with Showtime," *Los Angeles Times*, 7 September 1983, part 4, 2.

96. David Crook, "Merger Challenges HBO Pay-TV Supremacy," *Los Angeles Times*, 16 August 1983, part 6, 7.

97. Kagan, 1.

98. "Arbitron Says 39% of Homes Tied to Cable," *Daily Variety*, 5 March 1984, 12.

99. "Vid Rentals Dilute Cable Owners Pulled in by Prices," *Daily Variety*, 27 July 1983, 16.

100. Rudell, *Behind the Scenes*, 155–56.

101. Michael I. Rudell, "The Financing and Distribution of Feature Motion Pictures: Network Television, Pay Television and Other Forms of Home Video," in *The Financing and Distribution of Feature Motion Pictures*, 230–32.

102. David Crook, "'Tootsie' Sales Enliven Industry Pricing Debate," *Los Angeles Times*, 7 February 1984, part 6, 8.

103. "MTV: The Birth of a Rock Sensation," *Los Angeles Times,* 21 August 1983, part 6, 80–82.

104. Tom Girard, "Slim Pickings So Far for Indies in Pay-TV," *Daily Variety,* 11 June 1984, 46.

105. Harmetz, *Rolling Breaks,* 166.

106. Cook, Isgur, and Londoner, 46.

107. Harris, "HBO Takes Best Seat," 14.

108. Tom Bierbaum, "Homevideo Licensing Fees Can Return 25% of Budget for Pix Costing $8–10 Mil," *Daily Variety,* 11 June 1984, 32.

109. Silverman, "Fox Chairman Hirschfield Takes Aim," 10.

110. Ken Terry, "1990 Homevid Market Put at near $10 Bil," *Daily Variety,* 16 February 1984, 25.

111. Crook, "Schroeder's Pep Talk," 7.

112. Will Tusher, "Addition of Ancillary Market to Theaters Gets No Opposition at ShoWest," *Daily Variety,* 23 February 1984, 8.

113. Ibid., 24.

114. Harmetz, "Of '83 Movie Winners and Losers," D11.

115. Michael London, "Theater Owners Push Cassettes," *Los Angeles Times,* 25 February 1984, part 5, 1–2.

116. Crook, "'Tootsie' Sales," 8.

117. Rudell, "The Financing and Distribution," 230–32.

118. Semel, 50–51.

119. Will Tusher, "Syufy Circuit Deals with Paramount for Pilot Program to Sell Tapes in Theaters," *Daily Variety,* 13 February 1984, 1, 13.

120. "Ritter-Geller Testing Rental of Video-Cassettes in Markets," *Daily Variety,* 9 April 1984, 8.

121. Dale Pollock, "Stealing the Show," *Los Angeles Times,* 8 July 1984, part 6, 14–15, 17, 20–22.

122. *"Universal City Studios, Inc. v. Sony Corporation of America,"* in *The Financing and Distribution of Feature Motion Pictures,* 390.

123. Tusher, "Predicts Dire Consequences," 23.

124. Jim Mann, "Home TV Taping Legal, Court Says," *Los Angeles Times,* 18 January 1984, part 6, 1.

125. Paul Harris, "High Court Rules Homevid Taping Does Not Violate Current Copyright Laws," *Daily Variety,* 18 January 1984, 1.

126. Penny Pagano, "Video Battle Will Now Go to Congress," *Los Angeles Times,* 18 January 1984, part 4, 1.

127. Kathryn Harris and David Crook, "Film, Television Producers Dismayed by Court Ruling," *Los Angeles Times,* 18 January 1984, part 1, 7.

128. Joe Smith, "Pirating," in *The Growth and Financing of Filmed Entertainment,* 31–32.

129. Will Tusher, "Film Security Office Head Raises Financial Red Flag in Address at ShoWest '84," *Daily Variety,* 24 February 1984, 1.

130. Tony Seidemann, "MPAA Wants Its Due from Inmates Sues Wisconsin, Claiming Prisoners Constitute 'Public Audience' for Videocassettes," *Daily Variety,* 22 August 1983, 1.

131. Tony Seidemann, "MPAA Puts the U.S. Air Force on Piracy List," *Daily Variety,* 24 January 1984, 1, 43.

132. Caulfield, "Studio Head Warns," 1, 6–7.

133. Silverman, "Fox Chairman," 10.

134. Will Tusher, "Enforcement Slowdown Seen as One Alternative to Threat of Videocassettes," *Daily Variety,* 7 February 1984, 1, 15.

135. Wilton R. Holm, "Technological Standardization in Motion Pictures," *Journal of Producers Guild of America,* June 1973, 15.

136. Knight, *The Liveliest Art* (1957), 142.

137. Jacobs, *The Emergence of Film Art,* 171–73.

138. Crowther, 32.

139. Knight, *The Liveliest Art* (1957), 188.

140. Balio, ed., 215.

141. Anthony Dawson, "Motion Picture Economics," *Hollywood Quarterly,* Fall 1947, 234.

142. Griffith, 372.

143. Knight, *The Liveliest Art* (1957), 252.

144. Balio, ed., 315.

145. Knight, *The Liveliest Art* (1957), 149.

146. Walter Lowe, "The Screen's Third-Dimensional Roundup," *Theater Arts,* 11 September 1953, 73.

147. James I. Limbacher, *Four Aspects of the Film* (New York: Brussel and Brussel, 1969), 116.

148. Ibid., 91.

149. Martin Quigley, Jr., *New Screen Techniques* (New York: Quigley, 1953), 142.

150. Knight, *The Liveliest Art* (1957), 293.

151. Ibid., 295.

152. "Digital Sound," 6.

153. Will Tusher, "Super 8 Deal Inked; Aimed at Theatres," *Daily Variety,* 25 October 1983, 1.

154. Frank Segers, "'Video Theatre System' Is Primed for Japan Launch; Export Market Planned," *Daily Variety,* 6 September 1983, 1, 11.

155. "Japanese Parking Lots Do Double Duty As Drive-Ins," *Daily Variety,* 19 March 1984, 7.

156. Dennis Wharton, "When Film Hits Your Eye Like a Big Pizza Pie ...," *Daily Variety,* 30 March 1984, 10.

157. Will Tusher, "Comedy Feature Will Test Aud Tastes," *Daily Variety,* 28 December 1983, 2.

158. Robert Russett and Cecile Starr, *Experimental Animation* (New York: Van Nostrand Reinhold, 1976), 201–2.

159. Harmetz, *Rolling Breaks,* 183.

160. Russett and Starr, 134.

161. Carole Spearin McCauley, *Computers and Creativity* (New York: Praeger, 1974), 70.

162. David Prince, *Interactive Graphics for Computer-Aided Design* (Reading: Addison-Wesley Publishing, 1971), 1.

163. Douglas M. Davis, "Art and Technology—The New Combine," *Art in America,* January-February 1968, 38.

164. Ralph Stephenson, *The Animated Film* (New York: A.S. Barnes and Company, 1973), 184.

165. Jasia Reichardt, *Cybernetics, Art and Ideas* (New York: Graphic Society Limited, 1971), 145.

166. Ibid., 11.

167. Charles M. Firestone, ed., *International Satellite Television: Resource Manual for the Third Biennial Communications Law Symposium* (Los Angeles: The Regents of the University of California, 1983), 213.

Chapter 8

1. Kenneth Ziffren, "The Structure and Negotiation of Distribution Agreements," in *The Fifth Annual UCLA Entertainment Symposium,* 186.

2. Ibid., 209.

3. "Women in Film Presents Hard Times: A Game Plan for a Changing Industry," 9 October 1982.

4. A.D. Murphy, "Distribs' B.O. Share below 40% Talent Generation Shift, Screen Expansion, Price War Contributing Factors," *Daily Variety,* 21 August 1984, 1.

5. A.D. Murphy, "21 Fundamental Aspects of U.S. Theatrical Film Biz," *Daily Variety,* 26 October 1982, 29.

6. Murphy, "Distribs' B.O. Share," 1.

7. Ibid., 15.

8. The Fifth Annual UCLA Entertainment Symposium," 5–6 December 1980.

9. Ed Colarik and William Madden, "Marketing and Distribution," 6 April 1983.

10. Murphy, "Distribs' B.O. Share," 15.

11. Byron Shapiro, "Marketing and Distribution," 11 May 1983.

12. Beaupre, "How to Distribute a Film," 50.

13. Kagan, 1.

14. Pollock, "From Depths to Heights," 28.

15. Steven Ginsberg, "'Jedi' Sets B.O. Records with Its Huge $6.2 Mil Bow," *Daily Variety*, 27 May 1983, 1.

16. "'Return of Jedi' Carves a Niche for Itself in the Ranks of All-Time Grossers," *Daily Variety*, 20 July 1983, 1.

17. Tromberg, 173.

18. Ball, 36.

19. Ziffren, 206.

20. "Future Shock," 4 April 1983.

21. Tromberg, 142.

22. "Exhibit C," in *The Financing and Distribution of Feature Motion Pictures*, 207-9.

23. Mike Medavoy, "Future Shock," 4 April 1983.

24. Benjamin W. Solomon, "Distribution: The Accountant's Role," in *The Movie Business*, 206.

25. Ibid.

26. Ibid.

27. Andrew Rigrod, "Marketing and Distribution," 15 June 1983.

28. Tromberg, 136.

29. Paul A. Baumgarten and Donald C. Farber, *Producing, Financing and Distributing Film* (New York: Drama Book Specialists, 1973), 141.

30. "Future Shock," 16 May 1983.

31. "Motion Picture Investments Seminar," 24 May 1984.

32. Leedy, *An Accountant's Perspective*, 23-24.

33. Michael Silverman, "Zupnik-Curtis Puts Its Money Where Its Enthusiasm Is for 1st Pic, 'Dreamscape'," *Daily Variety*, 11 June 1984, 56.

34. James Monaco, *American Film Now* (New York: New American Library, 1979), 40.

35. Ed Colarik, "Marketing and Distribution," 25 May 1983.

36. Gregory, 187.

37. Ziffren, 190–206.

38. Solomon, 207.

39. Silverman, "Zupnik-Curtis," 56.

40. "Marketing and Distribution," 25 May 1983.

41. Barbara D. Boyle, "Independent Distribution: New World Pictures," in *The Movie Business Book*, 289.

42. Ziffren, 194–95.

43. Ibid., 193.

44. Myers, "Foreign Distribution," 163.

45. Andrew Rigrod, "Marketing and Distribution," 15 June 1983.

46. Boyle, 289.

47. Ziffren, 198.

48. Alex Ben Block, "Survey Shows Movie Industry Has Bad Bookkeeping Image," *Los Angeles Herald Examiner,* 4 August 1983, A12.

49. "Silver Screen Partners Prospectus," 13.

50. *Statement of Financial Accounting Standards, No. 53, Financial Reporting by Producers and Distributors of Motion Picture Films* (Stamford: Financial Accounting Standards Board, 1981).

51. Block, "Survey Shows," A12.

52. Committee on the Entertainment Industries of the American Institute of Certified Public Accountants, *Accounting for Motion Picture Films* (New York: American Institute of Certified Public Accountants, 1973), 4.

53. Solomon, 205–9.

54. Tromberg, 156.

55. Solomon, 206.

56. "NATO Survey Says Most States Levying Taxes on Film-Going," *Daily Variety,* 14 November 1983, 1, 18.

Chapter 9

1. McClintick, 476.

2. "Future Shock," 4 April 1983.

3. Lee Beaupre, "Industry," *Film Comment,* July-August 1978, 68.

4. James Greenberg, "Tri-Star Blows Its Own Horn as 'Instant Major'," *Daily Variety,* 3 November 1983, 1, 3.

5. Dale Pollock, "Tri-Star Plans to Sell 25% of Stock to Public," *Los Angeles Times,* 4 October 1984, part 4, 1–2.

6. Kathryn Harris, "Biondi Leaves as HBO Chief over Dispute," *Los Angeles Times,* 13 October 1984, part 4, 1–2.

7. Pollock, "Tri-Star Plans," 1–2.

8. Gregg Kilday, "Ladd Stumbles in Quest for Prestige Movies," *Los Angeles Herald Examiner,* 22 April 1984, E-9.

9. Michael Pye and Lynda Myles, *The Movie Brats* (New York: Holt, Rinehart and Winston, 1979), 39.

10. Dave Kaufman, "Main Thrust of Studio Is in Bread-and-Butter Weekly Series, Says Frank," *Daily Variety,* 17 October 1983, 1, 10.

11. Sandra Salmans, "Movie Making Is an Uncertain Art," *Los Angeles Herald Examiner,* 29 May 1983, B4–8.

12. Sandra Salmans, "The Value of Old Films to Movie Studios," *Los Angeles Herald Examiner,* 8 April 1984, B5.

13. Peter J. Boyer and Dale Pollock, "MGM-UA and the Big Debt," *Los Angeles Times,* 28 March 1982, part 6, 1, 3–7.

14. Jack Searles, "Fifth Distribution Boss Is Studio Chief," *Los Angeles Herald Examiner,* 8 February 1983, C1, C4.

15. Pye and Myles, 53.

16. Dale Pollock, "That Smoke-Filled Room Leads to Clean Deals," *Los Angeles Times,* 26 May 1984, part 5, 1, 7.

17. Lawrence Cohn, "Major Distributors Line Up Lots of Big-Budget Features for 1984," *Daily Variety,* 16 January 1984, 8.

18. "'Story' Hits Roadblock on Way to Rebate," *Daily Variety,* 13 December 1983, 1, 18.

19. David Pauly, Peter McAlevey, and Marilyn Achiron, "Hollywood's Penny Pinchers," *Newsweek,* 9 April 1984, 83.

20. Alex Ben Block, "In Hollywood, Success Doesn't Always Equal Job Security," *Los Angeles Herald Examiner,* 1 May 1983, B6, B8, B10.

21. Aljean Harmetz, "Paramount's Gamble on Low-Budget Films Pays Off," *The Register* (California), 24 May 1983, D9.

22. Dale Pollock, "Behind Two Financial Eight Balls," *Los Angeles Times,* 28 March 1984, part 6, 4.

23. Ned Tannen, "Hard Times: A Game Plan for a Changing Industry" (Los Angeles: Women in Film Seminar, 9 October 1982).

24. Daly, 89–97.

25. Lee Beaupre, "Staying Alive with Word-of-Mouth," *Film Comment,* March-April 1984, 64.

26. Goodell, 233.

27. Caulfield, "Studio Head Warns," 1, 6–7.

28. Kagan, 3.

29. "Motion Picture Investments Seminar," 24 May 1984.

Chapter 10

1. Monaco, 203.

2. Knight, *The Liveliest Art* (1957), 28.

3. Ibid., 265.

4. Ibid., 259.

5. Dwight Macdonald, *Dwight Macdonald on Movies* (Englewood Cliffs, N.J.: Prentice-Hall, 1969), 312.

6. Knight, *The Liveliest Art* (1957), 267.

7. Ibid., 263.

8. Jonas Mekas, "Independence for Independents," *American Film,* September 1978, 39.

9. Amos Vogel, "Independent Film," *Film Comment,* May-June 1974, 37.

10. Walter Reade, Jr., "The Distributors: A Sound of Different Drummers," in *The Movie Business,* 193–96.

11. Moreno and Almond, 78.

12. Ibid.

13. Caulfield, "Studios and Art Films," 16–17.

14. Alicia Springer, "Sell It Again, Sam!" *American Film,* March 1983, 52.

15. Aljean Harmetz, "Financial Security Aids Sayles in Making Films," *New York Times,* 25 October 1983, Arts/Entertainment Section, 25.

16. Caulfield, "Studios and Art Films," 18.

17. Stephen Klain, "Orion Pictures Establishing Classics Arm," *Daily Variety,* 1 April 1983, 1, 22.

18. "'Country' Continues Orion Classics' Art-House Success," *Screen International,* 6–13 October 1984, 6.

19. B.J. Franklin, "Orion Classics Trio Aims towards Production," *Screen International,* 27 August-3 September 1983, 28, 34.

20. "Motion Picture Investments Seminar," 24 May 1984.

21. Caulfield, "Studios and Art Films," 16–18.

22. Springer, 55.

23. Rena Kleiman, "Classics Division and the Indie," *Hollywood Reporter,* 13 August 1982, S42–S46.

24. Caulfield, "Studios and Art Films," 17.

25. B.J. Franklin, "The Two 'Real' Classics Divisions," *Screen International,* 27 August-3 September 1983, 26.

26. James Greenberg, "James C. Katz Out as Prod'n Veepee for U," *Daily Variety,* 25 January 1984, 1, 6.

27. Caulfield, "Studios and Art Films," 16.

28. James Greenberg, "'Mr. Lawrence' Moves from U Classics," *Daily Variety,* 30 August 1983, 5.

29. Caulfield, "Studios and Art Films," 18.

30. Ibid., 16.

31. Franklin, "The Two 'Real' Classics," 26.

32. Jeff Trachtenberg, "Profits Spur Film Studios into Rereleasing Movies," *Los Angeles Herald Examiner,* 18 August 1983, C1.

33. Caulfield, "Studios and Art Films," 17.

34. Harlan Jacobson, "How the Classics Kids Snatched Foreign Film," *The Village Voice*, 29 November 1983, 74–76, 83.

35. Ibid.

36. Springer, 55.

37. Charles Teitel, "Art House Pic Booking Frustrations," *Daily Variety*, 13 June 1983, 16.

38. *The New American Cinema Conference* (Los Angeles: The Independent Feature Project, 4 April 1981), 84.

39. Caulfield, "Studios and Art Films," 17.

40. Jacobson, "The Classics Kids," 76.

41. Michael Berg, "Second-Hand Shows," *American Film*, June 1983, 46.

42. Michael Silverman, "'Little Guys' of Exhibition See Bad Times," *Daily Variety*, 4 November 1983, 1, 26.

43. Musun, 115–17.

44. Charles Teitel, "Who Said Distribution Is a Man's World?" *Daily Variety*, 11 June 1984, 86.

45. Lamont, 73.

46. Julia Reichert, *Doing It Yourself a Handbook on Independent Film Distribution* (New York: Association of Independent Video and Filmmakers, 1977), 5.

47. Trojan and Covert, 58.

48. Ibid., 16.

49. Ibid., 58–59.

50. Ibid., 97–99.

51. Amos Vogel, "Structures," *Film Comment*, January-February 1975, 6.

52. Amos Vogel, "The Vital Statistics of Media Centers," *Film Comment*, July-August 1979, 78–79.

53. Clarke Taylor, "New York's Film Forum for Independents," *Los Angeles Times*, 3 April 1983, part 6, 18.

54. Linda Gross, "Cannon Heads for Exit at Film Forum," *Los Angeles Times*, 16 January 1984, part 6, 5–6.

55. Jonas Mekas, "Free Cinema and the New Wave," *Film Culture*, Summer 1960, 408.

56. Vogel, "Independent Film," 37.

57. Charles Silver, "For a Fair Distribution of Film Wealth," *Film Comment*, Fall 1970, 4.

58. Stuart Samuels, *Midnight Movies* (New York: Macmillan Publishing Company, 1983), 7–12, 222.

59. Ibid., 24, 28.

60. Ibid., 58–61.

61. Ibid., 83–84.

62. Ibid., 92, 101, 104.

63. Ibid., 106.

64. Ibid., 11, 133–37.

65. Ibid., 153, 157, 181.

66. Ibid., 204–5, 218.

67. Jim Robbins, "Gotham Film Theatres Cater to Diverse Ethnic Populations," *Daily Variety,* 19 May 1983, 14.

68. Richard Corliss, "I'm Always in Money Trouble," *Time,* 23 February 1981, 82.

69. Todd Gitlin, "The Lyric Odyssey of Alain Tanner," *Harper's,* February 1984, 68.

70. Seldes, 42.

71. Will Tusher, "NATO Prez Resnick Unveils Details of Program for Limited-Market Theaters," *Daily Variety,* 20 March 1984, 1, 31.

72. Will Tusher, "Twinning Held Up as Boon to Limited-Market Houses," *Daily Variety,* 24 October 1984, 4.

73. Lipton, 231.

74. Springer, 50–51.

75. Robert Laemmle, "The Independent Exhibitor," in *The Movie Business Book,* 334–36.

76. Byron Shapiro, "Marketing and Distribution," 11 May 1983.

77. Bill Steigerwald and Kerry Platman, "The Winds of Change Hit the Revivals," *Los Angeles Times,* 27 February 1983, part 6, 5–7.

78. Audie Bock, "Local Heroes," *American Film,* April 1984, 38–39.

79. Ibid., 40.

80. Robert Cross, "Is Seattle the Filmgoing Capitol of the U.S?" *The Register* (California), 17 March 1983, D9.

81. Jim Robbins, "Robert Laemmle Pines for 'Self-Contained' Classics Divisions," *Daily Variety,* 26 July 1983, 4.

82. Caulfield, "Studios and Art Films," 17.

83. Steigerwald and Platman, 7.

84. Ibid., 5–6.

85. David Ehrenstein, "End of an Era for Revival Theaters?" *Los Angeles Herald Examiner,* 9 September 1983, D4–5, D10.

86. Mitch Tuchman, "Declaration of Independence," *Film Comment,* May-June 1980, 22.

Chapter 11

1. Moreno and Almond, 69–70.

2. Lee Beaupre, "Do-It-Yourself Distribution," *Film Comment,* July-August 1977, 48.

3. Sandy Climan, "Independent Filmmakers: Are We Merely Rearranging Deck Chairs on the Titanic?" *Hollywood Reporter,* 6 March 1984, S20.

4. Doug McClelland, *The Golden Age of "B" Movies* (Nashville: Charter House, 1978), 6, 14.

5. Moreno and Almond, 76.

6. Ed Colarik, "Marketing and Distribution," 25 May 1983.

7. Will Tusher, "Playdates: Perennial Problem," *Daily Variety*, 19 June 1980, 13, 96.

8. Michael F. Mayer, "The Journal Looks at Film Distribution Abroad," *The Journal of the Producers Guild of America*, March 1975, 4.

9. David Baughn, "Distributing Independent Feature Films," *Filmmakers Monthly*, September 1979, 19.

10. Moreno and Almond, 75.

11. Ibid., 79.

12. "Arista Found Prod'n Essential," *Daily Variety*, 11 June 1984, 78.

13. Moreno and Almond, 73.

14. Girard, "Slim Pickings," 46, 48.

15. Moreno and Almond, 77–78.

16. Ed Colarik, "Marketing and Distribution," 25 May 1983.

17. Gerry Putzer, "IFP Interview," *IFP West Newsletter*, October 1984, 2.

18. Alexander Auerbach, "He Built a Film Company on a Movie Scrap Heap," *Daily Variety*, 25 October 1982, 182.

19. Roger Ebert, "Cannes Game: Blind Dealer Shuffles Films," *Daily Variety*, 22 June 1984, 9.

20. Pirie, 90–91.

21. "History of American International Pictures—Twenty-Fifth Anniversary" (Los Angeles: American International Pictures, 1979), 1–6.

22. Ibid.

23. Pirie, 90–91.

24. Harmetz, *Rolling Breaks*, 129–30.

25. Pye and Myles, 35.

26. Kirk Honeycutt, "Time Aids AIP's 'Quickie' Films," *Valley News* (California), 29 July 1979, 1.

27. "History of American International Pictures," 1–6.

28. Honeycutt, 1.

29. Pye and Myles, 33.

30. John Cocchi, "AIP, Celebrating 25 Years, Looking Ahead to Quality Summer Releases," *Boxoffice*, 9 April 1979, 5.

31. Harmetz, *Rolling Breaks*, 134.

32. Ibid., 124, 131.

33. Pirie, 92.

34. Harmetz, *Rolling Breaks,* 124–26.

35. James H. Nicholson, "AIP Formula," *Daily Variety,* 27 October 1970, 50.

36. Judith McNally, "Lucrative Trash—The Dime-Store Movies," *Filmmakers Newsletter,* October 1974, 61.

37. Bridget Byrne, "Keeping an Eye on Business," *Los Angeles Herald Examiner,* 19 August 1974, B6.

38. Harmetz, *Rolling Breaks,* 123.

39. McNally, 63.

40. Pye and Myles, 36.

41. Arkoff, "Transcript of Publicists Guild Speech," 4.

42. "Samuel Z. Arkoff Biography" (Beverly Hills: American International Pictures, 30 March 1979), 2.

43. Honeycutt, 1–2.

44. Lee Grant, "Sho-West: Differing Outlooks for Films," *Los Angeles Times,* 11 February 1981, part 6, 1.

45. "History of American International Pictures," 7.

46. Pirie, 90–91.

47. Byrne, B6.

48. "History of American International Pictures," 8.

49. Harmetz, *Rolling Breaks,* 133.

50. Honeycutt, 5.

51. Harmetz, *Rolling Breaks,* 139.

52. Lee Beaupre, "Industry," *Film Comment,* March-April 1980, 71.

53. Harmetz, *Rolling Breaks,* 139.

54. Dale Pollock, "A New Team Gives a New Look to Embassy Communications," *Los Angeles Times,* 20 January 1982, part 6, 1, 4.

55. Richard Albarino, "Avemb out of Pic Financing, To Be Merchandiser: Chaikin," *Daily Variety,* 27 September 1974, 1, 3.

56. Ibid.

57. "Avco Embassy Unveils Its 1976 Releases, Policies," *Boxoffice,* 6 October 1975, 5.

58. Dan Yakir, "Industry Bob Rehme: New Power in Hollywood," *Film Comment,* July-August 1981, 74–76.

59. Martin Kent, "Avco Looks beyond Low-Budget Movies; Will Broaden Its Scope," *Hollywood Reporter,* 26 January 1981, 1.

60. Ibid.

61. Stephen Ginsberg, "Independent Feature Film Starts Are Down but the Future Is Still up for Grabs," *Daily Variety,* 7 June 1982, 8.

62. Todd McCarthy, "As Avco Develops New Policy Bigger Opportunities Appear Open to Other Independents," *Daily Variety,* 7 June 1982, 8, 50.

63. Yakir, 76.

64. "Perenchio, Lear Form Embassy; Horn Chairman," *Hollywood Reporter,* 21 January 1982, 4.

65. McCarthy, "As Avco Develops," 8.

66. Chute, "The New World of Roger Corman," 27.

67. Boyle, 285–86.

68. Deborah Caulfield, "What's New Is Old at the New New World," *Los Angeles Times,* 19 February 1984, part 6, 4.

69. Boyle, 286.

70. Chute, 27.

71. Boyle, 288.

72. Daly, 140–61.

73. Boyle, 287.

74. Chute, 29.

75. Boyle, 288.

76. Ibid., 289–90.

77. Ibid., 291.

78. Roger Corman, "Hard Times: A Game Plan for a Changing Industry Seminar" (Los Angeles: Women in Film, 9 October 1982).

79. Lee Reynolds, "Corman Probes Distribution; Ware Reacts to Indie Setbacks," *Hollywood Reporter,* 30 April 1973, 12.

80. Boyle, 291.

81. Roger Corman, "Hard Times," 9 October 1982.

82. Chute, 30.

83. Richard Klein, "Roger Corman: Emotional Ties Are with Production," *Daily Variety,* 13 June 1983, 80.

84. "The Mini-Mogul," *Forbes,* 28 February 1983, 12.

85. Jack Searles, "Corman Wins Big with Studio Sale, but Coppola on Verge of Losing It," *Los Angeles Herald Examiner,* 15 January 1983, B5.

86. Caulfield, "What's New," 5.

87. "New World Hopes Bigger Budgets Will Bring Bigger Pay-Offs," *Daily Variety,* 13 June 1983, 83.

88. Klein, "New World Targets," 69.

89. "New World Alters Course, Will Sign First DGA Contract," *Daily Variety,* 25 April 1983, 1.

90. Richard Klein, "New World Positioned to Go Public in Future," *Daily Variety*, 29 June 1984, 27.

91. Ellen Farley, "New World Pictures Gets Financing Deal," *Los Angeles Times*, 14 June 1984, part 4, 1, 5.

92. William Shields, "Women in Film," 18 April 1983.

93. Richard Klein, "Crown OK's Two More Youth Pix for '84 Prod'n," *Daily Variety*, 21 February 1984, 1, 22.

94. "Crown Celebrates 25th Anniversary, Introduces Two New Films at the Market," *Screen International*, 10–17 March 1984, 142.

95. Mark Tenser, "The Sale, Marketing and Distribution," 26 February 1983.

96. "Crown Expanding Horizons," *Daily Variety*, 19 June 1980, 6.

97. Bierbaum, 32.

98. "Tenser Boosts Crown's Prod'n Level, Stepping into Television," *Hollywood Reporter*, 9 August 1983, 8.

99. "Boost in Cash Flow Cues Crown Production Plans," *Daily Variety*, 13 June 1983, 58.

100. Richard Klein, "Crown Going Wide 1st Time with 'Tomboy'," *Daily Variety*, 11 June 1984, 92.

101. Ibid., 17, 92.

102. Ibid.

103. Mark Tenser, "The Sale, Marketing, and Distribution," 26 February 1983.

104. Klein, "Crown Going Wide," 92.

105. "Montoro at Mifed for Artists Releasing Corp.," *Screen International*, 29 October–5 November 1983, 236.

106. Richard Klein, "ARC Rolls First Pic via $16.6 Mil Production Pool," *Daily Variety*, 8 August 1983, 1, 14.

107. Ed Montoro, "The Sale, Marketing and Distribution," 26 February 1983.

108. "Indies Summer Looks Brighter," *Daily Variety*, 19 June 1980, 24.

109. "Film Ventures Lands 'Light,' 'Prey' Distrib'n," *Daily Variety*, 9 May 1984, 1, 16.

110. "Film Ventures' New Banner off to Good Beginning," *Daily Variety*, 13 June 1983, 66.

111. Lees and Berkowitz, 119–20.

112. "American Cinema Moves Up," *Daily Variety*, 13 July 1981, 101.

113. "American Cinema Values '81–82 Prod'n Program at $40 Mil," *Daily Variety*, 23 March 1981, 8.

114. Simonet, "Market Research," 68.

115. "Indies Summer," 24.

116. "Biggest Indie of All," *Daily Variety*, 7 June 1982, 10.

117. Todd McCarthy, "More Misses Than Hits Making Life Tougher for Independents," *Daily Variety*, 7 June 1982, 56.

118. Martin A. Grove, "Some 'Public' Lessons for Hollywood," *Los Angeles Times Herald Examiner*, 28 September 1981, A10.

119. Goodell, xxii–xxiii.

120. "Jensen Farley Decides to Keep Offshore Sales at Home under Swindler," *Variety*, 2 March 1983, 89, 142.

121. "Jensen-Farley Is Negotiating Reorganization," *Daily Variety*, 27 October 1983, 1, 17.

122. "Motion Picture Marketing Takes Plunge into Production," *Daily Variety*, 12 April 1983, 4.

123. "Breathing New Life into Old Features Is Motion Picture Marketing Forte," *Daily Variety*, 7 June 1982, 56.

124. "Indies Summer," 24.

125. "M.P. Marketing Hits Its Four-Year Mark," *Daily Variety*, 13 June 1983, 98.

126. McCarthy, "Distribs Miss a Chance," 84.

127. "Breathing New Life," 56.

128. McCarthy, "As Avco Develops," 50.

129. Goodell, xviii.

130. "Mastorakis Plans 'Rockaine' to Follow the Success of 'Blind Date'," *Screen International*, 10–17 March 1984, 80.

131. "The Evil Dead," Advertisement, *Variety*, 4 May 1983, 78.

132. "New Line Seeking Commercial Films to Aid Production," *Variety*, 4 May 1983, 16.

133. Jim Robbins, "New Line Using AFMarket to Push 3 New Projects," *Variety*, 2 March 1983, 258.

134. Ellen Farley and William K. Knoedelseder, Jr., "The Real Texas Chain Saw Massacre," *Los Angeles Times Calendar*, 5 September 1982, 1, 3–7.

135. William Wolf, *Landmark Films* (London: Paddington Press, 1979), 365.

136. Farley and Knoedelseder, Jr., "A Tangled Web," 3–5.

137. McCarthy, "Distribs Miss," 82.

138. Farley and Knoedelseder, Jr., "The Real Texas," 3.

139. Pirie, 93.

140. "The Making of a Modern-Day Movie Mogul," *Business Week*, 16 May 1977, 117.

141. Tusher, "Playdates," 96.

142. Pirie, 93.

143. "The Kids at Cannon," *Time*, 31 August 1970, 60.

144. Dennis Friedland, "The Distributors: A Sound of Different Drummers," in *The Movie Business*, 196–99.

145. Addison Verrill, "'Joe' Bonanza Over, Cannon Exex Tap Own Wallet to Help Finance Films," *Daily Variety*, 16 February 1972, 6.

146. Addison Verrill, "Cannon Films Run by Under-30s, Never Had a Loser; Shuns Trade's Obsolete Ways; Mulls Going Public," *Variety*, 25 February 1970, 4.

147. Verrill, "'Joe'," 6.

148. William Wolf, "The Sunshine Boys," *New York*, 12 September 1983, 89.

149. Terry Ilott, "Five Years on, Golan and Globus Make Cannon a Major Force," *Screen International*, 10–17 March 1984, 61–62.

150. Barry Rehfeld, "Cannon Fathers," *Film Comment*, November-December 1983, 21–24.

151. "Golan-Globus Operate Like a 1940s Movie Company," *Daily Variety*, 11 June 1984, 72.

152. Rehfeld, 23.

153. Gregg Kilday, "Yoo-hoo, Menachem, It's Hollywood Calling," *Los Angeles Herald Examiner*, 21 January 1983, D4.

154. "Golan, Globus Success Keeps Company Busy," *Daily Variety*, 26 October 1982, 120.

155. Hy Hollinger, "Cannon's Golan, Globus in Fast Lane," *Daily Variety*, 27 October 1983, 4.

156. "Cannon Piggy-Back," 20.

157. "Golan, Globus Trek to Film Market with 19 Pix in Tow," *Daily Variety*, 9 March 1984, 32.

158. David Friendly, "Hollywood's Rug Merchants," *Newsweek*, 31 October 1983, 60.

159. "Golan and Globus Lead Cannon Team in Fifth Anniversary Year," *Screen International*, 10–17 March 1984, 76.

160. Ilott, "Five Years," 62.

161. "Cannon '84 Slate Reps $170 Mil; 17 Films, 2 Miniseries, 4 Pickups," *Hollywood Reporter*, 9 August 1983, 3, 8.

162. Ilott, "Five Years," 62.

163. Joe Klein, "Sweet Sweetback's Wall Street Song," *New York*, 5 September 1983, 42–43.

164. Wolf, *Landmark Films*, 352–55.

165. "Indies Summer," 20, 24.

166. "Film Clips," *Los Angeles Times*, 23 September 1983, part 6, 6.

167. "Atlantic Releasing Takes Production Plunge," *Daily Variety*, 11 June 1984, 63.

168. Girard, "Slim Pickings," 53.

169. Alexander Auerbach, "Troma's Films Traumatize Critics, but Audiences Love the Stuff," *Boxoffice*, July 1982, 20.

170. N.R. Kleinfield, "Cecil B. in a West Side Walk-Up," *New York Times*, 19 April 1981, section 3, 6.

171. Auerbach, "Troma's Films," 20.

172. Kleinfield, "Cecil B.," 6.

173. Rena Kleiman, "Troma Pact Supplies $10 Mil for Six Films," *Hollywood Reporter*, 29 September 1983, 1, 8.

174. Jeffrey A. Trachtenberg, "Low Budget," *Forbes,* 26 March 1984, 116, 119.

175. Auerbach, "Troma's Films," 20.

176. "Troma Aiming for 'Careful Approach' to Pic Marketing," *Daily Variety,* 2 March 1983, 80, 135.

177. "'Stuck On You' Heads Troma List; Kaufman and Herz at MIFED," *Screen International,* 29 October-5 November 1983, 181.

178. Kleinfield, "Cecil B.," 6.

179. Goodell, xvii.

180. *Hard Cash: How to Finance Independent Feature Films* (Los Angeles: Independent Feature Project/Los Angeles, 1982), 167.

181. Ibid., 192.

182. McCarthy, "Distribs Miss," 84.

183. "I Just Want to Make Bigger-than-Life Films," *Film Comment,* January-February 1980, 21.

184. Roger Ebert, "Russ Meyer: King of the Nudies," *Film Comment,* January-February 1973, 35.

185. Lees and Berkowitz, 21.

186. Ebert, "Russ Meyer," 36.

187. Ibid., 41.

188. Russ Meyer, "The Low-Budget Producer," in *The Movie Business Book,* 44.

189. Stan Berkowitz, "Sex, Violence and Drugs: All in Good Fun!" *Film Comment,* January-February 1973, 48.

190. Lees and Berkowitz, 30.

191. Berkowitz, 51.

192. Lees and Berkowitz, 31.

193. Meyer, "The Low-Budget Producer," in *The Movie Business Book,* 47.

194. Baughn, "Distributing Independent Feature Films," 18-19.

195. Meyer, "The Low-Budget Producer," in *The Movie Business Book,* 48.

196. Meyer, "The Low-Budget Producer," in *The Movie Business,* 179-82.

197. Ebert, "Russ Meyer," 37.

198. Cary Brokaw, "High Profits from Low Budgets," 15 October 1983.

199. Michael London, "Progress: Good, Better, Beast," *Los Angeles Times,* 18 June 1983, part 5, 1, 6.

200. London, "Progress," 1, 6.

201. Lawrence Cohn, "Island Alive Lines Up Five Pix for Release," *Daily Variety,* 7 September 1983, 1, 14.

202. Ron Gold, "Untold Tales of Koyaanisqatsi," *American Cinematographer*, March 1984, 62–74.

203. Robert B. Frederick, "'Koyaanisqatsi,' against All Filmic Odds, Self-Distribs into Real Coin," *Variety*, 24 August 1983, 25, 30.

204. Jimmy Summers, "Island Alive Films," *Boxoffice*, August 1984, 12–13.

205. "Indies at the Box Office," *The Independent Feature Project*, Winter 1984, 1.

206. Summers, 12–13.

207. Cohn, "Island Alive," 1, 14.

208. "IFM: Alternative to Indie Producers," *Daily Variety*, 11 June 1984, 42.

209. Michael Burkett, "OC's First Movie Turns Out to Be a Cheap, Schlocky Rip-Off," *The Register* (California), 20 March 1984, D7.

210. William K. Knoedelseder, Jr., "K-Tel Files for Protection after Losing $33.8 Million," *Los Angeles Times*, 9 October 1984, part 4, 1, 3.

211. "Borde Bankrolls," *Daily Variety*, 13 July 1981, 42.

212. Stulberg, 101–6.

213. Toby Talbot, "Introduction," *New Yorker Films Catalogue*, 1982.

214. Tuchman, 21.

215. Goodell, xviii.

216. Raphael D. Silver, 293–300.

217. Axel Madsen, 99.

218. Raphael D. Silver, 293–300.

219. "Orion Classics Picks up Dom. 'Old' Distrib'n," *Daily Variety*, 27 March 1984, 1.

220. Lawrence Cohn, "Wenders Distributes 'State of Things'," *Daily Variety*, 17 February 1983, 7.

221. Axel Madsen, 99.

222. Ibid.

223. Monaco, 329.

224. Axel Madsen, 116.

225. Michael Ventura, "Coppola's Woes and the Zoetrope Revolution," *L.A. Weekly*, 13–19 February 1981, 7–10.

226. *Benji* and *For the Love of Benji* souvenir programs.

227. Marilyn Bender, "'Benji,' A Doghouse Hero," *New York Times*, 31 August 1975, 3.

228. Will Tusher, "'Benji' Topdog in B.O. Dog Fight with Disney," *Hollywood Reporter*, 18 July 1975, 1, 17.

229. Tusher, "'Benji,'" 1, 17.

230. Goodell, xix-xx.

231. Mulberry Square Productions Press Release, "Joe Camp, a Twenty-Year Overnight Success."

232. Wayne Kabak, "Industry," *Film Comment,* November-December 1975, 30–31.

233. Hurst and Hale, 78.

234. Kabak, 30–31.

235. Ibid.

236. Lee Beaupre, "Industry," *Film Comment,* September-October 1978, 68, 70.

237. Ibid.

238. Simonet, "Market Research," 66, 68–69.

239. Beaupre, "Industry," September-October 1978, 68, 70.

240. Kabak, 30–31.

241. Peter Funt, "For Some Films, It's No, No, New York!" *New York Times,* 10 March 1974, D9.

242. "Pacific Int'l," *Hollywood Reporter,* 24 March 1982, S-41.

243. Rob Fulcher, "A Maverick Defies Hollywood," *Los Angeles Times,* 28 December 1983, part 6, 2.

244. Ibid.

245. "Videocassette Film Review," *Daily Variety,* 28 June 1984, 6, 17.

246. Kabak, 30–31.

247. "Indies Summer," 24.

248. Ibid., 68, 70.

249. Kabak, 30–31.

250. Alex Ben Block, "The Lord Giveth . . . ," *Los Angeles Herald Examiner,* 7 February 1984, A2.

251. Lane Maloney, "Where Are They Now," *Daily Variety,* 13 July 1981, 30.

252. Goodell, xxi-xxii.

253. Lee Reynolds, "Winkler, Laughlin View Distrib System," *Hollywood Reporter,* 3 May 1973, 10.

254. Marie Brenner, "Who Does Tom Laughlin Think He Is? Billy Jack?" *New York,* 4 August 1975, 50.

255. Ibid., 51.

256. Ibid.

257. "The Two Faces of Tom," *Time,* 6 October 1975, 84.

258. Tom Laughlin, *How to Invest in Motion Pictures . . . And Why You Shouldn't!* (Tom Laughlin, 1972), 26.

259. Richard Kahn, "The Day Film Marketing Came of Age," *Daily Variety,* 30 October 1979, 38.

260. Ibid.

261. Kahn, "The Day Film," 38.

262. "The Systems Analysis Approach to Distribution," unpublished article, 1.

263. Kahn, "The Day Film," 38.

264. "The Systems Analysis Approach," 1.

265. Kahn, "The Day Film," 38.

266. Richard Albarino, "Billy Sequel's Grand $11-Mil Preem: Tom Laughlin Stuns Old Film Biz Pros," *Variety,* 20 November 1974, 61.

267. Brenner, 52.

268. Kahn, "The Day Film," 92.

269. Beaupre, "Industry," September-October 1978, 70, 72.

270. Albarino, "Billy Sequel's," 61.

271. Brenner, 52.

272. Albarino, "Billy Sequel's," 1, 61.

273. Beaupre, "Industry," September-October 1978, 68, 70, 72, 77.

274. Brenner, 48.

275. *Daily Bruin* (University of California at Los Angeles), 17 April 1975, 17.

276. Brenner, 48.

277. Gregg Kilday, "Laughlin—'You Either Like Me or Hate My Guts'," *Los Angeles Times,* 12 October 1975, Calendar section, 30.

278. "The Systems Analysis Approach," 4–5.

279. Kahn, "The Day Film," 38, 92.

280. Ibid., 92.

281. Ibid., 38.

282. Funt, D9.

283. "Tom Laughlin Is Hailed for Film Rental Plan," *Boxoffice,* 22 March 1976, 3.

284. Laughlin, *How to Invest,* 29.

285. *Daily Variety,* 22 February 1984, 8–9; 27 February 1984, 10–11; 1 March 1984, 14–15; 6 March 1984, 7; 9 March 1984, 25; 19 March 1984, 20–21; 21 March 1984, 21; 26 March 1984, 7; 2 April 1984, 5.

286. "Part V—So You Think You Can Run the Studio Better?" *Daily Variety,* 9 March 1984, 25.

287. "Part VII—So You Think You Can Run the Studio Better?" *Daily Variety,* 21 March 1984, 21.

288. "Part VIII—How Stars Can Create Their Dream Studio: The Impossible Dream Achieved," *Daily Variety,* 26 March 1984, 7.

289. "Part II—So You Think You Can Run the Studio Better?" *Daily Variety,* 27 February 1984, 11.

290. "Part III—So You Think You Can Run the Studio Better?" *Daily Variety,* 1 March 1984, 15.

Chapter 12

1. Lawrence Cohn, "Horror Film Output down from Record 1982 Numbers," *Daily Variety,* 18 February 1983, 6, 10.

2. Ibid.

3. Cohn, "AFMA's All-American Image," 6.

4. "Third AFM to Open in Hollywood," *Boxoffice,* March 1983, 48.

5. Cohn, "Companies Participating," 8.

Conclusion

1. Monaco, 14.

2. Ibid., 31–32.

3. Hy Hollinger, "Arkoff Issues Warning in Wake of Summer Box-Office Hits," *Daily Variety,* 13 July 1981, 3.

Bibliography

Books

A Code to Govern the Making of Motion Pictures. New York: Motion Picture Association of America, 1955.

Adler, Nathan, and Scherzer, Larry, eds. *The Growth and Financing of Filmed Entertainment.* New York: Arthur Young, 1983.

Atkins, Thomas R., ed. *Sexuality in the Movies.* Bloomington: Indiana University Press, 1975.

Balio, Tino, ed. *The American Film Industry.* Madison: The University of Wisconsin Press, 1976.

Baumgarten, Paul A., and Farber, Donald C. *Producing, Financing and Distributing Film.* New York: Drama Book Specialists, 1973.

Baxter, John. *Hollywood in the Thirties.* New York: A.S. Barnes and Company, 1968.

Bayer, William S. *Breaking Through, Selling Out, Dropping Dead and Other Notes on Filmmaking.* New York: Macmillan Publishing Company, 1971.

Bluem, A. William, and Squire, Jason E. *The Movie Business.* New York: Hastings House, 1972.

Brode, Douglas. *The Films of the Sixties.* Secaucus, N.J.: Citadel Press, 1980.

Brown, Les, and Walker, Savannah Waring, eds. *Fast Forward: The New Television and American Society.* Kansas City: Andrews and McMeel, 1983.

Cagin, Seth and Dray, Philip. *Hollywood Films of the Seventies.* New York: Harper and Row, 1984.

Committee on the Entertainment Industries of the American Institute of Certified Public Accountants. *Accounting for Motion Picture Films.* New York: American Institute of Certified Public Accountants, 1973.

Conant, Michael. *Antitrust in the Motion Picture Industry.* Berkeley: University of California Press, 1960.

Cowie, Peter, ed. *Eighty Years of Cinema.* New York: A.S. Barnes and Company. 1977.

———. *International Film Guide 1983.* London: The Tantivy Press, 1982.

Crowther, Bosley. *The Lion's Share.* New York: E. P. Dutton and Company, 1957.

Curtis, David. *Experimental Cinema.* New York: Dell Publishing Company, 1971.

Daily Year Book (1948).

Day, Beth. *This Was Hollywood.* New York: Doubleday and Company, 1960.

Dekom, Peter J.; Adler, Michael I.; Ginsburg, David; and Lauer, Michael H., eds. *The Fifth Annual UCLA Entertainment Symposium, the Selling of Motion Pictures in the '80s: New Producer/Distributor/Exhibitor Relationships.* Los Angeles: The Regents of the University of California, 1980.

Edgerton, Gary R. *American Film Exhibition and an Analysis of the Motion Picture Industry's Market Structures 1963-1980.* New York: Garland Publishing, 1983.

Eighteenth Chicago International Film Festival. Chicago: Illinois Department of Commerce and Community Affairs, Office of Tourism, 1982.

Ellis, Jack C. *A History of Film.* Englewood Cliffs, N.J.: Prentice-Hall, 1979.

Firestone, Charles M., ed. *International Satellite Television: Resource Manual for the Third Biennial Communications Law Symposium.* Los Angeles: The Regents of the University of California, 1983.

Georgakas, Dan, and Rubenstein, Lenny, eds. *The Cineaste Interviews on the Art and Politics of the Cinema.* Chicago: Lake View Press, 1983.

Goldman, William. *Adventures in the Screen Trade.* New York: Warner Books, 1983.

Goodell, Gregory. *Independent Feature Film Production.* New York: St. Martin's Press, 1982.

Gordon, George N. *The Communications Revolution: A History of Mass Media in the United States.* New York: Hastings House, 1977.

Gregory, Mollie. *Making Films Your Business.* New York: Schocken Books, 1979.

Griffith, Richard Arthur. *The Movies.* New York: Simon and Schuster, 1957.

Griffith, Richard; Mayer, Arthur; and Bowser, Eileen. *The Movies.* New York: Simon and Schuster, 1977.

Guback, Thomas H. *The International Film Industry.* Bloomington: Indiana University Press, 1969.

Hampton, Benjamin B. *A History of the Movies.* New York: Covici Friede, 1931.

Handel, Leo A. *Hollywood Looks at Its Audience.* Urbana: The University of Illinois Press, 1950.

Hard Cash: How to Finance Independent Feature Films. Los Angeles: Independent Feature Project/Los Angeles, 1982.

Harmetz, Aljean. *Rolling Break and Other Movie Business.* New York: Alfred A. Knopf, 1983.

Harrington, John. *The Rhetoric of Film.* New York: Holt, Rinehart and Winston, 1973.

Hendricks, Gordon. *Origins of the American Film.* New York: Arno Press and *The New York Times,* 1972.

Huettig, Mae D. *Economic Control of the Motion Picture Industry.* Philadelphia: University of Pennsylvania Press, 1944.

Hurst, Walter E., and Hale, William Storm. *Motion Picture Distribution (Business and/or Racquet?!?).* Los Angeles: Seven Arts Press, 1977.

Jacobs, Lewis, ed. *The Emergence of Film Art.* New York: Hopkinson and Blake, 1969.

———. *The Rise of the American Film.* New York: Harcourt, Brace and Company, 1939.

Katz, Ephraim. *The Film Encyclopedia.* New York: Thomas Y. Crowell, 1979.

Keyser, Les. *Hollywood in the Seventies.* San Diego: A.S. Barnes and Company, 1981.

Knight, Arthur. *The Liveliest Art.* New York: The New American Library, 1957.

———. *The Liveliest Art.* New York: Macmillan Publishing Company, 1978.

Laughlin, Tom. *How to Invest in Motion Pictures ... And Why You Shouldn't!* Tom Laughlin, 1972.

Lazarsfeld, Paul F. *The People Look at Radio.* Chapel Hill: The University of North Carolina Press, 1946.

Leedy, David J. *Motion Picture Distribution: An Accountant's Perspective.* Los Angeles: David J. Leedy, 1980.

Lees, David, and Berkowitz, Stan. *The Movie Business: A Primer.* New York: Random House, 1978.

Lewis, Howard T. *The Motion Picture Industry.* New York: D. Van Nostrand Company, 1939.

Limbacher, James L. *Four Aspects of the Film.* New York: Brussel and Brussel, 1969.

Macdonald, Dwight. *Dwight Macdonald on Movies.* Englewood Cliffs, N.J.: Prentice-Hall, 1969.

Macgowan, Kenneth. *Behind the Screen.* New York: A Delacorte Press Book, 1965.

Madsen, Axel. *The New Hollywood: American Movies in the '70s.* New York: Thomas Y. Crowell Company, 1975.

Madsen, Roy. *Animated Film Concepts, Methods, Uses.* New York: Interland Publishing, 1969.

Marek, Kurt W. [C.W. Ceram]. *Archaeology of the Cinema.* New York: Harcourt, Brace and World, 1965.

May, Lary. *Screening out the Past.* New York: Oxford University Press, 1980.

Mayer, Michael F. *The Film Industries.* New York: Hastings House, 1978.

McCary, James Leslie. *Human Sexuality.* New York: D. Van Nostrand Company, 1973.

McCauley, Carole Spearin. *Computers and Creativity.* New York: Praeger Publications, 1974.

McClelland, Doug. *The Golden Age of "B" Movies.* Nashville: Charter House, 1978.

McClintick, David. *Indecent Exposure.* New York: William Morrow and Company, 1982.

Monaco, James. *American Film Now.* New York: New American Library, 1979.

————. *How to Read a Film.* New York: Oxford University Press, 1977.

Motion-Picture Distribution Trade Practices—1956. Select U.S. Congress Senate Committee on Small Business. Washington, D.C.: Government Printing Office, 1956.

Motion-Picture Films. Hearing before a Subcommittee of the Committee on Interstate and Foreign Commerce, House. 74th Cong. Washington, D.C.: Government Printing Office, 1936.

Motion-Picture Films. Hearing before the Committee on Interstate and Foreign Commerce, House. 76th Cong., 3d sess. on S. 280, Washington, D.C: U.S. Government Printing Office, 1940.

New American Cinema Conference (Los Angeles: Independent Feature Project, 4 April 1981).

1982 Nielsen Report on... Television. Northbrook, Ill.: A.C. Nielsen Company, 1982.

Perlman, William, Jr., ed. *The Movies on Trial.* New York: The Macmillan Company, 1936.

Pildas, Ave. *Movie Palaces.* New York: Clarkson N. Potter, 1980.

Pirie, David, ed. *Anatomy of the Movies.* New York: Macmillan, 1981.

Polanski, Roman. *Roman.* New York: William Morrow and Company, 1984.

Prince, David. *Interactive Graphics for Computer-Aided Design.* Reading: Addison-Wesley Publishing, 1971.

Pye, Michael, and Myles, Lynda. *The Movie Brats.* New York: Holt, Rinehart and Winston, 1979.

Quigley, Martin, Jr. *New Screen Techniques.* New York: Quigley Publishing Company, 1953.

Ramsaye, Terry. *A Million and One Nights.* New York: Simon and Schuster, 1964.

————. *Vocational and Professional Monographs: The Motion Picture Industry.* Boston: Bellman Publishing Company, 1946.

Reichardt, Jasia. *Cybernetics, Art and Ideas.* New York: Graphic Society Limited, 1971.

Reichert, Julia. *Doing It Yourself: A Handbook on Independent Film Distribution.* New York: Association of Independent Video and Filmmakers, 1977.

Rembusch, Trueman T. *What the Public Wants to See.* Allied States Association of Motion Picture Exhibitors, 1949.

Robertson, Joseph F. *Motion Picture Distribution Handbook.* Blue Ridge Summit, Pa.: Tab Books, 1981.

Rosen, Marjorie. *Popcorn Venus.* New York: Coward, McCann and Geoghegan, 1973.

Rudell, Michael I. *Behind the Scenes: Practical Entertainment Law.* New York: Law And Business/Harcourt Brace Jovanovich, 1984.

Russett, Robert, and Starr, Cecile. *Experimental Animation.* New York: Van Nostrand Reinhold Company, 1976.

Samuels, Stuart. *Midnight Movies.* New York: Macmillan Publishing Company, 1983.

Schickel, Richard. *Movies: The History of an Art as an Institution.* New York: Basic Books, 1964.

Seldes, Gilbert. *The Great Audience.* New York: The Viking Press, 1950.

Sellin, Thorsten, ed. *The Annals (The Motion Picture Industry).* Philadephia: The American Academy of Political and Social Science, 1947.

Sklar, Robert. *Movie-Made America.* New York: Random House, 1975.

Squire, Jason E., ed. *The Movie Business Book.* Englewood Cliffs, N.J.: Prentice-Hall, 1983.

Statement of Financial Accounting Standards, No. 53, Financial Reporting by Producers and Distributors of Motion Picture Films. Stamford: Financial Accounting Standards Board, 1981.

Steinberg, Cobbett. *Reel Facts: The Movie Book of Records.* New York: Vintage Books, 1978.

Stephenson, Ralph. *The Animated Film.* New York: A.S. Barnes and Company, 1973.

Technical Report of the Commission on Obscenity and Pornography, Volume III. Washington, D.C.: Government Printing Office, 1971.

Temporary National Economic Committee. *Investigation of Concentration of Economic Power Monograph No. 43. The Motion Picture Industry—A Pattern of Control.* Washington: United States Government Printing Office, 1941.

The Financing and Distribution of Feature Motion Pictures. New York: Benjamin N. Cardozo School of Law, American Bar Association, Forum Committee on the Entertainment and Sports Industries, 17-18 March 1983.

The Public Relations of the Motion Picture Industry. New York: Department of Research and Education, Federal Council of the Churches of Christ in America, 1931.

Trojan, Judith, and Covert, Nadine, eds. *16mm Distribution.* New York: Educational Film Library Association, 1977.

Tromberg, Sheldon. *Making Money, Making Movies: The Independent Movie-Makers' Handbook.* New York: New Viewpoints/Vision Books, 1980.

Vance, Malcolm. *The Movie Ad Book.* Minneapolis: Control Data Publishing, 1981.

Wholesale Distribution Motion Picture Films. U.S. Dept. of Commerce Bureau of the Census. Washington, D.C.: Government Printing Office, 1932.

Wolf, William. *Landmark Films.* London: Paddington Press, 1979.

Articles

"Advertising Code for Motion Pictures." *The Motion Picture Monthly,* 1 July 1930, 3, 7.

Albarino, Richard. "Billy Sequel's Grand $11-mil Preem: Tom Laughlin Stuns Old Film Biz Pros." *Variety,* 20 November 1984, 1, 61.

"All the Ads Fit to Print." *Time,* 12 September 1977, 80.

Auerbach, Alexander. "Troma's Films Traumatize Critics, but Audiences Love the Stuff." *Boxoffice,* July 1982, 20.

Austin, Bruce A. "Do Movie Ratings Affect a Film's Performance at the Ticket Window?" *Boxoffice,* March 1983, 40–46.

———. "Motivations for Movie Attendance." *Boxoffice,* October 1984, 13–16.

"Avco Embassy Unveils Its 1976 Releases, Policies." *Boxoffice,* 6 October 1975, 5.

Baughn, David. "Distributing Independent Feature Films." *Filmmakers Monthly,* September 1979, 19–20.

Beaupre, Lee. "Do-It-Yourself Distribution." *Film Comment,* July-August 1977, 48.

———. "How to Distribute a Film." *Film Comment,* July-August 1977, 44–54.

———. "Industry." *Film Comment,* July-August 1978, 68–70.

———. "Industry." *Film Comment,* September-October 1978, 68, 70, 72, 77.

———. "Industry." *Film Comment,* March-April 1980, 69–73.

———. "Staying Alive with Word-of-Mouth." *Film Comment,* March-April 1984, 64.

Berg, Michael. "Second-Hand Shows." *American Film,* June 1983, 46–48, 62–64.

Berkowitz, Stan. "Sex, Violence, and Drugs: All in Good Fun!" *Film Comment,* January-February 1973, 47–51.

Bernstein, William. "Financing and Supplying Filmed Product." In *The Growth and Financing of Filmed Entertainment,* 2–9. Edited by Nathan Adler and Larry Scherzer. New York: Arthur Young, 1983.

Birge, Peter and Maslin, Janet. "Getting Snuffed in Boston." *Film Comment,* May-June 1976, 35, 63.

Blum, Stanford. "Merchandising." In *The Movie Business Book,* 379–84. Edited by Jason E. Squire. Englewood Cliffs, N.J.: Prentice-Hall, 1983.

Bock, Audie. "Local Heroes." *American Film,* April 1984, 38–39.

Boyer, Peter. "Risky Business." *American Film,* January-February 1984, 14, 76–77.

Boyle, Barbara D. "Independent Distribution: New World Pictures." In *The Movie Business Book,* 285-92. Edited by Jason E. Squire. Englewood Cliffs, N.J.: Prentice-Hall, 1983.

Brenner, Marie. "Who Does Tom Laughlin Think He Is? Billy Jack?" *New York,* 4 August 1975, 46–52.

Byron, Stuart. "The Industry." *Film Comment,* January-February 1980, 38–39.

Canby, Vincent. "The Power of the Times." In *The Cineaste Interviews on the Art and Politics of the Cinema,* 282–97. Edited by Dan Georgakas and Lenny Rubenstein. Chicago: Lake View Press, 1983.

Caranicas, Peter. "Hollywood Wakes Up and Smells the Coffee." *Channels,* July-August 1983, 43–45.

――――. "How Pay TV Got the Upper Hand." *Channels,* July-August 1983, 44.

Chambers, Robert W. "Need for Statistical Research." In *Annals (The Motion Picture Industry),* 169–72. Edited by Thorsten Sellin. Philadelphia: The American Academy of Political Science, 1947.

Chute, David. "The New World of Roger Corman." *Film Comment,* March-April 1982, 27–32.

Clarke, Gerald. "Dark Cloud over the Drive-Ins." *Time,* 8 August 1983, 64.

Cocchi, John. "AIP Celebrating 25 Years, Looking Ahead to Qualify Summer Releases." *Boxoffice,* 9 April 1979, 5.

Collart, Yanou. "The Deauville Film Festival." *American Premiere,* November 1982, 33.

Cook, Errol; Isgur, Lee; and Londoner, David. "The Growth of the Entertainment Industry: The Analysts' Perspectives." In *The Growth and Financing of Filmed Entertainment,* 34–47. Edited by Nathan Adler and Larry Scherzer. New York: Arthur Young, 1983.

Corliss, Mary. "Cannes Journal." *Film Comment,* September-October 1974, 2, 66.

Corliss, Richard. "I'm Always in Money Trouble." *Time,* 23 February 1981, 82.

Cort, Robert. "Advertising and Marketing of Theatrical Motion Pictures in the 1980s." In *The Fifth Annual UCLA Entertainment Symposium, The Selling of Motion Pictures in the '80s: New Producer/Distributor/Exhibitor Relationships;* 138–50. Edited by Peter J. Dekom, Michael I. Adler, David Ginsburg, and Michael H. Lauer. Los Angeles: The Regents of the University of California, 1980.

"'Country' Continues Orion Classics' Art-House Success." *Screen International,* 6–13 October 1984, 6.

Counts, Kyle. "U.S. Foreign Sales Agents." *American Premiere,* November 1982, 26–28.

"Crown Celebrates 25th Anniversary, Introduces Two New Films at the Market." *Screen International,* 10–17 March 1984, 142.

"'Cruising' Spurs a Test of Booking Films Blind." *Business Week,* 3 March 1980, 26–27.

"Current Status of Obscenity Laws." *Intellect,* September 1977, 99–100.

Davis, Douglas M. "Art and Technology—The New Combine." *Art in America,* January-February 1968, 38.

Dawson, Anthony. "Motion Picture Economics." *Hollywood Quarterly,* Fall 1947, 217–40.

Dudar, Helen. "All the Right Moves." *American Film,* March 1984, 36–42.

Durwood, Stanley H., and Resnick, Joel H. "The Theatre Chain: American Multi-Cinema." In *The Movie Business Book,* 327–32. Edited by Jason E. Squire. Englewood Cliffs, N.J.: Prentice-Hall, 1983.

Ebert, Roger. "Russ Meyer: King of the Nudies." *Film Comment,* January-February 1973, 35–45.

"'83 World Feature Rentals Reach New High.'" *Boxoffice,* October 1984, 28.

Epple, Ron. "Festivals: Independent Film-Makers Exposition." *Filmmakers Newsletter*, April 1974, 68, 70.

Evans, Robert. "The Producer." In *The Movie Business Book*, 13–20. Edited by Jason E. Squire. Englewood Cliffs, N.J.: Prentice-Hall, 1983.

"Exhibit C." In *The Financing and Distribution of Feature Motion Pictures*, 207–9. Edited by Nathan Adler and Larry Scherzer. New York: Arthur Young, 1983.

"Family Night." *The Motion Picture Monthly*, August 1930, 3–4.

Fellman, Nat D. "The Exhibitor." In *The Movie Business Book*, 313–22. Edited by Jason E. Squire. Englewood Cliffs, N.J.: Prentice-Hall, 1983.

Fellman, Nat D., and Durwood, Stanley H. "The Exhibitors: Show and Teller Time." In *The Movie Business*, 214–23. Edited by A. William Bluem and Jason E. Squire. New York: Hastings House, 1972.

"Five Ways in Which Pictures Bring Goodwill among Nations." *The Motion Picture Monthly*, September 1930, 8–9.

Flaherty, Robert. "Nanook." In *The Emergence of Film Art*, 215–21. Edited by Lewis Jacobs. New York: Hopkinson and Blake, 1969.

Franklin, B. J. "AFMA Pride at Four-Year Record of Achievement." *Screen International*, 10–17 March 1984, 8.

———. "Orion Classics Trio Aims towards Production." *Screen International*, 27 August—3 September 1983, 28,34.

———. "The Two 'Real' Classics Divisions." *Screen International*, 27 August—3 September 1983, 26.

Frederick, Robert B. "'Koyaanisqatsi' against All Filmic Odds, Self-Distribs into Real Coin." *Variety*, 24 August 1983, 25, 30.

Friedland, Dennis. "The Distributors: A Sound of Different Drummers." In *The Movie Business*, 193–99. Edited by A. William Bluem and Jason E. Squire. New York: Hastings House, 1972.

Friendly, David. "Hollywood's Rug Merchants." *Newsweek*, 31 October 1983, 60.

Geiger, Peter W. "The Bank and Feature Financing." In *The Movie Business Book*, 107–12. Edited by Jason E. Squire. Englewood Cliffs, N.J.: Prentice-Hall, 1983.

Gelling v. Texas (1952) 343 US 960, 96 L ed 1359, 72 S Ct 1002.

Gillette, Don Carle. "Distribution Faces Drastic Overhaul." *The Journal of the Producers Guild of America*, December 1970, 17–20.

Gitlin, Todd. "The Lyric Odyssey of Alain Tanner." *Harper's*, February 1984, 68–71.

"Golan and Globus Lead Cannon Team in Fifth Anniversary Year." *Screen International*, 10–17 March 1984, 76.

Gold, Ron. "Untold Tales of Koyaanisqatsi." *American Cinematographer*, March 1984, 62–74.

Goldwyn, Samuel. "Hollywood in the Television Age." *Hollywood Quarterly*, 4 (1949–1950), 145–51.

Guback, Thomas H. "Hollywood's International Market." In *The American Film Industry*, 387–409. Edited by Tino Balio. Madison: The University of Wisconsin Press, 1976.

Hanson, John. "The Theatrical Self-Distribution of 'Northern Lights.'" *Filmmakers Monthly*, October 1979, 19–24.

Harmetz, Aljean. "Burden of Dreams George Lucas." *American Film*, June 1983, 30–36.

Harris, Diane. "Want to Make a Movie?" *Financial World*, 15–31 July 1983, 50–51.

Hendricks, Gordon. "The History of the Kinetoscope." In *The American Film Industry*, 33–45. Edited by Tino Balio. Madison: University of Wisconsin Press, 1976.

Hollinger, Hy. "AFM Kicks Off As Hopes Soar." *Variety*, 2 March 1983, 13, 166.

Holm, Wilton R. "Technological Standardization in Motion Pictures." *Journal of Producers Guild of America*, June 1983, 15–17.

Howard, Edwin. "Why Films Silently Come, Quickly Go." *Journal of Producers Guild of America*, March 1972, 13.

Huettig, Mae D. "The Motion Picture Industry Today." In *The American Film Industry*, 228–55. Edited by Tino Balio. Madison: University of Wisconsin Press, 1976.

"I Just Want to Make Bigger-Than-Life Films." *Film Comment*, January-February 1980, 20–21.

Ilott, Terry. "Films Good, Weather Bad, Business in Between at 37th Cannes Festival." *Screen International*, 2–9 June 1984, 8.

———. "Five Years on Golan and Globus Make Cannon a Major Force." *Screen International*, 10–17 March 1984, 61–62.

"Indies at the Box Office." *The Independent Feature Project*, Winter 1984, 1.

Jacobson, Harlan. "Exhibition." *Film Comment*, January-February 1980, 39, 42.

———. "How the Classics Kids Snatched Foreign Film." *The Village Voice*, 29 November 1983, 74–76, 83.

"Japan Theatres Mull Ways to Recapture Their Auds." *Variety*, 4 May 1983, 335, 360.

"Jensen Farley Decides to Keep Offshore Sales at Home under Swindler." *Variety*, 2 March 1983, 89, 142.

Joseph Burstyn, Inc. v. Wilson (1952) 343 US 495, 96 L ed 1089, 72 S Ct 777.

Kabak, Wayne. "Industry." *Film Comment*, November-December 1975, 30–31.

Kagan, Paul. "A Primer on Pay TV and Motion Picture Economics." Published for the Paul Kagan Motion Picture Investments Seminar, 24 May 1984, 1–3.

———. *Motion Picture Investor*, 30 April 1984, Carmel, Calif: Paul Kagan Associates, Inc., 1–3.

Kilday, Gregg. "The Queue Factor." *The Movies*, September 1983, 76–77.

Klein, Joe. "Sweet Sweetback's Wall Street Song." *New York*, 5 September 1983, 42–43.

Kowinski, William Severini. "The Malling of the Movies." *American Film*, September 1983, 52–56.

Laemmle, Carl. "The Business of Motion Pictures." In *The American Film Industry*, 153–68. Edited by Tino Balio. Madison: The University of Wisconsin Press, 1976.

Laemmle, Robert. "The Independent Exhibitor." In *The Movie Business Book*, 333–37. Edited by Jason E. Squire. New Jersey: Prentice-Hall, 1983.

Laine, Ralph E. "International PR beyond the Glitter." *American Premiere*, November 1982, 25–26.

Lamont, Austin. "Independence Day." *Film Comment*, November-December 1981, 15–20, 69–76.

Landler, Edward. "IFP Interview with Ken Wlaschin." *IFP West Newsletter*, September 1984, 1–2.

Lazarsfeld, Paul F. "Audience Research in the Movie Field." In *The Annals (The Motion Picture Industry)*, 160–68. Edited by Thorsten Sellin. Philadelphia: The American Academy of Political and Social Science, 1947.

Lederer, Richard. "Management; New Rules of the Game." In *The Movie Business Book*, 136–41. Edited by Jason E. Squire. Englewood Cliffs, N.J.: Prentice-Hall, 1983.

Lees, David. "The Secret Life of Henry Plitt." *Los Angeles Magazine*, January 1984, 94–103.

Linck, David. "A Real Exhibitor's Dream." *Boxoffice*, March 1983, 16, 22.

Lipton, David. A. "Advertising and Publicity." In *The Movie Business*, 227–33. Edited by A. William Bluem and Jason E. Squire. New York: Hastings House, 1972.

Lowe, Philip M. "Refreshment Sales and Theatre Profits." In *The Movie Business Book*, 343–49. Edited by Jason E. Squire. Englewood Cliffs, N.J.: Prentice-Hall, 1983.

Lowe, Walter. "The Screen's Third-Dimensional Roundup." *Theater Arts*, 11 September 1953, 72–73, 92–93.

Lubow, Arthur. "How To Read a Movie Ad." *Harpers*, June 1983, 14–18.

Luther, Rodney. "Television and the Future of Motion Picture Exhibition," *Hollywood Quarterly*, 1950–1951, 164–77.

Mancini, Marc. "Pictures at an Exposition." *Film Comment*, January-February 1983, 43–49.

"Mastorakis Plans 'Rockaine' to Follow the Success of 'Blind Date.'" *Screen International,* 10–17 March 1984, 80.

Mayer, Michael F. "The Exhibition Contract—A Scrap of Paper." In *The Movie Business,* 210–13. Edited by A. William Bluem and Jason E. Squire. New York: Hastings House, 1972.

———. "The Exhibition License." In *The Movie Business Book,* 338–42. Edited by Jason E. Squire. Englewood Cliffs, N.J.: Prentice-Hall, 1983.

———. "The Journal Looks at Film Distribution Abroad." *The Journal of the Producers Guild of America,* March 1975, 1, 3–7.

McNally, Judith. "Lucrative Trash—The Dime-Store Movies." *Filmmakers Newsletter,* October 1974, 61–63.

Megel, Joe. "Foreign Presales: Can You Afford Them?" *American Premiere,* November 1982, 38–39.

Meisel, Myron. "Seventh Annual Grosses Gloss." *Film Comment,* March-April 1982, 60–66.

Mekas, Jonas. "Free Cinema and the New Wave." *Film Comment,* Summer 1960, 400–19.

———. "Independence for Independents." *American Film,* September 1978, 38–40.

———. "Statement." *Film Comment,* Winter 1964, 28.

Merritt, Russell. "Nickelodeon Theaters 1905–1914: Building an Audience for the Movies." In *The American Film Industry,* 59–79. Edited by Tino Balio. Madison: The University of Wisconsin Press, 1976.

Meyer, Russ. "The Low-Budget Producer." In *The Movie Business,* 179–82. Edited by A. William Bluem and Jason E. Squire. New York: Hastings House, 1972.

———. "The Low-Budget Producer." In *The Movie Business Book,* 44–50. Edited by Jason E. Squire. Englewood Cliffs, N.J.: Prentice-Hall, 1983.

"Montoro at Mifed for Artists Releasing Corp." *Screen International,* 29 October - 5 November 1983, 236.

Moreno, Frank J., and Almond, Paul S. "Life amongst the Giants." In *The Fifth Annual UCLA Entertainment Symposium, the Selling of Motion Pictures in the '80s: New Producer/Distributor/Exhibitor Relationships,* 69–81. Edited by Peter J. Dekom, Michael I. Adler, David Ginsburg, and Michael H. Lauer. Los Angeles: The Regents of the University of California, 1980.

Moss, Adam. "The Exhibition Game Ron Lesser on Owning the Theater near You." *Esquire,* July 1982, 96–99.

"Motion Pictures in Sound Condition." *The Motion Picture Monthly,* 1 December 1929, 2.

Myers, Robert. "Foreign Distribution." In *The Fifth Annual UCLA Entertainment Symposium, the Selling of Motion Pictures in the '80s: New Producer/Distributor/Exhibitor Relationships,* 151–83. Edited by Peter J. Dekom, Michael I. Adler, David Ginsburg, and Michael H. Lauer. Los Angeles: The Regents of the University of California, 1980.

"New Line Seeking Commercial Films to Aid Production." *Variety,* 4 May 1983, 16.

"Now Playing: Sipping Cinemas." *Time,* 27 April 1981, 55.

Patterson, Richard. "'Chan Is Missing' or How to Make a Successful Feature for $22,315.92." *American Cinematographer,* February 1983, 32–39.

Paul, William. "Hollywood Harakiri." *Film Comment,* March—April 1977, 40–43, 56–62.

Pauly, David; McAlevey, Peter; and Achiron, Marilyn. "Hollywood's Penny Pinchers." *Newsweek,* 9 April 1984, 83.

Perry, Simon. "Cannes, Festivals and the Movie Business." *Sight and Sound,* Autumn 1981, 226–32.

Pietschmann, Richard J. "'And Maybe He Should Be Smoking a Virginia Slims....'" *Los Angeles Magazine,* October 1981, 172–79.

Plotkin, Harris M. "Protolite Screen: Drive-In Breakthrough?" *Boxoffice,* March 1983, 64–65.

Pollock, Dale. "Hot Time! Summer at the Box Office." *American Film,* June 1983, 12.

Putzer, Gerry. "IFP Interview," *IFP West Newsletter,* October 1984.

Quigley, Martin. "Importance of the Entertainment Film." In *The Annals (The Motion Picture Industry)*, 65–69. Edited by Thorsten Sellin. Philadelphia: The American Academy of Political and Social Science, 1947.

Ramsaye, Terry. "The Rise and Place of the Motion Picture." In *The Annals (The Motion Picture Industry)*, 1–11. Edited by Thorsten Sellin. Philadelphia: The American Academy of Political and Social Science, 1947.

Ravaud, Don. "Italian Festivals and Us." *Framework*, Summer 1983, 54–55.

Reade, Jr., Walter. "The Distributors: A Sound of Different Drummers." In *The Movie Business*, 193–96. Edited by A. William Bluem and Jason E. Squire. New York: Hastings House, 1972.

Redstone, Sumner. "The Nature, Manner and Structure of Exhibition Arrangements." In *The Fifth Annual UCLA Entertainment Symposium. The Selling of Motion Pictures in the '80s: New Producer/Distributor/Exhibitor Relationships*, 210–39. Edited by Peter J. Dekom, Michael I. Adler, David Ginsburg, and Michael H. Lauer. Los Angeles: The Regents of the University of California, 1980.

Rehfeld, Barry. "Cannon Fathers." *Film Comment*, November - December 1983, 21–24.

Robbins, Jim. "New Line Using AFMarket to Push 3 New Projects." *Variety*, 2 March 1983, 80, 258.

Rudell, Michael I. "The Financing and Distribution of Feature Motion Pictures: Network Television, Pay Television and Other Forms of Home Video." In *The Financing and Distribution of Feature Motion Pictures*, 230–32. New York: American Bar Association, 1983.

Schallert, Edwin. "The Parable of the Climbing Girl." In *The Movies on Trial*, 99–112. Edited by William J. Perlman. New York: The Macmillan Company, 1936.

Scherzer, Larry. "An Accountant's Perspective." In *The Growth and Financing of Filmed Entertainment*, 20–24. Edited by Nathan Adler and Larry Scherzer. New York: Arthur Young, 1983.

Schneble, Sylvie, and Rainer, Tristine. "Financing and Foreign Distribution." In *The Movie Business Book*, 122–31. Edited by Jason E. Squire. Englewood Cliffs, N.J.: Prentice-Hall, 1983.

Semel, Terry. "Where Filmed Product Is Going." In *The Growth and Financing of Filmed Entertainment*, 48–51. Edited by Nathan Adler and Larry Scherzer. New York: Arthur Young, 1983.

Shapiro, Joe. "An Attorney's Perspective." In *The Growth and Financing of Filmed Entertainment*, 14–19. Edited by Nathan Adler and Larry Scherzer. New York: Arthur Young, 1983.

Silver, Charles. "For a Fair Distribution of Film Wealth." *Film Comment*, Fall 1970, 2, 4.

Silver, Raphael D. "Independent Distribution: Midwest Films." In *The Movie Business Book*, 293–300. Edited by Jason E. Squire. Englewood Cliffs, N.J.: Prentice-Hall, 1983.

"Silver Screen Partners Prospectus." (New York: E.F. Hutton and Company, 9 April 1983).

Simonet, Thomas. "Industry." *Film Comment*, January - February 1978, 72–73.

———. "Market Research: Beyond the Fanny of the Cohn." *Film Comment*, January-February 1980, 66, 68–69.

Smith, Joe. "Pirating." In *The Growth and Financing of Filmed Entertainment*, 31–33. Edited by Nathan Adler and Larry Scherzer. New York: Arthur Young, 1983.

Smith, Ralph Lee. "Birth of a Wired Nation." In *Fast Forward: The New Television and American Society*, 7–19. Edited by Les Brown and Savannah Waring Walker. Kansas City: Andrews and McMeel, 1983.

Solomon, Benjamin W. "Distribution: The Accountant's Role." In *The Movie Business*, 205–9. Edited by A. William Bluem and Jason E. Squire. New York: Hastings House, 1972.

Springer, Alicia. "Sell It Again, Sam!" *American Film*, March 1983, 50–55.

Stuart, Shelley R. *"Young v. American Mini Theatres, Inc."* New England Law Review, Fall 1976, 391–418.

" 'Stuck on You' Heads Troma List; Kaufman and Herz at MIFED." *Screen International,* 29 October - 5 November 1983, 181.

Stulberg, Gordon. "The Establishment of a Film Company." In *The Movie Business,* 101–8. Edited by A. William Bluem and Jason E. Squire. New York: Hastings House, 1972.

Summers, Jimmy. "Island Alive Films." *Boxoffice,* August 1984, 12–13.

Swerdlow, Harry B. and Jaffe, Judianne. "Current Antitrust Aspects of the Distribution/ Exhibition Relationship." In *The Fifth Annual UCLA Entertainment Symposium. The Selling of Motion Pictures in the 80s: New Producer/Distributor/Exhibitor Relationships,* 240–76. Edited by Peter J. Dekom, Michael I. Adler, David Ginsburg, and Michael H. Lauer. Los Angeles: The Regents of the University of California, 1980.

Talbot, Toby. "Introduction." *New Yorker Films Catalogue,* 1982.

Taub, Stephen. "Sunny Skies Ahead for the Old Dream Machine." *Financial World,* 15–31 July 1983, 46–51.

"The American Independent Feature Market." *American Premiere,* November 1982, 24, 32.

"The Evil Dead" Advertisement. *Variety,* 4 May 1983, 78.

"The Kids at Cannon." *Time,* 31 August 1970, 60.

"The Making of a Modern-Day Movie Mogul." *Business Week,* 16 May 1977, 117.

"The Market: Five Years Progress." *The Independent Feature Project,* Winter 1984, 2.

"The Mini-Mogul." *Forbes,* 28 February 1983, 12.

"The Motion Picture Industry." *Harvard Law Review,* March 1979, 1128–1147.

"The Two Faces of Tom." *Time,* 6 October 1975, 83–84.

"Theater Owners Work to Ban Blind Bidding." *Business Week,* 19 April 1978, 40.

"Third AFM to Open in Hollywood." *Boxoffice,* March 1983, 48.

Thompson, Toby. "The Twilight of the Drive-In." *American Film,* July-August 1983, 44–49.

Thompson, William. "Traditional and Non-Traditional Methods of Financing Filmed Product: A Banker's Perspective." In *The Growth and Financing of Filmed Entertainment,* 10–13. Edited by Nathan Adler and Larry Scherzer. New York: Arthur Young, 1983.

"Tom Laughlin Is Hailed for Film Rental Plan." *Boxoffice,* 22 March 1976, 3.

Trachtenberg, Jeffrey A. "Low Budget." *Forbes,* 26 March 1984, 116, 119.

Tuchman, Mitch. "Declaration of Independence." *Film Comment,* May-June 1980, 20–22.

"United States v. Columbia Pictures Industries et al." In *The Financing and Distribution of Feature Motion Pictures,* 355–77. New York: American Bar Association, 1983.

"Universal City Studios, Inc., v. Sony Corporation of America." In *The Financing and Distribution of Feature Motion Pictures,* 383–99. New York: American Bar Association, 1983.

"U.S. Releases." *Variety,* 7 March 1984, 414.

Vaines, Colin; Illott, Terry; Head, Anne; and McFarling, Tina. "Largest MIFED Turnout, Business Only Average." *Screen International,* 19–26 November 1983, 8.

Vajna, Andrew. "AFMA." *American Premiere,* November 1982, 16.

Valenti, Jack. "The Movie Rating System." In *The Movie Business Book,* 363–72. Edited by Jason E. Squire. Englewood Cliffs, N.J.: Prentice-Hall, 1983.

Ventura, Michael. "Coppola's Woes and the Zoetrope Revolution." *L.A. Weekly,* 13–19 February 1981, 7–10.

Verrill, Addison. "Cannon Films Run by Under-30s, Never Had a Loser; Shuns Trade's Obsolete Ways; Mulls Going Public." *Variety,* 25 February 1970, 4.

Vogel, Amos. "Independent Film." *Film Comment,* May-June 1974, 37.

———. "Independents." *Film Comment,* September-October 1978, 74–76.

———. "More Apocalypse Now." *Film Comment,* May-June 1983, 76–77.

———. "Structures." *Film Comment,* January-February 1975, 6, 8.

———. "The Vital Statistics of Media Centers." *Film Comment,* July-August 1979, 78–79.

Waters, John. "Whatever Happened to Showmanship?" *American Film,* December 1983, 55–58.

"What Blockbooking Does." *The Motion Picture Monthly,* December 1930, 9–10.

Wolf, William. "The Sunshine Boys." *New York,* 12 September 1983, 89.

Yakir, Dan. "Campaigns and Caveat." *Film Comment,* May-June 1980, 72–77.

_____. "Industry. Bob Rehme: New Power in Hollywood." *Film Comment,* July-August 1981, 74–76.

Ziffren, Kenneth. "The Structure and Negotiation of Distribution Agreements." In *The Fifth Annual UCLA Entertainment Symposium. The Selling of Motion Pictures in the '80s: New Producer/Distributor/Exhibitor Relationships,* 184–209. Edited by Peter J. Dekom, Michael I. Adler, David Ginsburg, and Michael H. Lauer. Los Angeles: The Regents of the University of California, 1980.

Unpublished Materials

Arkoff, Samuel Z. Ninth Annual Publicists Guild Awards Luncheon Speech Transcript, Beverly Wilshire Hotel, 7 April 1972.

Ball, Jimmy Lloyd. 1965. "Distribution of Theatrical Motion Pictures: The History and Contemporary Practices of Independent Producers." M.A. thesis, University of Southern California.

Benji and *For the Love of Benji* souvenir programs.

Daly, David Anthony. 1978. "A Comparison of Exhibition and Distribution Patterns in Three Recent Feature Motion Pictures." Ph.D. diss., Southern Illinois University at Carbondale.

"History of American International Pictures—Twenty-Fifth Anniversary." Los Angeles: American International Pictures, 1979, 1–6.

Kosower, Herbert. 1969. "A Study of an Independent Feature Film. 'You Don't Have Time.'" Ph.D. diss., University of Southern California.

[Laughlin, Tom.] "The Systems Analysis Approach to Distribution," 1–22.

Mulberry Square Productions press release, "Joe Camp, a Twenty-Year Overnight Success."

Musun, Chris. 1969. "The Marketing of Motion Pictures." D.B.A. diss., University of Southern California.

"Samuel Z. Arkoff Biography." Beverly Hills: American International Pictures, 30 March 1979.

Seminars

The Fifth Annual UCLA Entertainment Symposium (5-6 December 1980)

The New American Cinema Conference (4 April 1981)
The Independent Feature Project/Los Angeles in conjunction with Filmex

Women in Film Presents The Future of the Entertainment Industry: Where To? What Next? (10 October 1981)

The Sale, Distribution and Marketing of a Motion Picture, UCLA Extension (3-24 November 1981)
Moderators: Hy Hollinger—West Coast Editor, *Variety*
Harold Berlfein—Partner, Ernst and Whinney CPAs

Independent Feature Project/Los Angeles in conjunction with Filmex presents: HARD CASH How to Finance Independent Feature Films (27 March 1982)

Women in Film Presents Hard Times: A Game Plan for a Changing Industry (9 October 1982)

Motion Pictures from Acquisition to Exhibition, American Film Institute (19 February 1983)

The Sale, Marketing and Distribution of a Motion Picture, UCLA Extension (26 February 1983)

American Bar Association Forum Committee on the Entertainment and Sports Industries, Motion Picture Division Symposium, the Financing and Distribution of Feature Motion Pictures New York Statler (17-18 March 1983)

Independent Film: International Marketing and Distribution, The American Film Institute (9 April 1983)

Women In Film Meeting (18 April 1983)

Future Shock in the Motion Picture Industry (4 April - 6 June 1983) UCLA Extension
Instructor: Mike Medavoy, Executive Vice President, Orion Pictures

The Complete Independent Filmmaker: A Practical Seminar with Tom Laughlin, UCLA Extension (7 April - 9 June 1983)

Marketing and Distribution in the Motion Picture Industry, UCLA Extension Course (6 April-22 June 1983)
Instructors: Ed Colarik—President of International Marketing Consultants and Independent Distributor
William Madden—Former Vice President and General Sales Manager of MGM Distribution, Industry Consultant to the Federal Government

High Profits from Low Budgets: Making the Most from Independent Features, American Film Institute (15 October 1983)

Paul Kagan Associates, Inc., "Motion Picture Investments Seminar," on KaganCassette, Los Angeles (24 May 1984)

Index